INSIGHT GUIDE

Seattle

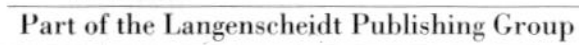

About This Book

Editorial

Editor
Scott Rutherford
Editorial Director
Brian Bell

Distribution

UK & Ireland
GeoCenter International Ltd
The Viables Centre , Harrow Way
Basingstoke, Hants RG22 4BJ
Fax: (44) 1256-817988

United States
Langenscheidt Publishers, Inc.
46–35 54th Road, Maspeth, NY 11378
Fax: (718) 784-0640

Canada
Prologue Inc.
1650 Lionel Bertrand Blvd., Boisbriand
Québec, Canada J7H 1N7
Tel: (450) 434-0306. Fax: (450) 434-2627

Australia & New Zealand
Hema Maps Pty. Ltd.
24 Allgas Street, Slacks Creek 4127
Brisbane, Australia
Tel: (61) 7 3290 0322. Fax: (61) 7 3290 0478

Worldwide
Apa Publications GmbH & Co.
Verlag KG (Singapore branch)
38 Joo Koon Road, Singapore 628990
Tel: (65) 865-1600. Fax: (65) 861-6438

Printing

Insight Print Services (Pte) Ltd
38 Joo Koon Road, Singapore 628990
Tel: (65) 865-1600. Fax: (65) 861-6438

First Edition 1993
Third Edition 2000

CONTACTING THE EDITORS
Although every effort is made to provide accurate information in this publication, we live in a fast-changing world and would appreciate it if readers would call our attention to any errors or outdated information that may occur by writing to us at:
Insight Guides, P.O. Box 7910,
London SE1 1WE, England.
Fax: (44 20) 7403 0290.
e-mail:
insight@apaguide.demon.co.uk

This guidebook combines the interests and enthusiasms of two of the world's best known information providers: Insight Guides, whose titles have set the standard for visual travel guides since 1970, and Discovery Channel, the world's premier source of non-fiction television programming.

Insight Guides' editors provide practical advice and general understanding about a place's history, culture, institutions and people. Discovery Channel and its extensive web site, www.discovery.com, help millions of viewers explore their world from the comfort of their home and also encourage them to explore it firsthand.

In this, the third edition of the guide, we take you around one of North America's most livable and embracing cities – the rain notwithstanding – known for its espresso, software entrepreneurs, and outdoor enthusiasts. We set out on the waters that surround Seattle to nearby islands and suburbs, from Vashon Island to the Eastside centers of Bellevue and Redmond. Ramblers that most of us are, we also explore the area from Victoria, B.C., to Mount St. Helens and the Cascades.

How to use this book

The book is carefully structured to convey a strong understanding of Seattle and its culture, and to guide readers through the city's sights:

◆ The Features section, with a yellow colour bar, covers the region's history and culture in lively authoritative essays written by specialists.

◆ The Places section, with a blue bar, provides full details of all the sights and areas worth seeing. The chief places of interest are coordinated by number with specially drawn maps.

◆ The Travel Tips listings section, with an orange bar, at the back of the book, offers a convenient point of reference for information on travel, accommodation, restaurants and other practical aspects of Seattle and the surrounding region. Information is located quickly using the index printed on the back cover flap, which also serves as a handy bookmark.

The contributors

This edition of *Insight Guide: Seattle* builds on previous editions supervised by **Martha Ellen Zenfell**, who worked closely with project editor **John Wilcock**, a contributor to numerous Insight Guides. Also closely involved in creating the title was Seattle resident **Giselle Smith**, who also worked on this new edition by updating the central Seattle chapters. She was assisted by resident **Leslie Anderson**, who also overhauled the extensive Travel Tips section. In Seattle, **David Williams** contributed new essays on geology and flora and fauna; **John Stevenson** updated the Eastside cities. In Tacoma, **Don Ranard** reworked the Puget Sound and South of Seattle chapters, while Victoria-based **Don Rutherford** wrote a new chapter on Victoria, updated the Olympic Peninsula, and overhauled several feature essays.

Contributors to the previous editions – and much of their work still appears in this new edition – included **Joel Rogers**, **Bodo Bondzio**, **Stanley Young**, **Brenda Peterson**, **Bruce Barcott**, **Eric Lucas**, **J. Kingston Pierce**, **Charles Smyth**, **Molly Dee Anderson**, **Carlene Canton**, **Kristen Nelson**, **Jamie Wakefield**, and **Anne Frichtl**.

Map Legend

▬ ▪ ▪	International Boundary
- - - -	State/County Boundary
	National Park/Reserve
- - - -	Ferry Route
✈ ✈	Airport: International/ Regional
	Bus Station
■	Parking
	Tourist Information
✉	Post Office
†	Church/Ruins
†	Monastery
☪	Mosque
✡	Synagogue
	Castle/Ruins
∴	Archaeological Site
∩	Cave
	Statue/Monument
★	Place of Interest

The main places of interest in the Places section are coordinated by number with a full-colour map (e.g. ❶), and a symbol at the top of every right-hand page tells you where to find the map.

INSIGHT GUIDE Seattle

Contents

Maps

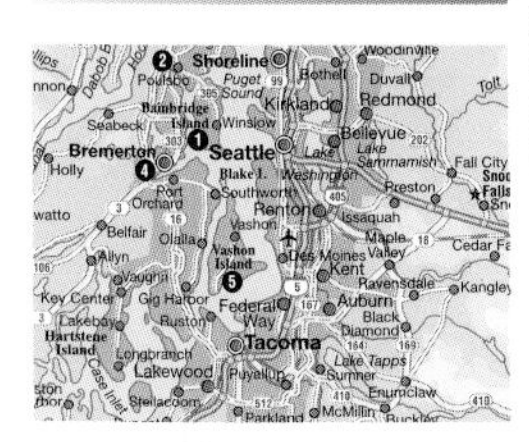

Introduction

History

Features

Seattle's exquisite skyline and the Space Needle.

Insight on ...

Information panels

Places

Travel Tips

◆ **Full Travel Tips index is on page 263**

No. 2 End

A City of Immigrants

Seattle's residents relish the perceptions held by outsiders about the city's style and mystique – and its smugness

For some years now Seattle has been a media darling, touted as a most livable city by numerous publications and written up kindly in magazines from the *Atlantic* to *Esquire* to *Newsweek*. And while longtime residents smugly shrug and say they knew it all along, some newcomers criticize the city for being less idyllic than they had hoped when they packed up and headed northwest. But it is those newcomers who will come to define the city, as did the immigrants who settled here before them, and those before them, stretching back a mere century and a half to 1852. Seattle is a city of immigrants, whether from California or Cambodia.

Like many growing cities, Seattle has problems. Arguments in favor of height restrictions on downtown skyscrapers culminated in a ballot initiative that passed by a narrow margin. An increasing crime rate has arrived along with the surge in population, as has an increase in the number – and therefore the visibility – of the homeless population. It remains a much safer city than many others, however, and is consciously working not to be just another big city.

What is it that sets Seattleites apart? According to *Seattle Times* columnist Jean Godden, they never carry umbrellas, never wash their cars, never shine their shoes and never turn on their windshield wipers unless it's absolutely pouring. Whatever the reasons for their distinctive identity, if such be the case, Seattle's coffee fanatics – and that seems to be most of the population – rationalize that they're synonymous with a preference for fine espresso. "Perhaps we're a bit independent and tend to taste things for ourselves," wrote an essayist in the city's *Cafe Ole* magazine.

The typical, stereotypical image of a Seattle resident is a modern mountain man clad in GoreTex, plaid shirt, sensible shoes and a beard. The reality is often not far from that. The Seattle-based outfitters Recreational Equipment, Inc. (REI) registers future brides and grooms for outdoor gear ranging from crampons to campstoves, but this city also sports a growing local arts scene that is demanding attention from East Coast and Southern California critics.

There's something about this city, though, a sense of style or good taste, that justifies most of the boasts concerning its quality of living. Seattle's sunny, polite disposition won't let most people dwell on any of the city's negative aspects for long. When the sun comes out in Seattle – after a day, a week or even a month of drizzle – most residents will tell you there is no better place to be. ❑

PRECEDING PAGES: outdoor art frames the ubiquitous Space Needle; the Space Needle's top rotates once an hour; ferry crewmen; Mount Rainier from Tacoma.
LEFT: float planes frequent the waters of downtown Seattle.

Decisive Dates

BEGINNINGS AND EARLY EXPLORATIONS

20,000 BC Small bands of Ice Age hunters cross the Bering Land Bridge from Asia.
7000–1000 BC Tribes of the Puget Sound become dependent upon fishing.
1592 Spanish ships visit the region.
1790 Chief Sealth – also known as Seattle – is born in the Puget Sound area.
1792 English navigator Capt. George Vancouver lands near present-day Everett, north of Seattle. His expedition explores Puget Sound, named for Peter Puget, a lieutenant on Vancouver's crew.

1805 Merriwether Lewis and William Clark finish their explorations of the Louisiana Purchase when they reach the Pacific Ocean.
1820s The Hudson's Bay Company expands its operations in the Pacific Northwest, based in Fort Vancouver, at the mouth of the Columbia River.
1833 The Hudson's Bay Company establishes Fort Nisqually in present-day Tacoma.

ESTABLISHMENT OF SEATTLE

1851 David Denny and a group of settlers arrive at Alki Point, in what is now West Seattle. They name their settlement Alki-New York.
1852 Disappointed by Alki Point's winter weather and poor port potential, Denny and his crew shift north a bit to Elliott Bay, near present-day downtown Seattle.
1853 The relocated town of Seattle is laid out and named for Chief Seattle, a friend of the settlers.
1854 A treaty with the local tribes provides for the newcomers to "buy" Indian land.
1855 Chief Seattle – leader of the Duwamish, Suquamish and other Puget Sound tribes – signs the Port Elliott treaty, giving away Indian land and establishing a reservation.
1856 Some Indians rebel against the treaty, but the rebellion is quickly quenched by the U.S. Army.
1861 The University of Washington is established.
1864 The transcontinental telegraph connects Seattle with the rest of the United States.
1866 Chief Seattle dies at the Port Madison Reservation, Washington.
1882 Nurtured by the economic depression, animosity against Chinese immigrants increases.
1883 Tacoma is incorporated.

SEATTLE BECOMES A CITY

1886 Racial violence breaks out against Chinese residents. Five men are shot and Chinese stores and homes are destroyed. 200 Chinese are forced onto a San Francisco-bound ship.
1889 A handyman tosses a bucket of water onto a flaming pot of glue in a paint store. The resulting explosion and fire destroys the entire 60-block downtown area of Seattle.
1890 The population of Seattle reaches 50,000; the city of Seattle erects a monument over Chief Seattle's grave.
1893 The Great Northern Railway arrives in Seattle, making it a major rail terminus.
1897 The S.S. *Portland* arrives in Seattle, carrying hundreds of thousands of dollars worth of gold from the Yukon's Klondike. Seattle's mayor resigns and heads north for the gold.
Late 1890s Japanese laborers begin arriving.
1900 In Tacoma, Midwesterner Frederick Weyerhauser buys 900,000 acres of Pacific Northwest timberland not wanted by the Northern Pacific Railroad.
Early 1900s Hills in the downtown area are removed by sluicing methods and the removed earth is used for harbor landfill. Ten surrounding cities and towns are annexed by Seattle.
1909 The Alaska-Yukon-Pacific Exposition is held in Seattle, at the site of the present-day University of Washington.
1910 Seattle's population reaches 250,000.
1914 The Panama Canal opens, increasing Seattle's importance as a Pacific port.

A CITY OF COMMERCE AND TECHNOLOGY

1916 The Lake Washington Ship Canal, linking the outer harbour of Elliott Bay with the inner harbour of Lake Washington, opens. William Boeing, a prosperous Seattle lumberman, flies a pontooned plane and incorporates Pacific Aero Products Company.

1917 Pacific Aero Products Company is renamed the Boeing Airplane Company.

1919 The country's first and longest general strike is held in Seattle, but it becomes a tactical error as some of its supporters are targeted as Communists.

1928 Boeing becomes part of United Aircraft & Transport Corporation, a merger of several aircraft manufacturers and airlines under Boeing's chairmanship.

1934 Antitrust rules force United Aircraft & Transport to break up. Boeing, newly incorporated, emerges along with United Airlines and United Aircraft.

1935 The B-17 *Flying Fortress* is first flown.

1940 Seattle's population is 450,000.

1941 The U.S. entry into World War II invigorates Seattle's importance, both in shipbuilding and in aircraft manufacturing.

1942 President Franklin D. Roosevelt signs an executive order permitting internment of Japanese-Americans. In Seattle, 6,000 Japanese-Americans are placed in Idaho internment camps. James Marshall Hendrix, a.k.a. Jimi Hendrix, is born in Seattle. The B-29 *Superfortress* begins flight.

1944 Seattle's mayor forms the Seattle Civic Unity Committee to promote racial accord.

1950 An economic recession is squelched by the Korean War; Seattle builds B-47 bombers.

1958 The Boeing 707 commercial passenger jet is introduced for regular service.

1960 Seattle's population exceeds 1 million.

1962 The Seattle World's Fair introduces the city – and the ubiquitous Space Needle, which becomes the city's most noted symbol – to the world.

1969 Boeing lays off 60 percent of its employees as the demand for commercial aircraft plummets. Seattle's economy heads into a tailspin.

1970 The Boeing 747 is put into service, with twice the carrying capacity of any previous passenger jet.

1980 Mount St. Helens explodes to the south of Seattle after being dormant for 200 years. The Pacific Northwest is blanketed with ash.

1982 The so-called Green River Killer begins his 49-person murder spree. He is never caught.

1992 Seattle becomes a music center as grunge music – Soundgarden, Nirvana, Pearl Jam – sweeps the nation.

1999 Safeco Field replaces the Kingdome to host major-league baseball. After years of acrimony, Canada and the U.S. sign a salmon-fishing treaty. ❑

PRECEDING PAGES: Northwest scene by Alfred Jacob Miller, c. 1858. **LEFT:** totem carving of a Northwest tribe. **ABOVE:** Port Gamble sawmill in the late 1800s.

SEATTLE PUTS DOWN ROOTS

The second choice for its original pioneer settlers, Seattle took root and with considerable luck – and a massive fire – became the Northwest's urban center

The impression that the typical visitor receives of Seattle today – a city that is stolid, self-confident, prosperous, and eminently livable – belies the eccentricity and gritty, ribald character that mark much of Seattle's brief – and early – history. Carved from the primeval forest beginning in 1851, Seattle has come into its own as a great American metropoli. But during its earliest days it more closely resembled the Indian village of "seven ill-looking houses" that Merriwether Lewis and William Clark found "situated at the foot of the high hills" when they concluded their transcontinental expedition on the Pacific coast, in 1805.

The Salish tribe of Puget Sound inhabited a paradise mild in climate and abundant in resources. The Duwamish, one of the Puget Sound tribes, occupied most of the present site of Seattle. They were a remarkably peaceful people. Fishing and hunting only on their own lands, they bought dressed deer and elk skins, using seashells as money, from more easterly inland tribes, whom the Sound people considered to be savages. In turn, of course, these mountain dwellers to the east, for their part, looked down upon the "fish-eaters."

Fish, especially the ubiquitous salmon, was significant in the lives of these coastal peoples. The man who caught the first salmon each spring invited all his friends to a feast; each guest received a small piece of the first salmon, except the host, who did not eat. The same ceremony greeted the first deer, berries, or fowl – the Duwamish were known to enjoy celebrating given any kind of excuse.

During the summer, the eastern inland tribes came down from the mountains to trade for the seafood they needed to help survive through the winter. Fishing, hunting, and berry-picking grounds were tribal territory, but requests to forage in another tribe's territory were usually accepted. Using a territory without the tribe's permission, however, was regarded as an invasion and frequently led to war.

When attacked by other tribes, as they often were by the more northerly Haida, Indians of the Puget Sound region preferred to retreat into the dense forests until the marauders left. Men unlucky enough to be caught unawares were killed and their women enslaved. Should a warrior kill an enemy in one of the more local conflicts, he was not allowed to touch food with his fingers for 10 days, and he often scratched his cheeks with a sharp stone to make them bleed. Among some Puget Sound tribes, a warrior who had killed an enemy had to paint his face black to avoid blindness.

The first Europeans to see the Seattle area, under the command of Capt. George Vancouver, an Englishman, landed near Everett, north of Seattle, in 1792. Later, furs drew the Europeans back to the Northwest. The Hudson's Bay Company, based to the south in Fort Vancouver on the Columbia River, along the present-day

PRECEDING PAGES: native village, Alert Bay.
LEFT: 19th-century Goomokwey tribal mask.
RIGHT: chief of a Puget Sound tribe.

border between Washington and Oregon, outfitted a rag-tag group of social outcasts to deal with the indigenous peoples and bring in the pelts of sea otters and beavers.

"The very scum of the earth, and the most unruly and troublesome gang to deal with in this, or perhaps any other part of the World," wrote Sir George Simpson, sent out in the 1820s to reorganize the company's holdings in the Pacific Northwest. For the next three decades, the Hudson's Bay Company dominated the Northwest, considering itself as steward in a foreign land – a bureaucracy owned by distant landlords interested in profits.

The discovery of gold in northern California in the mid-19th century and the opening of new trails to the West pushed out the corporate bureaucrats and fur-traders.

Soon the pristine reaches of the Pacific Coast were being carved up by zealous city builders and determined entrepreneurs. There were already a handful of settlers in Puget Sound when David Denny reached the sandy spit of Alki Point – just south of present-day downtown Seattle – in September of 1851. The settlers at the newly named Alki-New York (*alki* means "by-and-by" in the Chinook language, and New York was in honor of Denny's home town) had come by way of Illinois, and then

THE NORTHWEST PASSAGE

For almost a century, the Spanish had viewed the Pacific Ocean as their private lake. But the smugness was shaken – quite rudely – in 1579 when Englishman Francis Drake, a notorious English pirate, sailed up the South American coast, plundering Spanish ports of their gold and other bounty. Afterwards, Drake escaped to the north along the coast of North America to the Pacific Northwest and its atmosphere of the "most vile, thick and stinking fog." When Drake had retreated to the north, rather than south back around South America's tip, the Spanish speculated that he was retreating to the fabled and long-sought-after Northwest Passage, connecting the Pacific with the Atlantic. Had the British found it?

In fact, they had not. But tales of the Northwest Passage would persist for another 150 years, a catalyst for explorations of the Pacific Northwest. Russians, seeking markets for furs, had begun searching for the Northwest Passage decades before Drake escaped from the Spanish. The forays of the Russians from the north (now Alaska) threatened Spain and its claims to the Pacific. Spanish ships sailed to the Pacific Northwest to find that the Russians had no permanent settlements. But while Spanish ships had staked an early claim to the region, Spain never showed an interest in the region.

The legend of the Northwest Passage was enriched by a creative lie cooked up by a 60-year-old Greek ship's pilot. Apostolos Valerianos claimed to have been a pilot for the Viceroy of Mexico – traveling under the pseudonym Juan de Fuca – when the Viceroy searched for the Passage in 1592. Valerianos claimed that they had sailed along the Passage for 20 days to Europe's North Sea. The old Greek first spun his lie to Michael Lok, an armchair explorer, fortune hunter and frequent guest in English debtors' prisons. Lok, seeking backing to find the Passage (and escape from his debts), spread the story amongst the British aristocracy. Soon the imaginary voyage of Juan de Fuca had affixed itself in the collective mind of a hopeful Europe for a shortcut to the Pacific.

Two centuries later, Capt. James Cook undertook his third circumnavigation of the world in 1776, in part to search for the Northwest Passage, though he personally did not think it existed. Fur traders later frequented the area. One, Charles Barkley, arrived on the west side of Vancouver Island in 1787. He wrote of the great strait – now Juan de Fuca Strait – that was close to the latitude claimed by Apostolos Valerianos for the Passage. Thus the pseudonym of a man who sailed a fictitious voyage became a geographical name. Further explorations by a British captain, George Vancouver, and an American trader, Robert Gray, failed to find the Northwest Passage.

through Portland, which by that time already a congested burg of 2,000 people. But the Denny group preferred to establish their own city further north and with their arrival in Puget Sound, the formal history of Seattle begins.

Flattery and fraud

City-building was a commonplace American enterprise of the 19th century. A determined land developer laid claim to a location he believed held promise, designed a town plan, then used every means at his disposal – from bribery and exaggeration to flattery and fraud – to entice settlers and investors to fill out his vision of the future. Thus began Steilacoom, Olympia, Whatcom, Port Townsend, Tacoma and Seattle, each born with hope and determination; yet of these neighboring settlements, only Seattle would become a world-class city.

Seattle's early years were not auspicious. After a dismal winter, the Denny party discovered that Alki-New York was an entirely unsuitable site for a cabin, let alone a potential urban center. Windswept and far too shallow for shipping, all it provided was a breathtaking view and pleasant breezes compared to the dark swamps and dense forests that lined the rest of the area. But Denny knew that any successful city in the area would need at least a deep-water harbor, so he borrowed a neighbor's clothesline, tied several horseshoes to it, and spent several days in a dugout canoe plumbing the depths of the adjacent coastline until he found his deep water in Elliott Bay, opposite several acres of mudflats (which reeked when the tide went out) that were guarded by an impenetrable forest, steep cliffs and hills. Seattle had thus been discovered.

Denny, Charles Boren, and William Bell staked out claims on the waterfront and were soon joined by Dr. David Swinson Maynard, the first notable man of Seattle history. Medical doctor, lumberman, blacksmith, entrepreneur and all-around visionary – Maynard, like many of those arriving in the Northwest, came by way of the Oregon Trail. This 2,000-mile-long (3,200-km) trek from the Mississippi River through the Rocky Mountains to the mouth of the Columbia River was the route that thousands of eager settlers would take.

The trip along the Oregon Trail by ox-drawn covered wagon was fraught with death and disease, but it was an experience that bonded the pioneers. Maynard settled first in what is now Olympia, but he was driven out by fellow mer-

LEFT: spear fishing at Snoqualmie Falls.
ABOVE: the Oregon Trail, east of the Cascades.

chants who, despite their common experiences on the Oregon Trail, were upset that the kind-hearted Maynard's general store offered prices that were suicidally low and credit that was virtually unlimited.

When Maynard wandered down the Puget Sound for a new location, both groups – those who stayed at Alki-New York and the Denny trio on Elliott Bay – wanted Maynard to join them "for the benefit," as one of them later wrote, "a good man brings." Maynard believed that the new town on Elliott Bay was the more likely to succeed, and it didn't hurt that Boren, Bell and Denny offered to move their claims north by an eighth of a mile (200 meters) to make room for his.

The first store

Maynard measured out about 300 yards (270 meters) of the most southernly deep-water frontage and took the rest in marsh and hillside. He hired some local tribal men to construct a building down by the Sag, as they called the low land by the water. Within a few days, he was in his new store selling, as one flyer put it, "a general assortment of dry goods, groceries, hardware, etc., suitable for the wants of immigrants just arriving."

In Olympia, Maynard had earlier befriended an Indian *tyee* (chief) named Sealth (pronounced *see-alth* and sometimes *see-attle*), leader of the tribe living at the mouth of the Duwamish River, where it entered Elliott Bay. Dressed in a breechcloth and faded blue blanket, the 6-ft-tall (183-cm) chief with steel-gray hair hanging to his shoulders caused quite a stir among the settlers. Europeans in the region considered him among the most important tyee in the territory; they were certainly more impressed with Sealth than his fellow people were. The various tribes of the Sound had their differences but they were all agreed on one thing: a chief had little authority, being merely a rich man with some eloquence and whose opinions carried a little more weight than those of his fellow tribesmen. Even so, when it was time to name the new city, Maynard's suggestion of Seattle, in honor of his noble friend, replaced the native name used by the local authorities, Duwamps.

Ever since a ship captained by G. W. Kendall had nosed past the Strait of Juan de Fuca two years earlier in a misguided search for icebergs (to be used in drinks on the Barbary Coast in California) and had to settle for a load of piling, timber had become the region's cash crop. Maynard set some of the Indians to transforming a stand of fir behind his store into shakes, square logs, and cordwood, while others caught salmon and constructed crude barrels that were roughly hooped. When the ship *Franklin Adams* turned up at Maynard's tiny dock in October, the doctor-entrepreneur had ready for shipment 1,000 barrels of brined salmon, 30 cords of wood, 12,000 ft (3,700 meters) of squared timbers, 8,000 ft (2,400 meters) of piling and 10,000 roofing shingles.

Even though the salmon spoiled, ruining most of his profits, nothing dimmed "Doc" Maynard's extravagant enthusiasm and exuberant friendliness for long. Anything good for Seattle was good for Doc Maynard, and he did his best to make sure the town prospered. When Henry Yesler arrived in Seattle, scouting the Sound for the best location for a steam-driven sawmill to cut lumber, Maynard and Boren each gave up some of their land for the necessary waterfront frontage.

Skid Road

The determined city-founders knew that the settlement that got Yesler's sawmill would have a head start on the future, and the town's rugged residents built a log cookhouse and started on "Skid Road," a log slide that would allow the timber to slide down the hill to the sawmill on the waterfront. When Yesler returned from San Francisco and set up his equipment, Seattle took a large step forward. "Huzza for Seattle!" wrote the editors of the paper in Olympia. "The mill will prove as good as a gold mine to Mr. Yesler, besides tending greatly to improve the fine town site of Seattle and the fertile country around it, by attracting thither the farmer, the laborer, and the capitalist. On with improvement!" Within months, Seattle was named the government seat of King County, with Doc Maynard's little store the site of the post office and even the Seattle Exchange.

Though the local tribes at first had welcomed the outsiders – and their wonderful tools, blankets, liquor, guns, and medicines – they soon came to see that other things were less desirable: new diseases, a religion that said that many things the Indians had always done were wicked (though the reasons why were less than clear), and most perniciously, perhaps, the concept of private, individual property. By the time

FEMALE SLAVES

Women were in demand and Seattle became a center for traffic in white slaves, coaxed onto ships bound for the Northwest with promises of the good life.

FAR LEFT: Chief Seattle (Sealth); **LEFT:** Dr. David Maynard. **ABOVE:** steamships in Seattle's harbor.

Doc Maynard helped broker an arrangement to buy their land, they were in little position to bargain. In 1854, the treaty was explained to the assembled Indians by a drunken Governor Stevens in Chinook creole, a bastard tongue that had been developed by fur traders more suited to commerce than to the subtleties of diplomacy.

BING'S LEGAL HERITAGE

One of the two lawyers for the unsuccessful defense of the rebel leader Leschi was H. R. Crosby, who would later become the father of singer Bing Crosby.

The American government offered the Indian tribes $150,000, payable over 20 years in usable goods, and a reservation in return for 3,000 square miles (8,000 sq. km) of property. Chief Seattle, towering 12 inches (30 cm) taller than Stevens, answered the ultimatum on behalf of all the Indians in his language, Duwamish. The speech was recalled over three decades later by Dr. Henry Smith, an observer at the time much taken, as he put it, "with the magnificent bearing, kindness and paternal benignity" of Chief Seattle.

"The Big Chief at Washington sends us word that he wishes to buy our lands but is willing to allow us enough to live comfortably," goes Smith's version of Chief Seattle's speech. "His people are many. They are like the grass that covers vast prairies. My people are few. They resemble the scattering trees of a storm-swept plain. Every part of this soil is sacred in the estimation of my people. Every hillside, every valley, every plain and grove has been hallowed by some sad or happy event in days long vanished, and when the last Red Man shall have perished and the memory of my tribe shall have become a myth among the White Men, these shores will swarm with the invisible dead of my tribe."

The following year the treaty was signed and most Indians moved to the reservations across Puget Sound. Some of the Indians fought the agreement and in 1856 rebelled. There was a lot of gunplay but few casualties on either side. The U.S. Army easily defeated the small rebel group. When one of the rebel Indian leaders, Leschi, was later caught through the perfidy of a nephew, he was tried and convicted of ambushing and murdering an officer during the war. Leschi was hanged.

Today, Leschi is considered a regional hero, and he has a park and statue dedicated to his memory. The so-called Indian War was over and the whites had won, but many issues were left unsettled. Some, such as the continuing dispute over territorial fishing rights, remain disputed to this day.

Seattle was little more than an industrious village in these earlier years. Venison was caught and sold for 10 cents a pound in the "downtown" area, where 8-ft-thick (2.5-meter) trees still grew above all else. Angeline, the daughter of Chief Seattle, worked as a domestic helper – "a good worker", recalls Sophie Frye Bass, niece of founder David Denny, "but when she had a fit of temper she would leave, even though she left a tub full of clothes soaking." Meanwhile, Yesler's sawmill sent its lumber to San Francisco, while the sawdust was used to fill the swampy lowland south of the downtown area.

The Chinese were hard-working and uncomplaining. Without their labor, America's railroads would have taken far longer, but many unemployed Seattleites believed the Asian immigrants were also inherently inferior, unreliable, debased, immoral, given to gambling and smoking opium, and riddled with diseases like syphilis and malaria. The Knights of Labor, a white fraternal organization, wanted to eject the Chinese from the Northwest by force; in 1885, rampaging whites drove about 30 Chinese from Newcastle, a nearby town. The hate spread to Tacoma, and in early 1886 Seattle exploded in anti-Chinese violence.

LEFT: anti-Chinese riots in Seattle, late 19th century.
ABOVE: gold-rush miners on downtown street.

Racial problems

The mid-1880s turned out to be difficult times in Seattle. The city was hard hit by an economic depression affecting the entire country. Out-of-work fishermen, lumber workers and miners found themselves competing for jobs not only with unemployed city clerks and carpenters, but also with substantial numbers of Chinese laborers who had been discharged after the completion of the area's railroads. Not surprisingly, the Chinese workers became the scapegoat for the area's problems.

TELEGRAPH AND TRAINS

In 1864, the world became a smaller place for Seattle when the transcontinental telegraph arrived. But it was the coming of the Northern Pacific Railroad the same year – a spur was extended to Seattle from the terminus in Tacoma – that culminated in a brief period of unparalleled growth and prosperity. Immigrants poured in, lumber output expanded, building construction soared, electric streetcar lines opened up, and new districts were established. Areas such as Queen Anne, Madison Park, Lake Washington, Rainier Valley and West Seattle became substantial suburbs by the early 1890s and sharply expanded the boundaries of the city.

During the trouble, five men were shot, Chinese stores and homes were demolished, and 200 Chinese were forced to board a San Francisco-bound steamer. By March, when federal troops had restored order, the Seattle Chinese community of about 500 had been eliminated. In July, voters returned almost the entire slate of the anti-Chinese People's Party in municipal elections. It would be a decade before the Chinese community slowly built itself up to its previous numbers.

By 1890, Seattle's population had more than quadrupled, from 11,000 a decade before to 50,000. Three years later, the surge was over

but Seattle had become a very different place. The city was also developing a sense of place, a personality and identity.

An 1882 visitor had found it a "self-reliant, determined, well-governed" community with "exceptional public spirit." Other observers stressed the "marvelous enterprise" of the city's inhabitants, calling it a virtual "paradise" for anyone willing to work hard. One New Englander, after visiting nearly all the major urban centers of Puget Sound, found that Seattle, though it had "few flowers, less laughter, and a scarcity of tennis courts," in its "dogged determination and energetic push reminds me most strongly of Chicago."

The Great Fire

Nothing demonstrates this Seattle can-do attitude more than the city's reaction to John Back's unfortunate blunder on June 6, 1889. Back, a handyman, threw a bucket of water on a flaming pot of glue in the middle of a paint store. The building exploded in flames, and 12 hours later the entire commercial district – 60 city blocks – lay burned to the ground. "Oh, light-hearted, industrious Seattle," a reporter wailed in Friday's *Seattle Daily Press*, "to be reduced to ashes in a single afternoon."

In fact, the "Great Fire" was the best thing to happen to the city. The commercial section of pre-fire Seattle had been a pestilential morass. The downtown was built on mudflats and the sewers would back up when the tide came in, spewing raw sewage directly from toilets. Huge chuckholes and pools of mud would open up at major intersections, sucking in horses, carriages and even one unfortunate schoolboy. Typhoid and tuberculosis were rampant.

No wonder the populace called the fire a godsend, as it allowed them to overhaul the municipal systems and rebuild a city worthy of its industrious inhabitants. Civic improvement began three days after the fire, while the fire's embers were still warm. Three years later, a new Seattle – built of brick and stone – stood ready to lead the Pacific Northwest.

When the new, higher roadways were later built, they reached the second stories of the buildings but had to leave the sidewalks and the ground levels accessible 12 ft (4 meters) below. Ladders were placed at intersections so people could cross the street and the sidewalks covered over (creating "Underground Seattle").

The streets were realigned after the fire. New wharves, railroad depots, freight sheds, coal bunkers and warehouses in the mile-long waterfront strip were repaired or rebuilt. The sawmills moved out of town, leaving behind only the name Skid Road (now called Yeslers Way), a remembrance of the days when the logs would come tumbling down the pathway to Yesler's waterfront sawmills. In later years, as this area of town became a drab repository of broken men and women, the name Skid Road would be corrupted to Skid Row and used as a description of urban decay in other cities. ❑

LEFT: the Great Fire of 1889. **RIGHT:** Pioneer Building was built on the ashes of the Great Fire.

PIONEER SQUARE MA

PRESCRIPTIONS

SPECIAL SEATTLE NUMBER

THE COAST

ALASKA AND GREATER NORTHWEST

VOL. 18 NO. 3 SEPT. 1909.

LOIS
STO
CO.

SEATTLE
The METROPOLIS

The Coast Publishing Company
14th and Main St., SEATTLE, U. S. A.

AMERICAN ENGRAVING CO. SPOKANE

PRICE FIFTEEN CENTS

SKID ROW TO SPACE NEEDLE

The expression "Skid Row" was first used in Seattle. But now the city has grown rich, thanks to the aerospace and software industries

For much of the 1890s, Seattle was in a state of decline, its Skid Road crowded with the homeless and the poor. Business slumped to a fraction of its former strength, and Seattle might well have become a second-rate town were it not for the fortuitous arrival of the SS *Portland* in July of 1897. Fresh from Alaska, the *Portland* carried – as newspapers' headlines screamed across the country the following day – "A Ton of Gold Aboard."

When Seattle's then-mayor, W. D. Wood, heard news of the Yukon gold strike, he wired his resignation from San Francisco, where he was visiting, and headed for gold country. His reaction was quite typical as a kind of madness descended upon the Western world, as men from Sydney to Switzerland uprooted their lives on a moment's notice and sailed and walked to the frozen fields and primitive camps at Dawson, in the Yukon far to the north of Seattle. And many of these treasure seekers passed through Seattle.

Fortune seekers

The Yukon gold rush wrenched Seattle out of its commercial doldrums and propelled it into becoming the major center of the Northwest. Tens of thousands of prospectors and hopelessly naive and unprepared fortune hunters descended on the city to purchase supplies and transport northward. Schwabacher's Outfitters rose to the top of the provisioning industry and its supplies for the trek north lay stacked on the boardwalk in piles 10 ft (3 meters) high to keep up with demand. By spring and following the SS *Portland*'s arrival, Seattle merchants now raked in some $25 million, no small increase over the previous year's total revenues of $300,000. Hotels and restaurants were overbooked and Seattle's banks filled up with Yukon gold. Schools opened to teach mining techniques and classes were even offered in Seattle on how to drive a dog sled – in a city that rarely saw a snowflake.

And this transient gold-rush population wanted entertainment. John Considine, patriarch of the famous acting family, opened up the People's Theater and brought in famed exotic dancer Little Egypt, who, clad in diaphanous harem clothes, gave a lesson in international culture – dancing the muscle dance, the Turkish dance and the Damascus dance to wildly appreciative crowds almost every night of the year. These box-houses – so-called for the private plywood alcoves situated along the sides of the theater – had long been a part of Seattle's early entertainment nightlife.

The entry fee to a box-house was only 10 cents, with profits made on the drinks cajoled out of the male patrons by "women with dresses nearly to the point above the knees, with stained and sweaty tights, with bare arms and necks uncovered over halfway to their waists," as a reporter for *Coast* magazine wrote.

PRECEDING PAGES: Seattle's industry helped win World War II. **LEFT:** promoting Seattle, "The Metropolis". **RIGHT:** miners at Chilkoot Pass often began in Seattle.

Sitting in their box-houses equipped with electric bells to call for drinks, the women golddiggers would entertain the male goldminers while Little Egypt danced for the newcomers in the main hall of the theater. Those gold-digger-and goldmining couples who wished to continue their conversations about gold or other subjects of mutual interest could walk to nearby rooming houses.

Prostitution had always been a facet of early Seattle life, a natural result of the vicissitudes of a nearly all-male lumber town. As early as 1861, an enterprising rake by the name of John Pennell established the Illahee (Salish for "homeland") over the mudflats, close by the mill – and its male workers – and in full view of arriving ships. Pennell's bordello soon became a landmark in the young town. Locals renamed it the Madhouse and some scholars hold that its presence helped establish Seattle in its formative years, serving as "the best mouse trap in the woods."

The considerable demographic discrepancy between men and women prompted Asa Mercer, a carpenter who worked on the newly built Territorial University (and became its first president), to secure a $300 fee from lonely northwest bachelors with the assurance he

GIDDY OVER GOLD

The gold rush to Canada's Klondike region, in the western part of the Yukon Territory near the Alaskan border, began when an American prospector, George Washington Carmack, struck alluvial gold in 1896 after eight years of searching. Carmack found gold in Bonanza Creek, a tributary of the Klondike River, near Dawson. All of the Klondike gold would be taken from streams and rivers.

Reports of the strike reached the United States the following year, emphasized by the arrival of the *Excelsior* in San Francisco, carrying $750,000 in Klondike gold; three days later, the *Portland* arrived in Seattle with $800,000 of Klondike gold. By the end of 1897, $22 million worth of gold had been extracted by miners in the Klondike fields. By the end of 1898, 30,000 prospectors had descended upon the Klondike, half of them living in Dawson. (From 1898 until 1953, Dawson was the government seat of the Yukon Territory. Today, Dawson's population has shrunk to less than 1,000 people.)

The American author Jack London took part in the gold rush for a couple of years. When he returned home to the San Francisco Bay Area, he wrote of his experiences.

The mother lode peaked in 1900, but the area continued to cough up gold until 1966, by which time the Klondike fields had produced more than $250 million in gold.

would bring them marriageable young maidens from the East Coast. While he had promised delivery of some 500 women, he arrived in Seattle a year later with just 100, but he still managed somehow to placate his male clients. Mercer married one of his imports and promptly moved inland.

Bordellos persisted in the Skid Road area (in the area of modern-day Pioneer Square), helping solidify its already gamy reputation. Once the gold from the Yukon poured in, the local bawdy houses went upscale. One house of pleasure spent $200,000 on tapestries and velvet. Lou Graham, a famous madam, paraded her newest arrivals in fine carriages on Sunday afternoon. She also served as an unofficial banker, helping to start many a business in boomtown Seattle.

BORDELLO DECORUM

Honest Kate's "Parlor House" was subdued: no rowdy behavior or foul language in her salon. Customers and the ladies met and conversed in tones of utter propriety.

The gold rush in the Klondike also solidified Seattle's position as the center of trade in the Northwest, allowing it to surpass the older and then-larger city of Portland, to the south at the mouth of the Columbia River. The boom raised Seattle's population to 80,000 by 1900; with the arrival of three new railroad lines and a road over the Cascades, those numbers rose to a quarter of a million by 1910. Most of the immigrants were from the Midwest and from Europe, particularly Scandinavia. (Swedes, in fact, populated the then-separate sawmill city of Ballard, now in northern Seattle.) Laborers from Japan began arriving in large numbers in the late 1890s, an indication of Seattle's future position as a major shipping outlet to Asia and the Pacific.

Seattle was also growing increasingly legitimate. The entire downtown area was regraded to reduce the steep inclines of the original hills. Areas such as Capitol Hill became neighborhoods of the utmost propriety. The high-class bordellos and cheaper "crib-houses" were closed down, and John Considine moved out of his first box-house theater on Skid Road into a countrywide vaudeville-theater chain that soon extended from coast to coast and guaranteed performers 70 weeks of work. Alexander Pantages, who had also started with a single box-house theater during the uproarious Gold Rush days, rivaled Considine's chain and earned a reputation for booking superior acts. By 1926, Pantages, who had once worked as a

LEFT: the *Victoria* sails to Alaska from Seattle, 1900.
ABOVE: Lou Graham, notable local madam, at home.

bartender in a Dawson saloon during the Gold Rush, owned the largest chain of theaters in the country. He later sold the chain, but its name (in film theaters) lives on as a little-known memento to the days of the Seattle box-houses.

The birth of Boeing

Seattle already dominated the Alaskan shipping routes along the West Coast, and when the Panama Canal opened in 1914 and World War I brought an increased demand for navy vessels, Seattle was convinced that its future lay in shipbuilding and the sea. But there was one wealthy resident who disagreed. In 1910, at a makeshift airport south of Los Angeles, William Boeing attended the first international flying meet held in the United States. The scion of a wealthy Minnesota iron-and-timber family, he had made his own fortune in the timber of the Pacific Northwest.

Boeing's initial interest in flying may have been on a par with his decision to buy the Heath shipyards in order to finish a yacht. During tests over Lake Washington of a Curtiss-type hydroplane he had built with his friend and fellow Yale graduate Conrad Westervelt, he discovered a profession and a mission. In 1916, after some years of experimentation, the company of Boeing was incorporated in Seattle.

Boeing to United

In 1927, Boeing Air Transport flew the first commercial flight between Chicago and San Francisco. Later, Boeing Air Transport would become known as United Air Lines.

With the end of World War I in 1918, government contracts for ships evaporated. Seattle was saddled with 35,000 skilled but unemployed laborers who had been enticed to the city by the promise of high wages and permanent employment, but who now found themselves out of work. Rapid industrial expansion had provided fertile ground for the growth of strong labor unions and radical politics in the early decades of the century. The Northwest became a stronghold of organized labor, but some unions fared better than others. The International Workers of the World, better known as the "Wobblies," were often the target of violent suppression by the police, the American Legion, and the companies attempting to break the unions.

In Seattle, all the conditions were ripe for a confrontation, and in February of 1919 the Central Labor Council organized the country's first and – at five days – longest general strike, driving a spike of fear into the hearts of the propertied classes.

The fear exceeded any reality of danger and, in fact, the general strike proved to be a tactical error. Anarchists, socialists and communists were targeted as agents of the "Red Scare," and while Seattle and the state of Washington continued to be highly unionized, labor leaders prudently adopted a strategy of cooperation with management instead of confrontation. This union orientation and liberal heritage is still alive to this day – even many of the state's Republicans, nationally a conservative lot, are often progressive.

Yet even trade unions could not guard against the economic body blow that would follow in the wake of the Great Depression in the early 1930s, which hit Seattle harder than most cities. Skid Road saw an ever-growing population of the haggard and the hungry. A meal cost only 20 cents, but few down on Skid Road could afford it. Still, there was a surprising degree of order among the destitute. The city's so-called Hooverville (Depression-era shantytowns were given the generic name after then-Pres. Hoover), built on the tideflats in an abandoned shipyard, was among the largest temporary communities in the country. It also had its own self-appointed vigilante committee to enforce a sanitation code. The Unemployed Citizens' League, which reached a peak membership of 50,000 in 1931, formed a separate community – the so-called Republic of the Penniless – that used an elaborate system of work and barter to keep most of its members fed and housed. Those lucky enough to hold jobs were members of a well-organized network held in lockstep with the powerful teamsters.

When non-union beer from the East Coast began appearing in the Seattle area, the local teamsters refused to move it out of the warehouses. In turn, local breweries benefited, helping to establish the tradition of strong regional breweries in the Seattle area to this day.

LEFT: strikers carrying food, 1919. **ABOVE:** Seattle's sprawling Great Depression "Hooverville."

GLOBAL DEPRESSION

It began in October of 1929 when the stock market in the United States crashed, followed shortly in 1931 by the failure of the Austrian Credit-Anstalt. The global economic panic and depression – the Great Depression – led to a credit crunch that resulted in countless bankruptcies around the world and massive unemployment, 12 million jobless in the United States alone. World trade evaporated with the enactment of tariff restrictions by many governments. In the United States, President Herbert Hoover would not intervene with federal funds to alleviate unemployment and subsequently lost the presidency after one term to Franklin D. Roosevelt.

Big bombers and racial friction

With World War II came Seattle's second great economic boom. Although based partly on shipbuilding, this time the recovery was centered predominantly on one industry – aircraft – and one company – Boeing. Borne on the wings of Boeing's mass-produced B-17 Flying Fortress and B-29 Super Fortress bombers, the 1940 metropolitan population of about 450,000 would increase another 50 percent by 1950.

But the burgeoning Seattle economy was placed out of reach for the local Japanese population. When President Franklin D. Roosevelt signed Executive Order 9066 in February of 1942, 110,000 Japanese were summarily removed from their jobs and homes and placed in containment camps along the West Coast and in Wyoming and Idaho. In Seattle, 6,000 Japanese, many whose families had been settled in the city for half a century, lost everything they owned and moved out of Seattle to spend the next three years in an Idaho camp. Yet, like the Chinese before them, the Japanese returned to Seattle after their expulsion and the war's end, despite the often overt racism they encountered.

Race relations were always a matter of tension in Seattle. Long before the Asians, the immigrant Swedes were the first object of deri-

Tacoma: Long in Seattle's Shadow

There was a time, at the end of the 19th century, when Tacoma had a chance to become the region's urban center. Tacoma, for example, was chosen as the terminus for the Northern Pacific Railroad, which connected the two coasts.

In the battle for regional dominance, Seattle didn't beat Tacoma by itself. It had help – from Tacoma. After the financial panic of 1893 sent Tacoma into an economic tailspin, the city couldn't do anything right. When gold was discovered in the Yukon, Seattle sent a publicity man back East touting Seattle as the gateway to riches. In 1929, to great local acclaim, the *Spirit of Tacoma* attempted the first nonstop flight to Asia. The plane never got off the ground.

In 1940, Tacoma made national news when the Narrows Bridge – nicknamed Galloping Gertie for its tendency to sway in the wind – collapsed just four months after it was built. In the 1950s and 1960s, organized crime in high places, downtown decay and gangs, and Tacoma Aroma (from lumber processing) plagued the city's reputation.

Perhaps most galling to Tacoma's pride were the years when Tacoma tried to change the name of Mount Rainier, the region's most notable landmark, to Tahoma, a variation of the old Indian name for the volcano. Fearing benefits to its rival, Seattle opposed the name change, fighting to keep Mount Rainier, named after a long-forgotten Englishman.

sion. And after the Japanese were evacuated, the city faced its first real influx of blacks from the East Coast and southern states as wartime jobs appeared in factories. Most moved to the Central District, and in 1944 the mayor formed the Seattle Civic Unity Committee to promote racial accord.

Post-war elation led to a brief depression in 1950 that, in the Seattle area, was squelched by the Korean War and its demand for B-47 and B-52 bombers. With the civilian 707, Seattle confidently entered into the Jet Age, and nothing symbolized this attitude of onwards and upwards more than the skyline-embedded Space Needle, built as part of the 1962 World's Fair in Seattle, which introduced a resurgent Seattle to much of the world.

Unfortunately, Boeing had overestimated its market, and the city's fortunes plummeted almost overnight. In 1969 and 1970, the company was forced to lay off nearly two-thirds of its employees as the demand for commercial jets crumbled. Seattle seemed bereft. Aircraft engineers, unable to secure work anywhere else, opened up hamburger stands and drove taxis. When the unemployment rate hit one of every six workers in the city, tens of thousands subsequently left the city in which they thought they had lifelong security with Boeing.

Despite the bust at Boeing, Seattle continued to draw newcomers. By 1970, the population topped 1.2 million. Several attempts were made to raze the older sections of the city, but a growing population countered with an interest – and intent – in preserving what remained of old Seattle.

BOEING'S 10 PERCENT

Boeing's civilian 707 jet – a spinoff of a military tanker – turned Seattle into an industrial center. By 1960, Boeing was employing one in 10 workers in a city of 1 million people.

LEFT: a B-29. **ABOVE:** Elvis Presley in *It Happened at the World's Fair* (1963). **RIGHT:** Space Needle.

AIRBORNE BRIDAL SUITES

Boeing's legacy as an icon of international air transport began when now-defunct Pan American Airways used Boeing-built flying boats to bridge the seas. In 1935, the *China Clipper* arrived in Manila after flying over 8,000 miles (13,000 km), with four stops. Four years later, the *Yankee Clipper* began the first trans-Atlantic passenger service, between New York and Marseille, with 2 stops during the 26-hour flight. Initiating the service was delayed – Pan Am already had service to South America and Asia – because of differences with the British over landing rights. The Pan Am planes had a dining salon, sleeping berths, ladies' dressing room and a bridal suite.

Fire Mountain explodes

On May 18, 1980, nature took a stab at containing the growth of Seattle and the Pacific Northwest when Mount St Helens, south of Seattle, lived up to its American Indian name of Fire Mountain. After 200 years of being virtually dormant, the 9,665-ft (2,946-meter) Mount St Helens erupted, sending much of the mountain's summit peak 60,000 ft (18,000 meters) into the air.

The eruption came after warnings from scientists and attempts to evacuate the area, but the flow of molten rock and clouds of ash still resulted in almost 60 deaths near the mountain.

Damage was estimated at $1 billion. Within three days, the ash cloud had crossed North America; within two weeks, it had traveled right around the globe. Mount St. Helens itself was now 1,300 ft (400 meters) shorter than it had been before the blast. Ash fell throughout the Northwest in heavy amounts, hindering transportation, industry, and – for the short term – agriculture. (In the end, of course, the ash injected nutrients into the soil.)

Industrially, Seattle and the surrounding area has now become less dependent upon Boeing for the region's economy, developing an extensive high-tech industry in the suburbs that includes Adobe and Microsoft. But Bill Gates, Microsoft's co-founder and now America's richest man, has been criticized for using too little of his vast wealth to help the local community. In contrast, Paul Allen, the other co-founder, has gone on to spend much of his money in civic projects in the Puget Sound region. For example, he founded the Experience Music Project, a dynamic interactive music museum designed by architect Frank Gehry that opened in Seattle in 2000. He purchased the Seattle Seahawks football franchise, securing the team's long-term future in Seattle, and he embarked on a project to construct a world-class football-soccer stadium and exhibition center on the site of the old Seattle Kingdome and adjacent to Safeco Field, which opened in 1999. In 1997, Allen purchased and began work on preserving the historic Union Station, a century-old Seattle landmark.

Seattle is blossoming with even more ambitious new projects. The Seattle Symphony has a new home in Benaroya Hall, a state-of-the-art performance center featuring a 2,500-seat concert hall. The acoustics are magnificent. The Seattle Mariners now play ball in the new Safeco Field, a 47,000-seat stadium with a three-panel retractable roof designed to accommodate Seattle's unpredictable weather.

Traffic problems

All this growth has not come without cost. Seattle recently had the dubious distinction of being tied with Los Angeles as the nation's worst city for rush-hour traffic congestion. Like those in LA, people of Seattle like their cars, especially given the commute patterns of the region. The Interstate 5 corridor is particularly crowded and the problem is getting worse. To solve it, residents of the Puget Sound area have approved local funding for a 10-year regional transit plan. Sound Transit, the public agency charged with finding solutions to the Seattle area's traffic mess, is implementing a very ambitious mix of light-rail lines, regional bus routes, and new transit facilities. Meanwhile, Seattle's Metro bus system wins awards for the efficiency and friendliness of its services.

Seattle continues to draw new "settlers" to its wooded hills, drawn by Seattle's reputation as one of the nation's most livable cities. ❑

LEFT: aftermath of 1980 Mount St Helens eruption.
RIGHT: the 1962 World's Fair illuminated Seattle.

EATTLE
ORLD'S FAIR
CENTURY
21
EXPOSITION
EATTLE, WASH., U.S.A.
April 21-October 21
1962

ESPRESSO

SB
SEATTLE'S BEST COFFEE™
ESPRESSO MENU

NO CHECKS CASHED
WA SAM

TUMS

ZEST AND XENOPHOBIA

Just what makes Seattleites different – or, as they would insist, unique?

J. Kingston Pierce, a native Northwesterner, reveals all

Californians and Seattleites have a symbiotic love-hate relationship. They love us. We hate them. Both sides consider themselves to be virtuous. Actually, *hate* may be too strong a word to describe how Seattleites feel about visitors. We usually deny hating anything. We're too polite for that, thank you, a fact that might be traced to decades of Scandinavian influence. (Many local families can follow bloodlines back to Europe's emotionally reserved northern latitudes.) Or perhaps we are just reticent to voice any definite opinion, for fear that it will turn out to be politically incorrect. Locals worry about being labeled incorrigible hicks, because we're either too trusting or we're out of step with East Coast towns from which so many of us recently moved.

We were humbled greatly in the late 1980s when it was discovered that the organization chartered by the city to operate the popular Pike Place Market had apparently been selling off financial control of this historic civic cynosure to a New York investment company. Even the local press couldn't find words of rebuke for city officials. Seattle, it appeared, didn't have the fins to be swimming with sharks.

Origins of the Happy Face

Every once in a while there will be a splenetic public offensive here against something that wouldn't provoke so much as a yawn elsewhere – like nude-dancing clubs or the issue of whether guys who dress up as pirates during the summer's Seafair Festival and leer at beauty queens are actually encouraging sexual violence. But for the most part, Seattle wants to portray itself as upbeat and friendly. It was no mere coincidence that the Happy Face – that loony, lemony yellow, noseless symbol that now decorates everything from headlamp covers to boxer shorts to sanitation straps on motel toilets – was created in Seattle in the 1960s and for which we sometimes should apologize. This is a town that doesn't want to raise a ruckus, that likes to get along with everybody.

Everybody, that is, except all those carpetbaggers who've descended upon Puget Sound since the mid-1980s, fanning fistfuls of greenbacks they gleaned from selling homes in pricier areas and snapping up property here that would cost many times more elsewhere. Californians are a special focus of disgust, usually because we stereotype them as money-oriented, tasteless and self-obsessed. Oregonians struck back at them first, with their "Don't Californicate Oregon" bumper stickers, but Seattleites have followed at a heady clip. We live in a spot shoved far up into the northwest corner of the United States, at least 3,000 miles (4,800 km) away from the New York-Boston-Washington, DC corridor and 1,133 miles (1,823 km) from the floor show that is Los Angeles. We thought we were safe here from the attentions of the world. We were, unfortunately, dead wrong.

PRECEDING PAGES: Seattle window garden, and a store merchant. **LEFT:** Seattle happy face. **RIGHT:** many Seattleites are at home with writing and reading.

Exclusionists have done their utmost to discourage outsiders from seeing and then staying in Seattle. Their secret, if subtle, weapon was once rain jokes, playing on the frequent local drizzle as a deterrent. "Last year 299 people in Washington fell out of bed... and drowned," went one jibe. "What comes after two days of rain?" *Monday*, of course. "The most popular movie in Seattle?" *The Sound of Mucous.*

UNAPPRECIATED

If outsiders feel unfairly maligned, it's because they figure Seattle should be more grateful for their interest. California visitors rank number one among states.

But while it's true that in an average year Seattle records only 50-plus clear days, with another 90 registering as partly cloudy and the remaining 220 recorded beneath the rubric "cloudy," climate is not a part of the assorted ratings systems used to rank "livable" cities. Even if it were, that still wouldn't make Seattle look too bad: New York, Atlanta and Boston are all pummelled with more precipitation annually than is this city. While New Englanders and Midwesterners battle through their winters looking like leftovers wrapped securely for freezer storage, Seattleites enjoy moderate, if again rainy, conditions. Polls show that weather doesn't figure prominently in how locals measure quality of life. Besides, without the rain we wouldn't have all those fir trees.

Go back home

Recently, however, the calumny over new residents has intensified. Media across the nation picked up on the story of a young woman from Los Angeles who, shortly after relocating to the Puget Sound area, advertised in the *Seattle Weekly* personal columns "hoping to meet fellow Californians." Instead of dates, she received calls "from angry Seattle natives telling her in no uncertain terms to go back where she came from."

Emmett Watson, the *Seattle Times*'s curmudgeonly columnist and enthusiastic proponent of wrapping the city in an amber that's impenetrable to all but the longest-term Seattleites, constantly blames this town's ills on immigrants – and that means not only the traffic jams... and the gang violence... and the pollution... and the runaway housing prices, but even what Seattleites have labeled The New Rudeness. Time was when locals would sit patiently at stoplights for hours, watching one yutz after another try unsuccessfully to make a turn into heavy traffic, and nobody would utter one word. Now, car horns can actually be heard through downtown streets. Whatever happened to Seattle's storied mellowness?

Even big business has played a hand or two in the "We Hate Outsiders" game. Rainier Brewery, ranked behind Boeing Corporation and computer colossus Microsoft as one of the most-recognizable Seattle companies (even if it is owned by an Australian firm), erected billboards all over the city one recent summer that featured a bottle of Rainier Beer, along with the slogan "Californians Don't Get It." Indeed, Rainier isn't marketed below the Oregon border. Rainier's message took on a distinct – and peculiarly appealing – xenophobic air. Curiously enough, the advertising company that put together the ads was, itself, California-based.

Visitors come north to scope out the view from the Space Needle; to chug across Puget Sound in one of the many ferries that connect Seattle with its nearby island communities; to stare in curiosity as fishmongers shout forth the freshness of their catch at Pike Place Market; and to venture into tunnels beneath Pioneer Square and listen while tour guides explain that sidewalks in this historic district were at one time a full story lower than the roads, so people had to climb ladders just to cross the streets. Most important of all, they come to spend money, millions of dollars annually, and that's something that should put a shine on the image of even the snobbiest, most acquisitive, most tasteless tourist riding around through Seattle streets on four chrome wheels.

LEFT: ballet is one of Seattle's high-brow offerings.
ABOVE: street-side tunes come from all backgrounds.

Self esteem

Not that everybody is concerned with how Seattleites think of them. Indeed, it was only a few years ago that a columnist with the *San Francisco Examiner* called Seattle "a prim and proper, almost prissy, little city" and wondered why stay-put locals tend to stay put. He concluded finally that "There must be drugs in the water." There's nothing wrong with a little enmity from both sides in this case. After all, as essayist Roger Rosenblatt once pointed out in a *Time* magazine article, both people and places can be more clearly defined by the quality of their enemies, who "offer a criticism of one's conduct (albeit unsought) that is not always provided by friends... They also encourage self-esteem. How would we know the magnitude of our own worth without someone so worthless attacking it?"

In a weird way, then, Seattle's exclusionists are actually demonstrating their respect for Californians and others by casting them as spiritual and philosophical opposites. If the people of Puget Sound honestly did hate newcomers, we would do better to ignore them completely, as architect Howard Roark dismisses his arch-enemy, Ellsworth Toohey, in Ayn Rand's hypnotic novel *The Fountainhead*. "Why don't you tell me what you think of me?" Toohey asks in the book. To which Roark replies, "But I don't think of you."

Reading the Seattle papers, it seems that locals are constantly speaking and writing with anger about those souls who deign to encroach, like H. G. Wells' Martians, past our city limits. We're starting to act frightfully defensive about our place in the world.

publications, too, have bought into the most-livable-city notion of Seattle, although they know deep down that most of it is just tourist-oriented bunk.

These reports often seem loaded unnecessarily with jealousy. They make much of the high per-capita rates at which Seattleites buy books and attend the theater. They portray us accurately as dedicated in our regard for serious films and supportive of both fringe and established arts. We're fervent gardeners and astute in our understanding of cutting-edge architecture. (Hey, wasn't distinguished designer Robert Venturi brought all the way from

World-class city?

The word has gone out, right or wrong: Seattle is the coming place. Rare is the month when at least one national magazine doesn't now trumpet its virtues. "A City That Likes Itself," read the headline on a lengthy piece in *The Atlantic* that applauded the muted architectural scale, the preservationist attitude and even the "eccentric personality" of this place called the Emerald City. (Efforts to change Seattle's silly nickname have so far failed, although two substitutes – "Jet City," in recognition of our associations with Boeing, and "Lady Gray," playing on this area's drizzly climate – can be spotted occasionally in local writings.) Several local

SEATTLE'S NURTURING MUSE

Seattle boasts an artistic culture that would be the envy of a city twice its size. News of its creative climate, not to mention the moodiness of its weather, has acted like an artistic pheromone, drawing a young generation of talented writers, actors, artists and musicians. Both high and low flourish here: the Seattle Symphony Orchestra and Seattle Opera pack the Opera House, while fringe theaters and avant-garde rock groups are born and die on 6-month cycles. Seattle's creative forces are inspired by climate – a sky the color of raw oysters, dripping a steady curtain of rain – and driven by caffeine. If it were too sunny, it would be a dreadful day for the muse.

Philadelphia to create the Seattle Art Museum downtown?) And we're trend-setting in our relentless fondness for *caffé lattes*. So popular have these Italian espresso drinks become here, in fact, that one columnist now regularly refers to much of the Seattle area as Latteland, surely still better than L.A.'s La-La Land.

AN OLD IDEA

Free bus service has been considered and rejected as impractical by many cities, but in Seattle it is an idea whose time arrived long ago.

Seattle's character might best have been embodied in Ivar Haglund, the late and lovably cornballish entrepreneur who left behind a chain of seafood restaurants that bears his name. But we are more than that. We're Boeing line workers who rise before the sun each morning. We're ex-hippies or hippie wannabes who settle out on Bainbridge Island, just west of the city, where we're told all of our kind eventually end up migrating.

We're aspiring intellectuals who can quote Tolstoy and Shakespeare, but know just enough about local writer Tom Robbins (*Even Cowgirls Get the Blues*) that we don't look completely like square pegs. We're weekday software writers who spend every minute of our weekends in sailboats on Lake Washington. We're architects and journalists and ferry workers and just teenagers with high hormone counts who want to make something of ourselves in a town that's still trying to make something of itself.

An all-star lineup of Seattleites who've made a difference in the world would include Kung Fu cult hero Bruce Lee; Hank Ketcham, creator of cartoon character Dennis the Menace; Microsoft computer moguls Bill Gates and Paul Allen; expatriate author Alice B. Toklas; art photographer Imogen Cunningham; packaging whiz Jim Casey, the man who created United Parcel Service; musicians Jimi Hendrix and Kurt Cobain; cartoonists Gary (*The Far Side*) Larson and Lynda (*Ernie Pook's Comeek*) Barry; and modern dance choreographer Mark Morris. Even locals are often surprised to discover so many big names in such a small place.

What visiting writers don't see is that Seattleites, while we may survey out as enviable, can also be strident and humorless in our desire to be taken seriously. Rush-hour drivers in the Fremont neighborhood weren't at all surprised to discover a cab company billboard that suggested women whose dates become intoxicated "go home with another man" (a cabbie, that is),

LEFT: taking part in an Asian festival in the International District. **ABOVE:** Norwegian Day in Ballard.

sprayed over in black paint with the legend "sexist." But this stridency is not something that generally makes the public press and, even if it did, the modern correctness would, to some people, make Seattle look even more attractive than it already does.

Seattle is the Teflon City: nothing can harm its image. Yet we show a streak of fear when it comes to maintaining our image. You can see it in newspaper stories that compare other, now-burgeoning cities – notably neighbors Portland, Oregon, and Vancouver, British Columbia – with the Emerald City. Check to see how often those out-of-state places are described as "what Seattle used to be like." Seattle worries that it's losing its freshness.

So it is actually worrisome when national and international media speak so cheerily of Seattle as an aspiring "world-class city" (whatever that really means). Places that are already fit to carry such a mantle (New York, Tokyo, London) are also those that people so often try to run *from*, not *to*.

Disdain for the 'burbs

And it's funny that many stories spun out from Seattle make it sound, not inaccurately, like some large-scale possessor of the qualities that Americans used to prize in suburbs: cars parked neatly in rows, smiling automatons to greet you at clean movie theaters, neighborhoods where a BMW can be left unlocked overnight and not be discovered in the morning with its seat covers and stereo gone and its wheel-less chassis mounted on blocks. Any such comparison would be a blow to hard-core Seattleites, for we unfortunately regard our own 'burbs with mild (and sometimes not so mild) disdain or at least humor.

While they aspire to be cities – and, indeed, the metroplex of Bellevue and Kirkland on Lake Washington's east side is the fourth-largest population center in the state of Wash-

A CITY OF NEVERS

According to local columnist Jean Godden, Seattleites never carry umbrellas, never wash their cars, never shine their shoes and never turn on windshield wipers unless it's absolutely pouring. Godden also wrote that Seattleites seldom visit the Space Needle unless accompanied by visitors, seldom hail taxis, can describe 42 shades of gray, and think that a perfect day is 68°F, partly sunny, with a light breeze from the north. Seattleites also buy more sunglasses than residents of any other city in the United States, perhaps because they never expect to use them – only 50 days' sun on average each year – and thus invariably have left them at home.

ington – Seattle suburbs are only now beginning to receive some guarded respect from inner-city habituees. Those suburbs have the reputation of harboring money-oriented residents with minimal architectural tastes, who live in sprawling, characterless homes and carry on all their social rites in shopping malls. Perhaps that will change only as more and more urbanites move outward from Seattle proper to find affordable property, more responsive school districts and greater elbow room, and in the course of it help to reshape the 'burbs using a more urban vernacular of "city."

Jonathan Raban, a well-known British travel writer who relocated not long ago to Puget Sound, is less quick with his hosannas than are other students of Seattle. As Raban puts it, the people who've decided to settle in Seattle "could somehow recast it in the image of home, arranging the city around themselves like so many pillows on a bed." Despite more than a century of history, Seattle still seems very new, protean, waiting to be fully defined. "Pitched on a line of bluffs along Puget Sound, with Lake Washington at its back, Seattle had ships at the ends of its streets and gulls in its traffic. Its light was restless and watery, making the buildings shiver like reflections. It felt like an island and smelled of the sea."

All of this isn't to say that Seattle is a blank slate. Nor is it the proper capital of Ernest Callenbach's *Ecotopia* – a place bereft of trouble and cleaving to a relationship with nature. It's just another city, with all the strengths and weaknesses that label implies. Seattle's history is pocked by racial prejudice and the Ku Klux Klan, by terrifying conflagrations and threatened violence on the highways, by ups and downs at Boeing and the loss of civic attributes both built (like much of the old terracotta archi-

LEFT: ballet dancers in the park, and a tourist.
ABOVE: Seattleites are addicted to the outdoor life.

A BRITISH PERSPECTIVE

In his de Tocquevillesque non-fiction book, *Hunting Mister Heartbreak: A Discovery of America*, Jonathan Raban suggests newcomers see a polished-glass, confidence-driven façade of what this city is really like. "If you had the bad taste to look at Seattle from the back, all you'd see would be plain brick cladding and a zig-zag tangle of fire escapes." Yet even Raban makes Seattle sound honestly like the Emerald City it wants to be. "One could tell that Seattle was on a winning streak by the number of men in cranes who were trying to smash the place to bits with wrecking balls. The pink dust rose in explosive flurries over the rooftops and colored the low sky."

tecture downtown) and unbuilt (such as a downtown park on the present site of Westlake Center, which would have given Seattle the spiritual, if not geographical, center that it so needs). It is a place where homeless people – whose numbers grow alarmingly every year – share bottles of screwtop wine in gutters, while stockbrokers stride blindly by, comparing the expense of their automobiles. It's a place where floating bridges have been known to sink into Lake Washington just after planners insist that traffic problems are on the downswing.

"We're not all that serene and peaceful; we're cold and sullen," said *Misc.* editor Clark Humphrey in a recent edition of *Greater Seattle* magazine. "Imagine old Swedish-Americans whose silence doesn't come from being an alternative to New York noise but out of just not caring to be all that sociable and affable."

Yet locals love this place, and they don't even have to be influenced by drugs in the water. Notice the use of "locals" rather than "natives" to describe the majority of Seattleites. That's because so many residents here have logged fewer than 10 years within the city limits. Between 1980 and 1990, Washington State's population grew nearly 20 percent, or twice as fast as the rest of the country. The Seattle metropolitan area itself grew by 18 percent.

Remembering when

Although locals like to depict themselves as the only true Seattleites, anybody who's lived here for more than a month can sometimes be heard saying things like, "You know, so much is different here than it was. Why, I remember when…" Such is the fate of a city that's just seriously establishing itself: everybody wants to be thought of as present when the boom began.

So the first thing newcomers do after signing a mortgage here is to gather the trappings of established residency about themselves. They register for membership with REI (Recreational Equipment, Inc.), the consummate local wilderness outfitter. They procure a credit card from the clothing giant, Nordstrom, and subscribe to *Seattle Weekly* so they can share in gossip about politics, this city's burgeoning art scene and prominent restaurant closings.

If they're unmarried, they start dating someone with family connections to Boeing or Microsoft. They start drinking local craft beers and, once they find a brand they like, they zealously contend that it is *the best in the world* – bar none. They buy a dog (there are now 2.8 for every fire hydrant in this city). Even if they despise the game of baseball, newcomers are obliged to insult the now-demolished Kingdome at every opportunity as an inappropriate venue for America's Great Game.

If they live within the Seattle city limits, they go out on the rare sunny days and kick the tires on a Volvo station wagon, which the *Seattle Post-Intelligencer* proclaimed as "a perfect match" for the semi-individualist, seemingly liberal and sensible nature of locals. If they've chosen instead to locate in one of the (gasp!) suburbs on the other side of Lake Washington, they opt for a Jeep Cherokee, which in turn was acclaimed by the newspaper *Eastsideweek* as "the national car of the Eastside." It's all a part of fitting in, of course, a way of getting along with everybody else.

Finally, these new Seattleites try to close the gates behind them. As is true of anybody who discovers a fresh, barely trammeled place, newcomers want to keep it to themselves. "No more immigrants," they bellow, even louder than the people who've lived here for decades and are now beginning to feel crowded. ❑

LEFT: a young Asian-American with an upside-down world on her shoulders.

Seattlespeak

Mukilteo. Sequim. Humptulips. Enumclaw. Influenced especially by local Native American names, cartographers have made the state of Washington a minefield of barely pronounceable monikers. Skookumchuck? Puyallup? Pysht? The dangerous days when men spoke "with forked tongues" may be long gone, but they've been surviving in the city of Seattle by the era of the twisted tongue.

It's disappointing sometimes to learn that the most colorful place names have been taken from Chinook jargon, a regrettable mishmash of Indian dialects that white explorers and settlers used to communicate haltingly with the previous stewards of this land. Alki, for instance, which today graces a beach and an area of southern Seattle, means "by and by" in this jargon. La Push, referring to a town at the mouth of the Quillayute River ("river with no head"), is at least geographically correct: it means, simply, "mouth."

Other names are really garbled versions of Indian words. Snohomish, which refers to a city, a river and a county north of Seattle, does not exist in any known Native American language, according to linguists. Its suffix, however – *ish*, which translates as "people" – stands out on road maps like pimples on a high school kid. Sammamish means "the hunting people." Skykomish translates as "the inland people." Stillaguamish, Duwamish... The words may come from different native dialects, but they both mean "people living on the river." So prominently did rivers and other bodies of water figure in the language of Northwest Indians that if someone were to ask you what a peculiar-sounding Washington name means, you could say "water" and stand 50-percent chance of being right.

Lucile McDonald, a prolific historian living in the Seattle-area town of Enatai (meaning "crossing" or "across" in Chinook jargon), writes that "Skookumchuck, Entiat, Cle Elum and Skamania all have to do with strong, swift or rapid water.

"Walla Walla and Wallula mean small, rapid river; Washougal is rushing water; Tumwater, a waterfall; Wenatchee, a river issuing from a canyon; Selah, still water; Pilchuck, red water; Newaukum, gently flowing water; Paha, big water; Palux, a slough covered with vines; Yakima is lake water. Sol Duc is magic water. Chelan is deep water."

RIGHT: a newspaper vendor downtown.

Which is exactly what outsiders find themselves in when trying to pronounce the majority of these names. When in doubt, refer to the book *Washington State Place Names*, by James W. Phillips, which offers not only the source of local appellations, but – thank God! – pronunciations as well.

Locals sometimes look at these mispronouncable monikers as their special revenge against the accents in other regions of the country. After all, as linguists are wont to remind Seattleites, Northwesterners have no discernible accent.

The Northwest's language differences are more subtle than swallowed or drawled vowels. In New England, men who used to risk their lives cutting

down the forests of Maine were called "lumberjacks." In the Northwest, they're known as "loggers." Call somebody riding a horse in eastern Washington State a "cowpoke" and you're liable to earn a mean if not offended stare at best, a poke in the nose at worst. They prefer the name "buckaroo," pardner.

Despite its tenuous connections with the Old West of legend, Washington has appropriated some discernible Westernisms. It's not uncommon in farming country to hear someone say "That's as useless as tits on a boar hog" and, despite the fact that weather here is generally mild, one may describe a thick-headed outsider as being so dumb that he "couldn't drive nails in a snowbank." ❑

THE CULTURE OF THE NORTHWEST TRIBES

There are more than 25,000 Native Americans living in the Seattle area. Their heritage is commemorated in museums large and small

Apart from in place names, it can be difficult to find specific evidence of Duwamish natives (the original Seattleites, *see page 23*), but the city has many rich resources for learning about Native art and culture, particularly those of Southeast Alaska and British Columbia tribes.

The Burke Museum of Natural History and Culture (tel: 206-543-5590), on the University of Washington campus, has one of the country's largest collections of Northwest Coast native art. The art and artifacts, from British Columbia and Southeast Alaska, include totem poles, model canoes, baskets, tools and a house front.

The Seattle Art Museum (tel: 206-654-3100) also has a valuable Native American collection, with many fine Tlingit, Haida and Makah pieces.

Lastly, Daybreak Start Indian Cultural Center (tel: 206-285-4425), in Discovery Park, coordinates events and services for Seattle Native Americans, exhibits a permanent collection of contemporary Native art, and offers a small gallery.

▷ **MYTHICAL CREATURE**
This Haida wood carving represents the thunderbird. Carved totem poles are found all over Seattle, including a few in Pioneer Square.

△ **FISHING RIGHTS**
Laws entitle Native American tribes to half of the annual salmon catch in Northwest waters.

▷ **NATIVE HEADDRESS**
Museums and galleries throughout the Northwest include magnifcent examples of Native American headdresses.

◁ **CELEBRATING SALMON**
Tulalip Indians drum during a "first fish" ceremony. The tribe's ancestral home is at the mouth of the Snohomish River, north of Seattle.

△ **CHIEF'S DAUGHTER**
Edward S. Curtis photographed Native Americans in the 1800s, including this daughter of a Skokomish chief.

△ **CEREMONIAL GATHERING**
Tulalip Indians gather in their longhouse on the reservation near Marysville, to celebrate the first salmon ceremony.

▷ **BRIDAL FINERY**
Bride of the Wishram Tribe, photographed by Edward S. Curtis, depicts a young woman of the Chinook tribe of the Columbia River.

CHIEFJOSEPH OF THE NEZ PERCE

One of the most dramatic stories in Northwest Native American history is that of Chief Joseph, shown here in a photograph by Edward S. Curtis. He was a chief of the Nez Perce (Nimiipu).
In 1877, after the US government created a new treaty with the Nez Perce, stripping the tribe of valuable land, violence erupted. Several chiefs, including Joseph, refused to sign the treaty and a band, led by Chief Joseph, fled by horseback and on foot toward Canada. The natives were able to hold off the U.S. cavalry for 1,500 miles (2,400 km), surviving more than 20 battles along the way. The Nez Perce eventually surrendered in Northern Montana near the Canadian border, where Chief Joseph delivered his historic speech, concluding: "I will fight no more forever." Exiled to Oklahoma until 1885, Chief Joseph finally returned to the Pacific Northwest and lived on Washington state's Colville Reservation until his death in 1904.

GEOGRAPHY OF THE NORTHWEST

In few places is the collision of tectonic plates – and the erosion of glacial movement – more apparent than in the Pacific Northwest

For most Pacific Northwest and Seattle residents, their introduction to the dynamics of geology began on May 18, 1980. At 8.32am on that sunny Sunday, a magnitude 5.1 earthquake triggered a landslide on the north slope of Mount St. Helens, which had long been rumbling beneath. This released the pressure on a summit dome of magma that was growing outward at 6 ft (1.8 meters) daily. Within seconds, the dome was gone and a cloud of ash and rock escaped the volcano at 500 miles per hour (800 kph). Within half an hour, the mushroom-shaped cloud reached an altitude of 95,000 ft (30,000 meters). When the sky and dust eventually cleared, geologists discovered that Mount St. Helens had blown 1,300 ft (400 meters) of rock from its summit.

Closer to home, Seattle's own dynamic geology was unleashed in the winter of 1996–97. An unusually wet series of storms crashed into the city in autumn, creating soggy soils. In the weeks around New Year's, freezing rain, snow, and warm rain combined to push the soil to its saturation point, triggering hundreds of landslides on the numerous bluffs that surround the city. Mud destroyed houses, businesses, and railroad tracks. Unlike many regions on the continent, the Seattle area is constantly reminded of its geological foundations.

Origins in plate tectonics

Seattle's geologic history is young and dynamic. If one were to stand on the city's highest accessible point – the 73rd floor of the Columbia Center – little of the geology visible would be older than 100 million years, youthful in geological terms. In fact, the most dramatic landmarks, like Mount Rainier or Puget Sound, are less than 1 million years old.

Like the people of the region, few of the rocks originated in the Puget Sound area or in the inland Cascade Range; most arrived after forming someplace else. Some formed as volcanic islands, while others were deposited on the ocean floor before being carried here by the movement of tectonic plates.

The theory of plate tectonics argues that Earth's surface is made of a thin crust consisting of 10 large and several smaller pieces, or tectonic plates. This crust rests atop a partially molten mass called the asthenosphere. Deformation of the asthenosphere, from heat produced by radioactive decay within the planet, moves the plates across the surface of the Earth.

The interaction between these solid plates plays a central role in all geologic phenomena, whether it is the explosion of Mount St. Helens or the landslides on Seattle's bluffs. The plates of importance for the Northwest are the North American (made of relatively light, continental crust); the Pacific Plate (comprised of dense, basalt-rich oceanic crust); and the Farallon/Juan de Fuca plate system (also consisting of oceanic crust). The formation of the North Cascades

PRECEDING PAGES: glaciers and plate tectonics formed inland waterways; Mount St. Helens. **LEFT:** a dramatic setting. **RIGHT:** the geology means good climbing.

was the first great geologic event that sculpted today's Pacific Northwest, roughly 100 million years ago when Pacific Plate movement carried a group of islands into the North American continent. Geologists call rocks that crash into a continent "terranes." This was followed by the collision of another larger terrane that became Vancouver Island.

Most of this colliding land mass slid into a massive trench in the Pacific just off the continent, but the Vancouver Island terrane material – riding on top of the Pacific Plate – piled onto the land and compressed, folded and faulted the land, eventually creating the North Cascades. In fact, this collision was preceded by earlier ones, creating several periods of compression and folding of the land.

The San Juan and Gulf islands are also part of this "island" collision process and are some of the most complicated bits of geology in the region. Like the North Cascades, none of the San Juan rocks formed where they now sit. The San Juan islands range in age from 120 to 400 million years old and consist of basalt, deep water-deposited sandstone, and metamorphosed rocks originally deposited on the bottom of the ocean. Some may have formed in the vicinity of California and then shifted 600 miles (1,000 km) northward via tectonic plate movement.

Tropical swamps and oceans

Fifty-five million years ago, before the spectacular volcanoes of the Cascades and the Olympics existed, water dominated the region, with a sea to the west and rivers and swamps to the east of the land now occupied by Everett, Seattle, and Tacoma. These rivers deposited layer upon layer of sand in a vast swath of deltas, which formed at the sea-land boundary.

Palm trees, ferns, and magnolias flourished in a subtropical ecosystem, while large herons and small three-toed horses traipsed through the waterways. Although these deltas and swamps did not produce dramatic geologic layers, they

CRUSTY MOVEMENTS

Earth's continents have changed their positions over the past millions of years, a fact confirmed by studying, amongst other things, the magnetism retained within the rocks of the tectonic plates.

This movement of the earth's crust – the lithosphere – is generated further below within the earth. The earth's core and mantle are hot, but there are temperature differences, creating convection currents that circulate in the mantle, giving motion to the crust on top. When currents meet the crust in a downward direction, tectonic plates can meet and collide. When this happens, the earth is uplifted into mountains, or volcanoes may form.

have played an important role in the contemporary cultural history of Seattle. Compression of the carbon-rich plant material in the swamps converted it to coal, the mining of which became one of the earliest industries in the Seattle area. The first mine opened in 1853 and production peaked in 1907. (This coal-bearing past is reflected in the area names like Carbonado, Black Diamond, and Newcastle.)

YOUTHFUL CASCADES

The Cascades are less than 1 million years old (Mount St. Helens is 40,000 years old). The Rockies are 60 million years old and the Appalachian, 350 million years old.

The delta deposits, which eventually hardened into sandstone, became important to Seattle after the 1889 fire consumed most of the downtown business district. To prevent such a catastrophe again, the city rebuilt with stone and brick instead of wood. Some of this building material came from sandstone quarried near Bellingham to the north and Tacoma to the south. This tannish sandstone can still be seen in many buildings in the Pioneer Square area of downtown Seattle.

The stage was now set for the modern landscape to take shape. This began 20 million years ago with the docking of the Northwest's final terrane, produced by the slipping of the Farallon Plate under the western edge of the North American Plate. As in the earlier collisions, most of the plate disappeared under the continent, but a raft of basaltic seamounts (mountains that form on oceanic crust) and marine sediments didn't descend; instead, they were folded and thrust to the east. In that position, the less dense sedimentary rocks began to rise and fold further toward the east, creating the mountains of the Olympic Peninsula.

As the Farallon Plate (now called the Juan de Fuca Plate) continued to slip beneath the North American Plate, it encountered greater and greater temperatures and pressures and so started to melt. This molten rock or magma began to rise and eventually pierced the surface to create the volcanoes of the Cascade range, the oldest of which is Mount Adams at about two million years old.

To the geologist, the Cascades are composite volcanoes made from alternating lava flows and pyroclastic eruptions, or ash flows. Similar volcanoes are Japan's Mount Fuji and Italy's Vesuvius. Composite mountains are built by brief pulses of magma or ash expelling out of a cen-

LEFT: destruction aftermath, Mount St. Helens.
ABOVE: glacial residue, Fidalgo Island.

tral vent interspersed with longer periods of quiet. Most of the volcanoes in the Seattle area – Rainier, Adams, Baker, St. Helens and Glacier Peak – are considered dormant, not extinct. All are merely waiting for tectonic forces to reach a critical point and then they will explode to life again.

One of the last major eruptions on Rainier, only 5,000 years ago, produced a 300-ft-deep (100-meter) mud flow that cascaded 30 miles (50 km) down the mountain. Moreover, the peak was 2,000 ft (600 meters) higher only 75,000 years ago. Although Baker has not had a significant recent eruption, it did blow in 1880 and produced steam in 1975. And, of course, Mount St. Helen's 1980 blast displayed the most telling evidence of the swirling forces under these mountains.

Movements of glaciers

One of the fundamental rules of geology – and life – is that what goes up must come back down. In the case of our mountains, gravity and ice are the two agents that are bringing mountains down. Unlike today, the glaciers of the past were not restricted to lofty summits; instead, massive, continent-covering glaciers carved their way across the Puget Sound lowlands to create today's landscape.

Although this period of continental ice is often referred to as the Ice Age, geologists have evidence for 22 cycles of glaciers retreating and advancing in the Northwest over the past 2 million years. A warmer period followed each cycle of glaciation. The most recent retreat of the continental ice sheets started roughly 16,000 years ago. In the long term, the region is simply sunning itself in the warm period; the cycle of glaciation will continue.

The sheet of ice over what is now Seattle was between 3,000 and 4,000 ft (900–1,200 meters) thick 17,000 years ago, when the last glaciers were at their maximum, spreading south from Canada and splitting into two lobes. One lobe flowed between the Olympics and Cascades and ended at Olympia, while the other passed around the north end of the Olympics cutting the Strait of Juan de Fuca. The glaciers had two effects on Seattle: erosional and depositional. They sculpted the rounded hills of the city and rasped out Lake Washington, Puget Sound, and Hood Canal. The calving of Brobdingnagian-sized pieces of ice created the numerous kettle-lakes, like Green and Hallers, that dot the landscape. Torrents washing out from the

ABOVE: glacial silt is carried by rivers downstream.
RIGHT: glacier in Olympic National Park.

retreating glaciers cut many of the drainages and ravines that still carry water in Seattle.

The glaciers also deposited three layers of material: the recent and relatively impermeable (hardpan) gravelly sand with clay and scattered boulders. This layer generally caps the hills of Seattle. Below this is a thicker layer of poorly consolidated, well-drained sand and silt. A layer of dark gray, finely-bedded clay makes up the bottom of most regional hills. The contact zones between these layers are responsible for the area's landslides.

During a rainstorm, water percolates downward until it encounters the bottom clay-rich layer, where it builds up and starts to form a slick surface upon which the middle sandy layer can slide. Removal of vegetation exacerbates the resulting unstable earth. As Seattle continues to grow and people have more money to spend on houses overlooking the water, the landslides will only become more frequent.

Sometimes the earth shakes

Historically, Seattle has not been well-known for earthquake activity. Still, research in the 1980s and 1990s pinpointed three fault zones – the result of plate tectonics – in the area, all of which have a potential to cause massive

STILL IN THE TIME OF GLACIERS

Washington state contains more alpine or mountain glaciers than any state except Alaska. The North Cascades have over 300, the Olympics around 265, and Mount Rainier has 26, including Emmons, the largest glacier (4.2 sq. miles/11 sq. km of surface area) in the lower 48.

Glaciers are generally formed in areas of near-perpetual snow coverage. Accumulating snow is compacted into glacial ice over time. If accumulation is greater than melting or evaporation, the glacier increases in size.

Like the larger continental ice sheets, alpine glaciers continuously rasp and scour bedrock, creating the mountain landscape we see today.

Another important aspect of alpine glaciers is their use as an effective indicator of climate change. For example, during a several-century-long cold spell that ended around 1850, many of Mount Rainier's glaciers advanced down to their lowest point since the Ice Age 20,000 years ago. From 1850 to 1950, the glaciers retreated in response to a warming trend. This was followed by three decades of advance. The glaciers have again started to retreat in response to a general trend in global warming.

Twenty thousand years ago, most of North America and Europe looked as Greenland does today – covered in ice. One day North America and Europe will be, too. Again.

damage. Geologists estimate that movement along the zone where the San Juans slip beneath the North American Plate – and where two of the fault zones are located – could produce a quake as large as 8 or 9 in magnitude.

The third and most recently discovered zone runs directly under the downtown area in an east-west direction. Known as the Seattle Fault, it is a shallow fault – less than 12 miles (19 km) deep that was most recently active approximately 1,100 years ago, producing a *tsunami*, or tidal wave, that

DEEPLY MOVING

Two earthquakes in the Seattle area – a magnitude 6.5 on the Richter scale in 1965 and one over 7 in 1949 – occurred roughly 40 miles (65 km) below the surface.

inundated the Puget Sound region. Geologists estimate that the Seattle Fault could produce a magnitude 7 or larger earthquake. Damage from such an event would obviously be rather severe in the metropolitan area.

Climate

John Ruskin once wrote that "sunshine is delicious, rain is refreshing, wind braces up, snow is exhilarating; there is really no such thing as bad weather, only different kinds of weather." A fair description of Seattle, which is well known as rather rainy spot.

In fact, however, and contrary to popular belief, the city receives less precipitation than New York or Miami. Perhaps it is the lack of sunshine that spreads the misconception of Seattle's raininess. The average yearly total in Seattle is only 38 inches (96 cm), while the city averages only 50 clear days annually.

Most of those clear days come in summer, when only 3 or 4 inches (7–10 cm) of rain falls. Seattle receives 75 percent of its precipitation from October to March. The lack of sun and the abundance of rain may account for local residents' propensity for coffee, books, and more coffee still.

This unusual weather situation (few other temperate spots on Earth have such a disparity between a wet winter and a dry summer) is primarily driven by two pressure cells that lurk over the northern Pacific Ocean. During the summer, the prevailing winds are from the west and northwest, carrying dry, cool, and stable air. In winter, the low pressure cell in Alaska migrates south and replaces the summer's high-pressure cell, producing southwesterly to westerly air laden with moisture.

The region's weather is also affected by water and mountains. The Pacific Ocean is both source of moisture and – combined with Puget Sound and Lake Washington – regional thermostat.

Water absorbs heat during the day and, unlike land, which loses heat quickly, releases the heat slowly and thus creates a blanket of air that cools in the summer and warms in winter.

Wet air moving onto land encounters the Olympic and Cascade ranges and is forced to rise over them. The rising air cools and loses its ability to retain moisture. The moisture falls as rain at lower elevations and as snow higher up. If the Northwest was perfectly flat, the air mass would drop its precipitation gradually, instead of dumping it in belts along the western side of the mountain chains.

The mountains also create a rain shadow on

their lee or eastern side because the air loses most of its moisture on the western side.

The town of Sequim, on the northeastern side of the Olympics, averages 16 inches (41 cm) of rain annually, while more than 200 inches (500 cm) of rain fall only 10 miles (16 km) away in the Olympic range. This radical change in such a short distance is also commonly found on tropical islands with mountains: the windward side unloads moisture from clouds while the leeward side can have near-desert characteristics. ❑

LEFT: satellite view of central downtown Seattle.
ABOVE: early morning dew on rain forest plant.

SEATTLE'S STONE FOUNDATIONS

A stroll through downtown Seattle is a ramble along a geological time line – from 1.6-billion-year-old Finnish granite to 4-inch (10-cm) fossils in limestone walls. Seattle's use of stone, rather than wood, began after the 1889 "Great Fire", which consumed most of downtown. Seattle builders began with rock quarried near Tacoma, Index and Bellingham for streets, curbs, walls and foundations. As the city grew wealthier, stone was imported from, first, Vermont and Indiana, then Italy and Brazil.

Salem limestone, the most popular building stone in the U.S., comes from quarries in Indiana. This white-to-buff rock was used in the Empire State Building and Pentagon. In Seattle, it graces the exterior of the Seattle Art Museum. Embedded within the stone are fossils. This limestone was deposited around 300 million years ago, in a shallow tropical sea alive with small invertebrates. When they died, their bodies solidified on the sea floor into a layer 40 to 100-ft (12–30 meters) thick.

Chuckanut sandstone, like Index granite, is a local stone first quarried in the 1850s. Most of the Seattle buildings using this local sandstone center around Pioneer Square and include the Pioneer Building, built after the 1889 fire. The sandstone was deposited 40 to 50 million years ago when this region was warmer and flatter, 15 million years before the rise of the Cascades. Oceans, rivers and swamps deposited layer upon layer of sand in a vast swath of deltas. Along with this changed topography was a changing climate. Palm trees and ferns flourished in the subtropical lowlands; 25 million years ago, the region began to take on its modern climate of cooler temperatures.

Index granite, from a quarry east of Seattle and used at the base of Smith Tower, was formed 33 million years ago when a wedge of oceanic crust began to slither beneath the North American continent. Magma from the friction rose and melted the silica- and aluminum-rich crustal material, turning it into granite. (This same tectonic action created the Cascades.) Less attractive than the imported pink, green and red granites from elsewhere, Index granite soon lost its importance.

Building stone also came from overseas. **Finnish granite** – mostly reddish, pink or brown – has been used extensively downtown. Formed more than 1.6 billion years ago, Finnish granite often contains large feldspar crystals. **Italian travertine**, from quarries near Rome, was used not only in the Pacific Building and interior of Rainier Tower, but for the ancient Colosseum in Rome. The Jurassic-period **French limestone** on the ground at Westlake Center is embedded with the fossilized remains of assorted marine organisms, including sponges.

NORTHWEST MOUNTAINS: BEAUTY AND DANGER

The city of Seattle sits inside the Pacific's so-called "Ring of Fire," an area of volcanoes that have the potential to erupt at any time

Klickitat mythology tells the story of a pair of warriors, Wyeast and Pahto, who fought each other for the love of a beautiful maiden. Their monumental battle involved earthquakes and firing volleys of rock and fire across the Columbia River. To settle the earth, the gods transformed the warriors into mountains along the Cascade Chain: Wyeast became Mount Hood and Pahto became Mount Rainier.

Seattle sits on the Pacific Rim, where 850 active volcanoes in mountain ranges on all sides of the Pacific Ocean form a "Ring of Fire." This includes the Cascade Range, a 700-mile-long (1,100-km) chain of mountains that extends from northern California to southern British Columbia and runs north-south through Washington state.

The most recent volcanic eruption in the Cascades occurred in May 1980, when Mount St Helens gave a powerful demonstration of the natural forces that created much of the Northwest landscape. The eruption of ash and molten lava transfigured the hillsides surrounding the mountain, and sent a gray cloud across the state.

Other active volcanos in the Cascades include Mount Rainier, at 14,410 ft (4,400 meters) one of the most popular among climbers in the region. Also with the potential for activity are Mount Baker (north of Seattle), Mount Adams (in southern Washington, Mount Hood (near Portland), and Mount Shasta (near the Oregon-California state border).

▷ CASCADIA
The 700-mile (1,100-km) range includes Mount Rainier, Hood and Baker and stretches from northern California to southern British Columbia.

▷ MOUNT RAINIER NATIONAL PARK
This is one of the most popular national parks in the U.S. Visitors can walk to many viewpoints.

△ MOUNT BAKER
This long-dormant volcano is in the Cascade Range near the Washington/British Columbia border.

△ MOUNT HOOD
This 11,235-ft (3,424-meter) Cascade peak is in northern Oregon state. Here it is reflected in the water of Trillium Lake.

▽ LAVA DOME
The enormous lava dome on the volcano of Mount St Helens is still growing almost 20 years after its last eruption.

MOUNT ST HELENS ERUPTS

On May 18, 1980, skies darkened as far away as Seattle as Mount St Helens, in southwestern Washington state, literally blew its top. The explosion took a cubic mile off the summit, reducing the mountain's elevation from 9,677 ft (2,950 meters) to 8,364 ft (2,550 meters).

The volcano had shown signs of activity well before the blast, and although the region had been evacuated by all but the most stubborn of residents, the death toll reached almost 70, as lava and mud slides flattened 230 square miles (595 sq. km) of forest.

There was extensive damage to wildlife, and the ash-covered slopes and fallen trees still serve as reminders of the fateful day.

△ **SNOW-CAPPED PEAK**
When Seattle residents have a clear view of Mount Rainier, seen here from the south, they say, "The Mountain is out."

▷ **MOUNT RAINIER**
Mount Rainier National Park is popular with sightseers and hikers, as well as climbers of varying experience.

FLORA AND FAUNA

Even within the downtown parks, the wildlife and plants of the Pacific Northwest are intriguingly diverse and well-suited to the region's challenges

Where else does one find 300 to 400 million clams with grapefruit-sized shells, yellow slugs 12 inches (30 cm) long that can consume several times their body weight each night, or 300-ft-tall (90-meter) trees that can live for a thousand years? Although the present-day flora and fauna of the Seattle region do not rival the abundance of its pre-European discovery, they still can inspire awe.

If one had to choose a single plant and a single animal to symbolize the Seattle region, the choice would be easy. Douglas firs are the quintessential tree of this area, while salmon are the lynch pin of the animal world. From food to housing, salmon and Douglas fir trees have played essential roles for both humans and wildlife in the Northwest, and almost every early traveler and expedition to the region mentioned the two species.

When Seattle's first group of settlers landed in 1851, all they could see through the rain were trees, water, and more trees still. The Douglas firs that covered the hillsides were unlike any trees these pioneers had seen in their 2,000-mile (3,200-km) journey westward across the country – few plants on Earth rival a Douglas fir in size or age. According to one early writer, the trees were so tall it took "two men and boy to look to the top." Scientists, who like facts better than hyperbole, cite one 330-ft-tall (100-meter) tree and another with a 48-ft (15-meter) circumference. And the trees were old – the oldest Douglas fir around started to grow in the 6th century.

Skid Row

From an economic standpoint, Douglas firs were critical to the development of Seattle and its surroundings. Within one month of the city's founding, plans were made to ship the first boatload of Douglas fir trees to San Francisco. Seattle's first employer was Henry Yesler's sawmill, in what is today's neighborhood of Pioneer Square. The trees even contributed to the coining of the town's infamous moniker, Skid Road (later to beget Skid Row), a reference to skidding the massive trees down to Yesler's mill. Douglas firs were and still are the most important timber product in the Northwest; unfortunately, the high value of Douglas fir has led to extensive clear-cutting throughout the Northwest.

Only a handful of monumental Douglas firs can be found in Seattle. The best places are Seward, Carkeek, and Schmitz parks, but these

reserves pale in comparison to the Northwest's once-omnipresent old-growth forests, which are now limited to the area's national parks, a few remnants in national forests, and on state lands. Along with the western red cedar and western hemlock, the fir was the primary conifer of the old-growth ecosystem. These three species reached gargantuan proportions and are indigenous to the Seattle area. Cedars have always been the most important tree for the native people of the region, who used the wood for canoes and houses, and the bark for clothing.

ABOVE: loggers have long harvested Douglas firs.
RIGHT: madrona trees frame distant Mount Rainier.

The common name of the firs honors David Douglas, a Scottish botanist who was the first to bring seeds of the tree back to England. Douglas walked over 6,000 miles (10,000 km) through Washington and Oregon in 1825 and 1826 collecting indigenous seeds. He eventually introduced over 200 plants to England, describing his namesake tree as "one of the most striking and truly graceful in Nature."

Neighborhood namesake

Three neighborhoods in Seattle – Laurelhurst, Magnolia, and Madrona – are named after one of the area's most beautiful trees, the madrona. Madronas are in the same family as laurels. The neighborhood of Magnolia received its name in 1856 when Capt. George Davidson of the U.S. Coast Survey thought he saw magnolias on the bluffs overlooking Puget Sound. If he had been a better botanist, he would have clearly recognized the red-barked trees as madrona. No other tree resembles this shiny, dark-green-leaved, evergreen species that produces white flowers in the spring and orange fruit in late summer.

Madronas thrive on west-facing, well-drained exposures around Puget Sound. They often grow on bluffs overlooking the water, where they may have a twisted, wind-blown shape. Madronas can reach to heights of 90 ft (30 meters) and live for over 200 years. Good specimens grow in the Innis Arden neighborhood, and at Lincoln, Discovery, and Seward parks. At Seward, however, watch for the poison oak that often surrounds the trees.

Rhododendrons are a common and well-known relative of the madronas. In the Cascade foothills, they favor the shady understory of Douglas firs and western hemlocks. Like other "rhodies" in this 850-member-strong genus, the native varieties produce a spectacular flower that blooms pink in the spring. They have dark green leaves that curl under. Along with aza-

VOLCANOES AND WILDLIFE

The destruction of Mount St. Helens was a visually evident thing. Little, however, is said of the wildlife that disappeared during that cataclysmic 1980 explosion, in which a cubic mile of the summit disappeared. Over 200 square miles (500 sq. km) of forest was flattened. It is estimated that 5,000 black-tailed deer, 1,500 elk, over 200 black bears and a dozen or more mountain goats were killed. Uncountable were the mountain lions, bobcats, rodents, birds, fish and insects. The region's rare spotted owl population was wiped out. But in the decades since, flora and fauna have returned to Mount St. Helens, a biologist's perfect laboratory for research.

leas, which are in the same genus, rhododendrons are practically ubiquitous in yards, parks, and gardens around Puget Sound. The western rhododendron was chosen as the state flower of Washington in 1892.

Other understory plants include salal and Cascade Oregon grape. Salal is widespread and easy to identify by its leathery, oval leaves and quarter-inch-long (6-mm), bell-shaped flowers, which mature to black berries. They are in the same family (Heath) as rhodies and madronas. Like other members of the barberry family, Oregon grape has spiny, holly-like leaves. The purple fruit is edible but tart.

The Northwest has a well-deserved reputation as a land teeming with edible, juicy berries of all sorts. Depending upon the soil type, elevation, and aspect, one can find cranberries, several varieties of huckleberry, blueberries, squashberries, snowberries, salmonberries, twinberries, thimbleberries, dewberries, elderberries, and blackberries. One may also come upon strawberries. They have been eaten by humans since earliest times and are still an uncommonly good delicacy for those who visit the backcountry. Hikers must contend with bears, who may subsist on little else during late summer, when the berries are at their ripest.

A Proper Beach Walk

Beachwalkers unfamiliar with the area should consult a tide table. These indispensable charts, available in many places, detail the time of day and the magnitude of the two daily high and low tides.

At certain times, stretches of shoreline will be exposed to walkers and tidepool explorers. Six hours later, these same areas will be covered by several feet of ocean. By picking the low tide for an excursion, beachwalkers will have the best of explorations. Misjudging the time of the tides – and their changes – could result in a shoreline stranding. Indeed, Pacific Northwest tides can vary by over 10 feet (3 meters) in some places.

Marine mammals

Killer whales are a primary consumer of salmon. Roughly 90 individuals in three pods, or extended family units composed of mothers and their offspring, spend late spring to early autumn in the waters around the San Juan Islands. Also known as orcas, they do not, despite rumors to the contrary, attack humans. Their common name refers to their hunting ability, which positions them at the top of the marine food chain. They are efficient hunters and generally form cooperative groups to kill larger prey, such as gray or baleen whales.

Killer whales are the largest member of the dolphin family. They grow to 25 ft (7.5 meters) in length and weigh up to 6 tons (5,500 kilograms). Females typically live for 50 years, while a male's lifespan averages around 25 years. Orcas have a highly evolved social structure – living in groups called pods – and communicate via an extensive repertoire of vocalizations that include whoops, whistles, and chirps. In fact, each pod has a distinct dialect.

WHALE WATCHERS

One good spot to see orcas is at Lime Kiln Whale Watch Park, on San Juan Island. It is the only park in the country established expressly for whale-watching.

Look for the whale's back fin, 5 to 6 ft tall (1.5–1.8 metres), slicing through the water. The distinctive black-and-white whales may also be seen breaching the water. The Whale Museum, located at Friday Harbor, offers whale tours throughout the summer. Gray whales, minke whales, and Dall's porpoises may also venture into the Puget Sound.

The harbor porpoise, often seen around Puget Sound and the San Juan Islands, is the smallest oceanic cetacean. Unlike the bottle-nose dolphin, harbor porpoises are not terribly gregarious. Dall porpoises can swim at up to 30 knots and are sometimes seen preceding a ship's bow. The Pacific white-sided dolphin is a spirited daredevil, traveling in schools of over 50 members and leaping up to 20 ft (6 meters) into the air, complete with aerial somersaults.

Only along the ocean coast does one see the gray whale on its 12,000-mile (19,000-km) annual migration. Once endangered with just a few hundred gray whales on earth, protection has increased their numbers to 20,000 or so. Distinguishing it from other whales roaming the Pacific are the 10 to 14 "knuckles" along the ridge of its 40- to 50-ft (12–15-meter) back.

FAR LEFT: sea anemone. **LEFT:** a breeching orca. **ABOVE:** sea lions are a delicacy of orcas.

The most commonly sighted marine mammal in the region is the harbor seal, year-round resident of Puget Sound and coastal Washington. The mottled adults may reach over 6 ft (2 meters) in length. During summer months, mothers can be seen tending young pups. Like most marine mammals, harbor seals are wary of human contact. When surprised by walkers along the beach, they scramble en masse into the water, swiftly disappearing.

Often confused with seals, the Northwest's two sea lion species are distinguished by their ears. California and Steller's sea lions both have small, rolled-up ear flaps; harbor seals don't. Other differences often become apparent underwater. The lions employ their broad and flat front flippers to propel themselves, often with show-off acrobatics, through the water. Harbor seals, in contrast, choose to scull conservatively with their hind flippers. Male sea lions attain lengths of over 6 ft (2 meters) and may weigh 600 pounds (270 kg). Females are smaller, seldom exceeding 6 feet and 200 pounds. Steller's sea lions migrate from both California and British Columbia breeding grounds to share the Northwest with the California sea lion. They are easily recognized by size alone. Bull males approach 10 ft (3 meters) in length and 2,000 pounds (900 kg).

The simple life

Described by one ecologist as "a cruelly destructive pest, if there ever was one," slugs seem to be almost universally detested, except maybe in France where their close cousins, snails, are consumed. Slugs are champion herbivores using their tongue-like organ – the radula, covered with thousands of burrs – to rasp plants into minute edible nuggets.

This propensity to eat vegetable matter has led the slug to be abhorred by many Seattle gardeners. But this most common of visitor in area gardens is not a Northwest native. The nighttime raider of pea-patches and backyard gar-

THE SALMON'S ENDLESS CYCLE

One biologist wrote that salmon "reduce life to its simplest, most heroic terms." During its life, local salmon may travel up to 10,000 miles (16,000 km), swimming from a small freshwater stream in the Seattle area to Alaska, and eventually back again, where it will spawn and die. Other salmon start 2,000 miles (3,200 km) inland up the Columbia and Snake rivers.

Five species of salmon – chinook (king), coho (silver), chum (dog), sockeye, and pink – inhabit the Puget Sound region. Salmon range in size from 3 to more than 100 pounds (1.4–45 kg), and in color from mottled grey with tinges of red to brilliant red.

The life of a salmon ends where it began, in its birth stream. Before they die, the salmon release eggs and milt (sperm), which settle into the gravelly stream bed. After hatching, young remain nearby for up to two years before migrating out into salt water, returning up to seven years later to die where they were born. Overfishing, dams, logging (allows sediments to wash into streams and smothers the eggs), and suburban sprawl have all contributed to driving down the population.

The Puget Sound chinook was listed as an endangered species in 1999, the first listing of its kind in an urban environment in the United States.

dens, the European black slug is an alien that probably escaped from vegetation transported to the region from elsewhere.

The Northwest area has 23 species of native slugs, the best known of which is the banana slug, yellow-green inhabitants of forest ecosystems that can grow to 12 inches (30 cm) in length. Like all slugs, they are hermaphrodites, having both male and female organs. Although they can self-fertilize, most slugs mate with another slug, the notorious mucus helps grease the mating maneuvers.

TASTY GEODUCKS

Geoducks are sold at the Pike Place Market and in some supermarkets. A large geoduck can sell for $100 in Japan, where delicacies are often uncommon, like the geoduck.

"Once seen, never forgotten" could be the slogan for the state's only marine bivalve honored in song. The clam's most laudable attribute is also celebrated by the motto of Evergreen State College in Olympia, *Omni Extaris*, which translates to "let it all hang out." This clam is none other than Puget Sound's most ridiculed mollusk, the geoduck (pronounced *gooey-duck*). Unlike clams familiar to most people, the geoduck is not contained within its shell. The neck grows so large that its grey, tubular, wrinkled appendage may stretch to 3 ft (1 meter) in length. All geoducks spend the majority of their lives buried in the sand, basically immobile except for the contraction and extension of their neck.

Geoducks suck in water and food through their neck, which they extend ever so slightly above the sand. Any food in the water is filtered out as the water passes down one tube and up another within the neck. A typical geoduck weighs about 2½ pounds (1 kilogram), while some have topped the scales at 20 pounds (9 kilograms).

LEFT: salmon have long been important food.
ABOVE: coastal clams. **RIGHT:** Canada geese.

Wings aloft

With its combination of fresh and salt water, marshes, and forested hills, Seattle has an abundance of bird habitat right in the city center. Double-crested cormorants are commonly seen from fall to spring perched on buoys or bridge pilings with their wings outstretched. Glaucous-winged gulls are another bird that may be seen in either fresh- or saltwater settings. Mallards and coots live year-round in the numerous freshwater lakes that punctuate Seattle, along with great blue herons and pied-billed grebes. During winter, migratory waterfowl such as buffleheads, western grebes, and surf scooters are also common.

Two native birds – crows and Canada geese

– have so exploited the urban environment that many people would like to eliminate them. During the day, crows spread across the city *caaawing* and searching for food anywhere they can get it, which might include shrubbery, garbage cans, around park benches, or in cars with open windows. At night, they form communal roosts; the largest is on Foster Island in Washington Park Arboretum, where up to 10,000 birds may congregate.

We also can blame ourselves for the unchecked population explosion of Canada geese. In the early 1960s, when the goose population dropped to about 100, geese from the Columbia River were transplanted to the city. Unfortunately, it was a non-migratory population. They have never learned to migrate and why should they? With its abundant grassy fields and predator-free shoreline, the urban ecosystem is a perfect habitat for the birds.

The present population totals about 5,000 geese and they make the headlines on a regular basis. Canada geese have crashed into a jet landing in Renton, set off alarms at the Bangor nuclear submarine base north of Seattle, and forced the closing of several beaches on Lake Washington because of their bacteria-rich fecal matter. People have tried dogs to roust the geese, killing the birds, and transporting them back to eastern Washington. Nothing has worked.

Like many cities with large downtown buildings, Seattle also has a resident pair of peregrine falcons, which built a nest on the 56th floor of the Washington Mutual Tower (3rd Avenue, between University and Seneca). Peregrines dive at speeds of up to 200 mph (320 kph) to kill the abundant pigeons, sparrows and wrens that inhabit the urban corridor. The peregrine falcon has made a spectacular comeback after being endangered. Unlike many other cities, Seattle's falcon were not introduced but instead returned to the area naturally.

Bald eagles

Bald eagles are another large bird of prey that live in Seattle. Nesting pairs can be seen at Seward, Discovery, and Green Lake parks. They have built nests in all three parks and live there year-round, eating the abundant fish and waterfowl that live in the nearby waters. Several pairs have successfully raised young.

The bald eagle population grows appreciably in winter when migrants from the north move into the region. Several hundred eagles descend upon the Skagit River valley along Highway 2, about two hours north of Seattle, to take advantage of a nearly perfect combination of flora and fauna. The river teems with spawned-out and dying salmon, while Douglas firs growing along the river offer ideal perching spots for the birds to locate the fish. If one location could exemplify the importance of Douglas fir and salmon to the Northwest ecosystem, then along the Skagit River is the place. ❑

OWLS V. TIMBER INDUSTRY

At the center of an environmental controversy during the 1990s was the diminutive Northern spotted owl, declared by the federal government a threatened species in 1990. Biologists claimed that the bird's decline was the loss of habitat – ancient forests, woods that have never been cut and with trees several centuries old. Considered an "indicator species", the decline of the spotted owl reflected a decline of the ecosystem. In 1991, most timber sales were restricted in the Northwest. Logging towns were hard hit and a way of life was threatened. In the mid-1990s, a compromise was reached that cooled rhetoric but was completely satisfactory to neither side.

LEFT: the bald eagle has made a spectacular return.
RIGHT: wildflowers grace mountain foothills in spring.

TIMBER AND SALMON

For more than a century the industries of timber cutting and salmon fishing have anchored the economies of the Northwest. But things are changing

When pioneers first settled the Puget Sound area, they found a land carpeted with trees that strained one's belief and forced viewers to crane their necks. Douglas firs, hemlocks and cedars towered higher than twenty-storey buildings and measured 20 ft (6 meters) or more around at the base. They were magnificent and daunting, the world's greatest forest.

These trees were also in the way. With hand saws, axes and oxen, the first residents cut down the trees, dragged them to shore and turned them into docks, cabins and stores, or sold them to trade ships that passed by. For a while, at least, every settler was a logger.

Entrepreneurs saw the Northwest as a land of limitless resources and riches. Acre after acre of giant trees cloaked the landscape. Salmon, returning to spawn, filled every stream and river. Armadas of sardines painted coastal waters a shimmering silver. Valuable minerals – gold, silver and coal – could be dug from the ground.

The dream that died

Stories of those riches brought people across the continent by wagon train and around Cape Horn by ship. The coming of the railroads to Seattle and Vancouver late in the 19th century turned a trickle into a flood. The area must have seemed like Eden to the newcomers. The mild climate, spectacular natural environment, relatively abundant job opportunities, and world-class cultural and educational facilities were well nigh irresistible.

Today, the landscape is far different from that which greeted the early settlers. Clear-cut mountainsides, sometimes naked from ridge line to water's edge and scarred by logging roads, scandalize the eyes. The heavy rains of the Northwest have pounded the bare land, cutting gullies into the bare slopes, sweeping silt and the debris of clear-cutting into streams used by spawning salmon.

PRECEDING PAGE: forest undergrowth on the Olympic Peninsula. **LEFT:** mission accomplished on the Olympic Peninsula. **RIGHT:** lumbering, early 1900s.

The Northwest forests

Starting with the first settlers cutting down trees for their own use and to make room, logging has been the major industry in the Northwest. First trees were felled to build towns in Washington and British Columbia, then to build San Francisco and other North American

SHIFTING ECONOMIC ATTITUDES

As the state of Washington did in earlier decades, circumstances have forced a shift away from wealth created from the land to wealth created within the state's cities, especially in the Seattle and Puget Sound area. Leading the way is tourism, whose contribution to the economy has caught up with that of the resource industries of timber and fishing. The other economic stars in the province include business and financial services, technology industries such as Adobe and Microsoft, movie-making, value-added agricultural and timber products, the manufacture of consumer goods, and transportation, especially from the likes of Boeing.

cities, and now to construct buildings in Japan and elsewhere in Asia.

When environmentalists first began questioning forest practices in the Northwest, the British Columbia government ran print and television ads trumpeting that "Forests Are Forever". Many actually involved in the forest industry, including government employees, felt a real sense of mission – they were providing the renewable resource that the public demanded. And many forests really were managed as a renewable resources, mandated either by government regulation or company policy.

The reality of clear-cutting old-growth forests

is somewhat different from what government and industry public relations people put out. After replanting a clear-cut, it takes 60 or more years to raise harvestable timber. The ecosystems of the resulting tree farms are but a shadow of the diversity of life existing in the old-growth forests. Replantings may fail in poorer soils, steeper and more rugged terrains, and because of fungal infections. Even when ready for harvest, the replacement trees are mere toothpicks compared to the magnificent, straight-grained and ancient giants that they replaced. The old-growth forests are converted into tree farms with less non-monetary amenities like beauty, habitat and diversity.

REGIONAL ECONOMICS

In the state of Washington, a shift away from dependence on forestry began during World War II in 1941 and the growth of airplane manufacturer Boeing during the war years. Boeing became the major employer in the Puget Sound area. But there was a flip side. When Boeing's business cycle went into decline and the company laid off thousands, as it did from time to time, the Puget Sound area suffered severely. That has changed in the past decade with the spectacular growth of Microsoft and other high-tech industries, and with financial and commercial businesses. Tourism, too, has become a major player in the economy of the area. Declines in Boeing's fortunes still affect the area, but they don't call for signboards asking "Will the last person leaving Seattle please turn out the lights?" as it was in the early 1970s.

The economic recession in Asia during the 1990s had a significant effect on the demand for timber from the United States, particularly the state of Washington. The effects can be seen in the Grays Harbor town of Aberdeen on the Pacific coast. Aberdeen grew and prospered from the forest industry and became a major shipping port for Asia-bound timber. Since the Asian economic meltdown, businesses have closed and unemployment increased.

One cannot talk about the economies of Seattle or Washington State without considering the Canadian neighbor to the north, British Columbia. Economic interests and solutions are often intertwined between the two nations. In British Columbia, the shift from a resource-based economy did not begin until the late 1980s and early 1990s, when the forest and fishing industries went into sharp decline, a trend that continues. The problems in the region's forest industry can be attributed to a number of factors.

A principal reason is the decline of the economy of Japan, the region's – especially British Columbia's – principal customer for wood, and export quotas imposed by the United States. British Columbia is facing increased competition in the Asian market by inroads of wood from Scandinavia, the Baltic countries, Austria, Russia, and Japan itself. More fundamentally, the disappearance of old first-growth lumber before lumber becomes available from the second-growth tree farms exacerbates the economic problems.

The provincial government has increased stumpage fees and enacted more stringent environmental protection legislation. Both of these reduce profits for forest companies. Improvements to the health of the forest industry in British Columbia face three wild cards: Canadian-U.S. dollar exchange rates, U.S. tariffs on B.C. lumber, and a reduction in American housing starts.

The fisheries story

Beneath the surface of Pacific Northwest waters lies a mystery as ancient as the land. For thousands of years salmon have hatched in remote freshwater inland streams, traveled to the sea, and, after some years, returned to their birthplace to start the incredible cycle over.

Alive, mature salmon provided food for the original Native American inhabitants and predators of the Northwest, such as bears, eagles, orcas (killer whales) and seals. After spawning, dead salmon provided food for the scavengers, which included bears and eagles, as well as smaller organisms as the decomposing fish added nutrients to streams, thus promoting aquatic life.

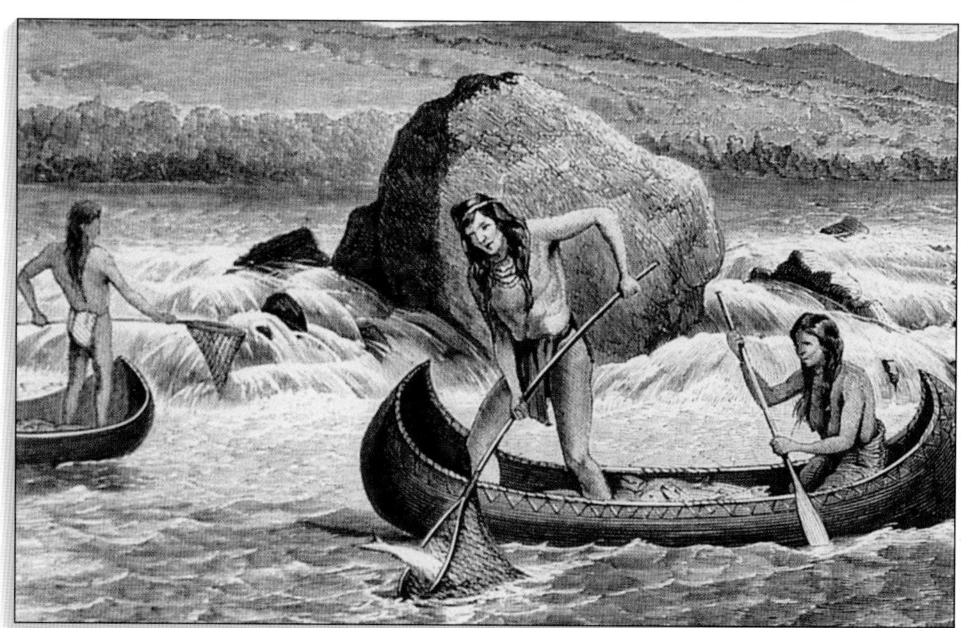

The most recent peoples to populate the Pacific shores of Washington and British Columbia, as well as Alaska and Oregon, have intercepted homeward-bound salmon, building an industry worth more than $1 billion annually and creating more than 60,000 jobs. In so doing, and by allowing virtually uncontrolled growth, we have tampered with salmon's magic cycle of life, perhaps fatally.

Not only have we overfished the salmon populations, we have lowered water quality in salmon streams by raising water temperatures and adding toxic pollutants and silt through agriculture and logging. Salmon habitats have also been destroyed by building dams, clear-cutting forests, overgrazing grasslands, and confining streams to concrete channels.

In particular, dams built to generate hydroelectric power and to provide water for irrigation have caused major damage to salmon populations. The Columbia-Snake river system once hosted the largest salmon migration in the world. Now it is an obstacle course of dams and turbines that kill approximately half of the

LEFT: supporting old-growth forests.
ABOVE: Indians netting salmon from canoes.

JAPANESE TIMBER DEMANDS

Japanese timber demand has much to do with Japanese aesthetics. Japanese houses have a lot of exposed beams, so they value the Northwest's old-growth timber with its great length and strength, and clear, straight grain. Most American and Canadian mills were unwilling to find out what kind of products the Japanese wanted and to retool to produce those products, so the Japanese bought unprocessed logs from the Pacific Northwest and did the secondary manufacturing in Japan – work that could have employed North Americans. A few smaller mill owners understood this and milled timbers to Japanese specifications. They did quite well.

salmon returning to spawn. Some nine out of ten young salmon returning to the sea don't make it. Turbines chew up the salmon and warm slow-moving water stress them, usually resulting in death.

Protecting Eden

Perhaps there is cause for optimism. Environmental activists have had some success in halting the clear-cutting of ancient forests. The U.S. Forest Service is becoming more environmentally sensitive and more responsive to public desires. Pressure by environmentalists forced the British Columbia government to cancel logging rights and protect some magnificent, centuries-old, first-growth, temperate rain forests, principally on southwest Vancouver Island.

THE LAST SALMON?

A century and a half ago, an estimated 30 million salmon migrated as spawning adults from the Pacific Ocean to rivers and lakes they had left some years before. With the coming of the white man came the realization that salmon were a source of wealth. The first salmon cannery went into operation in 1867 and packed away almost 450 tons annually. Other canneries followed. By 1883, over 20,000 tons of salmon annually were being canned from the Columbia River alone. A century later, the world – America, Canada, Japan and Russia – had taken such a huge bite out of the Pacific salmon population that salmon were faced with extinction.

In the United States, the new chief of the U.S. Forest Service is a fishery biologist, indicative of a shift at the upper levels away from timber-oriented management of the national forests. Other indicators include the recent announcements of a moratorium on new forest road construction – used as access roads for timber companies – and a program to close many forest roads and to restore them to a natural state. The Forest Service has implemented a natural resource agenda, intended for the 21st century, that will focus on four key areas: watershed health and restoration, sustainable forest ecosystem management, forest roads, and recreation. Of particular interest is that not one of these is to "get the cut out," the rallying cry since World War II for a generation of Forest Service employees and not a few members of Congress.

In 1999, the Pacific Salmon Treaty between the United States and Canada was renewed after a lapse of several years. For years American and Canadian salmon fishermen had battled over fishing rights and quotas.

The so-called salmon wars of the past few years included a blockade of an Alaskan ferry and finger pointing all around for the decline of salmon. British Columbia blamed Washington and Alaskan fishermen for overfishing British Columbia salmon. British Columbia and Washington blamed Alaska for overfishing "their" salmon. Alaska maintained that salmon knew no boundaries.

The signing of a new 10-year U.S.-Canada treaty regarding salmon has brought mixed reviews. Washington, Oregon and Alaska generally approve of it. The British Columbia government and British Columbia commercial fishing interests maintain that the Canadian government, which did not consult them during negotiations with the Americans, sold them out. The British Columbia sports fishing community and the British Columbia chapter of the Sierra Club, on the other hand, think it's a good thing. One can only hope that, in the long run, the treaty is good for the region's salmon. We'll just have to wait. ❑

LEFT: log storage yard at lumber processing plant.
RIGHT: moss-draped trees in the rain forest.

LIFE WITH WATER

Although other American cities have a lot more rain, Seattle's reputation as a wet, wet, wet place is embraced by the region's residents in a local pact

If landscape is character, then Northwesterners are most like water, shaped by the voluptuous shores and salt tides of Puget Sound and the deep currents of the Columbia, Salmon and Snake rivers. Finally, they are held back from falling off the proverbial edge of the world by a Pacific coastline whose rain forests and rocky peninsulas face the sea like protective guardians.

So, surrounded by water, Northwesterners cannot impose rhythms on nature as easily as a bulldozer does on a Southern California canyon or asphalt across a Southwestern desert.

This distinction – that Northwesterners are more changed by environment than it is by them – is crucial to understanding the Northwestern character. Northwesterners are a dreamy lot, in a fine tradition of dreamers.

Anticipation of change

According to the Wasco Indians along the Columbia River, the tribe knew well before the white men came to settle at Alki Point, in today's southern Seattle, in 1851 that a change was coming. As told in Ella Clark's classic *Indian Legends of the Pacific Northwest,* one of the Wasco elders dreamed that "white people with hair on their faces will come from the rising sun." The strangers, it was prophesied, would bring with them "iron birds that fly" and "something – if you just point it at anything moving, that thing will fall down and die." These strangers also brought modern new tools such as axes and hatchets; they even brought stoves to cook on. Along with this new technology, the newcomers brought a philosophy of individual ownership of land.

The Indians felt that the land could never be owned, just as it was impossible to section off the vast and winding lengths of the emerald-clear Puget Sound. Even now, after a century of non-Indian dominance, Puget Sound property rights ebb and flow according to the tides, not the set boundaries of so-called land owners. If even ownership of Northwest land is called into question by the changing and shifting of tides, how much more deeply are we affected by the water's relationship with us?

Physicists suggest that by observing something, we subtly change it whether intending to do so or not. Does what we gaze upon then also change us? Northwesterners not only reckon with water shaping our physical boundaries, but they must also learn to live most of the year as if underwater.

Rain is a Northwest native and perhaps is all that shelters locals from the massive population and industrial exploitations of California to the south. The rain is so omnipresent, especially between late October and even into June, that most Northwesterners disdain umbrellas, the true sign of any tourist.

Widely acclaimed Port Angeles poet Tess Gallagher tells it this way: "It is a faithful rain.

PRECEDING PAGES: Union Lake houseboat resident soaking up the water. **LEFT:** kayak and Seattle's skyline. **RIGHT:** still more houseboats in Seattle.

You feel it has some allegiance to the trees and the people... It brings an ongoing thoughtfulness to their faces, a meditativeness that causes them to fall silent for long periods, to stand at their windows looking at nothing in particular. The people walk in the rain as within some spirit they wish not to offend with resistance."

One must be rather fluid to live underwater; one must learn to flow with a pulse greater than one's own. A tolerance for misting gray days means an acceptance that life itself is not black and white, but in between. Gray. If the horizons out of one's window are not sharply defined but ease into a sky intimately merged with sea and soft landscape, then perhaps shadows are not so terrifying.

After all, most of the year Northwesterners can't even see their own shadows cast on the ground... They live inside the rain shadow, tolerating edges and differences in people and places perhaps because the landscape blends and blurs as it embraces.

Fluid heritage

The Northwest character is flexible. There are not the rigid social strata of New England or the South. Even the first American Indians were known not as warriors so much as fishermen.

CURRENTS AND WINDS, AND THE SALMON

The interactions between ocean currents and weather are complicated and not completely understood. Together, and when considered for the entire planet, the complexity of this "global engine" is staggering.

We are only now beginning to understand the part nature plays in the rise and decline of salmon populations, for example, and the populations of other creatures in the sea. Only in recent years have biologists, oceanographers and climatologists come to realize that something is going on in the northern Pacific that has a profound effect on the sea life. That something is a low-pressure weather system in the Aleutian Islands and the Gulf of Alaska.

When the low is strong, food in the Gulf of Alaska and Bering Sea is plentiful and western Alaska salmon thrive. Simultaneously, food in the coastal waters of the Pacific Northwest becomes scarce and Pacific Coast salmon populations decline. When the low is weak, as it has been in recent years, the reverse is true. During that time, salmon in the Pacific Northwest should have been plentiful. This has not been the case, however. Salmon stocks have been listed as endangered and fisheries closed. Are overfishing and salmon habitat destruction to blame? Well, partly, at least, but there may be longer-term cycles of that low at work that effect salmon populations.

While there were battles for territory, there was also a diversity and abundance of food that was quite a different story from the Southwest tribal struggles over scarce resources. Amidst this plenitude Northwest art flourished – and so did tribal storytelling.

In keeping with the landscape's watery changes, native stories of the region are full of legends in which animals change easily into people and back again. For example, the Salmon People are an underwater tribe who also spend a season on land; the whales and seals can metamorphose into humans as easily as the ever-present mist and clouds change into different shapes. Many Northwest coast tribes tell of merpeople – part human, part mammal – who mediate between the worlds to keep a watery balance. One of the most respected native gods was named Changer, a name perhaps explained by the local adage that if you don't like the weather, wait five minutes and it will change.

Many tribes began their mythologies with water, floods and seas creating what we now call "the people." A Skagit story details this beginning when Changer decided to "make all the rivers flow only one way" and that "there should be bends in the rivers so that there would be eddies where the fish could stop and rest. They decided that beasts should be placed in the forests. Human beings would have to keep out of their way."

Water before human

Here in the Northwest it is the human, not water, who must keep out of the way. People here tend to pride themselves, perhaps a little too arrogantly at times, on living within nature's laws, on listening to the environment. It is, after all, here in the Northwest where the

LEFT: on the water, Quinault Indian Reservation.
ABOVE: one in six Seattle residents owns a boat.

SEATTLE'S SOUND

Puget Sound, called Whulge by the local tribes, was explored in 1792 by Captain George Vancouver, who named the sound for Peter Puget, a lieutenant in his expedition who probed the main channel. The southern terminus of the Inside Passage to Alaska, Puget Sound is a deep inlet stretching south for 100 miles (160 km) from Whidbey Island (north of which are the straits of Georgia and Juan de Fuca). Hood Canal, which defines the Olympic Peninsula, is an extension of the sound. Rivers that enter the sound include the Skagit, Snohomish, and Duwamish. Puget Sound has several deep-water harbors: Seattle, Tacoma, Everett, and Port Townsend.

last nurturing old-growth forests still stand in the lower 48 states, a focus of sharp, ongoing economic and social debate.

Oil spills sometimes blacken the beaches and several species of salmon are endangered. Gray whales are sometimes found on their migrating courses belly-up from pollution in Puget Sound. There have been major closures of shellfish beds throughout the region because of toxic contaminations from industrial waste.

ESCAPE TO SEA

In the early 1990s, during the first days of the Gulf War, it was remarked by more than a few that there were more fishing boats on Puget Sound than usual.

There is a growing movement among corporations whose headquarters are in this area to give back some of their profits to protecting the wilderness. Recreational Equipment Inc. (REI) and Eddie Bauer are two such businesses that believe in investing in local environmental resources. Unfortunately, beyond its own lush Redmond campus, the unfathomably cash-rich Microsoft does little in comparison.

Just as Northwesterners claim closeness with their natural world so, too, they claim to be close to their history. The non-native history here is less than 200 years compared with thousands of years of Skagit, Suquamish, Muckleshoot, Okanogan and other tribal roots. Some of the myths favored by Indians calmly predict that "the human beings will not live on this earth forever." This prediction is an agreement between Raven, Mink, Coyote and what the Skagits call "Old Creator," concluding that human beings "will stay only for a short time. Then the body will go back to the earth and the spirit back to the spirit world."

Human worries and foibles seem to carry less weight in this region surrounded by water. It is typically Northwestern that this gone-fishing-while-the-world-falls-apart attitude prevails, while in New York City or Washington, DC, a population is transfixed by the news. It is not that Northwesterners aren't involved, it's just that nature can be an antidote to such strong doses of conflict. Nature can also remind us that there are other mysteries at work in the world that just might hold more power than our own.

If water defines the Northwest character and the rain is its temperament, it follows that those who stay long in the Pacific Northwest have developed a deep inner life to sustain them through the flow of changing gray days. ❑

ABOVE: journeys by ferry are a way of life in Seattle and Puget Sound.

Writin' in the Rain

Rain, or its absence, has always made the front pages in Seattle. It is the same story told with variations about a subject beloved by columnists and headline writers alike.

"This January, Wettest Ever, Getting Wetter" proclaimed the *Seattle Times* in 1953, announcing that a 40-year-old record for 27 January (9.8 inches/25 cm in 1914) had been beaten that day. "Rainless Seattle: Will We Become Another Tucson?" asked columnist Don Hannula in June 1985, alleging misleading under-reporting of rain by the Weather Bureau. "Drop In the Bucket: That Splatter Didn't Matter" was a 1987 headline in the *Seattle Times*.

In a city with only 50 totally clear days per year it is actually the lack of rain that seems to provide the most vivid stories. "How long, O Lord, How Long?" bemoaned columnist John Hinterberger in 1973, a year that clocked up only about half of the city's usual annual downpour. "What is giving us all this troublesome, lovely weather?"

Good – or at least exceptionally rainless – summer weather could indeed be troublesome for Seattle, lowering the level of the Cedar River up which 300,000 salmon travel from Lake Washington to spawn, not to mention slowing the turbines to half speed at the Diablo Lake plant which supplies much of the city's power. "There isn't enough water to cover all the gravel [in the river]," complained a fisheries department spokesman.

But that was a rare year. Later in the decade people were once again calling Seattle the rain capital of America, prompting a defensive story by writer Sharon Lane, who quoted from the 1978 World Almanac to show that Seattle's annual rainfall of 39 inches (99 cm) had been exceeded in the previous year by at least 125 American cities, including Miami (59.8), Atlanta (48.3), Houston (48.1), Nashville (46) and New York City (41.6).

What seems to make the difference here is the rain's ubiquity, a sheer, steady saturation slanting down from what a 1902 columnist called "the humid vats of heaven." It rains so frequently yet so unobtrusively in Seattle that few people wear coats or even admit to owning umbrellas (although the Bon Marche department store alone sells 13,000 each year and the Metro system reports that more than half that number are left on buses). Almost a decade ago a *Seattle Weekly* writer commented poetically that "drizzle and gray become the badge of pride for those who stay, and the curse that drives others away."

Even the legendary Craig Cappuccino, credited with setting up Seattle's first outdoor espresso cart, waited in the rain week after week until the customers came, building up that mystic relationship between sipping and soaking that has become the hallmark of the true espresso aficionado.

This perverse affection for rain sometimes suggests overly macho overtones. "Here if the sun doesn't shine we don't consider the day lost," says Walter Rue, author of *Weather of the Pacific Coast*. "People here don't complain about a little rain."

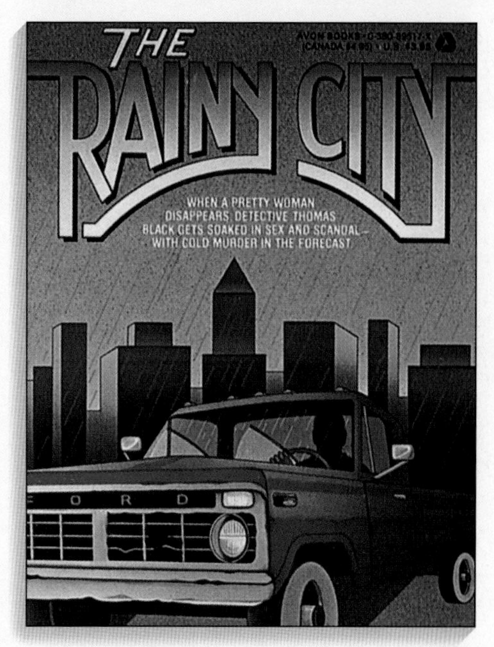

RIGHT: a writer's effort in the rain.

And the *Weekly* quoted a visitor from Kansas: "People actually get nervous when it's sunny. They feel exposed.They like the gray days; they wrap up in them like a security blanket."

All this, of course, plays right into the hands of the Lesser Seattle Movement, a tongue-in-cheek campaign promoted by veteran *Seattle Times* man Emmett Watson, who has repeatedly advocated a disinformation program to discourage would-be Seattleites. A couple of decades ago columnist Jean Godden gave his cause a hand with her playful list of 38 Things To Do In the Rain. "Write letters to all your friends," she urged her readers, "and tell them how horrible the weather is. Tell them this isn't even a nice place to visit..." ❑

U.S. AIR FORCE
USAF
N1343

NC19893
GOING

22
E-526
NO SMOKING
CONTROL

WINGS OF SEATTLE

Although upstarts like Microsoft have embedded themselves in the region's economy, it's Boeing that has, over the years, defined the area's industrial foundation

For a company that has produced most of the world's jetliners and has major military and space projects, Boeing maintains an unusually low profile in the Seattle area. No shining skyscraper, emblazoned with the company name and logo, reaches for the sky among the others that have transformed the Seattle skyline. Not only is the company studiously low-key, it is mysteriously inconspicuous in its home city. It's the company's own invisibility that is so puzzling to outsiders – in all respects, Boeing is a behemoth.

Its annual sales exceed $50 billion and, except for 1997 when Boeing had its first loss in five decades, the company is profitable. Boeing exports more goods than any other U.S. company: the annual figure has exceeded $26 billion. Its business backlog is over $100 billion, the largest in industrial history. When times are good (that is, no current layoffs), it employs well over 100,000 workers in the Puget Sound area and 230,000 worldwide. It owns thousands of acres of property and owns or leases more than 20 million sq. ft of office space.

If a gleaming downtown tower does not house Boeing's headquarters, what does? The executive offices, in fact, can be found in a drab, three-story building on an industrial street south of the city. The structure is as nondescript as most of Boeing's hundreds of buildings. Drive south on Interstate 5 from downtown Seattle. You'll see an airfield with dozens of new jets lined up alongside the runway – Boeing Field. There, Boeing workers prepare 737s and 757s for delivery. The headquarters is on the other side, hidden from view, and the airport's actual name is King County Airport.

Without a plush skyscraper headquarters, where do company executives give shareholders the word at the annual meeting? In the main cafeteria at the nondescript headquarters, where stockholders and directors alike sit in folding chairs and discuss their global enterprise. That's an apt allegory for Boeing's political power. It contributes faithfully but moderately to candidates, largely eschewing issues. It rarely takes public stands, although in the Washington State Legislature Boeing is described as a 1,000-pound gorilla. If your legislation is in trouble,

the axiom goes, the timber industry doesn't like it. If your bill vanishes without a trace, Boeing didn't like it. That's what the Seattle government discovered in the late 1970s when it aspired to annex the company's headquarters. Just a few weeks later the legislature abruptly changed the annexation rules to make the city's scheme impossible.

Boeing's planes, and the parts that comprise them, are made in large, helter-skelter complexes that reflect the hopscotch way the company grew from its beginnings in a red barn on the shores of Lake Union in 1916. Only in one place would you know at a glance that one of the world's biggest industrial enterprises is

PRECEDING PAGES: Boeing's Museum of Flight.
LEFT: Boeing's 747 plant in Everett.
RIGHT: earlier efforts of Boeing's engineers.

housed therein. That's in Everett, 45 minutes north of downtown Seattle. Here is the plant where 747s, 767s and 777s are assembled. The original 747 hangar, built in 1968, enclosed 200 million cubic ft (5.7 million cu. meters), the world's largest building at the time and one of the few grandiose claims Boeing allows itself. It has since doubled in size. Tours are offered daily – the only Boeing site open to the public.

Visitors, 140,000 a year, find themselves amazed by the sheer size of the planes and the plant, and by the apparent lack of activity. Assembling the world's largest commercial jet appears to be a leisurely process; on each fuse-

lage a few workers are driving rivets or bolting flanges. In the whole place there's no more than 700 workers on any shift. How on earth do a 747's 4 million separate parts coalesce into one massive plane that can take 450 people a third of the way around the globe in half a day?

Actually, most of the parts are pre-assembled. The planes are pieced together methodically during a 21-day journey through the assembly hangar. Every few nights the graveyard shift moves the line. That means picking up and shifting every single 747. They emerge at the other end ready to be painted for delivery to the international airlines. According to one popular legend, the 747 is the most universally recognized manufactured product in the world. This is also the world's most expensive commercial plane at some $170 million per airplane, the foundation of Boeing's finances.

On thin ice

Most Seattleites think of the 747 as the force that almost drove the company down, and the city with it. In 1970, Boeing had over-committed itself to develop the jumbo jet, investing more in the project than the corporate net worth. Banks refused to lend Boeing more money; when the government cancelled the supersonic transport (SST) project in 1971, it was a double blow that provoked catastrophic action. In less than two years, Boeing pared down more than 60,000 Seattle-area workers, shrinking its work force from 105,000 to 39,000 people.

Boeing was at the brink – and so was Seattle. With one in four jobs, directly or indirectly, beholden to Boeing, the behemoth had a profound impact on the area's economy. Thousands of families packed up and left; houses went begging. Houston, where unemployed engineers sought jobs in the space program, was known as Seattle South. A billboard on the city's outskirts exhorted "Will the last person leaving Seattle please turn off the lights?"

As a result, today the company hoards cash, keeping several billions on hand. It owns no executive jets and its few limousines are reserved for customers. Advertising is sparse.

The early years

Boeing is partly responsible for the region's evolution into a middle-class domain, the home of the neighborhood espresso cart. How did a manufacturing company transform a working-class city?

It began in 1947, when new Boeing President William Allen broke a long and bitter strike by out-bluffing the International Association of Machinists with a threat to replace workers. The company's simultaneous shift toward high-tech aerospace started its evolution from a blue-collar to a white-collar corporation, a key change. In 1942, at the height of the World War II bomber production effort, there were three hourly employees for every salaried worker.

Then came Boeing's first big boom, the postwar union struggles, the growth of high-tech and defense work. By the 1970s, Seattle was home ground for U.S. Senator Henry "Scoop" Jackson, the prototypical conservative Democrat who never met a defense project he didn't like. Scoop and colleague Warren Magnuson together wielded immense power in the U.S. Senate and funneled all the defense work to Boeing that they could manage, including the Minuteman nuclear missiles and the immense fleet of B-52s, still the heart of the US intercontinental strike force. The Air Force intends that the B-52, having been around for more than 40 years, will be kept in the inventory for another 40.

TOP HEAVY?

In contrast to Boeing's early days, it now takes far more designers and technicians to build a modern commercial airplane than it does production workers.

But when Congress killed its multi-billion-dollar funding of the supersonic transport (SST) project, Boeing found itself with no other direction to take but the one that led it to its status as the world's leading maker of commercial jets.

Of the 12,000 or so commercial jets flying today, over 10,000 have been built by Boeing and are by far the leading Washington state export. Not apples, not wheat, not wood. And it's all an accident of history.

LEFT: the famous Red Barn. **ABOVE:** assembling the fuselage of a 747 jumbo jet.

Bill Boeing, the company's founder, was a prosperous Seattle lumberman who developed a fascination with planes. In 1916, he asked George Westervelt, a Navy engineer, to design one – a pontooned biplane made of spruce and linen. Though Westervelt was transferred before the plane was built, Boeing called it the B&W for the two men's initials. Only two B&Ws were built, but they impressed the government and earned the fledgling Boeing Company new contracts to build military trainers during World War I.

Between the world wars, Boeing built and developed several fighters for the U.S. military and developed an all-metal, low-wing transport. In 1934, the U.S. Army Air Corps wanted a very heavy long-range experimental bomber. Boeing developed and built the XB-15, a four-engine monster with a wing spread of 149 ft (45.4 meters). This led to the legendary Boeing 314, for Pan American Airways Clipper fleet. The Boeing "Clippers," if slow by today's standards, provided a standard of luxury in commercial air travel that has never been surpassed.

The company earned world prominence with the B-17 and B-29 bombers of World War II fame. Thousands were built in factories in the

Seattle and Wichita, Kansas. An army of "Rosie the Riveters" turned out as many as 362 B-17s a month. In one 24-hour period, 16 B-17s rolled out of the Seattle plant.

Following the war, Boeing designed and built the B-47, the Air Force's first swept-wing jet bomber. The B-52 followed in 1952. Three years later, Boeing's executive suite almost had collective heart failure as they watched test pilot Tex Johnson barrel-roll the jet-powered "Dash 80." The plane was a big gamble for Boeing, but the gamble paid off. The Dash 80 was the prototype for the 707, the first successful passenger jet, which flew in 1958. Boeing won commercial dominance with the 707 and the company has never relinquished it, although Europe's Airbus threatened Boeing's lead by the end of the 1990s. A whole armada of Boeing jetliners followed – 720, 727, 737, 747, 757, 767, and 777. Some of these types were also adapted for military use.

Entering the new millennium

The 1990s saw two important mergers for Boeing. In 1996, Boeing merged with Rockwell International's aerospace and defense units to form Boeing North American. The following year, Boeing and McDonnell Douglas merged to form a single company of more than 200,000 employees. Creating a new corporate culture from the disparate cultures of McDonnell Douglas and Boeing was a major challenge. The goal was to move away from Boeing's command-and-control type of management to create a team culture, a process still on-going.

The year 1997 brought mammoth production problems. A dramatic increase in production goals led to parts and materials shortages and production inefficiencies due to the influx of thousands of new workers. The re-engineering of the production lines to increase efficiency at the giant Everett plant was almost the *coup de grace*. Boeing's Atlas-like burden of problems caused the shutdown of the 747 and 767 lines for a month. Delivery schedules slipped, upsetting customers. Boeing's annual report showed a loss for the first time in five decades. Wall Street expressed its displeasure.

The meltdown of the Asian economies in the 1990s was bad news, too. Asian airlines were among the prime customers for the 747, one of Boeing's largest sources of income. Rescheduling of delivery dates and some cancellations resulted. Despite its problems, Boeing delivered a record 559 jetliners in 1998, up from 374 the previous year. Even so, jobs were lost the following year as the airline business found it hard to predict future demand.

Visiting the old days

Some of Boeing's history can be seen at the Museum of Flight, a facility just down the street from Boeing headquarters. There, one of the world's major modern industrial endeavors is compressed into a compact, airy space. Some of the Museum's exhibits are housed in the original Red Barn, a more flamboyant structure than any of Boeing's present buildings. The Museum also displays aviation history.

The museum is in Seattle because Boeing is – the company donated the land – but at no point in the eight-decade history of the company has Seattle proved crucial to Boeing. In fact, a 1948 study found no economic reason why the company should operate in Seattle at all. But operate it does. Boeing is as pervasive as rain, and the company and the region regard each other like an old married couple, hardly ever stopping to take a close look. ❑

LEFT: Boeing is a prime contractor in the new International Space Station.

Golden Gates

Microsoft chairman Bill Gates's personal wealth reached $100 billion – in Microsoft stock – in 1999. His company reached $500,000,000,000 of valuation at around the same time. (As a handy reference, note that there isn't that much U.S. currency in circulation in the entire world, whether in New York banks or Third-World black markets.)

Microsoft's worth at the beginning of the 21st century is 50 percent more than the value of all the land in Washington State, where in Redmond (east of Seattle) Microsoft calls home, and only eight nations, with Spain number eight, have economies that are larger than the value of Microsoft. The irony of this half-trillion-dollar valuation is that Microsoft considered it to be too low and unreflective of Microsoft's Internet holdings. Corporate officials believed it should have been valued considerably higher, especially its Internet efforts.

William H. Gates III, son of a successful Seattle attorney, gained his first programming experience at the city's posh Lakeside School in 1968, when he was 12. At the age of 19, having dropped out of Harvard, he joined with friend Paul Allen to found Microsoft. They bought a basic operating code known as DOS for a few thousand dollars and then proceeded – through business acumen and arm-twisting – to make it the industry standard over the years. Allen and Gates recognized early that software, not hardware, is where the leverage – and profits – would be.

Microsoft's success is founded on a 1981 coup in which Microsoft won IBM's contract for the operating system in Big Blue's new line of personal desktop computers. Since Microsoft went public in 1986, Allen has sold stock valued at more than $7 billion and Gates at $7.6 billion. In 1986, Gates sold some of his stock at $21 a share; in 1999, he sold nearly 10 million shares at $86 a share. Nowadays, Gates's worth increases by an average of $1 million a second. A minimum-wage worker would have to work 40-hour weeks for 8.6 million years, twice as long as humanity's existence, to match the wealth of Bill Gates.

Much is made of Gates's wealth, and of Allen's philanthropy in the Seattle area, but little is made of the scores of employees made millionaires through stock options. This generation of wealth has made the neighborhoods surrounding Redmond, where Microsoft has its global headquarters, thick with millionaires. Gates's home on the shores of Lake Washington has a movie theater, underground parking, and a dining pavilion for 100 people. Large, flat-panel screens in each room display images from his electronic collection of art.

While Microsoft rose to power based on its computer operating system, when the Internet began to gain momentum in the mid-1990s, Gates engineered one of the swiftest corporate realignments in history, shifting the company's focus towards the blossoming Internet. Not only did Microsoft enter the browser war, but it also developed strategic alliances with the likes of NBC News, creating MSNBC, a cable-TV and online service. Its web browser set out to annihilate its Netscape rival, and its holdings range from WebTV to Hotmail.

RIGHT: William H. Gates III.

IBM and Microsoft have long parted ways, the former at one point allying itself with erstwhile enemies Apple and Motorola to take on Gates – and Intel. But owning the operating system that powers more than 90 percent of the world's personal computers makes Microsoft formidable, and it ended the 20th century fighting anti-trust proceedings threatening to break it up. At the Justice Department, the antitrust chief going after Microsoft may well have reflected that he would have to work for 42,000 years to earn what Gates makes in a single day. ❑

CAUTION
LOW
FLYING
FISH
FRESH
KING SALMON STEAKS

FRESH SALMON!
SOCKEYES
BAR-B-Q
FRESH
CAT FISH
WE HAVE

PLACES

A detailed guide to the entire city, with principal sites clearly cross-referenced by number to the maps

Seattle is a city of distinct neighborhoods. They may not be defined by their ethnic populations, but the individual areas do characterize the city, and longtime residents are often as loyal to their neighborhood as to any cultural ties. Residents of any one neighborhood chauvinistically tend to feel their local friends are more pleasant than those in other parts of the city, their views more picturesque and their local restaurant chefs more talented. Families with children are likely to label their neighborhood "a good place to raise the kids." If they are unmarried, they boast that it is exactly the right area for singles.

Specific differences between neighborhoods, however, are rather challenging to pin down for an outsider. The University District, surrounding the University of Washington, is understandably academic and student-oriented, the northern Fremont area is labeled funky, and the sprawling suburban neighborhoods in Bellevue and Redmond are called upscale. If one had any doubts that Ballard, north of downtown, was the city's Scandinavian center, you only need pick up a bottle of Ballard Bitter, made by Red Hook, the local micro-brewery, and read the label: "Ya sure, ya betcha," it says.

Residents of Wallingford argue with Queen Anne residents about whose homes offer the most spectacular views over downtown. And residents of Magnolia and West Seattle offer similar arguments about their views of Puget Sound, Vashon, Blake and Bainbridge islands, not to mention the Olympic Mountains to the west.

Because of the city's strong and diverse communities, some maintain, much of downtown Seattle is empty in the evenings because so many people find what they want closer to home. This couldn't be further from the truth. Pioneer Square and Belltown have exuberant after-dark entertainment, and the reliable Pike Place Market bustles with activity every weekend.

One of Seattle's specialties is the outdoors – fjord-like waters in Puget Sound, rain forests on the Olympic Peninsula, volcanoes in the Cascades to the east, and even a convenient foreign country – Canada – just a couple of hours to the north. To visit Seattle without immersing one's self into the surrounding geography is, somehow, sad. Even a few hours on a ferry skimming the waters of Puget Sound enrich the experience of Seattle. ❑

PRECEDING PAGES: Seattle skyline at dusk and the Space Needle; ferries connect the many islands; Pike Place Market's "flying" fish.
LEFT: sailing beneath the ever-present Space Needle.

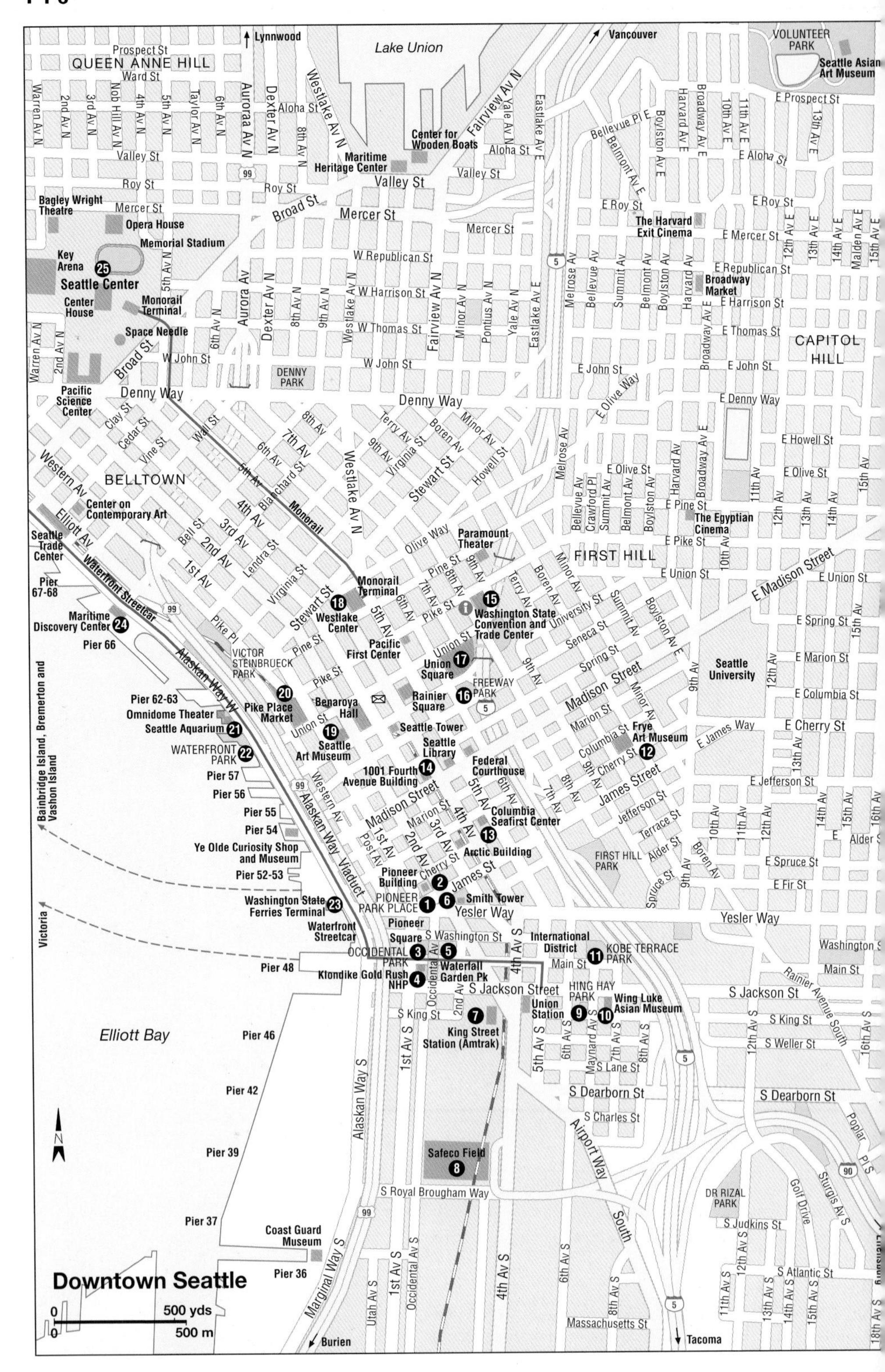

Downtown Seattle
0
500 yds
0
500 m
Lake Union
QUEEN ANNE HILL
CAPITOL HILL
FIRST HILL
BELLTOWN
Elliott Bay
Seattle Center
Key Arena
Space Needle
Pike Place Market
Seattle Art Museum
Seattle Aquarium
Westlake Center
Washington State Convention and Trade Center
Pioneer Square
International District
Safeco Field
King Street Station (Amtrak)
Union Station
Smith Tower
Seattle University
Frye Art Museum
Wing Luke Asian Museum
Klondike Gold Rush NHP
Washington State Ferries Terminal
Maritime Discovery Center
Seattle Asian Art Museum
Coast Guard Museum
Lynnwood
Vancouver
Tacoma
Burien
Victoria
Bainbridge Island, Bremerton and Vashon Island

OLD SEATTLE

Rather young by global standards, the old core of Seattle nonetheless has an architectural ambience that lends itself to tall tales, some real tales, and tall totems

Map on page 116

Modern Seattle began in February of 1852 when Arthur and David Denny, along with a score of other pioneers, moved up from Alki Point, on which they had first landed only three months earlier. They named their new home Seattle after an Indian chief – Noah Sealth, of the Duwamish and Suquamish tribes – who was among the settlement's first visitors.

The businessmen who came later were less respectful to the locals, however. A group from the Seattle Chamber of Commerce visited Alaska's Fort Tongass in 1899 and stole a Tlingit tribal totem pole while the men of the village were out on a fishing expedition. For 40 years this totem pole stood at First and Yesler in Seattle until it was vandalized. Shamelessly, the city shipped the pole back to Alaska and asked for a replacement. When the tribe said it would cost $5,000, the city sent a check. The reply came from the Tlingit tribal chief: thanks for finally paying for the first one – and the second one will also cost $5,000. The city duly paid for the second.

The 60-ft (18-meter) replacement pole stands today on a triangular brick plaza where First, James and Yesler intersect in front of the Pioneer Building (*see page 120*). This plaza is commonly – and mistakenly – called **Pioneer Square**, a name that actually refers to the encompassing 20-square-block neighborhood, which is a designated historical park. The official name of the triangular park is **Pioneer Park Place ❶**. However, even native Seattle residents call the park Pioneer Square. Regardless, the restored buildings of the area contain amongst the city's highest concentration of galleries and stylish restaurants.

Pioneer Square was the founding area that the settlers chose when they left Alki Point in 1852 for the superior harbor at Elliott Bay. The totem pole above is close to James A. Wehn's bust of Chief Sealth. Wehn, who arrived in Seattle not long after the 1889 fire that destroyed a large part of the Pioneer Square neighborhood and lived in Seattle until he died in 1953, also designed the city's seal, which bears Chief Sealth's profile. When Chief Sealth died in 1866, he was buried on the Suquamish Indian Reservation on the Kitsap Peninsula, northwest of Seattle.

The text of Sealth's only known peroration has become disputed because a century later, a Texas screenwriter created a speech for a mythical Native American into which he dropped a few of the chief's words – and now some people aren't certain which lines are original and which not.

At First and Yesler, where the street surface is genuine cobblestones, the Pioneer Square plaza – Pioneer Park Place – has long been dominated by an ornate Victorian iron-and-glass pergola built in 1905 and which once sheltered the patrons of the 1.3-mile (2.1-km) cable-car

PRECEDING PAGES: mood in a well-worn bar.
BELOW: Pioneer Park Place.

route that, until 1940, ran between Yesler Way and Lake Union, to the north of downtown. Behind the pergola is the Merchant's Cafe, the city's oldest restaurant and which in Gold Rush times served 5-cent beer to miners waiting their turn at the upstairs brothel. Seattle's great fire in 1889 wiped out most of the bar's neighbors in the 20-block Pioneer Square area, but rebuilding began immediately.

Architect Elmer Fisher, responsible for at least 50 of the new buildings built to replace those damaged by the fire, set the predominant style – one example of his work is the elegant **Pioneer Building** ❷. On James Street opposite the plaza, its turn-of-the-century tenants included several dozen mining companies above a saloon once operated by Dr. David Swinton "Doc" Maynard, one of the area's first settlers and among the most influential.

Doc Maynard's saloon is currently the headquarters of the Underground Tour, a 90-minute inspection of the shops and rooms that were abandoned when this part of town was rebuilt. To eliminate what had been persistent flooding, some of the buildings were raised as much as 18 ft (5 meters) and the unused subterranean city was sealed off until an enterprising newspaper columnist started to organize tours. The Underground Tour, which has been in business for decades, offers a refreshingly irreverent survey of Seattle history. "Henry Yesler had no moral or ethical values whatsoever," a guide announces. "Naturally he became our first mayor." On another occasion the guide adds, "That's the true Seattle spirit – even if it's a lousy deal, we'll stick with it."

Beginning in the restored 1892 Doc Maynard Saloon, the tour descends into the warren of musty, debris-lined passageways and rooms that were once at ground level. Passing under the glass-paneled sidewalk at First and Yesler, the tour ends in a tiny museum stocked with old photos, magazines, artifacts and

BELOW: Seattle as it looked in 1883.

scale models of the area when Yesler Way was three times as steep as it is today. On sale are books by columnist Bill Speidel, who originated the tours. Funky old bars and restaurants dot this area, and music from rock to blues to jazz can be heard almost any night of the week.

Map on page 116

Occidental Park

Occidental Avenue gives way to a brick pedestrian mall-park between South Washington and Jackson streets. The enticing aromas of a bakery beside the rear door of the Grand Central Building drift out into **Occidental Park** ❸ (also sometimes called Occidental Mall). Nobody's quite sure what to do with this area, where a curiously designed structure seems to attract only the homeless.

The four cedar totems in Occidental Park were carved over a 10-year period by Duane Pasco, a Washington State master carver with an international reputation, and are sited to follow the traditional custom of having their faces to the sea and hollowed backs to the forest, the latter in this case being represented by the skyscrapers of the city. It is speculated that the Northwest Indians followed this totem orientation as they often felt an affinity toward creatures of the sea, their primary source of food. Historical photographs from the southeastern Alaskan coast also show totems facing the sea. The tallest one in Occidental Park – *Sun and Raven* – depicts the Raven with the moon in his beak, bringing light to the world. Further down the 35-ft (11-meter) pole is the Chief of the Sky's daughter giving birth to the Raven, and the Chief himself holding the sun in his hands and the box that held "light." The second totem *Tsonoqua* is a human figure with outstretched arms; the other two totems are *Bear* and *Man Riding on Tail of Whale.*

Also on Main Street, across from Occidental Square, is the misleadingly

Unusual protection near Pioneer Square.

BELOW: Pioneer Building, and lunch amidst the sun.

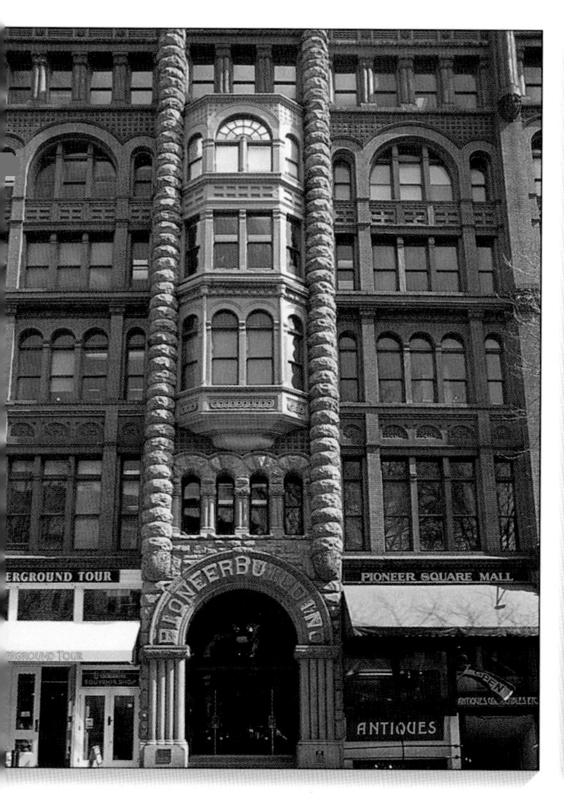

Totem pole.

named **Klondike Gold Rush National Historical Park** ❹ (open daily 9am–5pm; tel: 206 553 7220; free), administered by the National Park Service with units in southeast Alaska (the town of Skagway and the Chilkoot Trail), as well as this storefront museum. The museum has exhibits and photographs recounting the saga of the hectic 1890s, when half of Seattle caught Gold Rush fever.

Thousands left their jobs in Seattle (including the mayor) to undergo the rigorous journey over forbidding mountains and up treacherous rivers 1,500 miles (2,400 km) north to Alaska. Few of the spur-of-the-moment adventurers struck it rich, however, with most of the claims being already staked long before the newcomers' arrival. Many of those who stayed behind in Seattle did better – at Canada's insistence, prospectors were obliged to take with them a year's supply of goods and provisions (400 pounds of flour and 25 cans of butter, for example), and thus many of the city's early businesses did quite well.

Dating from before the 1889 fire is the **Maynard Building**, at Washington and First Avenue, the site now occupied by the Elliott Bay Book Company and where once stood the hospital established by Doc Maynard. It was Maynard who donated part of his land for Seattle's first industry: a steam-powered lumbermill built by an early arrival, German-born Henry Yesler. It was installed at the top of what is now Yesler Way, which began as Skid Road, the steep ramp down which the lumber was sped to the sawmill. In Yesler's day, the mill ran day and night, employing almost half the people in town. Yesler's house nearby was on the site of what is now the King County Courthouse. The Mutual Life Building at Yesler Way and First Avenue went up in 1897 where Yesler's busy cook-house once stood. At the waterfront end of Yesler Way is the Washington State Ferries Terminal, at Pier 51 (*see page 136*).

After World War II, Skid Road was a forgotten home of cheap hotels and

BELOW: the strength of Uncle Sam.
RIGHT: streetside cafe in Pioneer Square.

homeless winos. In the 1960s, artists began to move their studios into the low-rent lofts. Prevented from rebuilding by the city's rejection of wholesale urban renewal, property owners remodeled building interiors in wood and brass. High-priced condominiums melded in with the pensioners living cheaply.

The city's first horsecar line began running along neighboring Second Avenue in 1884, and the electric car followed five years later. For at least a couple of generations First Avenue was renowned not only for its low-rent stores, prostitutes, X-rated bookstores and taverns, but also for pawnbrokers, whose stock varied from jewelry and watches near Pike Place to more prosaic guns, radios and typewriters nearer to Pioneer Square.

Waterfall Garden Park

Savvy lunchtime brown-baggers walk a block east up Main Street to the enclosed **Waterfall Garden Park** ❺, which must surely take a prize for one of the best miniature parks in the country. It was funded as a tribute to the employees of the United Parcel Service (UPS), a company founded in Seattle, in 1907, by local resident James Casey. The park's tables are set amidst flowers and trees in front of a glorious waterfall designed by Masao Kinoshita, which drops 22 ft (37 meters) onto huge boulders and recycles 5,000 gallons (20,000 liters) of water every minute.

At the end of the 19th century, Lyman Cornelius Smith arrived in Seattle after his wife fell in love with the town. Smith, already wealthy from the sale of his gun company (later Smith & Wesson) and then his revolutionary new typewriter (later to be Smith Corona), promptly bought several blocks around Main Street and First Avenue. In 1901, he built the L. C. Smith Building. It was badly damaged by fire a year or two later, and Smith at first announced plans

Map on page 116

By the 1930s, Skid Road had become known as Skid Row, a term adopted elsewhere for an area frequented by the homeless or the hopelessly drunk.

BELOW: Waterfall Garden Park.

for a 12-story replacement. Goaded by the plans of a business rival, however, he ambitiously plotted the 42-story **Smith Tower** ❻. When completed in 1914, this was the tallest building in the world outside New York. Gradually, the distinction was whittled away until, at the time of the World's Fair in 1962, its last remaining title – tallest building in Seattle – was taken by the 605-ft (184-meter) Space Needle. (*See box on Smith Tower, page 139.*)

Although nobody has ever been able to count all the supposed 42 stories, Smith Tower remains a sentimental favorite with Seattle residents. Attempts over the years to "modernize" the building have always met with angry protests.

On First Avenue at Cherry Street is Metsker Maps, the best place in the city to buy travel books and maps. A plaque on the **Hoge Building**, Cherry and Second, identifies this as the site of Carson D. Boren's 1852 home, "the first cabin built by a white man in the city." There are some sturdy, old structures around here but none more noteworthy than the **Arctic Building**, at Third Avenue and Cherry, with its row of sculpted walruses adorning the upper levels. Believing the original terracotta tusks to be a potential danger to pedestrians walking outside below, the building's owners removed them some years ago and replaced them with epoxy versions.

Apart from a handful of patient souls (scarcely enough, one would imagine, to keep the espresso stands in business except at rush hours), the city's **Amtrak King Street Station** ❼ (on Second Avenue and King) is sometimes like a ghost town. Observant visitors will note the resemblance between its tower and the campanile of St. Mark's in Venice, after which it was modeled. Much of the surrounding terrain, including that under Safeco Field, is reclaimed land from what was once the bay. As much as 60 million cubic ft (1.7 million cubic meters)

BELOW: Smith Tower was completed in 1914.

AN ARTFUL BUS LINE

Seattle's Metro buses are well-known for being free downtown and for being ecologically efficient. Metro's most outstanding achievement, perhaps, has been its sponsorship of public art. Scores of works are distributed throughout the five stations of the $450-million bus tunnel, which passes beneath midtown Seattle. Granite stairs are colored: white for north, black for south, green for east, and red for west.

As far as possible, art is appropriate to the specific station in which it is located. The designers and artists studied what was above ground before adorning underground. Under Pioneer Square, engineers have placed a relic from the cable-car system that once ran along Yesler Way: a huge, cast-iron flywheel more than 11 ft (3.5 meters) in diameter. This has been supplemented with contemporary artwork, including a ceramic mural incorporating Indian baskets and a dugout canoe.

The quotations here are from Chief Sealth (Seattle) and Seattle pioneers Arthur Denny and Doc Maynard. The station at International District has tiles created from designs by children of the neighborhood and an enormous origami work of painted aluminum. The open plaza above is tiles with symbols of the Chinese zodiac.

of earth was used for foundation landfill and to raise the level of the old city.

Just to the south is **Safeco Field** ❽, a retractable-roofed stadium opened in 1999 at a final cost of just over half a billion dollars and in which the Mariners play baseball. With cedar-lined dugouts and a real field of Kentucky bluegrass and ryegrass, it is Major League Baseball's most expensive stadium in history. Before Safeco Field came on line, Seattle's baseball venue for 22 years was the creaky and gloomy **Kingdome**, a skyline landmark since 1976 and once described by *Sports Illustrated* as having the "ambience of a port-a-john". It was demolished the year after Safeco Field hosted its first ball game and an open-air football stadium is planned one day on the site of the Kingdome.

Map on page 116

Old-fashioned time.

International District

Known for more than a century as the city's Chinatown (Chinese were among Seattle's earliest residents), the area now called the **International District** – and never called Chinatown – has grown both geographically and culturally to include residents representing numerous Asian groups, especially the Chinese, Japanese, Vietnamese, Filipino, Korean and Southeast Asian.

A man named Wa Chong is credited with building – in 1871 – the third brick structure in the city and was also responsible for the first building to go up after the 1889 fire. The Wa Chung Tea Store, at the corner of Washington and Third, advertised in 1877 that contractors, mill owners and others requiring Chinese labor "will be furnished at short notice." And, as an afterthought, the store offered "the highest price paid for live hogs." A front-page announcement in that same paper by Tong Wa Shing & Co,, dealers in Chinese Fancy Goods, offered tea, rice – and opium.

By the turn of the century, Chinatown, riddled with secret passages and tunnels, had become a city within the city that saw few white faces except for the occasional adventurous opium smoker. Violent *tong* or gang wars were not uncommon. A story in the *Post-Intelligencer* in 1902 described well-guarded Chinese gambling houses from which whites were barred.

Long before World War II, the community stabilized, largely because of the influence of such civic bodies as the Chung Wa Association, of which all prominent Chinese were members. But the notorious gambling dens survived until 1942.

On Sixth and Jackson, brightly colored figures from traditional Chinese legends cover the wall of United Savings, one of many banks that safekeep family funds that, in an earlier era, might have gone into private safes (or under floorboards). Once preferred by Chinese over banks, these safes might be shared by up to 10 people, each having a key that could be used only in conjunction with the other partners.

Two fearsome white-stone dragons guard the sidewalk in front of Chung Kiu antique shop, outside which sometimes unfamiliar Asian vegetables spill over from the neighboring grocery store. A common sight around here are the rows of jars displaying herbs, flowers and roots – peony, honeysuckle, chrysanthemum, ginger, ginseng, and especially licorice, which for centuries have been used to build strength and

BELOW: one-stop merchant.

Jimi Hendrix was born in Seattle.

"balance the body's energy." The Bush Hotel here might be a good choice for budget-minded visitors who enjoy being in the center of a genuinely authentic and quite diverse ethnic area.

Behind the hotel, **Hing Hay Park** ❾ holds an ornamental arch that dates from 1973 and was designed in Taiwan by architect David Lin. The dragon mural at Hing Hay Park is a larger-than-life depiction of local Asian events. The park is also the setting for occasional martial-arts exhibitions and Chinese folk dancing, and even a little early-morning *taiqi*. A block away, at the corner of Maynard and Weller, is the region's largest Asian department store, Uwajimaya, which stocks everything from furniture to fruit and exotic vegetables.

Named after the first publicly elected Asian-American – Wing Luke, elected to the Seattle city council in 1962 – official in the Northwest, the **Wing Luke Asian Museum** ❿ (open Tues-Fri 11.30am-4.30pm, weekends noon-4pm, closed Mon; tel: 206 623 5124; admission fee) serves all the various ethnic communities by rotating shows about different parts of the Pacific region – exhibits have ranged from Balinese masks to Japanese textiles or Persian miniatures. The permanent collection includes historical photographs and artifacts such as a 50-ft (15-meter) dragon boat, used for festival races in China, and a mock-up of an old Chinese apothecary. Wing Luke died in a plane crash in 1965, before the end of his first term.

About a block north of the museum is what began as Nihon-machi, or Japan Town, as the area was called, centered around **Kobe Terrace Park** ⓫ at the top of the hill. The Japanese area was denuded of most of its population by the U.S. government internment policies of World War II, in which Japanese-Americans were shipped off to camps in Idaho or eastern Washington. Presidential Order

BELOW: gardens in the International District.

Map on page 116

9066, forcibly relocating Japanese-Americans on the mainland (most in Hawaii were left alone) to these internment camps, was signed by President Franklin D. Roosevelt in February of 1942. It was revoked in December of 1944. Of the Japanese interned during that period, about 7,000 of them were Seattle residents.

The old Japanese area was later decimated by construction of the Interstate 5 freeway. The park, from which there's a fine panoramic view, contains tiny gardens tended by low-income neighborhood residents and also a stone lantern donated by Seattle's sister city of Kobe, in Japan.

Asian influx

The red-brick **Nippon Kan Theater** (630 S. Washington) began in 1909 as the Astor Theater and has been designated as a National Historic Site. Although some Japanese still live nearby, the area has seen a heavy influx of other Asians in recent years, especially Cambodians, Laotians, and Vietnamese.

East of the freeway, the streets around the Japanese-owned Asian Plaza shopping mall at Jackson and 12th are sometimes referred to as Little Saigon and house a good proportion of the hundreds of Vietnamese-owned businesses in Seattle. The area is still expanding to the north.

Off on its own from the International District and to the northeast several blocks, the **Frye Art Museum** ⓬ (open daily; tel: 206 622 9250; free) was dramatically remodeled and expanded in 1997 and now offers frequently changing exhibits as well as poetry readings, chamber music and other performances. The museum originally showcased 19th-century German paintings from the collection of the late Charles and Emma Frye; now exhibits are more diverse and might include metaphorical paintings as well as the Frye's salon paintings. ❑

BELOW: origami art in International District bus stop.

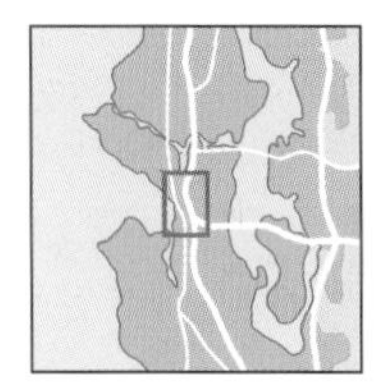

DOWNTOWN SEATTLE

A city with a delightful, if not a distinctive, personality, Seattle has a center graced with hills, refined architecture, public sculpture, lapping waves and seagulls – and the odd colorful character

North of the Pioneer Square area and International District is the downtown and financial district, with the imposing **Federal Courthouse** a few blocks to the northwest. Hilly terrain is this. On Fifth Avenue nearby is the *Fountain of Wisdom* by George Tsutakawa, a 9-ft-tall (2.7-meter) sculpture that integrates water and bronze. Tsutakawa is a local artist whose works grace many of the city's public areas. Many of the large hotel chains have located their local properties on Fifth and Sixth avenues, only a block or two from the immense towers of the financial district that have changed the city's skyline in the past decade.

Seattle's tallest building today – in fact, the tallest in the West – is the 76-story **Columbia Seafirst Center** ⓭, which rises 954 ft (291 meters) and is served by 46 elevators. There is an observation room on the 73rd floor with an impressive but not panoramic view. However, the vista from the top-floor (private) women's restroom is reputed to be superlative. Below street level at the center are carpeted, picture-lined corridors – one leading to the AT&T Gateway Tower next door to the east – and an attractive mall lined with shops, classy snack bars and tables.The Starbucks coffeeshop here serves 500 customers an hour during its morning rush and claims to be the world's busiest espresso bar, though doubtless other Seattle espresso counters are in contention. The **1001 Fourth**

BELOW: unusually sunny park in downtown Seattle.

Avenue Building ⓮ offers what some people consider to be the best free observation perch in town, from the 46th-floor foyer.

Enormous skyscrapers began to rise in downtown Seattle in the late 1960s and early 1970s, but the really big boom didn't get underway until the following decade, when the Columbia Seafirst Center was followed by the 62-story AT&T Gateway Tower; the 44-story Pacific First Center, at Sixth and Pike; the 56-story Two Union Square, 600 Union; the 55-story Washington Mutual Tower, at 1201 Third; and the domed Second and Seneca Building, whose local nickname – Ban Roll-On Building – suggests a brand of underarm deodorant. Aesthetic opinions about these structures vary a great deal, but the buildings have been a boon for sculptures under the city's 1973 "one-percent-for-art" ordinance, which requires that 1 percent of funds appropriated for municipal construction projects be set aside for art in public places, resulting in some spectacular work.

One of downtown's many high-rises.

The art controversy

The Henry Moore work *Three Piece Sculpture: Vertebrae*, outside the 1001 Fourth Avenue Building, predates the ordinance, however, and is only one of the bank's collection of 12,000 artworks. This one was donated to the Seattle Art Museum (*see page 131*) when the bank changed hands some years ago. Seafirst's big art-buying spree peaked just before the bank moved into its new headquarters, with its directors apportioning $200,000 for interior works to decorate the building's lower floors and a further $300,000 for public spaces, more than 50 percent of which was spent on the Henry Moore work. (The bank attracted some criticism for this, accused of making an unduly unconservative, even extravagant choice.) The offices were furnished both with works of local artists and such nationally

BELOW: downtown underground bus tunnel.

NEARLY AGELESS STONE

Walking through downtown Seattle is a walk along a geological time line, beginning with 1.6-billion-year-old Finnish granite at 1000 2nd Avenue to the Seattle Art Museum and its young, 300-million-year-old limestone walls. Further along are fossils, some up to 4 inches (10 cm) long, embedded in grey limestone at the Gap store on 4th Avenue. And this is just the beginning.

Around the corner and underground in the Westlake Center bus station is the burnt oatmeal-colored travertine deposited less than 2 million years ago near the Rio Grande River in New Mexico.

Seattle's use of stone, rather than wood, for building began soon after the 1889 fire that destroyed much of the city's downtown business district. Initially, Seattle started with local rock quarried in the Puget Sound region, especially near Tacoma and Bellingham. Stone spread throughout the city into streets, walls and foundations.

As the city grew and became more wealthy, and more worldly, builders sought out stone from Vermont and Indiana. Finally, with better and economical transportation systems and stone-cutting technology, local and regional geology became somewhat obsolete as contractors ordered stone from South Africa, Brazil and Italy.

Seattle George, a sculpture by Seattle artist Buster Simpson.

known painters as Karel Appel, Kenneth Noland and Jules Olitski, a policy that one local magazine – approvingly – dubbed "enlightened capitalism."

The Sheraton is flanked by the **Washington State Convention and Trade Center** ⓯, which looks as if it's built from green-glass cubes. The center's ground-floor **Tourist Office** (open Mon–Fri, 8.30am–5pm; tel: 206 461 5840) is a good place to pick up maps and brochures. On the building's second level, hanging above an otherwise sterile walkway to Pike Street, are a series of bells from schools, churches and other landmarks in each of the state's 39 counties. Controlled by an intricate computer system, the bells are played on the hour each day, with special performances twice daily.

In the walkway park adjoining the convention center itself is a remarkable aluminum sculpture – *Seattle George* – by Seattle artist Buster Simpson, combining silhouetted heads of George Washington and Chief Seattle, the latter destined to "become a memory" as ivy gradually grows over it.

The convention center – airy, spacious and spotless – segues into the curious **Freeway Park** ⓰, an oasis of greenery and waterfalls straddling over busy Interstate 5, which runs undisturbed beneath trees and several feet of turf and concrete. Both projects span the freeway in an imaginative use of air rights. The park is delightful. Tree-shaded paths wind past a multi-level "canyon" in which invigorating cascades of water pour down sheer walls into pools, spitting and gurgling before being recycled endlessly. Although the park's ingredients are little more than flowers, grass, trees, water and cement blocks, their imaginative placement results in one of the most restful oases in town.

Between Freeway Park and the Sheraton is Two Union Square, a pleasant office building that is part of **Union Square** ⓱ and with shops on the main

BELOW: Westlake Center.
RIGHT: the *Nutcracker Suite.*

level. Higher up, huge 56th-floor windows look out over the freeway and an outdoor plaza with another waterfall. Across the street, the Pacific West Center has comfortable chairs arranged inside an attractive atrium.

An underground walkway runs from Union Square to **Rainier Square**, two blocks west. The most accessible collection of photographs of old Seattle is found along the carpeted walkway running under the Skinner Building, which forms part of the Rainier Square complex. The collection includes pictures of the Moran Brothers' shipyard in 1906, prospectors of the Alaska Gold Rush, and some that celebrate the history of Boeing.

A major hotel area is half a dozen blocks northeast with the two biggest – the twin-towered Westin and the 840-room Sheraton respectively – north and southeast of **Westlake Center** ⓲ (between Pine Street and Olive Way, and Fourth and Fifth avenues). The southern terminus of the city's monorail line is on the top floor of Westlake Center, from where it powers north 1.3 miles (2.1 km) to the Seattle Center and Space Needle; like the Seattle Center and Space Needle, the monorail dates from the 1962 World's Fair.

Seattle pedestrians are rather well behaved. People here wait for lights to change at crosswalks even when there isn't a car in sight. Police issue an average of 10 jaywalking tickets a day in the city.

Seattle Art Museum

Three blocks west towards the waterfront, the **Seattle Art Museum** ⓳ (open daily 10am–5pm, Thurs to 9pm; tel: 206 654 3100; admission fee), at University and First, was designed by Robert Venturi, winner of architecture's highest award, the Pritzker Prize, and who was credited with the wry observation that "less is a bore." The $27-million museum is a 1991 addition to downtown, allowing the museum's former home (now the Seattle Asian Art Museum; *see page 146*) in Volunteer Park to better display its incomparable collection of Asian art ranging from

BELOW: the Seattle Art Museum.

Exterior lines of the Seattle Art Museum.

4,000-year-old Japanese tomb art to 19th-century Chinese snuff bottles. About the new limestone-and-sandstone Seattle Art Museum building, its exterior inlaid with richly-hued terracotta, Venturi says: "We think civic architecture should be popular; it should be liked by a range of people. It should not be esoteric." Galleries in the museum are devoted to collections that include Japanese art (as well as an authentic bamboo-and-cedar teahouse), African art, and Pacific Northwest Indian art, and also special exhibitions from around the world. A 300-seat auditorium hosts a film festival as well as musical performances.

Pike Place Market

Seattle's anchor and primary visitor destination started with half a dozen farmers bringing their produce to Seattle in 1907, moving into space the city had set aside for a commercial market in response to the public's demand for lower prices. Over the years, the number of farmers has varied from a high of several hundred in the 1930s to a low of 30 in 1976. Developers wanted to demolish the market but locals got the issue placed on the ballot and voted overwhelmingly to retain it. Since then, the number of visiting farmers has stabilized at around 100, but **Pike Place Market** ⑳ has become so famous for its multitude of other attractions that its role as one of the oldest continuously operating daily-produce markets in the country is sometimes overlooked for the overt tourism that it attracts.

Pike Place Market runs between Union and Lenora streets and envelops Pike Place, a short avenue sandwiched between First and Western avenues. Pike Place and Pike Street intersect at the main entrance to Pike Street Market. (Worry not – everyone confuses all the Pikes.) Most of the fruit and vegetable stalls, as well as those displaying gleaming banks of fish, are in the semi-open

BELOW: traditional entrance to Pike Place Market.

Map on page 116

arcade along Pike Place and centering around Georgia Gerber's life-size bronze sow piggy bank *Rachel*, under the Market sign at Pike Street and Pike Place and on whose back there always seems to be a child posing for a photograph. Rachel, who gets lots of fan mail, arrived at the Market in 1986 and collects about $7,000 annually for charities through the slot in her back.

But not everybody comes to the Market at the front entrance (at First and Pike) here; many approach from the waterfront, either via **Victor Steinbrueck Park** on Western Avenue at Virginia and named for the architect who revived the market in the 1970s, or else up the **Hillclimb** steps from the foot of Pike Street (not to be confused with Pike Place). Musicians tend to gather at this spot, on the stairs leading up to Pike Place Market from Western Avenue, perhaps because of the fine acoustics, as well as a half dozen other places where musicians with permits (around 50 are issued each year) are authorized to play. Many of the regulars – among them a classical music trio, gospel singer and a man who wheels around his own piano – can be found somewhere near the neon billboard clock at the Market's main entrance, at Pike Street and Pike Place.

Just north of the entrance clock and sign, around the uncovered stalls, craftspeople assemble each morning to be allocated a place for the day. Some of them have been attending the market for years and seniority plays a role; there are hundreds of people on the waiting list who move up only if existing craftspeople turn up less than two days a week.

Eating at the Market is a joy because it offers so many choices: home-style diner cooking, fine dining with views of the bay, French cuisine, Bolivian fare, fresh-baked pastries, or overstuffed sandwiches at a deli counter. The Corner Market, Post Alley Market and Sanitary Market (no horses were allowed) are

BELOW: fresh fish at Pike Place Market.

joined by walkways with eating spots on all levels. Don't overlook the Soames Dunn Building on the city-side of Pike Place, between Stewart and Virginia, which houses a few restaurants as well as the planet's first Starbucks, in what has since become a worldwide chain of espresso counters. You'll find it helpful to have a map of the market, which you can get at the information booth by the main entrance at First and Pike.

Seattle's diversified economy includes aerospace, forest products, electronics, food processing, biomedicine, and banking and finance.

The major fresh fish stalls are here; at one of them they are so used to visitors with videotape machines they'll borrow your camera and take some dramatic footage of the fish being thrown straight at the lens (into the safe hands of a colleague). If wanting to take some of the Northwest's fresh fish back home with you, stop on the Market en route to the airport and arrange to have your salmon packaged in dry ice for the journey home. Some visitors find it so frustrating to be unable to take the fresh produce from the Market home to cook that one local magazine recently ran a listing of Seattle accommodations with cooking facilities.

Under the Pike Street Market's main arcade (on the water-side of Pike Place) is a labyrinth of corners, corridors, cubbyholes, shops, stalls, stairs and empty spaces. Magical tricks, old posters, talking birds, Australian opals, Turkish pastries, books, funky clothes... they're but a few of the thousands of items for sale. No chain stores or franchises are allowed so everybody's an individualist, and there's no shortage of characters. Even some of the tiles on the floor are eccentric. Locals were invited to pay $35 for their own design some years ago and one mathematician's wife listed all the prime numbers under 100.

There's an expensive but very popular 65-room hotel, the Inn at the Market, at the corner of First Avenue and Pine Street and a superlative kitchenwares

BELOW: vegetable stand, Pike Place.

shop. There is in this 6-block area, in fact, virtually anything that you might need. Except a parking space. Leave the car behind and come by the (free) bus.

Map on page 116

Along the waterfront

The delightful **Seattle Aquarium** ㉑ (open daily 10am–7pm in summer, to 5pm at other times; tel: 206 386 4320; admission fee), a visitor-friendly attraction on Pier 59 just west of Pike Place, features 200 varieties of fish native to Puget Sound, plus environments that simulate the region's rocky reefs, sandy seafloor, eelgrass beds and tidepools. A working fish ladder explains the salmon life cycle and other exhibits demonstrate the paths that water travels before reaching Puget Sound.

Vividly striped lion fish, lethal electric eels, chameleon-like flatfish, octopus, dogfish and salmon dart by to the enjoyment of visitors, all side by side with irresistibly entertaining otters and seals. The twice-daily oceanic tides that flood Puget Sound mixing with fresh water from ample rainfall has nurtured "an unequaled estuarine haven for plants, animals and humans," according to one of the many educational captions.

Seattle's waterfront flanked by its downtown high-rises.

Sharing Pier 59 with the aquarium, the **Omnidome Theater**, with its giant screen overwhelming viewers with stupendous images of erupting volcanoes and explorations beneath the Great Barrier Reef, may be the best show in town.

What was once Pier 58 is now **Waterfront Park** ㉒, a relaxing place to sit on weekends or to watch the sun set. Green-and-white Foss tugs – nearly a local icon, as almost all tugboats on the Sound belong to the local tug company Foss – ply the waters of the Sound, hauling timber, sand and gravel as they have been doing for the past century since Thea Foss, a Norwegian immigrant, started

BELOW: nightlife.

Waterfront offerings.

the company with her husband by renting boats to fishermen. (Foss was allegedly the model for Norman Reilly Raine's Tugboat Annie in a series of 1930s movies.)

On Pier 54 is **Ye Olde Curiosity Shop and Museum** (tel: 206 682 5844) with its bizarre collection of carny attractions such as Siamese twin calves, mummies, shrunken heads, shark jaws and pins engraved with the Lord's Prayer. The shop-museum is still owned by the descendants of Joe Standley, who opened it in 1899, later selling his ethnological collection to New York's Museum of the American Indian.

Sharing Pier 54 is a bronze statue – *Ivar Feeding the Gulls* – by Richard Beyer of the late restaurateur Ivar Haglund feeding seagulls. A lovably irascible character who opened the city's first aquarium in 1906, Seattle-born Haglund began his career playing guitar and singing on local radio and TV. He later made a fortune with his seafood restaurants, including the one here, and which collectively sell a quarter million clams each year. The tramcar stop across the street from Ivar's is called Clam Central Station.

The **Washington State Ferries Terminal** ㉓ (Pier 51) at the waterfront end of Yesler Way might be America's busiest water-bound commuter route. The 25 ocean-going boats of the Washington Transportation Department's Maritime Division each year carry over 20 million passengers and almost 10 million cars, about half of them crossing Puget Sound to or from their island homes in under 35 minutes. The ferries run at a loss of around $1 million per week.

The splendid Joshua Green Fountain outside the ferry terminal at Pier 52, on Alaskan Way, is named after the late centenarian Joshua Green, who arrived in Seattle in 1886, operating steamboats on Puget Sound before helping to establish

BELOW: statue of Ivar Haglund.

SOUND FERRIES TO EVERYWHERE

Commuters with unbrushed hair and teeth in the early morning, rushing to the ferry, are not an uncommon sight at the Bainbridge Island ferry terminal. Ferry commuters are a breed with a gentle perspective on life. The Washington State Ferry System is a vital link for both Puget Sound and Seattle residents and travelers. Thousands of islands of inlets wrinkle the coastlines of Puget Sound, making travel, other than by sea, not only costly but also time-consuming.

Although ferries come in assorted sizes, the ferries from downtown Seattle to, say, Bremerton and Bainbridge Island carry over 200 cars and 2,000 people. Large, comfortable lounges and food services make journeys pleasurable. Most major ferry routes have boats departing hourly during daylight hours, with fewer boats at night. On most routes, frequency is greater during the summer months. In winter, check on schedules before making plans on a tight schedule. The *Victoria Clipper*, between Seattle and Victoria, B.C., has a greatly abbreviated timetable in winter.

If you are planning to hop around the Sound via ferry, make sure that accommodations are available – and reserved – on the smaller islands. Some of these smaller islands have very limited lodging possibilities.

one of the city's first banks. It is another of the fountains created by the redoubtable local sculptor George Tsutakawa, also responsible for the fountain outside the Seattle *Post-Intelligencer* building further north along Elliott Avenue about a mile. Between the newspaper offices and Pier 70, another public sculpture can be admired in the form of casually arranged boulders in Myrtle Edwards Park.

Map on page 116

Northward

Pier 66 was an $84-million development that includes a large plaza on the water, a lively promenade, the excellent, family-oriented **Maritime Discovery Center** ㉔ (open Sun–Wed 10am–9pm and Thur–Sat 10am–5pm in summer, at other times daily 10am–5pm; tel: 206 374 4000; admission fee) and, on clear days, a rare glimpse of Mount Rainier 60 miles (100 km) through viewfinder binoculars (which are free).

A couple of blocks north of downtown and Pike Place, along First through Fifth avenues, is the trendy and growing **Belltown** area. The area was once better known as the Denny Regrade because it was once Denny Hill, but the hill was removed to provide much of the landfill that raised downtown's muddy streets. Today the former hill is covered with apartments, office buildings and media offices such as those for two TV stations.

Actually, Belltown and the Denny Regrade are technically different, but most people now use the terms synonymously. The name Belltown comes from pioneer William Bell, who hoped to create a vital commercial nexus in the area but left town before he could do much to promote that development. The Denny Regrade name actually applies only to the area once occupied by Denny Hill.

Beginning in the first decade of the 20th century, Seattle's first city engineer,

BELOW: fireboats and ferry on the waterfront.

Reginald H. Thomson, started tearing away at Denny Hill because he thought it blocked the city's northward expansion. The regrading was completed in two stages – most of it completed within five years, but the eastern slope not regraded until 1929 and 1930.

Belltown boasts several fine restaurants, a couple of hotels, interesting shops and popular nightclubs. Belltown might accurately be described as the birthplace of grunge music, as it was in some of these local hotspots that young Seattle-based rock bands such as Nirvana, Pearl Jam and Soundgarden first started out. At the northern end of downtown sits 74-acre (30-hectare) **Seattle Center** ㉕. Only one World's Fair has ever been the site of a movie starring Elvis Presley and that is the one held in Seattle in 1962. It brought more attention to this Pacific Northwest city than anything since the Klondike Gold Rush in the late 1890s. Most Seattle residents are proud of the fair's long-lasting legacy: the Seattle Center with its internationally recognized Space Needle, not to mention one of the only monorail systems in America. This Seattle single-rail train travels back and forth on its 1.3-mile (2.1-km) elevated track from Westlake Center downtown to the station under the Space Needle.

Chief Sealth and the Space Needle.

The Space Needle

The 605-ft (184-meter) **Space Needle** (open daily 8am–midnight; tel: 206 443 2111; admission fee) understandably offers some of the best views of the city, especially from the rotating restaurant at the top: Lake Union, the immensely larger Lake Washington and the distant Cascade Range to the east; Elliott Bay opening into Puget Sound westwards with the Olympic Mountains fronted by verdant islands; and, southeast on any clear day, the snow-capped peak of 14,411-ft (4,392-meter) Mount Rainier 60 miles (100 km) away. The revolving restaurant one floor up from the observation deck makes a revolution every hour.

There's an amusement park with rides and arcade in Seattle Center, along with theaters, arts and crafts centers, a giant fountain, plus a flag-lined plaza for events ranging from business exhibits to displays of old Studebaker cars. The enormous Center House contains a children's museum, shops and restaurants all surrounding a dance floor. The Opera House, which was the origin of the whole project, is said to have some of the world's best acoustics.

Also here are the performance halls for Pacific Northwest Ballet, the Seattle Repertory Theater and Seattle Children's Theater.

What really takes time to do full justice to – and is more than worth the effort – is the fascinating and imaginative **Pacific Science Center** (open daily 10am–5pm, weekends to 6pm; tel: 206 443 2880; admission fee), which includes a laserium and two IMAX theaters screening larger-than-life films.

Originally erected as part of the 1962 World's Fair, the Science Center has kept up with technology, making learning fun along the way. Hands-on math and basic science exhibits still appeal to school children, but other demonstrations now feature virtual reality, computers and robots. A shop offers interestingly designed, one-of-a-kind gifts and souvenirs. ❑

BELOW: Pacific Science Center, from the 1962 World's Fair.

Smith Tower

When L. C. Smith's tower went up in downtown Seattle in 1914, it was touted as the tallest building in the West. Picture postcards depicting the 500-ft (150-meter) structure claimed that from "the world-famous catwalk surrounding the Chinese temple may be seen mountain ranges 380 miles (600 km) in the distance." Well, not quite. The mountain ranges in view – the Olympics and the Cascades – are about 60 miles (100 km) away. But 4,400 people flocked to the opening anyway, paying 25 cents each to be whizzed past offices mostly rented by local government agencies and to admire the view from the observation deck.

"A work of art worthy of the builders of the awe-inspiring cathedrals of the Middle Ages," boasted the tower's historian, Arthur F. Wakefield, who revealed that New York's American Bridge Company had taken 20 weeks to make the building's steel, transported cross-country from their Pittsburgh, Pennsylvania, plant in 164 railcars.

Smith spared no expense. The $1.5 million building's 600 rooms had steel doors, teak ceilings, walls of Alaskan white marble or tinted Mexican onyx, elevator doors of glass and bronze and, on the 35th floor, an expensive Chinese temple decorated with bronze lanterns, Oriental furniture and 776 semi-porcelain discs. A throne-like Chinese chair, reputed to have been a gift from the Empress of China, was actually obtained from a waterfront curio shop but did spawn its own legend. One year after Smith's daughter posed sitting in the chair, she got married, convincing other would-be brides that to sit in the "Wishing Chair" would bring them a husband. Even today, occasionally a couple will hold their wedding reception in the room.

One year after the tower's opening, some of the office tenants looked from their windows to see a one-armed parachutist go by, and a year or two later watched Harry – The Human Fly – scale the building. "I gave him a little help by hanging ropes over the cornices," recalled William K. Jackson, just before his retirement as building superintendent in 1944. Jackson, then 72, had worked in the tower since it opened, during which time Seattle had changed from "a friendly, clean little city to a town of strangers going so fast you can feel the tempo of wartime even in your own building." Recording the city's changes by what he'd seen in the harbor – first lumber barges and fishing boats, then liners, freighters and navy ships and now "mostly smoke" – he observed that the city "sort of grew up under me." The tower was still getting 300 visitors a day, was still the tallest building in the West, and on most days still offered a clear view of Mount Rainier.

Stunts abounded. In 1938, two high school students ran up stairs to the 36th floor in less than 10 minutes (and down again in four); four years later, a proud grandfather announced his new domestic status by running up a flag reading, "It's a girl."

Smith Tower was bought in 1985 by a San Francisco firm, whose partners remodeled it with respect, even acquiring special parts and equipment to retain the original copper, brass and glass elevators. ❑

RIGHT: Smith Tower.

WATER, WATER EVERYWHERE

Water is a constant feature of life in Seattle – and not just the stuff that falls liberally from the sky. It's no wonder than one in four people own a boat

It's water that keeps Washington green (a popular slogan on highway signs), and which also supports such a healthy fish, bird and sea mammal population. It also provides plenty of opportunities for recreation. It is estimated that one in four Seattleites owns a boat – whether it's a rowboat, a sailboat, a yacht or a kayak. With saltwater Puget Sound and a handful of in-city freshwater lakes, plus an eight-mile ship canal linking the Sound to Lake Washington (via Lake Union), Seattle has more than enough places to cruise, paddle or sail.

FERRY FIRST

For visitors who don't come to Seattle with a boat in tow, one of the easiest ways to get out on the water is on a Washington State Ferry. The state's ferry system is the largest in the United States, with 25 ferries carrying 21 million passengers (and almost 10 million cars) every year. Popular routes link downtown Seattle's Coleman Dock and Bainbridge Island, and downtown and Bremerton. Passenger-only ferries transport commuters between downtown and Bremerton, and downtown and Vashon Island.

▷ SEATTLE'S TOMB
The Tomb of Chief Seattle, after whom the city was named, stands like a sentinel overlooking the Puget Sound, in Suqamish, 45 minutes from Seattle.

△ FOR THE BIRDS
Waterfront restaurants attract flocks of seagulls clamouring for crumbs. Residents have a love-hate relationship with the birds.

▷ AGAINST THE STREAM
Fish ladders, such as this one at Hiram Chittenden Locks, offer views of wild salmon fighting their way against the current to spawn in inland streams.

◁ **FERRY LIFE**
A Washington State Ferry cruises across Elliott Bay. The state's ferry system is the largest in the US, attracting 21 million passengers every year.

△ **SEALIFE**
Puget Sound's cold saltwater environment supports a variety of mammals. Look for Dall's porpoises, orcas, sea lions, seal and otters.

△ **CLEAR NIGHTS**
Despite Seattle's famous reputation for rainy weather, the city has less annual precipitation than New York, Boston, Atlanta and Miami.

▷ **SKYLINE VIEWS**
Some of the best views of Seattle's skyline are from a ferry as it leaves or arrives at Coleman Dock, particularly at night.

THE PLEASURES OF PADDLING

Several in-city companies rent kayaks by the hour or day. Northwest Outdoor Center (NWOC) (tel: 206-281-9694) is on the west side of Lake Union. The Agua Verde Paddle Club (tel: 206-545-8570) is just below Cafe Agua Verde, a great spot for Mexican food. For canoeing, contact the University of Washington Waterfront Activities Center (tel: 206-543-9433). From the center on Union Bay, at the Lake Washington end of the Montlake Cut, you can explore the Washington Park Arboretum from a duck's perspective. A tamer watery experience is available from Green Lake Boat Rentals (tel: 206-527-0171). For something more adventurous, ask about NWOC's tours to the San Juans, or contact the Washington Kayak Club (tel: 206-433-1983).

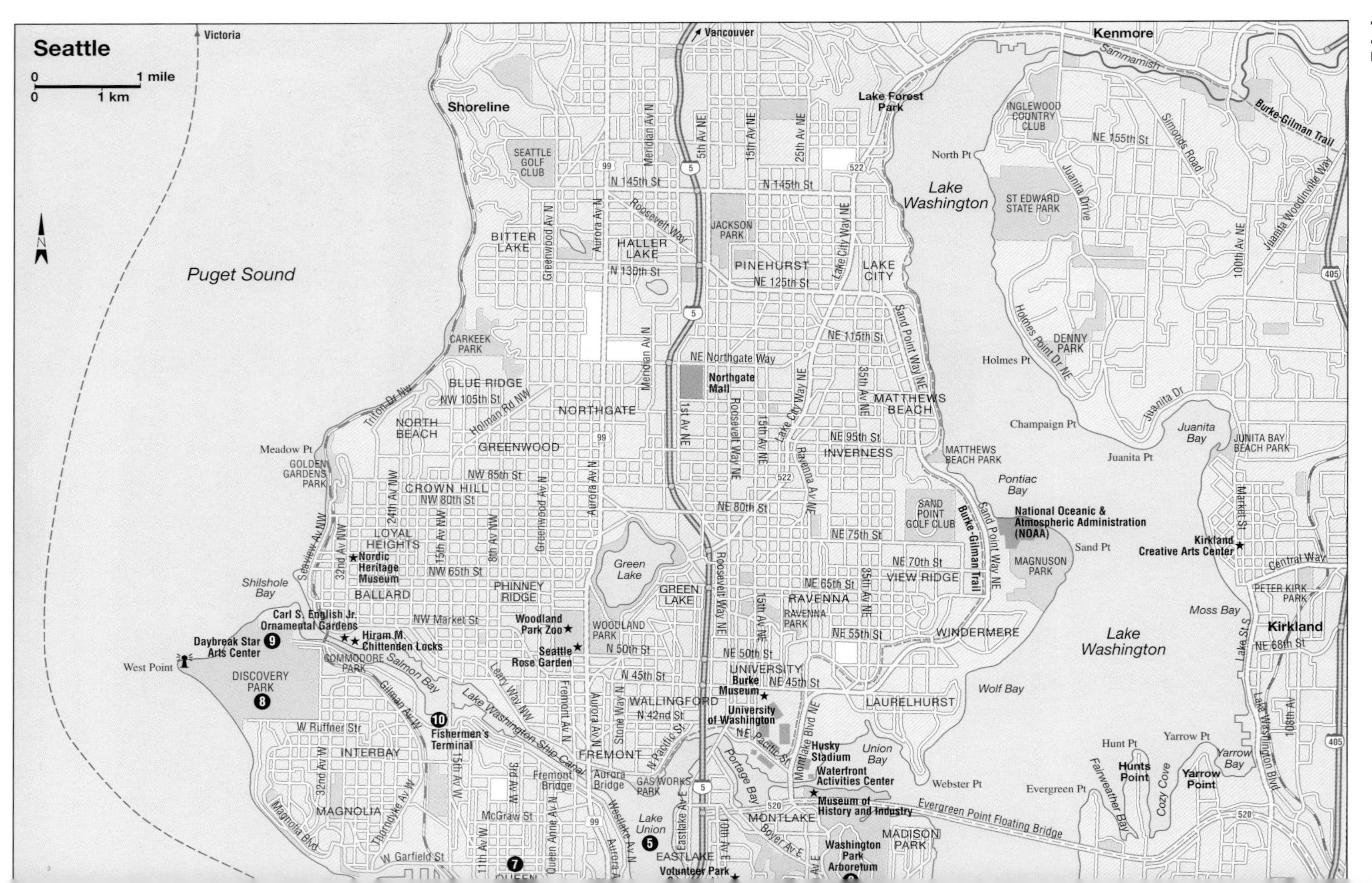
Seattle
0 1 mile
0 1 km
N
Victoria
Vancouver
Kenmore
Sammamish
Burke-Gilman Trail
Shoreline
Lake Forest Park
INGLEWOOD COUNTRY CLUB
NE 155th St
Simonds Road
Juanita Woodinville Way
North Pt
Lake Washington
ST EDWARD STATE PARK
Juanita Drive
100th Av NE
405
SEATTLE GOLF CLUB
99
Meridian Av N
5th Av NE
15th Av NE
25th Av NE
522
5
N 145th St
Roosevelt Way
Aurora Av N
Greenwood Av N
BITTER LAKE
HALLER LAKE
JACKSON PARK
PINEHURST
Lake City Way NE
LAKE CITY
Puget Sound
N 130th St
NE 125th St
Sand Point Way NE
Holmes Point Dr NE
DENNY PARK
CARKEEK PARK
NE 115th St
NE Northgate Way
Holmes Pt
Northgate Mall
BLUE RIDGE
NW 105th St
Triton Dr NW
Holman Rd NW
NORTHGATE
1st Av NE
Roosevelt Way NE
15th Av NE
35th Av NE
MATTHEWS BEACH
Juanita Dr
NORTH BEACH
Champaign Pt
Juanita Bay
JUNITA BAY BEACH PARK
Meadow Pt
GOLDEN GARDENS PARK
GREENWOOD
NE 95th St
INVERNESS
MATTHEWS BEACH PARK
Juanita Pt
NW 85th St
Ravenna Av NE
Pontiac Bay
CROWN HILL
NW 80th St
NE 80th St
SAND POINT GOLF CLUB
National Oceanic & Atmospheric Administration (NOAA)
Market St
24th Av NW
LOYAL HEIGHTS
15th Av NW
8th Av NW
NE 75th St
Sand Pt
Kirkland Creative Arts Center
Seaview Av NW
32nd Av NW
Nordic Heritage Museum
NW 65th St
Green Lake
NE 70th St
MAGNUSON PARK
Central Way
Shilshole Bay
BALLARD
PHINNEY RIDGE
GREEN LAKE
NE 65th St
VIEW RIDGE
PETER KIRK PARK
RAVENNA
RAVENNA PARK
Moss Bay
Carl S. English Jr. Ornamental Gardens
NW Market St
Woodland Park Zoo
WOODLAND PARK
WINDERMERE
Kirkland
Daybreak Star Arts Center
Hiram M. Chittenden Locks
Seattle Rose Garden
N 50th St
NE 55th St
Lake St S
NE 68th St
West Point
COMMODORE PARK
Salmon Bay
NE 50th St
UNIVERSITY
DISCOVERY PARK
Leary Way NW
N 45th St
Burke Museum
NE 45th St
Wolf Bay
Gilman Av W
Lake Washington Ship Canal
Fremont Av N
Stone Way N
WALLINGFORD
N 42nd St
LAURELHURST
University of Washington
Lake Washington Blvd
108th Av
W Ruffner St
Fishermen's Terminal
N Pacific St
NE Pacific St
Montlake Blvd NE
Hunt Pt
Yarrow Pt
Husky Stadium
Union Bay
Yarrow Bay
INTERBAY
FREMONT
Portage Bay
Hunts Point
Yarrow Point
32nd Av W
15th Av W
3rd Av W
Fremont Bridge
Aurora Bridge
GAS WORKS PARK
Waterfront Activities Center
Webster Pt
Evergreen Pt
Fairweather Bay
Cozy Cove
Museum of History and Industry
Evergreen Point Floating Bridge
Magnolia Blvd
MAGNOLIA
Thorndyke Av W
McGraw St
Queen Anne Av N
Westlake Av N
Lake Union
Eastlake Av E
520
MONTLAKE
Boyer Av E
MADISON PARK
W Garfield St
11th Av W
EASTLAKE
10th Av E
Washington Park Arboretum
Volunteer Park
5
7
8
9
10

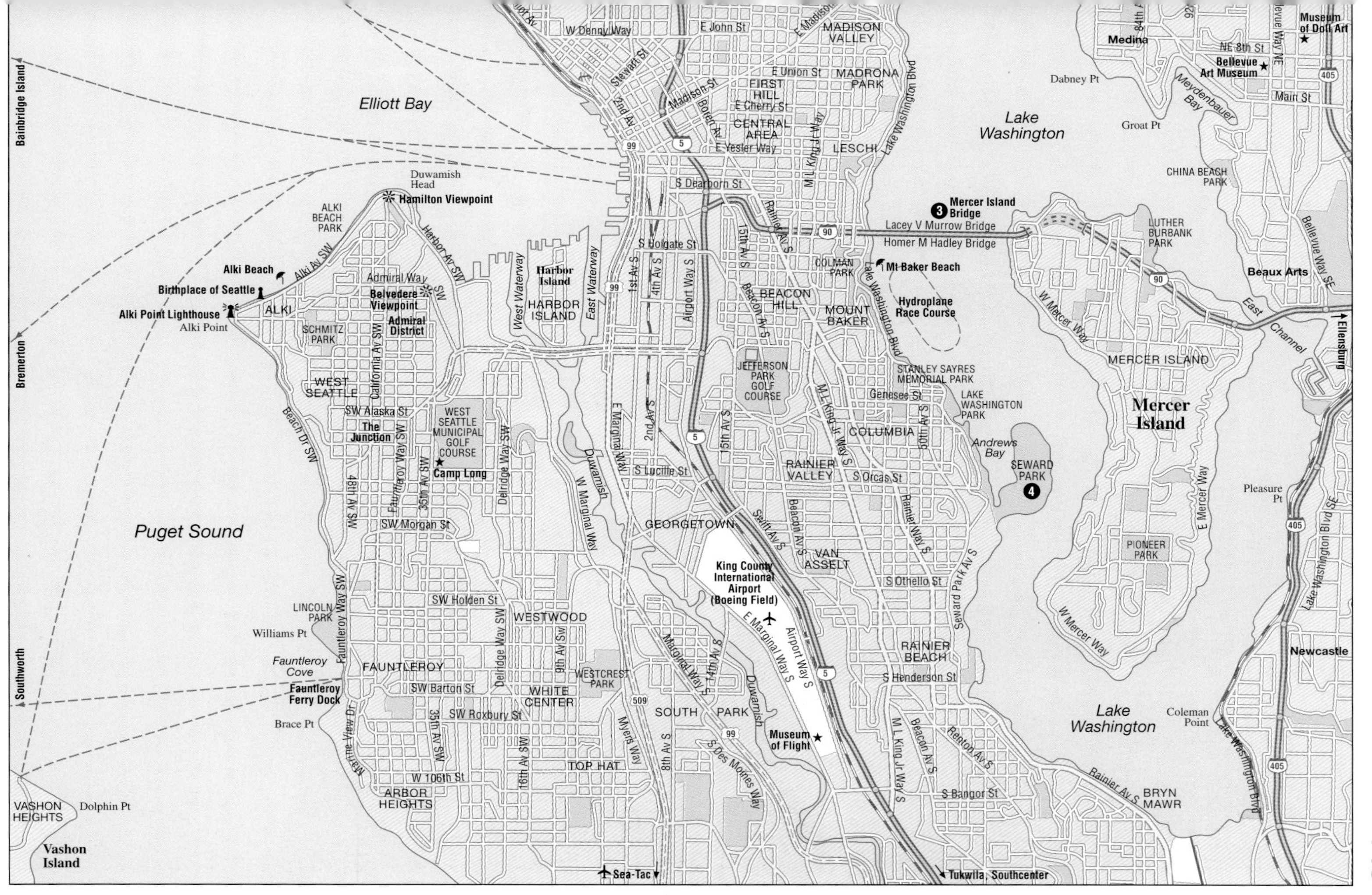
Elliott Bay
Puget Sound
Lake Washington
Bainbridge Island
Bremerton
Southworth
Duwamish Head
Hamilton Viewpoint
ALKI BEACH PARK
Alki Beach
Birthplace of Seattle
Alki Point Lighthouse
Alki Point
ALKI
SCHMITZ PARK
WEST SEATTLE
Admiral Way
Belvedere Viewpoint
Admiral District
Harbor Av SW
California Av SW
SW Alaska St
The Junction
WEST SEATTLE MUNICIPAL GOLF COURSE
Camp Long
Beach Dr SW
48th Av SW
Fauntleroy Way SW
35th Av SW
SW Morgan St
Delridge Way SW
West Waterway
Harbor Island
HARBOR ISLAND
East Waterway
W Denny Way
E John St
Stewart St
2nd Av
Madison St
Boren Av
FIRST HILL
E Cherry St
CENTRAL AREA
E Yesler Way
E Union St
MADISON VALLEY
MADRONA PARK
LESCHI
M L King Jr Way
Lake Washington Blvd
S Dearborn St
S Holgate St
1st Av S
4th Av S
Airport Way S
15th Av S
Rainier Av S
Mercer Island Bridge
Lacey V Murrow Bridge
Homer M Hadley Bridge
COLMAN PARK
Mt Baker Beach
Hydroplane Race Course
BEACON HILL
Beacon Av S
MOUNT BAKER
JEFFERSON PARK GOLF COURSE
STANLEY SAYRES MEMORIAL PARK
Genesee St
LAKE WASHINGTON PARK
COLUMBIA
50th Av S
Andrews Bay
SEWARD PARK
RAINIER VALLEY
S Orcas St
Rainier Way S
E Marginal Way
2nd Av S
S Lucille St
Duwamish
W Marginal Way
GEORGETOWN
Swift Av S
VAN ASSELT
King County International Airport (Boeing Field)
E Marginal Way S
Airport Way S
S Othello St
Seward Park Av S
RAINIER BEACH
S Henderson St
LINCOLN PARK
Williams Pt
Fauntleroy Way SW
Fauntleroy Cove
FAUNTLEROY
Fauntleroy Ferry Dock
Brace Pt
SW Holden St
WESTWOOD
9th Av SW
WESTCREST PARK
SW Barton St
WHITE CENTER
SW Roxbury St
Marginal Way S
14th Av S
SOUTH PARK
Myers Way
8th Av S
S Des Moines Way
Museum of Flight
Marine View Dr
35th Av SW
W 106th St
16th Av SW
TOP HAT
ARBOR HEIGHTS
VASHON HEIGHTS
Dolphin Pt
Vashon Island
Sea-Tac
Tukwila, Southcenter
M L King Jr Way S
Beacon Av S
Renton Av S
S Bangor St
Rainier Av S
BRYN MAWR
Medina
84th
Museum of Doll Art
NE 8th St
Bellevue Way NE
Bellevue Art Museum
Main St
Dabney Pt
Meydenbauer Bay
Groat Pt
CHINA BEACH PARK
LUTHER BURBANK PARK
Beaux Arts
Bellevue Way SE
East Channel
Ellensburg
W Mercer Way
MERCER ISLAND
Mercer Island
E Mercer Way
PIONEER PARK
Pleasure Pt
Lake Washington Blvd SE
Newcastle
Coleman Point
Lake Washington Blvd

NEIGHBORHOODS

With names like Capitol Hill, Queen Anne Hill, Madison and Magnolia, the neighborhoods' conservative names mask the sophisticated spunkiness of Seattle's personality

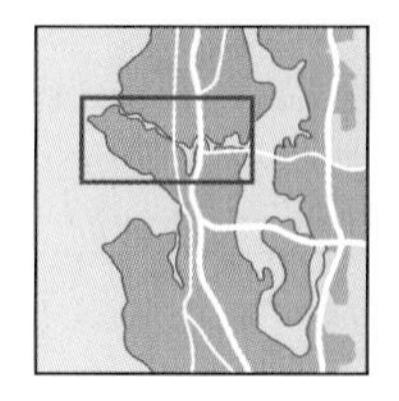

North of the International District and east of downtown, **Capitol Hill** gets its name not from any seat of government, here or in Washington, D.C., but from Denver, Colorado. Real estate promoter James A. Moore, whose wife was from that city, came up with the name – after the Capitol Hill in Denver – in 1901. The area is culturally, economically and racially mixed, with the hill being home to a substantial gay and lesbian population. A heavy concentration of apartment buildings supplements the mansions of Millionaires' Row (14th Avenue East, between Mercer and Prospect streets).

Broadway (Pine Street to East Roy Street) is the hill's leading thoroughfare and commercial district; it is also one of the few places in town where one can find casual strollers on the street as late as midnight, even on weeknights – much of Seattle turns in early. In an age of multiplex cinemas in shopping malls (there's one here, too, in the multi-level Broadway Market), the Egyptian on East Pine Street and the Harvard Exit on East Roy Street are handsome survivors from an earlier era of film cinemas. Both specialize in first-rate foreign films and host shows during the annual Seattle International Film Festival (May and June). Another distinctive neighborhood movie theater, the beloved Broadway, gave way years ago to a local discount store, which still retains the theater marquee. Now, instead of first-run films, the sign beckons passersby with promises of sale prices on lawn chairs.

Traffic is heavy on Broadway at almost any time of day and parking is all but impossible to find. But with its ever-changing assortment of shops and restaurants, the street is a good one for walking. Walkers can even learn some traditional dances by following sculptor Jack Mackie's bronze footsteps embedded in the sidewalk, part of the city's public art program. Several blocks east, Fifteenth Avenue East hosts another Capitol Hill shopping district, one that's less congested and less flamboyant than Broadway and with a handful of good restaurants representing varied cuisines, several interesting shops, and the obligatory espresso cart or two.

PRECEDING PAGES: life in north Seattle.
LEFT: sculpture.
BELOW: St. Joseph Church, Capitol Hill.

Volunteer Park

A few blocks north of the retail district on 15th lies one of Seattle's largest and loveliest parks, 45-acre (18-hectare) **Volunteer Park** ❶. Originally a cemetery for the city's early pioneers, the land became Lakeview Park when it was decided in 1887 to put a reservoir (which holds 20 million gallons of water) at the southern part of the property. The bodies were moved a few hundred feet north to what's now called Lakeview Cemetery. In 1901, the park was renamed Volunteer Park in honor of Seattle men who served in the 1898 Spanish-American War.

With an elevation of 445 ft (135 meters), the park

Khmer stone head, Asian Art Museum.

offers magnificent views of the Space Needle, Puget Sound and the Olympic Mountains. The park's major attractions are the 1932 Art Deco building that houses the **Seattle Asian Art Museum** (open daily 10am-5pm, Thur to 9pm, closed Mon; tel: 206 654 3100; admission fee) and the **Volunteer Park Conservatory**, with its three lush greenhouses. After the Seattle Art Museum (*see page 131*) moved downtown in 1991, the original building in Volunteer Park was renamed and renovated to display the museum's extensive Asian art collections, including 14th- to 16th-century ceramics from Thailand and *netsuke* from Japan.

Madison

East of Capitol Hill lies Madison Valley. The area west from Lake Washington Boulevard to 23rd Avenue East along both sides of Madison Street underwent a transformation in the 1980s and 1990s. Two-story retail complexes now anchor the intersection of Madison and Lake Washington Boulevard. A few consistently top-rated restaurants, an expansive gardening store and several pleasant delis and cafes, along with numerous new condominiums lining the hillside, signal the resurgence of this formerly overlooked neighborhood.

At the eastern foot of Madison Street – Seattle's only waterfront-to-waterfront street, running east to west from Elliott Bay to Lake Washington – sits the lovely, slightly quaint, unmistakably affluent waterfront community of **Madison Park**, once the western terminus of a passenger-boat line connecting Seattle to the east side of Lake Washington. Here are restaurants that range from trendy to a local-favorite bakery, as well as a village of shops. The park itself has a pair of lighted all-weather tennis courts and a beach, populated on hot summer days by an interesting urban mix from surrounding neighborhoods.

BELOW: Seattle Asian Art Museum.

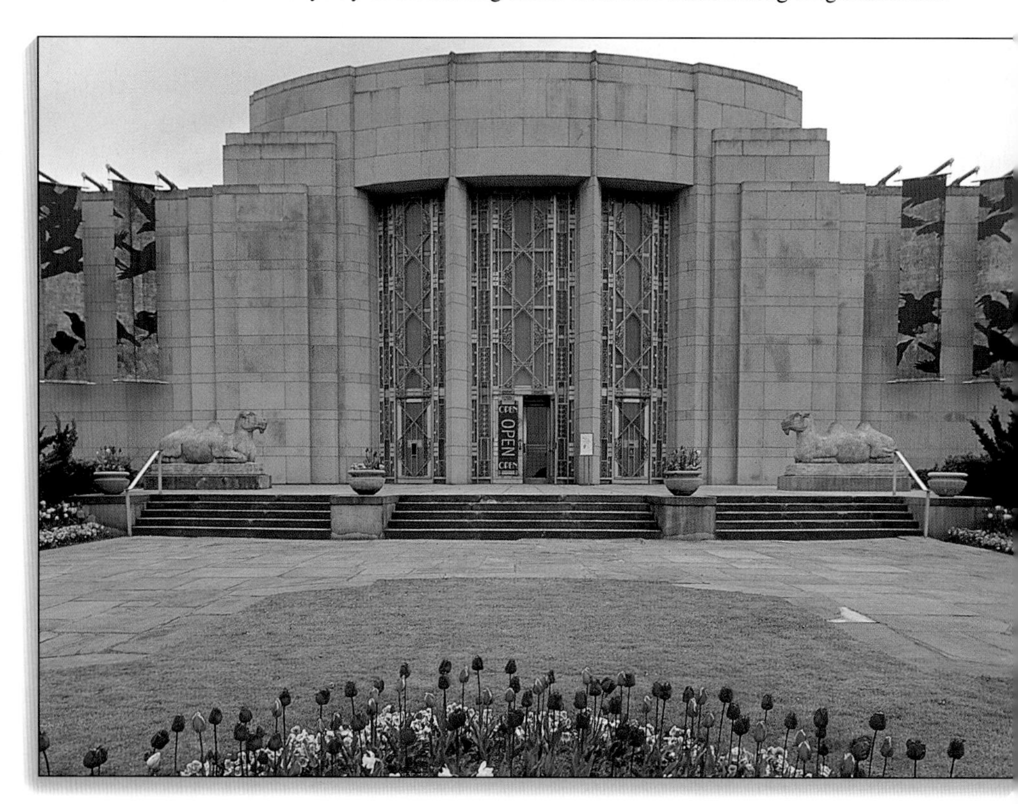

In the past couple of decades, a steady influx of younger people has moved into Madison Park, joining the more settled older residents in a comfortable enclave of lakefront apartments, condos and townhouses, and increasingly expensive, but pleasant, single-family homes.

Adjacent to Madison Park is the **Washington Park Arboretum ❷**, a 200-acre (80-hectare) public park and botanical research facility for the University of Washington. Highlights include the Japanese Garden and Azalea Way, a wide, grassy strip that winds through the park and is lined by blooming azaleas, dogwoods and flowering cherry trees in the spring.

Just up the hill from Madison Park reigns the wealthy – on some blocks, extravagantly wealthy – neighborhood of **Washington Park**. Particularly noteworthy in this residential area of stately homes and doted-upon lawns is the majestic thoroughfare of 36th Avenue East, extending south between Madison and East Mercer streets. Towering trees on both sides of 36th Avenue arch toward each other high above the street to form Seattle's most magnificent natural cathedral. Here too is the handsome brick mansion of the president of the University of Washington, at 808 36th East, with (one hears) a lovely rose garden, although you have to be an invited guest to see it.

Opposite 36th Avenue on the north side of Madison Street is the private residential community of **Broadmoor**, complete with a fine golf course. Behind gatehouses and armed guards at both entrances, bank presidents, corporate lawyers, financiers, city fathers and others of the upper crust take refuge from urban clash and clatter.

A sparkling waterfront neighborhood south of Madison Park along the western shore of Lake Washington, **Leschi** is named after a Nisqually Indian chief

Map on pages 142–3

BELOW: Volunteer Park Conservatory.

who liked to camp here and was said to have been among those who gathered in 1856 to plan an attack on the city of Seattle as part of the so-called Indian Wars, which broke out after some tribes signed treaties and were moved to reservations. The first automobile ferry, the *Leschi*, started regular service from here to the eastside of Seattle in 1913.

At 6,560 ft (2,000 meters) long, the Mercer Island Floating Bridge is classified as a concrete-pontoon bridge. The first known floating bridge was in 480 BC, built by Persian engineers to carry Xerxes' invasion army across the Hellespont.

At one time considered a social hot spot, Leschi is today a quiet neighborhood of waterfront homes, condominiums and apartment buildings, with a public beach, small-sailboat marina and the lushly green Leschi Park – once an amusement park at the terminus of the Yesler Street cable-car line. There are a couple of attractive restaurants that offer waterfront dining.

On the other side of Beacon Hill is Lake Washington, flanked on the west all the way to Seward Park by the boulevard that begins at the University of Washington Arboretum in North Seattle. Along the way, the road offers eastward views of the Cascade Range as it meanders past the Lake Washington parks, a string of grassy beachfronts along the lake's western shore. An adjacent bike path follows the road for some miles.

The stretch of lake shoreline from just south of the **Mercer Island Floating Bridge** ❸ to Andrews Bay is hydro-heaven during the Rainier Cup Hydroplane Race in August. The races, part of the city's Seafair celebration and first staged in 1950, have become a Seattle tradition, drawing thousands of spectators despite the horrendous noise of engines on 150mph (240kph) boats. Seafair's official viewing beach is **Stanley Sayres Memorial Park** (where the hydro pits are located), but many fans watch from homes along the lake and hundreds pay a per-foot charge to tie their boats up to log booms along the challenging course.

In **Rainier Valley**, named for the vistas of Mount Rainier that it offers, once stood Seattle's baseball stadium, replaced by a hardware store. Neighborhoods near the Duwamish River as it winds south from Elliot Bay include Holly Park, Highland Park, South Park and, further south, Burien. To the east on Lake Washington is **Rainier Beach**.

BELOW: Lake Union and Seattle skyline.

The Lake Washington parks culminate in **Seward Park** ❹, 277 acres (112 hectares) of greenery, trails and waterfront, and home to a pair of breeding bald eagles. The park has an art studio, fish hatchery, outdoor amphitheater and a short lakeside trail for cyclists and runners. Like Alki, and several other Seattle parks, Seward Park closes at 11pm each night because of citizen and police concerns about drug and gang activity.

West of Lake Union

Cut off from Capitol Hill by Interstate 5 and north of downtown along the east side of Lake Union, the **Eastlake** district is a lively mix of historic homes, multi-family dwellings and a thriving houseboat community sharing the neighborhood, uneasily at times, with ever-changing commercial and industrial properties. The Boeing Company got its start here in 1915 when William Boeing began building – in a hangar at the foot of Roanoke Street – seaplanes that he tested on Lake Union. Boeing moved his company to the south end of the city two years later, but the hangar survived until 1971, when it was demolished to make way for a

Map on pages 142–3

projected, but aborted, condominium project, in the end defeated after a fierce 13-year legal battle fought by a coalition of determined neighborhood groups.

The south end of **Lake Union** ❺, once exclusively an industrial area, has seen an explosion of development in recent years, which doesn't please all residents. A small group of restaurants rings the south end of the lake, most with outdoor decks overlooking the water and docking facilities. More are planned for the future. The **Center for Wooden Boats** ❻ (open Wed–Mon; tel: 206 382 2628; free) at the south end of Lake Union is a nostalgically charming maritime museum with some 75 sailboats and rowboats, many of which can be rented. Indeed, rowing or paddling around the lake is by far the best and most enjoyable way to appreciate the lake's diversity of activity, as well as being the only way to admire from nearby the multi-styled houseboats lining the northeast and northwest shorelines.

A **Maritime Heritage Center** adjacent to South Lake Union Park is planned to open sometime in the early 2000s on property currently occupied by a U.S. Naval Reserve Station. Lake Union is also home to several commercial seaplane services that offer flights to the San Juan Islands, as well as to the Canadian cities of Vancouver, Victoria and other destinations on Vancouver Island.

Sole truck of its kind.

Queen Anne Hill

Northwest of downtown and west of Lake Union awaits the area known as Lower Queen Anne, as it marks the bottom of **Queen Anne Hill** ❼. Real estate prices decrease with a drop in elevation, and it's apartment and condo country down here, with none of the grand homes that grace the hilltop. An interesting assortment of shops, coffeehouses and restaurants occupy Roy and Mercer streets, as well as Queen Anne Avenue just south of Mercer.

Queen Anne Hill, in the words of Seattle photo-historian Paul Dorpat, "is cleansed by winds, girdled by greenbelts, and topped by towers and mansions." The hill rises sharply on all four sides to a summit of 457 ft (139 meters), the second-highest elevation in the city; 35th Avenue SW in West Seattle reaches 514 ft (157 meters). Seattle pioneer Thomas Mercer, who arrived in 1853, filed the first claim on Queen Anne Hill and had to cut through a virtual forest in order to build. The hill got its name when Rev. Daniel Bagley referred to it as "Queen Anne Town," a jocular reference to the lavish mansions some of the city's prominent citizens built on the hill in the 1880s, in an American variation of the Queen Anne style of architecture found in England.

Bounded by Mercer Street on the south, Lake Union on the east, Lake Washington Ship Canal on the north, and Elliott Avenue on the west, the Queen Anne district is home to around 30,000 residents. Because of its great height, the hill offers spectacular views in all directions: Puget Sound, the Olympic Mountains and dramatic sunsets to the west; Lake Union, Capitol Hill and the Cascade Range to the east; Elliott Bay, downtown and Mount Rainier to the south; the Ship Canal and Mount Baker to the north.

Queen Anne boasts some of the loveliest residential streets in the city. For a good look at one of them,

BELOW: University area seen from Queen Anne Hill.

Map on pages 142–3

head west on Highland Drive from Queen Anne Avenue, about halfway up the hill. After passing gracious apartment buildings on both sides of the street, Kerry Park is a narrow stretch of green with wide-open views of the Space Needle, downtown office towers, the Elliott Bay harbor, and perhaps Mount Rainier, if the weather permits. The views from here are just as good at night as they are during the day. West of the park, stately mansions line both sides of Highland Drive, which ends in beautiful Parsons Garden, a tiny, secluded public park.

Magnolia

In 1856, the U.S. Coast Survey named the southern bluff overlooking Puget Sound for the magnolia trees growing along it. But the trees turned out to be madrona trees. The community liked the name **Magnolia** better than Madrona, however, and decided to keep Magnolia to identify the neighborhood. Northwest of downtown, Magnolia is an affluent, well-ordered, conservative neighborhood of mostly single-family homes resting on expansive lots. Magnificent waterfront properties along the western edge, south of Discovery Park, are protected from view by vegetation and long driveways. Magnolia Village, the neighborhood's shopping district (West McGraw Street between 32nd and 35th avenues), has recently undergone some dramatic changes after remaining much the same for years. In addition to the usual banks and real estate offices, there are now several fashionable shops and watering holes.

At 527 acres (213 hectares), **Discovery Park** ❽ is Seattle's largest green open area. In 1964, the United States government declared 85 percent of this land, which had been the site of Fort Lawton, an army base, to be surplus. Eight years later, after Congressional legislation made it possible for cities to obtain surplus federal property at no cost, the city of Seattle acquired the land. The park was named for the ship of the English explorer Captain George Vancouver, who, during his 1792 exploration of Puget Sound, spent several days with the HMS *Discovery* at anchor within sight of this land.

A 2½-mile (4-km) loop trail around the park winds through thick forests and crosses broad meadows and high, windswept bluffs with spectacular views of Puget Sound and the Olympic Mountains. Wildlife is abundant here: bald eagles are often seen in the treetops, and in 1982 a mountain lion was discovered lurking in the park.

A major attraction is the **Daybreak Star Arts Center** ❾ (open daily 9am–5pm, weekends from noon; tel: 206 285 4425; free) inside the park, which sponsors American Indian events and exhibits of contemporary Indian art. Discovery Park also has picnic areas, playgrounds, and tennis and basketball courts.

Fishermen's Terminal ❿, located on West Thurman Street on Magnolia's northern side, provides an opportunity to admire the boats of a major fishing fleet. This is home port for more than 700 commercial fishing vessels, many of which fish for salmon, halibut or crab in Alaskan waters and range in size from 30 ft (9 meters) to 300 ft (90 meters). One can sample the day's catch at one of the restaurants in the complex or purchase some at the fish market.

BELOW: enjoying one of 50 sunny days of the year. **RIGHT:** Lake Union.

U.S.
MAIL
ACHT
ALES
SHIP
U.S.
MAIL
SHOP
WESTERN YACHT
SALES INC
1115

VICTORIA

NORTH SEATTLE

Anchored by the pleasant campus of the University of Washington, the northern part of Seattle mingles the outdoors with some accommodating neighborhoods and subtle history

The 8-mile-long (13-km) **Lake Washington Ship Canal** ❶ separates the northern neighborhoods of Seattle from the city core. Completed in 1917, the artificial water route winds through the Ballard, Fremont, Wallingford, University and Montlake districts linking salty Puget Sound with the fresh waters of lakes Union and Washington. A series of locks (*see page 164*) raise and lower ships making the transit. Six bridges cross the canal, leading into a cluster of neighborhoods that make up North Seattle. These districts, born as independent townships in the 19th century, mostly maintain their individuality.

The **Burke-Gilman Trail**, a 12-mile (19-km) biking and hiking route, begins in Fremont, swings along Lake Union past the Gas Works, winds through the University of Washington campus and courses north on the left bank of Lake Washington. The innovative and scenic track follows the course of the lakeshore railroad, which connected these communities a century ago, an imaginative "recycling" that is part of a national "rails-to-trails" movement.

PRECEDING PAGES: *Fremont Troll.* **LEFT:** University of Washington. **BELOW:** the Coast Guard on Lake Washington Ship Canal.

The University District and beyond

The University District is an eclectic commercial center thriving on the cultural, education and athletic amenities afforded by the University of Washington. University Way Northeast, affectionately called "the Ave" by locals, is a busy strip of shops, theaters, newsstands, bookstores, pubs and eateries. Seattleites regard this animated district with caution, as an increasing number of panhandlers, rebellious youth and homeless bring with them a sometimes shadowy sub-culture. But the diverse community of students, businesspeople, academics and vagrants indisputably creates a certain vitality.

The **University Bookstore**, a resident of the Ave since 1925, carries a huge selection of contemporary fiction as well as textbooks, school and art supplies and T-shirts. Up and down the street are used bookstores, import shops, new and used clothing stores, jewelry stores, music stores, and a changing array of specialty stores.

Six blocks west of the Ave, on N.E. 45th Street, is the venerable **Blue Moon Tavern**, opened in 1934 and which apartment developers almost managed to demolish several years ago. This seedy, smoky den of glory – denizens have included the late poet Theodore Roethke and novelist Tom Robbins – fought back against development and won, not only with new historical landmark status but also a 40-year lease.

A few blocks to the east of the Ave is the 640-acre (260-hectare) **University of Washington** ❷ campus itself. Started on a 10-acre (4-hectare) plot that it acquired – and still owns (and from which it generates

George Washington's university statue.

huge rents) – in downtown Seattle on University Street in 1861, the university moved to its present site in 1895. More than 35,000 students and 17,000 staff come here to the state's finest public university, best known for its medical and law schools, and for its fine research facilities. Pick up a self-guided walking tour from the **Visitors' Information Center** (tel: 206 543 9198) at 4014 University Way.

Much of the original campus was designed by the Olmsted family, famous for New York's Central Park. Drumheller Fountain sits at the top of the Rainier Vista Mall, the gateway to the Gothic-style Quad, where in April rows of cherry trees burst into pink and white blossoms. The Allen Library (1990) expands by 40 percent the capacity of Suzzallo Library, the Gothic-style cathedral-like hall that opened in 1927 and was dubbed the soul of the university by then-president Henry Suzzallo. The addition was built with a $10 million donation from Paul Allen, co-founder of Microsoft, who bought the city's football team and created the Experience Music Project museum (which opened in 2000 at the Seattle Center). The red-tiled plaza adjoining Suzzallo was added in 1969 and is dubbed Red Square.

On summer evenings at the **Observatory** (open Mon and Thur in evenings, variable hours; tel: 206 543 0126; free), near the north campus entrance, one can stargaze through a 6-inch (15-cm) telescope.

The **Burke Museum** ❸ (open daily, 10am–5pm, Thur to 8pm; tel: 206 543 5590; donation), the Northwest's premier museum of natural and cultural history, has the only dinosaur skeletons in the Pacific Northwest, as well as housing the region's most comprehensive collection of Native art of the Northwest Coast tribes. The impressive anthropology, geology and zoology collections combined total more than 3 million specimens and artifacts. The museum underwent a remodeling in the late 1990s and now boasts a "walk-through" volcano,

BELOW: University of Washington's Suzallo Library.

in addition to two permanent exhibits, one looking at 500 million years of regional history, while the other highlights Pacific Rim cultures.

Not far from the Burke is the **Henry Art Gallery** (open daily 11am–5pm, Thurs to 8pm, closed Mon; tel: 206 543 2280; admission fee). Expanded and renovated in 1997, the gallery has 46,000 sq. ft (4,300 sq. meters) of exhibit space to show its 19,000 pieces of 19th- and 20th-century art, including Japanese ceramics and the American and European paintings from the collection of Horace C. Henry, a real estate and railroad magnate for whom the museum was named in 1927.

To the southeast rises **Husky Stadium**, the largest in the Pacific Northwest, with a capacity of 72,000 spectators. Just below, on Union Bay, weekend water-warriors rent rowboats or canoes at the **Waterfront Activities Center** ❹ (open daily, 10am–9pm, from 9am on weekends; tel: 206 543 9433).

Gas Works Park

The hulking specters of a bygone age dominate **Gas Works Park** ❺, situated on a southerly knob of land jutting boldly into Lake Union, the front door to North Seattle. The Seattle Gas Light Company began manufacturing heating and lighting gas in this factory on the 20-acre (8-hectare) knoll in 1906, fueling a rapidly growing city and earning a reputation as a filthy, foul-smelling killer of vegetation and wildlife. The plant closed its doors for good in 1956.

When the site was proposed as a park in the early 1960s, the city council hired landscape architect Richard Haag to create a lush, arboretum-type park. Instead, Haag submitted a plan incorporating much of the old gas plant. His design – with the rusting hulks of the gas works in the middle of an undulating lawn – triumphed after a storm of controversy from those wishing for a more tra-

Gas Works Park.

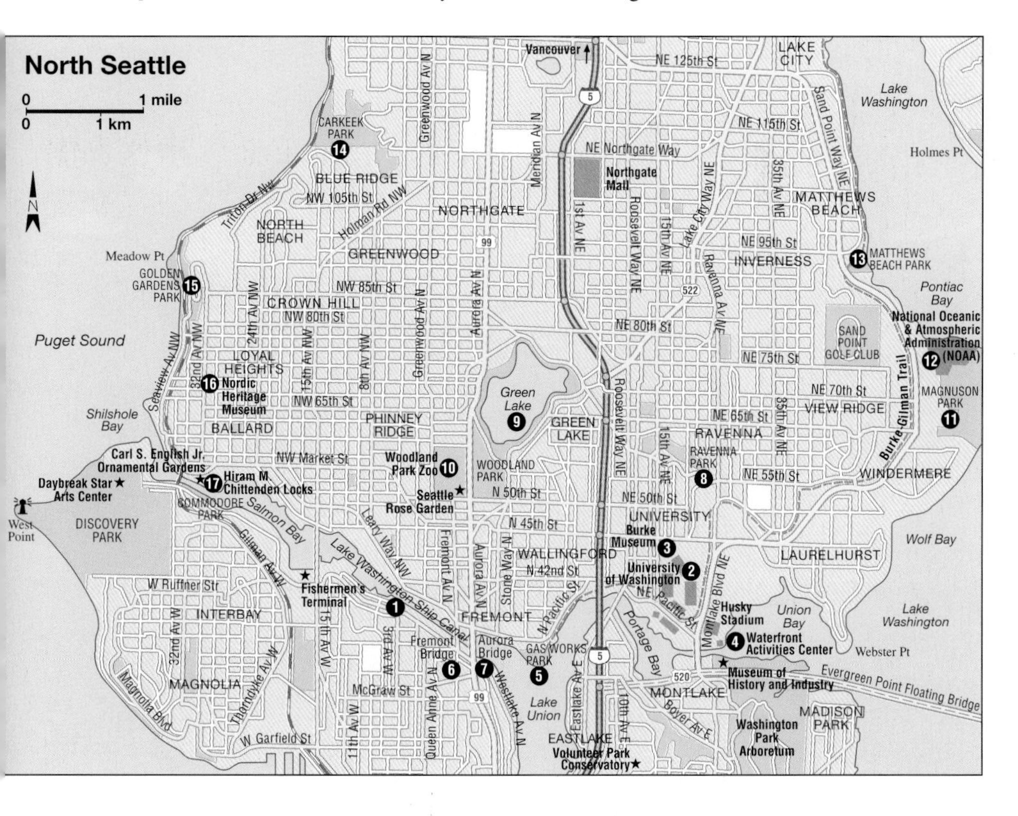

ditional park. The industrial-site conversion park was opened in 1975. Although concerns are still occasionally raised about contaminants in the soil under the park's green layer of grass, the city hasn't seen fit to close or restrict its use.

A medley of kites fly high over the park's Grand Mound, a grassy hill built west of the park's core from abandoned industrial waste. Picnickers and joggers share the space along an incline, and at the crown, visitors admire a mosaic sun and moon dial. The crest offers a great panorama of inner Seattle – downtown, Queen Anne Hill, the Aurora Bridge (where Highway 99 crosses the Lake Washington Ship Canal) to the west, and Capitol Hill to the east. To the north, the park gives way to the University of Washington and the pretty residential houses of Wallingford and Fremont.

Fremont doorway.

Fremont

Apparently no bridge on the planet opens more often than the **Fremont Bridge** ❻, completed in 1917 over the Lake Washington Ship Canal. Since then, it has opened its arms in a three-minute prayer to the clouds more than 500,000 times as of 1991 and perhaps 50,000 more times by the beginning of the new millennium – every 10 minutes on a busy summer day, it has been estimated. Watch boats go under the vibrant blue-and-orange drawbridge from a peaceful overlook at the **Fremont Canal Park**, a walkway on the north side of the waterway that features outdoor public art by local artists. Just east of the bridge on the north side sits the headquarters of Adobe Software.

The close-knit community of **Fremont**, strategically located at the northwest corner of Lake Union, was once a busy stop on the 1880s Burke-Gilman's SLS&E Railway, which carried lumber, coal and passengers between down-

BELOW: tavern suitable for rainy nights or days.

town and Ballard (*see page 164*). The railway's Edgewater station at the foot of Stone Way, near Lake Union, can still be seen today.

During Prohibition, Fremont's thriving taverns and hotel salons were closed, though the basement speakeasies flourished despite police raids common during Prohibition. **Aurora Bridge** ❼ opened in 1932, bypassing Fremont.

By the 1960s, hippies and unemployed drifters had taken over the Fremont and Triangle hotels, but the 1970s brought a long-awaited local renaissance. Artists moved into the cheap brick studios in lower Fremont, setting up the kind of eclectic galleries, shops and cafes that define the neighborhood today. Fremont got funky. Now, nary a tale is told of Fremont without the alliterative description "funky." Funky vintage collectibles are sold in the neighborhoods second-hand stores; funky furniture, housewares, gifts and local crafts are available at several specialty shops; and funky musical instruments can be found at a store specializing in drums and hand-crafted acoustical instruments.

Fremont's tavern life has survived intact throughout the decades. Choices range from a biker atmosphere, to young adults on the prowl, to nonsmoking pubs serving microbrews and occasional live music. Excellent restaurants here serve cuisine ranging from the healthy, vegetarian-leaning fare, to Asian, to Greek, to upscale fine dining.

On 34th Street just north of Aurora Bridge, the funky Fremont statue that has come to represent this area is *Waiting for the Interurban*, artist Rich Beyer's sculpture of five life-size adults, a baby in arms and a dog (said to have the face of a former mayor), all supposedly waiting for the electric trolley, which until the 1930s ran north to the town of Everett. Although some art critics are appalled by this sculpture, it is beloved by the general public, who regularly dec-

Map on page 157

BELOW: *Waiting for the Interurban* being immortalized.

Paddle boats at Green Lake.

orate the people, and the pergola above them, with T-shirts, balloons and streamers wishing friends happy birthday or good luck. A few blocks northeast, the 15-ft-high (4.6-meter), one-eyed *Fremont Troll* – a public sculpture of concrete – hunkers down under the Aurora Bridge clutching a Volkswagen.

East of Fremont is **Wallingford**, whose residential history is mired in memories of the sounds and stench that rose from the gas works at the bottom of the neighborhood. The district attracted working-class people who took special pride in their schools. The earliest school in the area, Latona, was founded in 1889. The Home of the Good Shepherd, a girls' orphanage started in 1906 by the Sisters of Our Lady of Charity, is now a cultural and community center.

North of the University District

The city of Seattle is young enough that residents still wistfully imagine the land as it was a century ago – a wilderness of virgin forests and crystal waterways. Just north of the University of Washington lies lush **Ravenna Park** ❽, an unspoiled, deep and wooded gorge far from the cosmopolitan life. Standing in silence next to a towering tree or a spill of green fern, it is not hard to envision early settlers meeting a grizzly bear on the track or gathering herbs for healing. Both the town and the park were named Ravenna after the Italian city on Italy's northern coast, which once stood on the edge of an ancient forest.

The shimmering waters of **Green Lake** ❾ ripple against grassy shores amidst the high-density neighborhood of the same name. It's a lake in a city surrounded by water, an algae-tinged reservoir born of glacial gougings 15,000 years ago. Walkers and roller-bladers zip along the busy 3-mile (5-km) perimeter path in all weather. Rent a pair of blades or admire the (sometimes aggressive) ducks

BELOW: views across Green Lake.

at the Waldo Waterfowl Sanctuary. Also keep a look out for the resident great blue heron and a visiting eagle. A community center and its environs include such facilities as football fields, tennis courts, a swimming pool, gym, beach and rowboat and canoe rentals. Restaurants around the lake range from trendy watering holes to fine Italian dining to fish and chips.

The neighborhood of Phinney Ridge and Greenwood blend easily together into an area known as The Ridge. Greenwood Avenue, once touted as Seattle's Antique Row, mixes traditional antiques and second-hand stores with modern merchants and specialty-food stores. There are galleries offering contemporary Northwest art, home-style cafes and several popular drinking establishments.

Almost 300 animal species dwell in the hills tucked between Phinney Ridge and Green Lake at the **Woodland Park Zoo** ❿ (open daily 9.30am-6pm, to 4pm in winter; tel: 206 684 4800; admission fee). The former wilderness estate of Guy Phinney, a leading Seattle real estate developer in the 1880s, this 92-acre (37-hectare) park pioneered the concept of creating naturalistic habitats for animals. Through ongoing efforts to convert old-style, iron-bar enclosures to larger, environmentally accurate enclosures, the zoo demonstrates a true commitment to a cageless future. Eight bioclimactic zones provide greater comfort for the animals and encourage natural behavior. Already, the Asian Elephant Forest and African Savannah have earned international recognition, and the Northern Tundra area is a favorite of visitors. Just outside the zoo's southeast exit, take time for the magnificent and free Seattle Rose Garden, originally laid out in the 1890s by old man Phinney himself.

In the neighborhoods bordering Lake Washington to the east, large contemporary homes built on landscaped hillsides capture sweeping views of the Cas-

Map on page 157

Giraffe at the zoo.

BELOW: maples in Woodland Park.

cades and Mount Rainier. On the southern stretch of the **Sand Point** peninsula, which juts out into Lake Washington north of the university, at least 87 species of birds and numerous kinds of wildlife frequent the recontoured terrain of **Magnuson Park** ⓫, once a naval air station and now filled with bluffs, sports fields, trails, and long, serene stretches of beach. On the same delta extending into Lake Washington, Bill Boeing flew his first airplane in 1916. In 1921, the first around-the-world flight began and ended here – four Navy aircraft left here on April 6 and three returned here on September 28.

In 1974, the city of Seattle granted the **National Oceanic and Atmospheric Administration** (NOAA⓬) the northern 114 acres (46 hectares) of what had been the naval air station for NOAA's **Western Regional Center**. It is now this country's largest federal center engaged in atmospheric and oceanic research. Many of the facilities are open to the public through tours, but arrangements should be made first: **National Weather Service**, tel: 206 526 6095, and the **Pacific Marine Environmental Lab**, tel: 206 526 6810.

Walkers are invited to saunter down the Shoreline Walk to see five publicly funded environmental artworks, so successful that the project has attracted national attention for public art. Earth, wind and water are the artists' media: a concrete spiraling dome with views in every direction; a viewpoint over the lake with chairs and sofas made from cut boulders; a bridge lettered with excerpts from Moby Dick; a multi-surfaced berth lapping up waves on the curve of the shoreline; and a sound garden of lacy towers and tuned organ pipes that make music from the wind.

About a mile to the north of Magnuson Park is Seattle's largest freshwater bathing beach (a lifeguard is on duty) at **Matthews Beach Park** ⓭, just off of

BELOW: old-fashioned hangout.

the Burke-Gilman Trail. At the south end, cross the footbridge above Thornton Creek to reach the tiny but charming **Thornton Creek Natural Area**, where wildlife find a convenient urban retreat.

In the tiny hamlet of Pontiac, a railroad worker once hung a sign that said "Lake" on a shed near the tracks of Northern Pacific Railroad. The name stuck, and **Lake City** was annexed by Seattle in 1954. Here, as in the surrounding neighborhoods, reasonably priced starter homes can be found relatively close to the urban core. The blur of chain restaurants, car lots, gas stations and supermarkets lining Lake City Way may not make an impression in the annals of history, but the region has a few worthwhile spots. A flagpole dedicated to World War II veterans sits in what is the smallest official city park, and a Will Rogers Memorial (12501 28th Ave. NE) honors the Oklahoma-born wit and philosopher, who spent one of his last days alive playing polo here. He then left Seattle for Alaska, where he was killed in a plane crash.

To the west

If access to the jeweled shores of Puget Sound means prosperity, then Seattleites are rich indeed, for 216-acre (87-hectare) **Carkeek Park ⓮**, on the coast of Puget Sound and northwest of Green Lake, winds and plunges down into a maze of wooded pathways, over the Burlington Northern Railroad tracks and onto an unfettered stretch of beach. The park was named for Morgan and Emily Carkeek, early Seattle contractors and philanthropists. Locals are laboring to re-establish the park's Piper's Creek as a salmon spawning site.

Follow the railroad south and you're on your way to proud-hearted Ballard. The tracks run through **Golden Gardens Park ⓯**, neatly dividing it into two distinct

Map on page 157

The Northern Pacific was chartered by the U.S. Congress in 1864, with the mandate to connect Lake Superior in the Midwest to a Pacific port. The final link to Seattle was made in 1883, when the line connected to the Oregon Railway in Helena, Montana.

BELOW: simple housing along Lake Washington.

sections: a forested hillside and a golden beach stretching along **Shilshole Bay**, Seattle's coast-of-blue. Sunbathe, scuba dive, dig for clams or watch the sailboats breezing out toward the Puget isles. Wind up Golden Gardens Drive and go south until a "scenic drives" sign at NW 77th denotes the aptly named Sunset Hill.

Ballard

Salmon painted on a Seattle wall.

After developers discovered this region in the mid-1880s, Scandinavian immigrants were drawn here by the abundant fishing, lumber and boat-building opportunities to be found in a majestic and watery region, much like their homeland. Thickly accented Scandinavian tongues can still be heard in local coffee shops. When downtown Seattle was rebuilt after the great fire of 1889 and Washington entered the Union as the 42nd state, Gilman Park, now a community of nearly 2,000 residents, hurried to be the first to incorporate, naming their boomtown **Ballard**. At the turn of the century it was the largest producer of red-cedar shingles in the United States (though little evidence of this production exists today). Early Ballard was a bastion of pioneer revelry, said to hold 27 saloons on a four-block strip. It has fewer today, but Ballard still sports its share of saloons and plays a key role in Seattle's hot music scene.

This thriving community of 15,000 inhabitants, coveted by Seattle officials for its major industrial district and access to water routes, was annexed to the city in 1907 and has been a major commercial fishing port ever since. The "Dream of America", a major exhibit at the **Nordic Heritage Museum** ⓰ (open daily 10am–4pm, Sun from noon, closed Mon; tel: 206 789 5707; admission fee), tells a graphic story of the immigrants' travel to the new land. Five ethnic rooms survey the cultural legacy of Sweden, Norway, Iceland, Finland and Denmark.

BELOW: one of Seattle's permanent residents.
RIGHT: a rainy climate makes the indoors pleasant.

Every year, about 100,000 commercial and pleasure vessels navigate through the 1917-era **Hiram M. Chittenden Locks** ⓱, two masonry gates on the north bank of the canal and opposite Discovery Park, which raise and lower boats between the saltwater of Puget Sound and the freshwater of Lake Washington.

About 500,000 sockeye, chinook and coho salmon use the same channel to get to their spawning grounds in Lake Washington and streams farther along in the Cascade Range to the east, climbing a 21-level fish ladder built to preserve the migrating runs. In summer, watch their passage upstream through six lighted underwater viewing windows, a moving portrait of creatures driven by a mandate of nature and against all odds back to their birthplace.

The issue of salmon runs came to the political and social foreground in 1999, when the U.S. Government listed nine types of salmon under the Endangered Species Act. This act, widely supported in Seattle and the Puget Sound area, will place limits on new building (and thus population and geographical growth) and probably raise taxes. Never had a listing affected such a large geographical region anchored with major metropolitan areas.

The terraced lawns and rose bushes of the waterside **Carl S. English, Jr. Ornamental Gardens** – named for one of the region's top horticulturalists in the early 1900s – make a fine picnic spot. ❑

GRAVITY
APPLES
PEARS

wonder
hat youre at!

SOUTH SEATTLE

Few visitors give southern Seattle much of a thought, other than for the international airport. But the area known as West Seattle (in south Seattle) is perhaps the city's funkiest outback

It was on the windswept shores of what is now Alki Beach that Seattle's pioneers first built a community. The area's original residents, led by Arthur Denny, came from the state of Illinois, in the American Midwest, seeking a better life. After one blustery winter on Alki, however, most of the Denny party moved away from the beach's winds to the shelter – and superior anchorage – of Elliott Bay. That long-ago exodus seems unbelievable given Alki's current popularity. In summer, the sandy beach is a mass of tanned bodies, and on sunny days year-round, the footpath and its adjacent bike-and-skating path are crowded with promenading, strutting people.

Geographically the southern part of the city, known locally as West Seattle, is situated on a peninsula, separated from downtown Seattle by the Duwamish River. The West Seattle bridge, which connects the area to the rest of the city, arcs over busy Harbor Island and the Duwamish River, which flows into Elliot Bay, like the back of a brontosaurus, its tail the Spokane Street Viaduct, its neck the sweep of the freeway up a tree-covered hill dotted with houses. Harbor Island, at the river's mouth where it empties into Elliott Bay, is an artificial industrial island and storage depot for much of the equipment serving the busy Port of Seattle.

The present high-level bridge, still called the "new bridge" by longtime residents (although completed in 1984) replaced a pair of bascule bridges that too often stopped traffic when they opened to let sailboats and freighters pass down the river.

PRECEDING PAGES: juice bar clientele. **LEFT:** taking a break from bicycling. **BELOW:** gentle look.

The Junction

Downtown West Seattle, as it is sometimes called, is best known as **The Junction** ❶. It is centered around California Avenue Southwest and Southwest Alaska Street. This central shopping area has had its ups and downs; a number of businesses have made passing appearances while several others have stood unchanged for more than 50 years. The Junction's display of murals is remarkable: more than half a dozen wall-sized painting decorate the exteriors of retail and business buildings, most of them depicting the area as it looked over a century ago, in the 19th century. The best of these, on the wall at California and Edmunds, looks as if one could walk right into a turn-of-the-century street scene.

North of the junction on California is the **Admiral District**, named for Admiral Way, which climbs up the hill from the West Seattle Bridge on the east and slides down to Alki Beach on the west. The district is home to the last of West Seattle's movie theaters, the Admiral Theatre, which shows second-run films at discount prices. Here, too, is a lovely old brick public library, a few Italian restaurants, coffee shops and West Seattle High School.

This part of Seattle is located on two hills, Gatewood and Genesee, which give it an abundance of view-enhanced property. Homes on the west sides of both hills overlook Puget Sound and the Olympic Mountains; those on the east overlook downtown and Harbor Island. At the top of Genesee Hill are a number of scenic outlooks including Hamilton Viewpoint, at the north end of California Avenue, and Belvedere Viewpoint, on Admiral Way.

Alki Beach

The closest thing Seattle has to a Southern California strand is **Alki Beach ❷**, which, for many years, was the summer place where teenagers headed for in their cars. Anti-cruising laws passed in the 1980s restricted drivers to one pass along the beach's Alki Avenue every four hours, thus cutting down considerably on the noise and traffic that plagued local residents – many of whom occupy shiny condominium complexes across from the beach. The beach park is technically closed between 11pm and 6am, mid-April through September. In summer, however, Alki still attracts a fair share of shiny cars, bronzed bodies in bikinis and teenagers out to see and be seen. Volleyball courts are usually filled with players and lined with spectators.

In the fall, winter and spring, Alki is still a wonderful place for a beach stroll under swirling clouds amidst squawking gulls. And when the wind and rain that drove the Denny party to the other side of the bay get to be too much, the area also offers plenty of places to eat, ranging from bakeries and delis to a chain seafood restaurant with an excellent view of the downtown skyline.

The oldest landmark here is a concrete column marking the beach as the "Birthplace of Seattle." It was presented to the city in 1905 by Arthur Denny's

BELOW: volleyball is always a focus at Alki Beach.

daughter and now stands at 63rd Avenue SW and Alki Avenue. In 1926, when the column was moved from its original location on the other side of the street, a piece of the actual Plymouth Rock, the Massachusetts boulder towards which the Pilgrims sailed in 1620, was embedded in its base.

At the southern end of the beach – just before it becomes residential – is the **Alki Point Lighthouse** ❸, first established in 1881 and marking the southern entrance to Seattle's harbor. The present lighthouse, standing on a small reservation behind apartments and condominiums, dates to 1913. The lighthouse is open to visitors for regular tours on weekends; group tours can be arranged Tuesday through Friday.

Schmitz Park ❹, just east of Alki, is a 50-acre (20-hectare) nature preserve with narrow trails through thick woods but with no picnic areas or playgrounds. Just off 35th Avenue Southwest, the hillside West Seattle Municipal Golf Course offers views of downtown Seattle, Elliott Bay and the Duwamish waterway. This 18-hole, par-72 course was built in 1940.

Continue along the waterfront, which becomes Beach Drive, passing beachside homes both extravagant and funky, as well as apartment buildings and open spaces such as Emma Schmitz Memorial Park. Beach Drive culminates in the lower part of Lincoln Park, at the foot of Gatewood Hill. Alki may be the most visible of this area's city parks, but it is certainly not the least of them. Most prominent is 130-acre (50-hectare) **Lincoln Park** ❺, designed by the Olmsted brothers, creators of New York's Central Park, and with miles of wooded and waterfront trails. Colman Pool is a heated 50-meter Olympic-size outdoor pool open only in summer. Filled partly with chlorinated freshwater and part saltwater, Colman Pool is accessible only on foot; the roads through the park are

Map on page 171

Wearing one's social commentary.

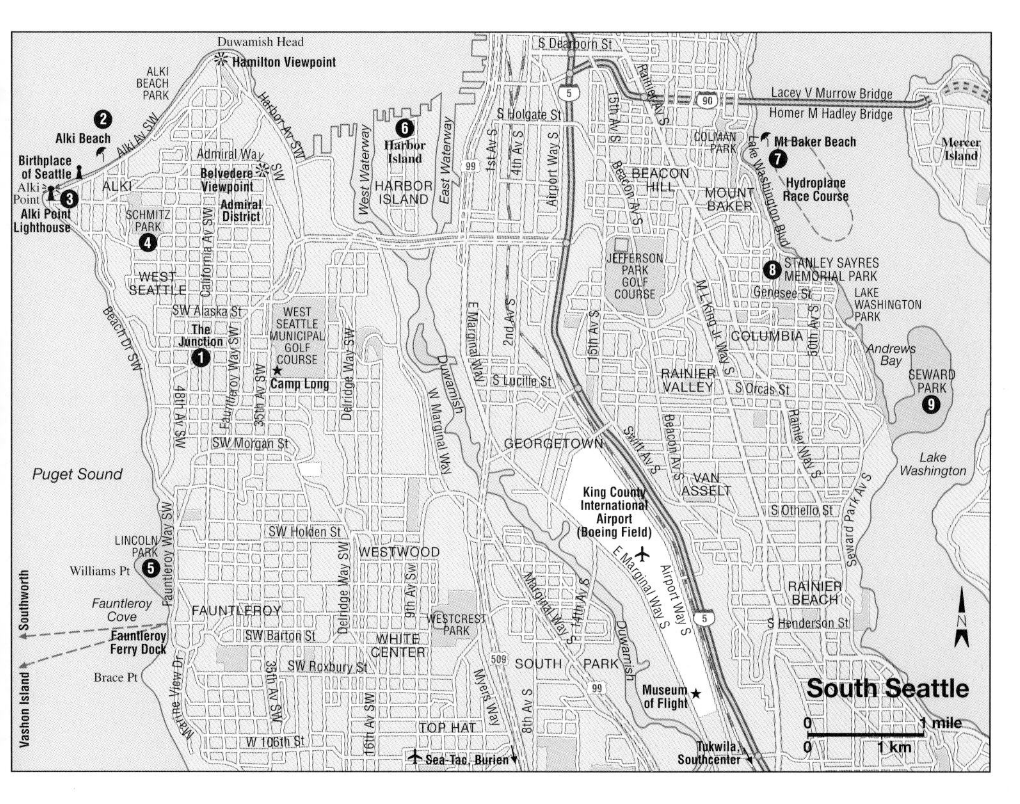

Sailboats pepper all of Seattle's water.

restricted to park vehicles. At the south end of Lincoln Park is the **Fauntleroy Ferry Dock**, where you can catch a boat for Vashon Island (*see page 222*) or Southworth. Either place makes a pleasant day trip. Vashon, just 20 minutes from the dock, is a charming rural area far from the rush of city life. Many residents farm as a hobby and make the daily commute to Seattle or Tacoma via ferry; others have found work on the island itself, working in such industries as ski manufacturing, orchid growing or food processing.

One of the city's few parks to offer overnight facilities, **Camp Long**, just off 35th Avenue SW at Dawson, is 68 acres (27 hectares) of wilderness. Open to organized groups for camping and wilderness-skills programs, Camp Long is a popular site for weddings and also features a decent rock wall for climbing practice and instruction.

Just Southeast of West Seattle is the area known as White Center, named in the early 1990s for George W. H. White, a partner in the railway that served this part of Seattle. Back then, White Center was a rugged logging area. Government housing projects went up after World War II and, later, taverns were built here just outside the city limits, thus earning White Center the nickname Rat City in the 1960s. Nowadays, White Center is one of the few nearby places left with affordable real estate for first-time home buyers, partly owing to its placement adjacent to a low-income housing development.

South of Safeco Field

The region immediately south of the baseball stadium, Safeco Field, which marks the southern edge of downtown, is mainly industrial. Shops here often sell carpeting, building supplies and reduced-rate furniture. Farther south is the

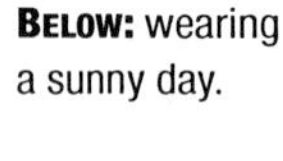

BELOW: wearing a sunny day.

FISH, BERRIES, NUTS AND APPLES

The only other city in western America that stands against Seattle for cuisine is San Francisco, which in many culinary ways rises far above Seattle. And like San Francisco, much of the cuisine found in Seattle and elsewhere in the Pacific Northwest has touches, if not a legacy, of Asian traditions. As in Australia, California and Hawaii, the Northwest's chefs have blended Asian, Continental and American into a cuisine often referred to under the umbrella Pacific Rim Cuisine.

But when it comes to seafood, Seattle and the Pacific Northwest reign supreme. Pike Place Market in Seattle abounds in fresh crab, salmon (sometimes from Alaska and not local) and oysters, all of it direct from the sea and well priced. Shellfish, especially clams and oysters, are also popular and worth trying while in the Northwest. Other fish taken from local waters include cod, tuna, flounder, halibut and snapper.

Inland, berries punctuate the flora, from strawberries and raspberries to some exquisite blueberries and cranberries. Visitors will find berries appearing in everything from jam to pie. Walnuts and hazelnuts add to the Northwest inventory. The state of Washington is also the country's largest grower of apples.

equally industrial area of Georgetown, which has fans who believe it's due to be discovered one day and become somewhat trendy.

Those already in the know come to visit the Seattle Design Center, a must-stop for interior designers, and Expresso by Design, an espresso stand next door in a little pink house. Several small restaurants here serve chili dogs, Mexican food, pho, teriyaki, Thai or diner food.

Harbor Island ❻, between downtown and southern West Seattle, is home to the city's shipyards as well as loading facilities for freighters. It is landfill of more than 25 million cubic yards (19 million cubic meters) of sludge pulled from the Duwamish River. At the time of its completion in 1912, Harbor Island was the largest artificial island in the world. Shortly after the island was created, the meandering Duwamish was straightened, allowing plenty of room on its banks for industrial development. South from Elliott Bay, past busy Harbor Island and through Seattle's industrial corridor, the river passes salvage ships, commercial shipping lanes, Boeing Field and the town of Tukwila.

On the east side of Interstate 5 is **Beacon Hill**, an affordable residential area with a diverse ethnic mix. Highlights here are the city-owned Jefferson Park Golf Course (where pro Fred Couples learned to play), the Latino community center El Centro de la Raza, and an authentic Asian grocery with tanks of live fish and foods from Asia.

East of Beacon Hill is the comfortable neighborhood of **Mount Baker**, which has several fine old homes, a few interesting shops and cafes, and a diverse population. Wind down the hill through Mount Baker and you'll find yourself on the shores of Lake Washington. At **Mount Baker Beach** ❼, a large, blue boathouse holds numerous rowing shells, which are taken out daily by rowers

Map on page 171

BELOW: Mercer Island Floating Bridge carries Interstate 90.

young and old. The city parks and recreation rowing program hosts classes and races for junior and masters rowers.

Along the west side of the lake runs Lake Washington Boulevard, which begins at the University of Washington in North Seattle (*see* North Seattle *chapter, page 155*) and continues all the way down to Seward Park. Along the way, the road offers eastward views of the Cascade Range, the road meandering past the Lake Washington parks, a string of grassy beachfronts along the lake's western shore. An adjacent bike path follows the road for some miles.

May through September the road is closed on some weekends to automobiles from Mount Baker Beach to Seward Park for "Bicycle Saturdays" and "Bicycle Sundays" (usually the second Saturday and third Sunday of each month). It's a beautiful ride at any time, but this Seattle Parks and Recreation Department-sponsored event makes it safer and that much more appealing.

Like Alki and several other Seattle parks, Seward Park closes at 11pm each night because of police and community concerns about possible drug and gang activity in the parks.

The stretch of lake shoreline from just south of the Mercer Island Floating Bridge (which carries Interstate 90) to Andrews Bay is hydro heaven during the Rainier Cup Hydroplane Race in August. The races, part of the city's annual Seafair celebration and first staged in 1950, have become a Seattle tradition, drawing thousands of spectators despite the horrendous noise of engines on 150-mph boats. Seafair's official viewing beach is **Stanley Sayres Memorial Park** ❽ (where the hydro pits are located), but many fans watch from homes along the lake and hundreds pay a per-foot charge to tie their boats up to log booms along the challenging course.

The Lake Washington parks culminate in **Seward Park** ❾, 279 acres (113 hectares) of greenery, trails and waterfront. It is also home to a pair of breeding bald eagles – and a flock of now-wild parrots, once domesticated birds that escaped and congregated here. The park has an art studio, an outdoor amphitheater and a short lakeside trail for cyclists and runners.

Further south towards Boeing Country

In **Rainier Valley**, named for the vistas of Mount Rainier it offers, once stood the old Sicks Stadium, home successively to baseball's Seattle Rainiers and the Seattle Pilots but now the site of a chain hardware store. Neighborhoods near the Duwamish River as it winds south from Elliott Bay include Holly Park, Highland Park, South Park, Beverly Park and, farther southwest, Burien. To the east on the edge of the lake is Rainier Beach.

Limited real estate in the city's International District prompted some Asian immigrants to seek other areas for development, including the area just south of the old Kingdome (now replaced by Safeco Field) and which now has a substantial Asian population, mostly Vietnamese, and several good ethnic restaurants. Many more Asian restaurants can be found on Pacific Highway South as it makes its way toward Sea-Tac International Airport. Southcenter, at the southern confluence of Interstates 5 and 405, is one of Seattle's largest covered shopping malls. This 75-acre (30-hectare) complex houses some 160 stores, anchored by department stores Nordstrom and the Bon Marché. Specialty apparel and gift stores, plus a busy food court, sell everything from toys to tacos.

This area – officially in the city of **Tukwila** – is a shopper's paradise, particularly if one is looking for discount and outlet stores, especially of most chain furniture, clothing and electronics stores, as well as a generous buffet of chain restaurant choices. Here, too, is the giant IKEA store in an old Boeing warehouse building, selling houseful of Swedish furniture.

The region south of Seattle is Boeing Country and is home to the aerospace firm's test field, at the south end of Lake Washington (*see "South of Seattle," page 199*). Other plants are in Renton, Auburn and Kent. ❑

Right: fresh smile from Seattle.

Short Horned Lizard

Balloon
Depot

BEYOND SEATTLE

There's more to Seattle than Seattle. Outside of the city are other communities that claim an identity of their own

Unlike most cities where the city's center slowly metamorphoses into neighboring cities and finally into suburbs, the city of Seattle is defined on two sides by bodies of water. This gives the city a sense of a finite place, as well as giving neighboring cities and towns distinctive autonomy from Seattle. To the east, on the other side of Lake Washington, is the area known as Eastside, while to the north are the bedroom communities of Edmonds and Everett (which is also home to one of Boeing's immense manufacturing plants). To the south, beyond the airport, is the sister city of Tacoma and the Washington State capital of Olympia.

The Eastside lands across Lake Washington were once rural and considered an outdoor adventure for residents of Seattle. Times do change. Bellevue is urban and glossy and high-tech, with an increasingly rising skyline of its own. Nearby Kirkland has long assured its residents plenty of outdoor spaces and waterfront access, something that many cities fail miserably at doing. Redmond once had little that would distinguish it from Seattle or any other urban center. Now it has Microsoft, with its headquarters here and an increasing number of Microsoft millionaires settling in surrounding neighborhoods. Further to the east, the steel and concrete slowly dissipate as the roads lead towards the jagged Cascade Range. Issaquah and then Carnation have a rural contour, and vineyards in the region produce some of the nicest wines in the Pacific Northwest.

North of Seattle has little to positively lure the traveler, but the affluent bedroom communities that make up the area are increasingly vital to the economic well-being of the region. In Everett, Boeing has built one of the world's largest manufacturing plants to assemble its jumbo jets.

South of Seattle is a corridor that begins at the Sea-Tac International Airport – Sea-Tac being constructed from Seattle and Tacoma – and passes through Tacoma, a city in its own right that has long lived in the shadow of Seattle. A little further along is the truly sleepy town of Olympia, the governmental center for the State of Washington. From the southern parts, one can easily head to the Olympic Peninsula or coastal areas of southern Washington. ❑

PRECEDING PAGES: towering reflections abound in Eastside; a casual kiss.
LEFT: hot-air ballooning in the farmlands to the east of Seattle.

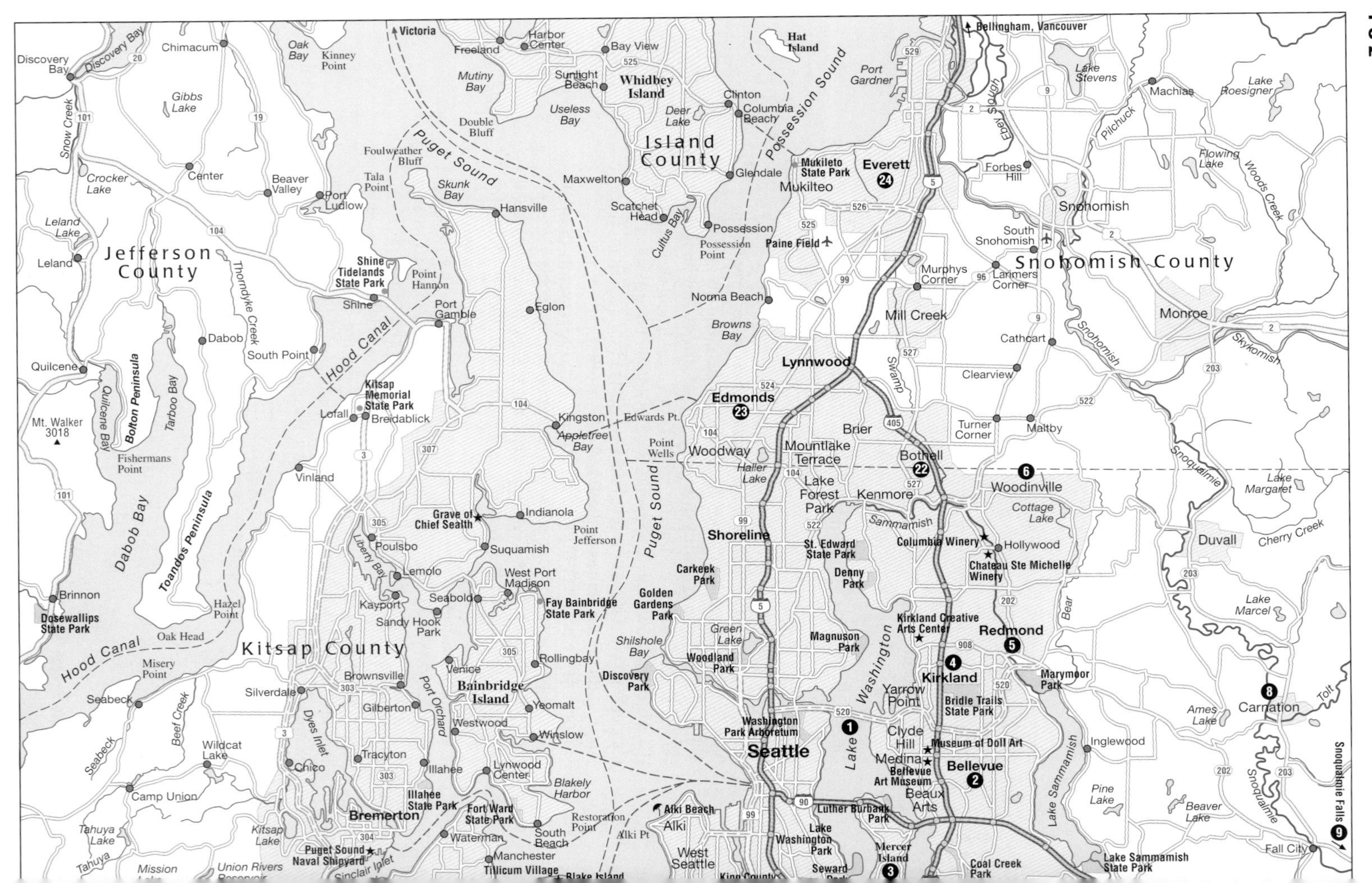
Victoria
Bellingham, Vancouver
Snoqualmie Falls
Jefferson County
Island County
Snohomish County
Kitsap County
Discovery Bay
Chimacum
Oak Bay
Kinney Point
Freeland
Harbor Center
Bay View
Hat Island
Port Gardner
Lake Stevens
Machias
Lake Roesigner
Gibbs Lake
Mutiny Bay
Sunlight Beach
Whidbey Island
Clinton
Columbia Beach
Possession Sound
Snow Creek
Useless Bay
Deer Lake
Double Bluff
Ebey Slough
Pilchuck
Flowing Lake
Woods Creek
Foulweather Bluff
Puget Sound
Crocker Lake
Center
Beaver Valley
Tala Point
Port Ludlow
Skunk Bay
Maxwelton
Glendale
Mukileto State Park
Everett
Mukilteo
Forbes Hill
Snohomish
Hansville
Scatchet Head
Cultus Bay
Possession
Possession Point
Paine Field
South Snohomish
Leland Lake
Leland
Shine Tidelands State Park
Point Hannon
Murphys Corner
Larimers Corner
Thorndyke Creek
Shine
Port Gamble
Eglon
Norma Beach
Mill Creek
Monroe
Browns Bay
Dabob
South Point
Hood Canal
Cathcart
Snohomish
Skykomish
Quilcene
Bolton Peninsula
Tarboo Bay
Quilcene Bay
Lynnwood
Swamp
Clearview
Kitsap Memorial State Park
Lofall
Breidablick
Edmonds
Mt. Walker 3018
Kingston
Appletree Bay
Edwards Pt.
Point Wells
Woodway
Brier
Turner Corner
Maltby
Mountlake Terrace
Bothell
Fishermans Point
Vinland
Haller Lake
Lake Forest Park
Kenmore
Woodinville
Snoqualmie
Lake Margaret
Dabob Bay
Toandos Peninsula
Grave of Chief Seatlh
Indianola
Sammamish
Cottage Lake
Duvall
Cherry Creek
Point Jefferson
Shoreline
St. Edward State Park
Columbia Winery
Hollywood
Poulsbo
Suquamish
Chateau Ste Michelle Winery
Liberty Bay
Lemolo
West Port Madison
Denny Park
Brinnon
Seabold
Fay Bainbridge State Park
Carkeek Park
Golden Gardens Park
Kirkland Creative Arts Center
Redmond
Lake Marcel
Bear
Dosewallips State Park
Kayport
Hazel Point
Sandy Hook Park
Oak Head
Green Lake
Magnuson Park
Shilshole Bay
Woodland Park
Rollingbay
Venice
Kirkland
Marymoor Park
Misery Point
Brownsville
Discovery Park
Lake Washington
Silverdale
Port Orchard
Bainbridge Island
Yarrow Point
Bridle Trails State Park
Carnation
Tolt
Seabeck
Gilberton
Yeomalt
Westwood
Washington Park Arboretum
Ames Lake
Beef Creek
Wildcat Lake
Dyes Inlet
Winslow
Clyde Hill
Museum of Doll Art
Inglewood
Tracyton
Seattle
Medina
Bellevue Art Museum
Bellevue
Chico
Illahee
Lynwood Center
Lake Sammamish
Camp Union
Blakely Harbor
Beaux Arts
Pine Lake
Illahee State Park
Fort Ward State Park
Restoration Point
Alki Beach
Luther Burbank Park
Beaver Lake
Bremerton
Alki
Tahuya Lake
Kitsap Lake
Waterman
South Beach
Alki Pt
Lake Washington Park
Mercer Island
Puget Sound Naval Shipyard
West Seattle
Fall City
Manchester
Coal Creek Park
Lake Sammamish State Park
Tahuya
Mission
Union Rivers
Sinclair Inlet
Tillicum Village
Blake Island
Seward Park
King County

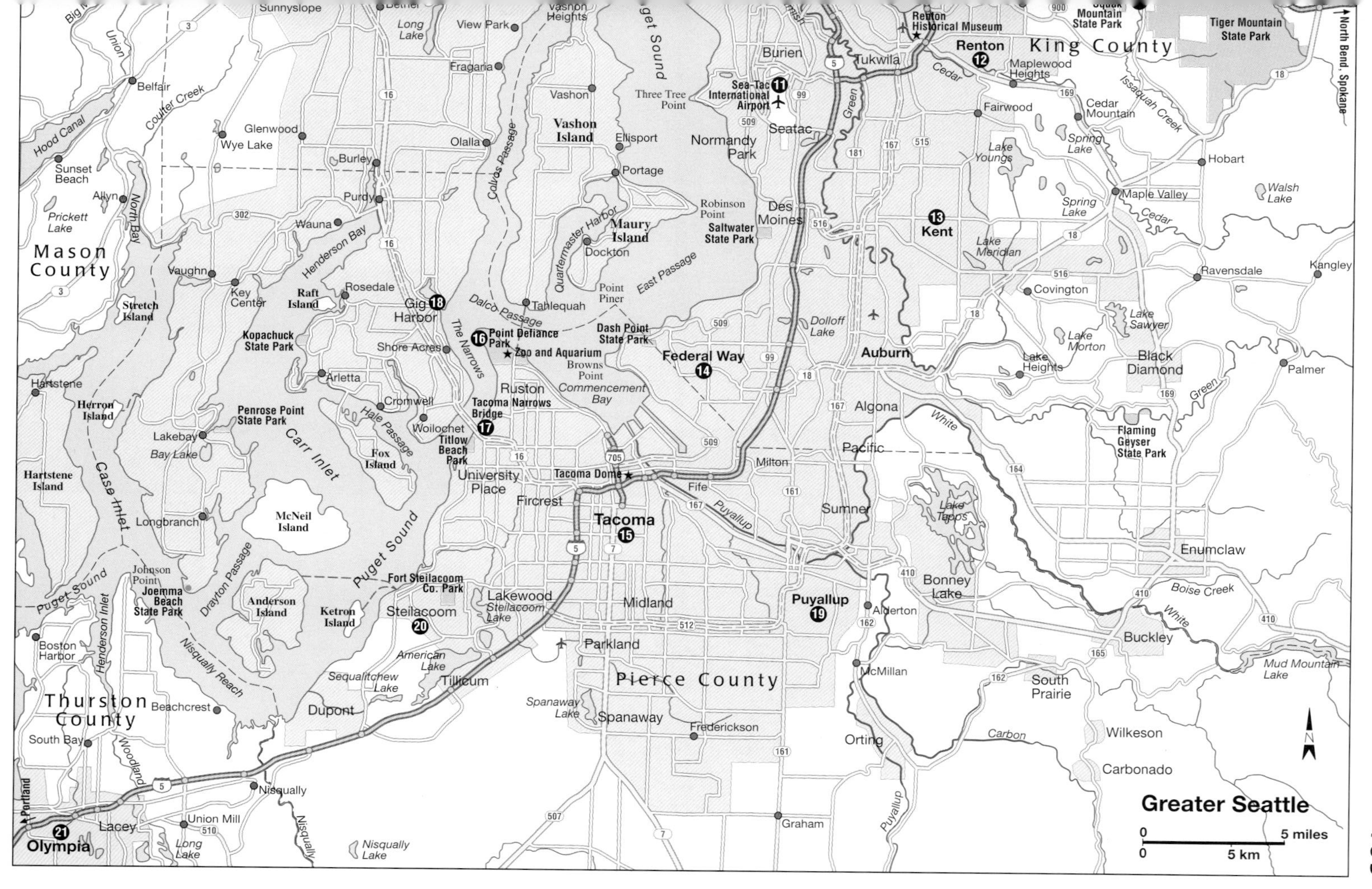
Greater Seattle
0 5 miles
0 5 km
North Bend, Spokane
Portland
King County
Pierce County
Mason County
Thurston County
Tiger Mountain State Park
Renton Historical Museum
Renton 12
Kent 13
Federal Way 14
Tacoma 15
Point Defiance Park 16
Zoo and Aquarium
Tacoma Narrows Bridge 17
Gig Harbor 18
Puyallup 19
Steilacoom 20
Olympia 21
Sea-Tac International Airport 11
Saltwater State Park
Dash Point State Park
Tacoma Dome
Titlow Beach Park
Fort Steilacoom Co. Park
Flaming Geyser State Park
Kopachuck State Park
Penrose Point State Park
Joemma Beach State Park
Vashon Island
Maury Island
Raft Island
Fox Island
McNeil Island
Ketron Island
Anderson Island
Stretch Island
Herron Island
Hartstene Island
Puget Sound
East Passage
Colvos Passage
Dalco Passage
The Narrows
Commencement Bay
Quartermaster Harbor
Hale Passage
Carr Inlet
Henderson Bay
Drayton Passage
Nisqually Reach
Case Inlet
Henderson Inlet
North Bay
Hood Canal
Tukwila
Burien
Seatac
Des Moines
Normandy Park
Auburn
Algona
Pacific
Sumner
Milton
Fife
Ruston
Fircrest
University Place
Lakewood
Midland
Parkland
Spanaway
Frederickson
Graham
Orting
McMillan
Alderton
Bonney Lake
Buckley
Wilkeson
Carbonado
South Prairie
Enumclaw
Black Diamond
Covington
Lake Heights
Ravensdale
Kangley
Palmer
Hobart
Maple Valley
Cedar Mountain
Maplewood Heights
Fairwood
Vashon
Vashon Heights
Ellisport
Portage
Dockton
Tahlequah
Point Piner
Browns Point
Robinson Point
Three Tree Point
View Park
Fragaria
Olalla
Burley
Purdy
Wauna
Rosedale
Shore Acres
Cromwell
Wollochet
Arletta
Sunnyslope
Glenwood
Wye Lake
Key Center
Vaughn
Lakebay
Longbranch
Johnson Point
Belfair
Allyn
Sunset Beach
Hartstene
Boston Harbor
South Bay
Lacey
Beachcrest
Union Mill
Nisqually
Dupont
Tillicum
Lake Tapps
Lake Youngs
Lake Meridian
Lake Sawyer
Lake Morton
Spring Lake
Walsh Lake
Dolloff Lake
Steilacoom Lake
American Lake
Sequalitchew Lake
Spanaway Lake
Nisqually Lake
Long Lake
Bay Lake
Prickett Lake
Mud Mountain Lake
Issaquah Creek
Boise Creek
Coulter Creek
Cedar
Green
White
Puyallup
Carbon
Nisqually
Woodland
Union

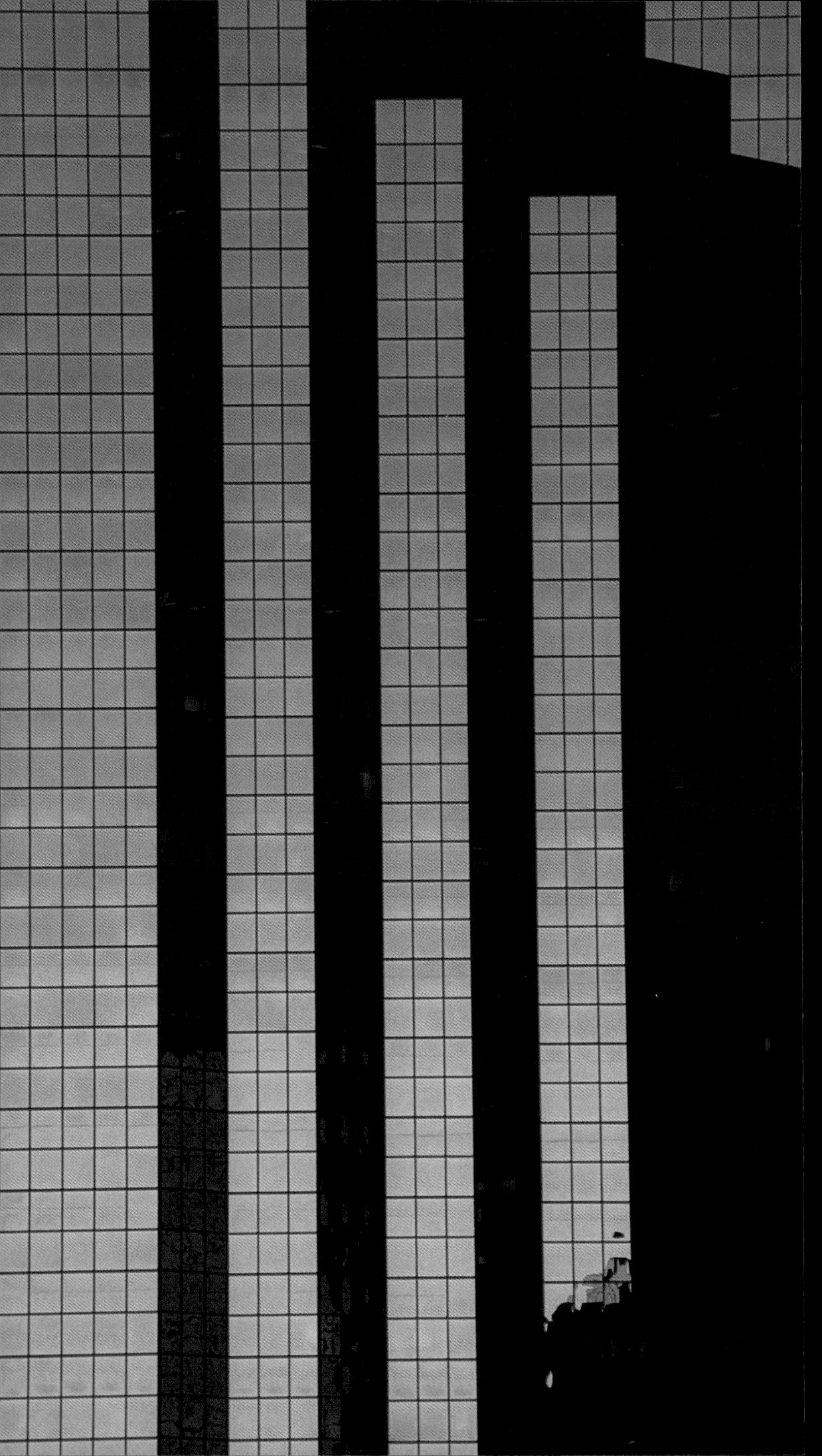

EASTSIDE

Once thought of as out in the sticks and suitable for excursions into the wild, Eastside – east of Lake Washington – is a high-tech, glossy area known for Microsoft billions and fine wines

Map on pages 182–3

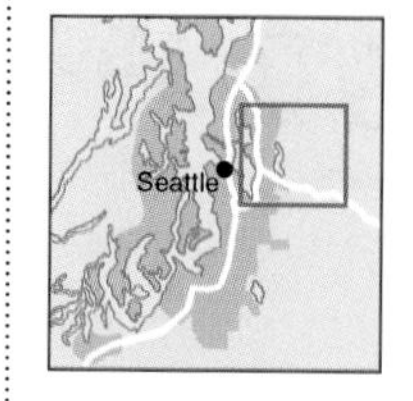

Stroll along the Kirkland waterfront, latte or espresso in hand. Stop for an outdoor lunch on a sunlit deck overlooking Lake Washington. Head to downtown Bellevue for an afternoon at the Bellevue Art Museum. Visit the velodrome in Redmond's Marymoor Park and cheer on world-class cyclists. Drive into Issaquah for an evening of professional theater or head out to Woodinville for an afternoon of wine tasting and music at the delightful Chateau Ste Michelle Winery, regionally renowned for its white wines. Although these scenarios are increasingly taken for granted by Eastsiders and Seattle residents alike, they can be inadvertently overlooked by visitors intent on seeing the area's sights.

By the late 1880s, Seattleites were already referring to the area that would later become Bellevue and Kirkland as "East Seattle." An influx of population after the Great Fire of 1889 was supplemented by new homesteaders coming to the shores of Lake Washington from many other parts of the country. As the decades passed and the population grew, agriculture, logging and mining gave way to housing, and the Eastside increasingly took on the role of bedroom community. Today, many Eastside cities are discovering identities of their own as financial or technology centers (Bellevue and Redmond) or as increasingly sophisticated regional recreation centers (Kirkland and Woodinville). More and more companies previously based in Seattle are making the leap across the lake and choosing to locate on the Eastside. Bellevue, for instance, has the distinction of attracting numerous financial, electronics and computer companies to its city limits.It wasn't long ago that, to most people in Seattle, visiting the Eastside meant packing a picnic lunch and going for a drive in the country. Still, most urban dwellers were familiar with the Eastside mainly as a place to get through on their way to the Cascades.

Today all that has changed. Seattleites zip back and forth across Lake Washington to the east side of the lake (20 minutes one-way, if the traffic gods are with you, over an hour if they're not) without feeling the need to pack a first-aid kit or a canteen. In fact, increasing numbers pack up and move to the Eastside each year and then make the trip across the lake twice a day as commuters.

LEFT: Bellevue's skyline is glassy. **BELOW:** lakeside retreats are classy.

Lake Washington

It's **Lake Washington** ❶ that provides the frame of reference for the term "Eastside," a designation that applies to the very individual cities, towns and rural areas that dot the hills and valleys to the east of the lake. A generally accepted definition of the Eastside includes the cities of Bellevue, Mercer Island, Kirkland, Redmond, Issaquah and Woodinville. As escalating house prices push acceptable commuting times to the outer eastern limits, cities such as North Bend,

Fall City, Duvall and Carnation surface in conversations about the Eastside.

Navigating the waterways and highways of the Eastside requires a few main reference points, most notably the bridges that run east and west across Lake Washington. The **Evergreen Point Floating Bridge** (SR 520) connects downtown Seattle from just south of the University District in northern Seattle to Kirkland and continues on to Redmond.

The **Mercer Island Floating Bridge** (Interstate 90) connects southern Seattle with southern Bellevue via Mercer Island, a residential community about midway across Lake Washington. The main north-south route on the east side of the lake is Interstate 405, which runs the length of the state and goes directly through Bellevue, Kirkland and north on to Bothell and Woodinville. The road eventually ends up in Vancouver, British Columbia, about three hours north across the Canadian border.

In many ways the Eastside owes its development to the bridges that connect it to Seattle in a truly love-hate relationship. These bridges can be the scenes of some of the most horrendous traffic and some of the most spectacular scenery imaginable. In fact, one could probably make a good case that the scenery causes some of the traffic problems. Area residents never seem to grow blasé about the beauty of Lake Washington. A boat skimming the water on a sunny day can still clog traffic on the bridges as motorists slow down to cast envious glances at the scene.

Bellevue

Given the beauty of Lake Washington and the finite aspect of its waterfront, it's no surprise that from **Bellevue** ❷ north to Bothell, waterfront property is prime

BELOW: music in the mall, Bellevue.

real estate. Properties with private docks, private beaches and multi-level houses cascading down the hills can be seen from the highways. They look even more spectacular, unsurprisingly, from the vantage point of a cruiseboat on the lake. (If cruising on the lake, keep a lookout for the mega-mansion in Medina built in the 1990s by Bill Gates, the mega-billionaire founder of Microsoft.)

Bellevue's **Meydenbauer Bay**, an area of luxury homes and condominiums on Lake Washington west of Bellevue's downtown, is named for William Meydenbauer, a Seattle baker. North of Meydenbauer Bay, the exclusive communities of Medina, Yarrow Point and Clyde Hill are other prominent Bellevue-area waterfront places. Public beach access to Lake Washington in Bellevue is limited, but Chism Beach offers swimming, trails and picnic facilities. Other good beaches in Bellevue include Meydenbauer, Newcastle and Enatai.

Aside from Lake Washington, the strongest attraction in Bellevue for visitors is **Bellevue Square**, known to locals as Bel Square. Among the teen set, a day of shopping at Bel Square is known as "squaring off." Opened in 1946 as one of the first suburban shopping centers in the country, Bellevue Square doubled in size in the early 1970s. Take the glass elevator to the top floor and the **Bellevue Art Museum** (open daily; tel: 425-454 3322; admission fee). A delightful surprise to find in a shopping center, the museum specializes in the decorative arts and frequently features traveling national art exhibits.

One of Bellevue's most popular annual events, the Pacific Northwest Arts Fair, began the same year the shopping center opened. What started in 1946 with a few paintings on display on the sidewalk is now one of the largest outdoor art shows in the western United States. Always slated for the last weekend in July (one of the weekends of the year when rain is least likely to fall), the

Map on pages 182–3

Another museum you may want to visit is the Rosalie Whyel Museum of Doll Art. Located in downtown Bellevue, the museum features antique dolls, toys, and miniatures.

BELOW: life on Meydenbauer Bay, Bellevue.

TIP

Public boat launches in both Bellevue and Kirkland make Lake Washington accessible to all kinds of floating vehicles, from sailboats and motorboats to cabin cruisers and canoes.

show attracts artists, exhibitors and the curious from all over North America.

If the performing arts are more to your liking, you'll want to check the schedule of the **Meydenbauer Center**, one of Bellevue's more recent downtown attractions. This convention facility features a 36,000-sq.-ft (3,350-sq.-meter) exhibition hall and a 410-seat performing arts theater.

Across the street from the southern side of Bellevue Square is Bellevue's **Downtown Park**, a 17-acre (7-hectare) site in the heart of the shopping district. It includes a 10-ft-high (3-meter) waterfall, a canal enclosing a large meadow and a 28-ft-wide (8-meter) promenade.

Just south of the park is **Old Bellevue**, the city's main shopping district before the advent of Bel Square. Highlights of the two-block area are a Christmas shop conveniently open year-round, cafeteria-style Mexican café, and several art galleries. Also in Old Bellevue is The Fountain Court, a delightful restaurant serving elegant lunches and dinners in an older home, complete with a picturesque courtyard and fountains. Keep in mind that in Bellevue "old" means dating to about 1940.

At Bellevue's **Kelsey Creek Farm**, pigs, horses, chickens and rabbits can be admired if not appreciated up close, and there are trails, picnic tables, and plenty of room to roam. A Japanese garden dedicated to Bellevue's sister Japanese city of Yao is also located on the farm.

Mercer Island

Named for Aaron Mercer, one of the first two homesteaders in Bellevue, **Mercer Island** ❸ sits directly to the west of Bellevue, about midway in Lake Washington between Bellevue and the southern part of Seattle. A thriving community

BELOW: Bellevue's skyline and towers.

of 21,000, it was incorporated in 1960. There are still people around who remember when Mercer Island was a summertime vacation area accessible only by ferry. The Mercer Island Floating Bridge of Interstate 90 that linked the island to the Eastside and to Seattle changed all that. Today, it's a residential community known for some incredible luxury homes (including the $30 million home built by Microsoft co-founder Paul Allen) and an excellent theater.

Definitely worth a stop on Mercer Island is **Luther Burbank Park**. Originally a private estate, today the park features 77 gorgeous acres (31 hectares) of lake front, tennis courts, an outdoor amphitheater and a playground for kids. Picnic tables, barbecues and a swimming area with sandy beach add up to a great spot for summer fun.

Kirkland

Just north of Bellevue, with much of its shopping, restaurants and commercial areas hugging the shore of Lake Washington, is **Kirkland** ❹. This city of 40,000 has more public access to waterfront through parks, open space and walkways than any other city in the state of Washington; public access to the waterfront has been a priority here since the city was first incorporated in 1905. A walk along Lake Street passes by a series of grassy lakeside parks providing public access to the lake and to numerous waterfront restaurants. The popular Foghorn provides its very own dock for restaurant patrons.

A central part of Kirkland's downtown is **Peter Kirk Park**, with tennis courts, a ball field, one of the few public outdoor swimming pools on the Eastside and a children's playground. On summer evenings, the lighted baseball field is a big draw. Parkplace Shopping Center offers movie theaters, gift shops, a bookstore,

Map on pages 182–3

The region is truly multicultural.

BELOW: outdoor sculpture, Bellevue.

toy stores and a wide variety of places to eat. Downtown, the Antique Heritage Mall displays the merchandise of many dealers. Art walks are periodically scheduled when galleries stay open late, and the public is invited to meet the artists whose work is on display.

Parrot's best friend.

The **Kirkland Creative Arts Center** offers classes and exhibits for children and adults. Kirkland also boasts numerous outdoor art works. **Carillon Point**, a waterfront complex that includes a luxury hotel, restaurants, waterfront walkways and docks as well as shops and restaurants, is a mile or two south of downtown. Two large office towers and a hillside of condominiums caused some initial complaints from nearby residents, but the view from the hotel, the restaurants and the docks is spectacular.

A few miles north of downtown (from the northern end of Lake Street turn left onto Central Way, right onto Market and then left onto Juanita Drive) is **Juanita Bay Beach Park**, a county-run beach complete with summertime lifeguards, roped-off swimming areas and a snack bar. The park is open year-round. There are picnic areas, a children's playground and a series of piers into the lake. Other Kirkland beach parks include O. Denny, Waverly and Houghton. **Bridle Trails State Park**, right in the middle of residential neighborhoods, is a heavily wooded haven for horseback riders and hikers who don't mind sharing their trails with horses. The park is located in south Kirkland near the Bellevue border and can be accessed off 132nd Avenue NE.

Redmond

In the past two decades **Redmond** ❺ has tripled its population to nearly 50,000 people and shows no signs of slowing. Fortunately, there's still enough open

BELOW: sculpture in Kirkland's park.

space in parts of the city for one of its signature activities to continue: hot-air ballooning. Look out toward the northern part of the city along the Sammamish River area on just about any summer or fall evening and chances are you'll see colorful hot air balloons drifting peacefully in the sky. Balloon rides are available from several companies and in varying styles: some offer "red carpet" romantic rides complete with champagne and gourmet lunches or dinners; others offer family prices.

The **Sammamish River** (often called the Sammamish Slough) winds its way south from Bothell to Marymoor Park, passing through Redmond and Woodinville. An asphalt pathway alongside the slough makes a perfect course for bicyclists, and on weekends the place gets quite a mix of visitors with widely varying skills in bicycling.

Toward the southern end of Redmond, the Sammamish River travels past **Marymoor Park**, a 500-acre (200-hectare) county-operated park that includes a museum housed in an old mansion, plus bike and hiking trails. Marymoor is also the home of the **Redmond Velodrome**. One of only six of its kind in the United States, the banked racing course attracts professional cyclists from all around the world.

Since the 1980s, Redmond has probably been best-known around the world as the galactic headquarters of the software colossus Microsoft, unquestionably the Pacific Northwest's most phenomenal business success story. Construction on its 26-acre (10-hectare) corporate campus at One Microsoft Way is continuous, as buildings are continually raised to accommodate Microsoft's ever-expanding workforce. Unfortunately for the curious, ambitious or desperate, the campus is closed to the public and highly guarded.

Map on pages 182–3

By the close of the 20th century, Microsoft was valued at $500,000,000,000 – or half a trillion dollars for those lacking patience to count zeros.

BELOW: favorite lakeside pastime.

The Chateau Ste Michelle Winery.

Woodinville

There are several interesting sights in **Woodinville ❻**, including the **Chateau Ste Michelle Winery**, just west of the Sammamish River and a frequent stop for bicyclists on the slough route. The internationally acclaimed winery, the largest in the state of Washington, has 87 acres (35 hectares) of picnic grounds, a pond with ducks and swans, a tasting room and test vineyards. Musical concerts are staged here each summer and the facilities are popular for weddings and receptions. Tours of the winery's operations (its main vineyards are actually located in eastern Washington) are offered daily, along with free wine tastings. Antique lovers will want to visit a large mall called Woodinville Antique Gallery, located not far from Ste Michelle Winery.

Across the street in a large, gingerbread-style building is **Columbia Winery**, formerly housed near downtown Bellevue and another contender for excellent regional wine. Also in the Woodinville area is the **Silver Lake Winery**, which welcomes visitors with an interest in wine. Although long known for white wines, the wineries of western Washington are increasingly producing finer table wines, both red and white.

From Woodinville hikers can catch the Tolt Pipeline trail, either westward to Bothell or eastward to the Snoqualmie Valley. Its wooded and open terrain makes it a popular hiking spot.

Molbak's Greenhouse and Nursery is probably the most popular downtown stop. Thousands of varieties of plants, a greenhouse, fountains and flowers are the attractions. At Christmas, when the greenhouses are filled with seemingly endless rows of blooming poinsettias, it's a local holiday tradition to head for Molbak's to be photographed against the colorful background.

Below: native carver in Issaquah, and recycling.

Issaquah

Southeast of Bellevue nestled in a valley between Squak, Tiger and Cougar mountains is the little town of **Issaquah ❼**, whose developers decided on a village theme for its shopping center. They scoured the area for old clapboard-style homes, moving them into a village setting at the edge of downtown. Then they built wooden boardwalks, planted flowers and set to work attracting a special kind of retailer. The result is Gilman Village, a "destination shopping center" of specialty shops and restaurants that draws people from many miles away.

Also downtown is the Village Theater, on Front Street, which puts on regular dramatic performances popular with locals. A few blocks east of Gilman Village is Boehm's Candy Kitchen, a family-owned candy-making operation that has been in Issaquah since 1956. Delectable Swiss-style chocolate candies are still made here the old-fashioned, hand-dipped way. Next to Boehm's is a winery, Hedges Cellars, which offers individual and group tastings as well as tours of the winery itself.

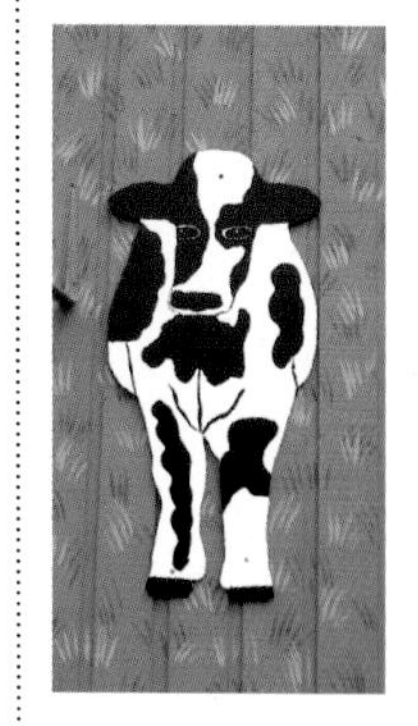

An immortalized contented cow.

Wildlife enthusiasts can enjoy the **Cougar Mountain Zoo** (open Fri–Sun 10am–5pm, Mar to Oct; tel: 425-391 5508; admission fee), formerly known as the Washington Zoological Park. At the **Issaquah State Salmon Hatchery** (tel: 425 391 9094) salmon head up Issaquah Creek via a fish ladder in autumn. The Salmon Days Festival, usually held the first week in October, celebrates the return of the salmon.

Lake Sammamish State Park, just north of downtown Issaquah, provides access to the south shore of Lake Sammamish with its trails, baseball fields, picnic tables and barbecue spots. Lake Sammamish is a popular boating spot in the summer, despite the incessant engine noise from the boats of waterskiers.

BELOW: contented cows in Carnation.

Map on pages 182–3

Further to the east

Continuing past Issaquah on Interstate 90, the farther east one travels, the more rural the experiences can become. In the Carnation and Fall City areas, for example, there's enough to merit at least one full day's visit, if not an entire weekend. Snoqualmie Falls is a dramatic sight that is worth considering.

In the heart of the scenic Snoqualmie Valley in **Carnation** ❽, Carnation Farms is sometimes open to the public, except in winter. Known as the home of the contented cows, this is a 900-acre (360-hectare) working dairy farm where free, self-guided tours lead through the maternity and calf barn, petting area, milking parlor and formal gardens. The tour takes about 40 minutes and can be topped off by making use of the picnic facilities in nearby John A. MacDonald Memorial Park.

One mile south of the town of Carnation is Remlinger U-Pick Farms, a great place to stop and prove to the kids that there really is some connection between the land and the food they eat. Here, during summer months one can pick berries and take them home in buckets. Remlinger offers fruits and vegetables aplenty, a restaurant, viewing and petting farm, and frequently a new litter of kittens or puppies that will soon be looking for good homes.

Not far away in **Fall City** is the Herbfarm, a combination of working herb farm, country store and nursery. Highlights include 16 herbal theme gardens and special events keyed to major holidays. The gourmet restaurant, burned down in 1997 but reopened in 1999, focuses on edible herbs and plants grown on the premises. There are also regular classes held on the farm in the growing, use and crafting of herbs.

Duvall, the outer limits of the Eastside, celebrates its rural atmosphere with Duvall Days every spring, the weekend after Mothers' Day. The one-street downtown area sports several antique stores. A street fair, parade and pancake breakfast highlight the annual celebration.

BELOW: another Seattle-area smile.

Into the mountains

Seattle's location induces a euphoria of the outdoors in most residents and visitors. If one doesn't take to the water that embraces the city, mountains beckon. To the east of the city are the Cascades. If wanting to explore just a bit further, consider heading east a little more. (*For more incisive excursions into the mountains, see* The Cascades *chapter, pages 255–60.*)

Worth a visit is sensational **Snoqualmie Falls** ❾, a fine 268-ft (82-meter) avalanche of water (100 ft/30 meters higher than Niagara Falls), above which sits the internationally famous **Salish Lodge**, known worldwide for its appearance in the *Twin Peaks* television series but better known locally for its fabulous Paul Bunyan-size country brunches. The small town of **North Bend**, on Interstate 90, is where much of the television series was shot, and where the former Mar-T Cafe became known for cherry pies.

While fall-gazing is about the only pastime here, 25 miles (40 km) further is 3,022-ft (921-meter) **Snoqualmie Pass**, a good place for finding trailheads into the mountains or skiing at the three easily accessible winter ski areas near the summit. ❑

Wines

The Pacific Northwest is known for its pioneering spirit, as is its wine industry. The Northwest's wineries have established themselves in world tasting circles in just a couple of decades; no small feat for an industry known for its picky noses. The region had fewer than 10 wineries in 1975; today there are well over 200. In fact, the Northwest is the nation's second-largest producer of *vitis vinifera* grapes – the premium European wine varieties, including cabernet sauvignon, pinot noir, chardonnay and merlot.

While often processed in the Seattle region, Washington-grown grapes are mostly nurtured on the eastern side of the Cascades in an arid environment featuring long, warm, sunny days and cool nights. Washington leads the Northwest in wine and grape production. Just a little over 10 percent of the estimated 150,000 acres (60,000 hectares) in the state suitable for vineyards are used. Oregon wines, in contrast, are grown on the western side of the mountains, in the wetter Willamette Valley, likened to a cooler, wetter Napa Valley in California. Despite the diversity of growing conditions between Oregon and Washington, the Northwest is the only region in the United States – outside of California, of course – where growing conditions are considered ideal for premium wine grapes.

Northwest wineries are primarily family-owned operations, tucked into farmland, hillsides, forests of fir, or sagebrush-dotted desert and defined by the Cascade Range.

Washington's potential for premium wine was "discovered" in 1966 when renowned wine critic Andre Tchelistcheff first sampled a homemade Washington Gewurztraminer and called it the best produced in the U.S. In 1974, a 1972 Chateau Ste Michelle Johannisberg riesling won first place in a blind tasting by the *Los Angeles Times*.

Seattle-area wineries: Several wineries and tasting rooms are convenient to Seattle. Chateau Ste Michelle, the largest winery in the Pacific Northwest, has its headquarters in Woodinville, in Eastside (*see Eastside chapter, page 185*). Fashioned after a French country manor, over 200,000 people visit it annually. Nearby Columbia Winery is one of the oldest wineries in the state. It also owns the Paul Thomas Winery in Bellevue. Another Woodinville winery is French Creek Cellars, with a salmon creek and picnic area.

Puget Sound wineries: A bit farther from Seattle, the wineries of the Puget Sound area are still within a couple of hours of the city. Snoqualmie Winery is sited within a mile of the magnificent Snoqualmie Falls (*see Eastside chapter, page 194*). Quilceda Creek Vintners, just a few miles from the rural Snohomish community of Quilceda, is open by appointment only. Owner Alex Golitzen's winemaking talents were nurtured by his uncle, world-famous winemaker and critic Andre Tchelistcheff. Bainbridge Island Winery, on one of the main ferry routes to the Olympic Peninsula, is open for tastings several days a week. The rugged Olympic Mountains offer a dramatic backdrop for the appropriately named Olympic Cellars, nestled near the harbor town of Port Angeles. ❑

RIGHT: easy drinking.

D
E
EXIT 133
SOUTH NORTH
City Center
MUST EXIT

MUST
EXIT

SOUTH OF SEATTLE

The corridor south from Seattle to Olympia, the oft-forgotten government seat of Washington, begins with old airplanes and the international airport and ends with the sleepiest of capitals

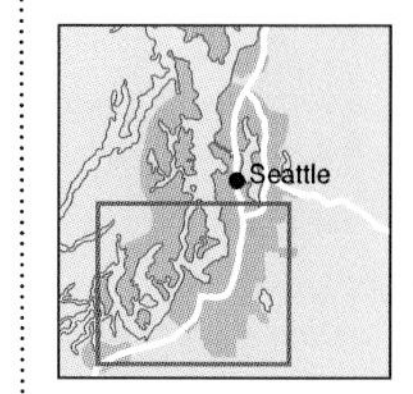

A region of challenging contrasts, the region south of Seattle is a place of rapid growth yet enduring natural beauty. Once largely overlooked by travelers, the area increasingly rivals Seattle as a destination. Whether or not one has a particular interest in the technology that brings people to Seatac, no visit to Seattle is complete without a visit to the **Museum of Flight** ⑩ (open daily, 10am–5pm; tel: 206-764 5720; admission fee), at **Boeing Field**, just south of Seattle.

The museum's impressive collection – the largest on the west coast – represents the entire aircraft industry, not just the local influence on it. Occupying the original Boeing building known as the Red Barn – built in 1909 as part of a shipyard along the Duwamish River – and the adjacent Great Gallery, built in the 1980s, the museum chronicles the history of human flight. Inside the Red Barn are a few restored early planes, historical photographs and drawings. The gallery features a main hall with 6-floor-high ceilings from which hang an assortment of flying craft, ranging from hang-gliders to fighter jets, including an F-104 Starfighter and a Russian MiG 21. Interesting exhibits include an airplane car that looks like (and in fact is) a shiny, red sports car with wings; a flight simulator (actually, a simulation of a simulator); and, just outside the gallery, the country's first presidential jet, a Boeing 707. From the museum is a clear view of Boeing's airfield, where commercial aircraft produced by Boeing are prepped and tested prior to delivery to an airline.

As most visitors usually arrive in Seattle by air, they will first touch down in one of the state's newest cities – aptly, if unpoetically, named **Seatac**, after the **Sea-Tac International Airport** ⑪, a hybrid name culled from Seattle and Tacoma.

PRECEDING PAGES: Tacoma Dome.
LEFT: meditating for the right meow.
BELOW: the B52 was built here.

Renton

Renton ⑫, a city of 65,000 at the southern end of Lake Washington, is home to two Boeing facilities producing 737 and 757 jets and a municipal airport. Among its attractive green offerings is Liberty Park beside the Cedar River, the site for the annual Renton River Days, and Gene Coulon Memorial Beach Park, on the lake. The **Renton Historical Museum** (open daily, 1–4pm, 9am–4pm Tues, closed Mon; tel: 425 255 2339; donation), not far from Liberty Park, recounts the city's birth as Black River Bridge, a coal-mining community. On view are a number of old photographs and some mining equipment, as well as maps showing the mining shafts that criss-cross under the expensive contemporary homes now perched on Renton Hill.

The valley around **Kent** ⑬, south of Renton and which used to produce much of the Puget Sound area's agriculture, is fast becoming one of the world's largest trade distribution centers, with countless manufacturing plants and warehouses. Farther south are

Even here, in the most developed region of the state, nature is never far away. Rent a canoe or kayak and put in at one of several spots along the Duwamish River to follow the river back to its source.

the waterfront communities of Normandy Park (where many Boeing employees live) and Des Moines, named by a founder from Des Moines, Iowa, who persuaded friends in the Midwest to finance his venture in 1887.

Federal Way ⓮, south of Seattle along Interstate 5 and named for federally funded Highway 99, was incorporated in 1990. It is home to Dash Point State Park and the Wild Waves Water Park and Enchanted Village, popular summer attractions for children. Also in Federal Way are the **Rhododendron Species Botanical Gardens** (open daily, except Thur, seasonal hours; tel: 253-661 9377; admission fee), at Weyerhauser Corporate Headquarters. One of the world's largest collections of rhododendron species, the 22-acre (9-hectare) gardens feature 450 varieties of the rhododendron – the state flower of Washington – from the 100-ft-high (30-meter) trees of the lower Himalaya to the ground-hugging species of Tibet and China. Adjacent to the rhododendron gardens is the **Pacific Rim Bonsai Collection** (open daily, seasonal hours; tel: 253-924 3153; free), with more than 50 examples of bonsai plants from Asia and North America.

Tacoma

Just south of Federal Way and an hour's drive south of Seattle, **Tacoma** ⓯ is the state's third-largest city, with around 200,000 people. Approaching the city with the bay in front and Mount Rainier behind, one can understand why the city founders had such high hopes for Tacoma. It is one of the few cities with a setting that rivals – surpasses, locals would argue – Seattle in beauty. In the quality and variety of its architecture, Tacoma also stands out; just about every major architectural style of the past 100 years, from neo-classical to art deco to post-modernism, can be found in the city and in many adjoining neighborhoods.

BELOW: a typical Victorian house.

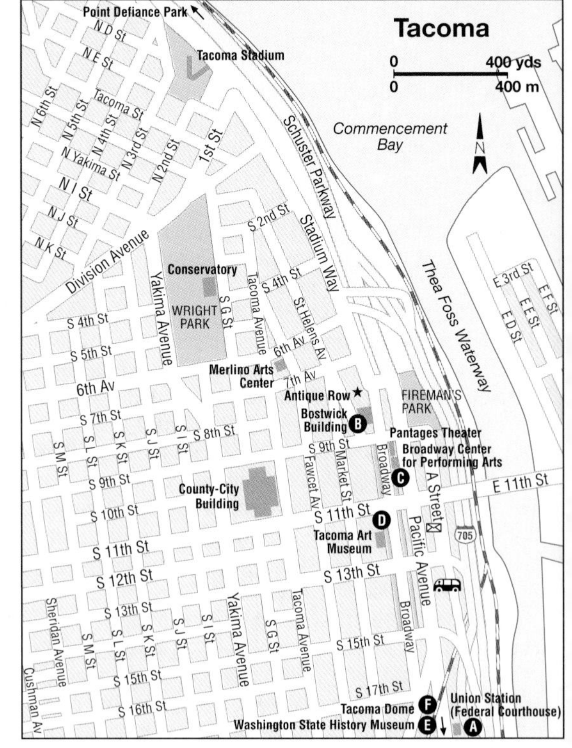

Maps:
Area 182
City 200

Originally named Commencement City – after Commencement Bay, in turn named because it was the origin of an 1841 surveying expedition – Tacoma was named after the Nisqually and Puyallup tribal name for Mount Rainier, 40 miles (65 km) to the southeast. It began as a 19th-century timber boomtown that in its 1890s heyday rivaled Seattle in importance. But the city went bust in the nationwide slump of 1893 and has been trying to catch up with Seattle ever since. In its heady, early days, Tacoma dubbed itself the City of Destiny, but for much of the 20th century, Tacoma's nickname has seemed amusingly at odds with reality. Its smelly air (known as "Tacoma Aroma" and derived from pulp-mill emissions), crime rate, and defunct downtown have long made it the designated butt of Seattle jokes.

People who mock Tacoma haven't been paying attention lately. Quietly and without much notice, Tacoma has been transforming itself from a blue-collar mill town with bad air, downtown decay, and LA-style gangs to an economically diverse and environmentally aware city with a vibrant cultural life. The economic center of a larger metropolitan area of more than 600,000 people, Tacoma serves as a major port facility in the Pacific Northwest and as a gateway to two of the Northwest's most popular attractions: the Olympic Peninsula and Mount Rainier National Park (*see pages 229 and 255*).

After a suburban mall stole business from the city center in the 1960s, downtown Tacoma was on its way to becoming an architecturally interesting ghost town. An effort to revive downtown is bringing back commerce and culture to the city center. To the surprise of no one who has been watching Tacoma's quiet rebirth, the magazine *Money* in 1998 rated it the second-best medium-sized city in the West. (First place went to Boulder, prompting the local quip: Who would want to live in a place named after a rock rather than a mountain?) Yet

Traffic in Tacoma's efficient harbor.

BELOW: Tacoma's setting rivals Seattle's.

Good rock and roll at the Java Jive.

despite the changes, Tacoma stubbornly holds on to its unpretentious, slightly eccentric ways. One can still get a burger and shake at Frisko Freeze and listen to rock and roll at the coffee-cup-shaped Java Jive.

Today, an energetic preservation movement is finding new uses for Tacoma's old buildings and breathing new life into the city center. The movement began with the transformation of the long-vacant Beaux Arts **Union Station** Ⓐ into an elegant venue for the Federal courthouse. Across the street, once-empty warehouses serve as the locale for a new University of Washington campus.

On Broadway, at the entry to so-called Antique Row, the triangular-shaped **Bostwick Building** Ⓑ, built in 1889 as a hotel, has been revitalized downstairs as a popular coffee shop and jazz club; antique stores and specialty shops make up the rest of the block. A brass plaque on the Bostwick makes an eccentric claim to fame. It was here, during a meeting of the Washington Commandery of the Loyal Legion of the United States in 1893, that civil war veteran Russell O'Brien began the tradition of standing during the national anthem.

Cultural attractions

A lively arts scene also contributes to the downtown revival. The **Broadway Center for the Performing Arts** Ⓒ puts on dance, music and stage productions at the restored Pantages and Rialto theaters and at the post-modernist Theater On the Square. A 1,100-seater vaudeville palace dating back to 1916, the ornate Panatages is the oldest building designed by B. Marcus Priteca, a European-trained architect noted for his neo-classical style and the designer of more than 150 theaters throughout North America.

Housed in a former downtown bank, the small but ambitious **Tacoma Art**

BELOW: former Northern Pacific headquarters and the old city hall.

Museum **D** (open daily except Mon, 10am-5pm; tel: 253-272 4258; admission fee) hosts a number of good traveling exhibitions and is building one of the world's top collections of works by Northwest artists; on permanent display is a collection of glass works by world-renowned, Tacoma-born artist Dale Chihuly. The museum, slated to move in 2002 into a new building designed by architect Antoine Predock, bills itself as "interactive". Visitors, inspired by the art they have seen, can make art in a studio downstairs using professional material provided free of charge. The **Washington State History Museum** **E** (open daily, 10am–6pm; tel: 888-238 4373; admission fee), housed in a handsome brick building next to Union Station, has a large collection of pioneer and American Indian exhibits from the Pacific Northwest.

Popular culture and sports have a venue at the **Tacoma Dome** **F**. Built in 1983 in the old warehouse district, the 152-ft-tall (46-meter) dome, one of the world's largest wooden-domed structures, is known for its good acoustics. A popular venue for rock acts, the arena seats up to 27,000 people and has hosted events ranging from the Billy Graham Crusade and the Spice Girls to truck-and-tractor pulls. Because it is city-owned, the dome can also afford to occasionally host local – and unprofitable – events: A night of wrestling at the Tacoma Dome does not necessarily mean Hulk Hogan and professional wrestling; it might mean local high school wrestlers vying for the state championship.

If you dislike malls, consider a mall that isn't one. A 10-minute walk from the dome, **Freighthouse Square** is a contradiction in terms: a mom-and-pop mall. A freighthouse for the Milwaukee/St. Paul Railroad in the early 1900s, the three-block-long building was converted in 1987 into a marketplace. Managed by the owner with assistance from his mother, Freighthouse Square is made up

Maps:
Area 182
City 200

While Tacoma's economy is focused on lumber, the city also has shipyards, smelters, and food-processing facilities. Its waterfront is of docks and wharves.

BELOW: Mount Rainier and Tacoma Dome.

Stadium High School, featured in the 1999 film Ten Things I Hate About You.

of small specialty stores, New Age health services, and an international food court with everything from Korean barbecue to Greek salads.

Tacoma is made up of diverse and distinctive residential neighborhoods. The oldest, North End, is evidence of Tacoma's glory days when the new city on the hill held promise of becoming the West Coast's center of industry and finance. Stroll along broad, tree-lined Yakima Avenue past colonnaded mansions built by Tacoma's 19th-century industrial barons. The neighborhood's most famous building (at 111 North E Street) is a French chateau lookalike, complete with towers and turrets. The building was begun by the Northern Pacific Railroad in 1891 as a hotel for its passengers after Tacoma became the terminus for the railroad; before the building was finished, the railroad went bankrupt and the hotel became (and still is) Stadium High School. Scenes from the 1999 movie *Ten Things I Hate About You*, a 1990s teen take on *The Taming of the Shrew*, were filmed at Stadium.

Below the North End, along the south shore of Commencement Bay, **Ruston Way** has trails, parks and piers as well as enough waterfront restaurants to earn it the nickname Restaurant Row. Follow Ruston Way inland a few miles to one of Tacoma's most appealing landmarks, **Point Defiance Park** ⓰. Located on a finger of land jutting out into Puget Sound, the 700-acre (280-hectare) wilderness park is one of the largest urban parks in the United States. It offers formal gardens, a swimming beach, a replica of a 19th-century trading post, a children's storybook park, a zoo and aquarium, and a logging camp, complete with a 1929 steam train that chugs around the camp.

BELOW: dolphin at the Point Defiance Aquarium.

Founded in 1888, the **Point Defiance Zoo and Aquarium** is both animal- and people-friendly; it isn't unusual to encounter a llama, a pig or even an elephant on an afternoon walk with its keeper. With a Pacific Rim focus, the zoo is internationally renowned for its humane and innovative approach.

On the west side of Tacoma, the **Tacoma Narrows Bridge** ⓱ is the fifth-largest suspension bridge in the world. The original bridge, constructed in 1940 across the Tacoma Narrows, was dubbed Galloping Gertie because of its tendency to undulate in the winds that whipped through the narrows. Gertie galloped too much, however, and just a few months after opening collapsed. ("We knew Gertie would make a splash," said a local wit, "but not this kind.") Sections of the old bridge and the marine life that it attracts now draw scuba divers to the cold waters far below the present-day 5,979-ft-long (1,822-meter) bridge, which has been firmly in place since 1950. Just across the Narrows Bridge is **Gig Harbor** ⓲, a lovely harbor town with old-fashioned specialty shops and restaurants and several bed-and-breakfast inns.

Puyallup

This is one of those Washington place names whose pronunciation separates locals from outlanders: *pyew-allup*. Although much of the surrounding farmlands has been lined with strip malls, **Puyallup** ⓳ is still primarily a farming community. In the 1880s, the fertile valley was the world's largest producer of hops, the plant used for brewing beer. Most of the hops from here were exported to Europe. Later, hop yards were converted to berry and rhubarb farms. Today, the area produces daffodils, tulips and Christmas trees.

An effort to revive the downtown has brought back some of the small-town ambience, lost a few years ago when a mall was built on the outskirts of town. Contributing to the effort is the Arts Downtown program, a changing exhibit of outdoor art by local and outside artists. Displayed in parks, shops, and in front of public buildings, the pieces range from a local artist's rendition of his pet pig, assembled from pieces of scrap metal, to an elegant tribute in bronze to a mother's love by a Russian-born artist from Olympia.

So many of Puyallup's older buildings have been torn down that a walking tour of historic buildings is sometimes called the parking-lot tour. Yet the town is in the process of painstakingly restoring the Ezra Meeker mansion, a 17-room, Italianate Victorian house built in 1890 by Puyallup's first mayor. Meeker's importance is more than just local. In 1906, 54 years after crossing the Oregon Trail in a covered wagon, Meeker made the trip in reverse at age 76, clearing the overgrown trail and marking it in stone for posterity; some of his markers still remain. He continued on his eastward journey, by foot and covered wagon, until he reached Washington, D.C.

Maps on pages 182–3

During Steilacoom's popular Apple Squeeze festival in October, antique hand-cranked apple presses make fresh cider, while barbershop quartets make old-time music.

Steilacoom

A 20-minute drive southeast of Tacoma, **Steilacoom** ⑳ (pronounced *stilacum*) is Washington's oldest incorporated town. It is hard to believe that this small waterfront village was once a busy frontier port and governmental seat. Steilacoom boasts an impressive list of firsts, claiming, among other things, the first Protestant church in Washington Territory, the first school, drugstore, and library in the county, and the first courthouse north of Colombia. It is also one of the first places in the area to develop a sense of its own historic importance. Years ago, its preservation-minded citizens registered the downtown as a national historic site, ensuring that Steilacoom would escape development. The town's old drugstore, Bair Drug & Hardware – a combination pharmacy, hardware store, post office and gathering place – has been turned into a museum and cafe. The museum displays patent medicines and other original drugstore items, while the cafe serves ice-cream sodas from the store's 1906 marble-topped soda fountain.

The small but interesting **Steilacoom Historical Museum** (open daily except Mon, 1–4pm; tel: 253-584 4133; donations) meticulously documents early town life with realistic displays of a living room, kitchen and parlor in a late 1890s-era home. At the block's other end, the **Steilacoom Tribal Museum** (open daily except Mon, 10am–4pm; tel: 253-584 6308; admission fee) tells the story of the American Indian in the state from the tribal point of view and is one of the few tribal-run museums in the state.

BELOW: the Art of hamburgers.

Olympia

Thirty miles (50 km) south of Tacoma at the southernmost point of Puget Sound, the Washington state capital of **Olympia** ㉑ brings to mind a comment made about another capital, Washington, D.C. – it's a city for people who don't like cities. The city's low-rise architecture – nothing is more than a few stories high – and leisurely pace gives the place a friendly, small-town feel, while Evergreen State College, a progressive liberal arts college established in 1972, provides enough of a countercultural edge to keep things interesting.

After Washington became a territory in 1853, Olympia was named the capital and spent the next 40 years fighting off claims to the title by Vancouver, Tacoma and Seattle, among others. It wasn't until 1890 that Olympia was officially named Washington's state capital, but it took another 60 or so years for it to wrestle several state government offices away from Seattle.

The Capitol area

It is easy to forget that Olympia is a state capital until confronting the **State Capitol** Ⓐ grounds. The beautifully landscaped grounds and stately buildings, on a hill overlooking the water with the snow-capped Cascades in the distance, make it one of most impressive capital sites in the country.

Dominating the 55-acre (22-hectare) campus is the Legislative Building. Built in 1927, the handsome Romanesque structure, with its 287-ft (87-meter) dome, brings to mind the capitol building in Washington, D.C. The chandelier hanging in the rotunda was designed by Louis Tiffany, an American artist and designer who established a firm in New York specializing in glass work and whose father founded the venerable Tiffany and Company. Under it, embedded in the floor, is the state seal with an image of George Washington worn smooth from the feet of visitors. Harry Truman, on a visit to the capital during his presidency in the late 1940s, objected to the defacing and ever since the state seal has been cordoned off.

BELOW: State Capitol building in Olympia.

Other buildings include the 1908 governor's mansion, the state library, which houses a collection of art work by Northwest artists, and the state greenhouse, providing all of the flowers and plants for the capital complex. War memorials and works of sculpture also grace the grounds.

On the edge of the capitol grounds, the **Hands-On Children's Museum** (open daily except Mon, 10am–5pm; admission fee) offers enough activities to keep children busy for an afternoon. A few blocks south, in a residential neighborhood of lovely old homes, adults can learn about Washington's early history at the **Washington State Capitol Museum** Ⓑ (open daily except Mon, 10am–4pm; tel: 360-753 2580; admission fee), housed in an 1920s Renaissance Revival-style mansion. Among the museum's American Indian artifacts is a collection of rare baskets by the Nisqually, Puyallup and Skokomish, all tribes of southern Puget Sound.

Olympia is a town where people hang out, and one of the oldest hang-outs is the Spar Restaurant, dating from 1935. Even write-ups in *The New York Times* have not turned this eatery, with its exceptionally long counter, into just a tourist spot. Today, it remains a popular gathering place for locals, although its demographics have shifted with the times. Once filled with millworkers and longshoremen, today the Spar harbors state government workers, civil servants, attorneys, retirees and college students.

Tourists and locals mingle at **Percival Landing Park**Ⓒ, a waterfront park and boardwalk, lined along its 1½ miles (2.5 km) with shops, restaurants and cafes. Next to the landing is the state's largest farmer's market. In a pole-frame barn, more than 80 vendors sell local produce and homemade crafts and foods. Rated one of the six best farmer's markets in the U.S. by the *Financial Times* of London, the market is also the site of summer music festivals. ❑

Maps: Area 182 City 207

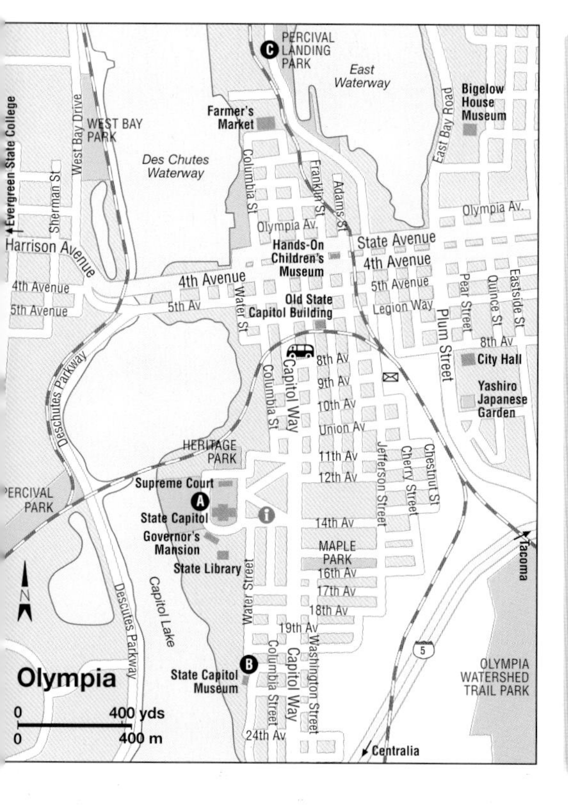

BELOW: container ship unloading.

Map on pages 182–3

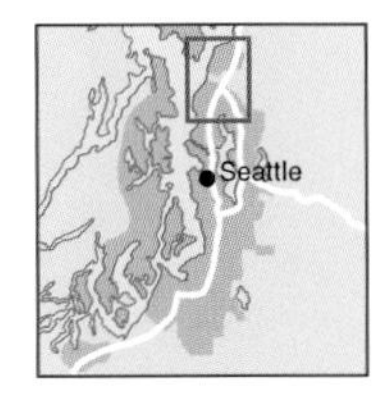

North of Seattle

Increasingly sought out by Seattle residents as a place to set down their roots, the northern towns of Bothell, Edmonds and Everett lure with subtlety and understated growth

After Seattle was named America's "most livable city" by *Money* magazine in 1989, much of Puget Sound's young and affluent population settled in the suburbs outside of the city limits, searching for that emblem of prosperity known as "quality of life." Indeed, from the northern frontier of Seattle at 145th Street to the city of Everett, 25 miles (40 km) north on Gardner Bay, a stretch of satellite communities with award-winning parks and progressive public schools seem to offer the culmination of migratory dreams.

Now, these bedroom communities on the northern tip of King County and the southern stretch of Snohomish County are some of the hottest growth regions in the nation – rapidly developing expanses of verdant rolling hills, tiny lakes and major streams. Snohomish County remains the fastest-growing county in the United States, its population of over half a million people still rising.

The earliest settlers – mill owners, homesteaders and land developers – relied on a steamship line known as the Mosquito Fleet for transport up and down Puget Sound, but railroads and electric trolleys soon speeded up the flow of goods and passengers. Today's commuters head to their jobs in downtown Seattle or, more likely, to any of the seven business parks on Technology Corridor, a path of commercial communities stretching along Interstate 405 between

Below: loading grain from the interior farmlands.

Bothell and Everett. The best known of the corridor's resident companies is Microsoft. More than 300 electronic, telecommunications and computer businesses cluster in campus-like neighborhoods where high-tech execs walk along groomed bike paths at lunch or work out in the company gym after hours.

Bothell ㉒ is the gateway to the corridor, a town of 12,500 people northeast of Lake Washington and nestled in the winding Sammamish River Valley, only 30 minutes' drive from Seattle or the Boeing plant in Everett. The Sammamish River biking and hiking trail joins the Burke-Gilman Trail (*see* North Seattle *chapter, page 155*) in Bothell and curves along 33 acres (13 hectares) of wetlands south of the river – a natural habitat for wildlife – and continues uninterrupted to Marymoor Park on the east side of Lake Washington. The trail connects by a pedestrian bridge to the north side of the river, where Bothell Landing serves as a focal point for the community.

The floats of a float plane, so common in the Seattle area (and not to be confused with a seaplane), can support 180 percent of the plane's maximum weight and are divided into seven compartments, assuring buoyancy even if one or more are damaged.

Recreational areas

Also in the vicinity is **Kenmore**, best known for its watersports, a spectacular view of Lake Washington, and the Kenmore Air Harbor, the country's largest seaplane base (with scheduled flights to Victoria and Vancouver, in British Columbia). **Mill Creek**, especially affluent, began as a contained community when, in 1976, almost 3,000 homes were developed around a country club and private 18-hole golf course, tennis courts, swimming pools and nature preserve. It was incorporated as a city in 1983.

The National Park Service awarded a commendation to the town of **Mountlake Terrace** for its parks and recreation system – a lavish sprinkling of little neighborhood parks, pocket parks and a 9-hole golf course on Lake Ballinger.

BELOW: service at Kenmore Aviation.

The largest and one of the fastest growing commercial and manufacturing centers in the north is **Lynnwood**, sporting a large middle-class population, a good percentage of whom are commuters. Nearly half a million cars pass through the intersection at 196th Street and 37th Avenue daily, which is rated in traffic terms as "Level F", or beyond gridlock.

The only truly rural community around here is **Brier**, a small town of fewer than 1,000 people whose strict no-growth policy means that there are only two grocery stores, one café and occasional horse traffic on the main street.

Edmonds

Flower boxes and hanging planters dot the main street of **Edmonds** ㉓, the self-proclaimed "Gem of Puget Sound," a modern community of more than 30,000 on the shore 15 miles (24 km) north of Seattle. Property values here are such that probably few people under 40 can afford the taxes, much less the mortgage payments, in this growth-resistant town, and thus few big business interests bother with the area. But Edmonds, aiming to be the artsy-craftsy town of the Northwest, doesn't mind. Residents know that their prestigious Amtrak station, ferry terminal, waterfront shops, restaurants and stylish parks will continue to draw weekend visitors.

One of three waterfront parks in Edmonds' **Brackett's Landing** features the oldest and most popular underwater park in the state of Washington, dedicated as a marine preserve in 1971. Divers can explore the 300-ft-long (90-meter) DeLion dry dock, which dropped to the sandy bottom in 1935, and numerous other sunken structures. The dock creates a maze-like haven for schools of fish and plant life.

Visitors are encouraged to feel the texture of leaves, needles and tree bark at **Sierra Park**, innovatively designed with the aroma and fragrance of plants in mind. The park provides paths and braille signs for sight-impaired visitors. Views from Marina Beach include the Unocal oil refinery loading dock at Edwards Point just off the beach to the south and the port of Edmonds to the north. At Olympic Beach, inspect the sea-lion sculpture and watch activities at the **Edmonds Fishing Pier**, open year-round to fishing.

Other parks along this stretch of waterfront include the woodsy Meadowdale Beach Park and the high, sandy cliffs of Norma Beach Boathouse. At the center of Edmonds is **Old Mill Town**, a living museum with historic mementos, shops and the prosperous Edmonds Antique Mall, built in the old shingle mill, a wood building with plank floors and looming timbers. Among Edmonds' cultural attractions is a community theater featuring theater and a symphony.

The late U.S. Senator Henry "Scoop" M. Jackson spent most of his life in Everett until his death in 1984; the pristine Jackson Mansion remains the pride of the city.

Everett

Tacoma lumberman Henry Hewitt hoped the Great Northern Railroad would locate its western terminus where **Everett** ㉔ sits today. He persuaded investors to develop an industrial timber site on Port Gardner Bay, but although the town boomed in 1891, it went bust almost immediately afterward. This cycle continued to haunt the town through the next century. Eventually the city's emphasis on lumber shifted to an economy based on high-technology operations.

In 1966, Boeing constructed what was then the world's largest building, the **Boeing Assembly Plant** in Everett. Boeing now employs over 20,000 workers in its aircraft plant on a parcel of land next to **Paine Field**, a fog-free commuter airport. Half a dozen jumbo jets fit inside of the structure. Boeing, of course, came into being in the 1930s in Seattle, and was the world's largest manufacturer of commercial aircraft in the second half of the 20th century, its dominance blunted in the 1990s by the European consortium Airbus. Long the area's prime employer, its economy defined the Seattle area's economy. ❑

RIGHT: high-tech shadows.

FURTHER AFIELD

One of the main reasons people live in Seattle is, ironically, the ease with which they can go somewhere else

Escaping the urban bustle can be as easy as a brief trip on a ferry to nearby Bainbridge Island, or as bracing as a trek lasting several days across the majestic Olympic Mountains.

Toss a slightly mashed hat into the waters of Puget Sound, claims one writer, and it resembles the Olympic Peninsula. The tip of this peninsula is Mount Olympus, which towers 7,965 ft (2,428 meters) over the surrounding mountains. The crown is the 922,000-acre (401,000-hectare) Olympic National Park, with glacial rivers that roar down the folds to empty into the Pacific Ocean, the Strait of Juan de Fuca and Puget Sound itself. This park encompasses what may be the last remaining wilderness forest on the United States mainland. Wildlife, both in the mountains and on the shore, is abundant. Among the animals common to the area is the Olympic short-tailed weasel, around enough but found nowhere else in the world.

A good measure of rain and fog, coupled with a mild coastal climate, are the essential ingredients of a temperate rain forest. Sitka spruce are the dominant trees in Olympic National Park, and record-sized specimens are much in evidence. The overall impression is one of 80-ft high trees draped in moss, shot through by hazy sunlight. One of the first expeditions to cross the Olympic Mountains on foot took nearly six months, but now, over 100 years later, you can do it in four or five days.

On the way to the peninsula are picturesque towns, one of which, Port Townsend, was designed to be the city Seattle has become today. In the mid-19th century, Port Townsend was set to become the great port of Puget Sound. But when Union Pacific's trans-continental railroad failed to connect to the Port Townsend Southern Railroad, this community faded into elegant obscurity. It has been revived only in the past few decades.

The jewels of Puget Sound are the San Juan Islands. This archipelago gets more sunshine than the surrounding area, so in winter the weather is pleasant; in summer it's even better. Commercial ferries stop at four of the San Juans, which, if time allows, you should definitely explore.

Jagged mountain peaks, temperate rain forests, Victorian towns and remote, sandy islands: all of these are just a few hours from downtown Seattle. "We'll take you to someplace special," is the boast of Washington State Ferries' ads. But, in fact, you may just be there already. ❑

PRECEDING PAGES: sailing the Sound; a Northwest anemone field.
LEFT: seals off Lopez Island in the San Juans.

ACROSS PUGET SOUND

Just minutes and a ferry ride away from downtown Seattle are rural countryside, a naval shipyard and nuclear submarine base, and smallish towns laced with the traditions of Scandinavia

A good ferry system, a few artfully placed bridges, and excellent roadways link Seattle to the nearby islands, peninsulas and network of waterways that surround the city. Day trips can easily extend into longer excursions, as each point of interest leads to another, and all roads – and ferries – lead in a scenic route back to Seattle.

Some of the islands are developed and offer the usual amenities. Others allow an escape into the semblance of wild without an expedition into the outback. Accessible only by boat, the small, uninhabited island of Blake, for example, has a park with 16 miles (26 km) of trails and driftwood-strewn beaches; deer and bald eagles are among the park wildlife. Believed to be the birthplace of Chief Sealth, the Salish tribal chief for whom Seattle is named, Blake is the locale for Tillicum Village. Designed as a tourist attraction in the early 1960s, Tillicum Village features a Northwest American Indian longhouse, where guests lunch on salmon, baked in the traditional fashion on cedar stakes over alder fires, and watch a dance that interprets tribal myths and legends.

LEFT: Puget Sound is for the birds. **BELOW:** at anchor with Mount Rainier.

Bainbridge Island

Jurisdictionally, nearby **Bainbridge Island** ❶ belongs to rural Kitsap County (to which it is connected by Route 305), but culturally the increasingly upscale island, with its pricey homes and proliferating BMWs, is closer to Seattle, a pleasant 35-minute ferry ride away. At the end of the 19th century, little Bainbridge was home to the world's largest sawmill, at Port Blakely. Later, the economy turned to berry farming. Many of the farmers were Japanese immigrants – arriving in the 1880s as laborers at sawmills and later becoming farmers – whose internment in government camps (in California but mostly in Idaho) during World War II is the subject of a 1995 best-selling novel, *Snow Falling on Cedars*, by Bainbridge resident David Guterson.

The farmers, fishermen and wealthy "summer people" from Seattle who once populated the island are being replaced by Seattle-commuting professionals, artists, writers and retirees. The big berry farms that once anchored the island's economy are gone, though there are enough small farms left to justify a summer strawberry festival put on by the local Filipino-American community. Most of the summer homes have been turned into year-round residences or bed-and-breakfast inns.

Winslow, the island's only incorporated town, is a tidy cluster of gift shops, cafes and restaurants, with a hardware store, a drugstore and a Thriftway to remind visitors that people actually live here. A few miles inland, on Route 305, **Bainbridge Island Vineyards**

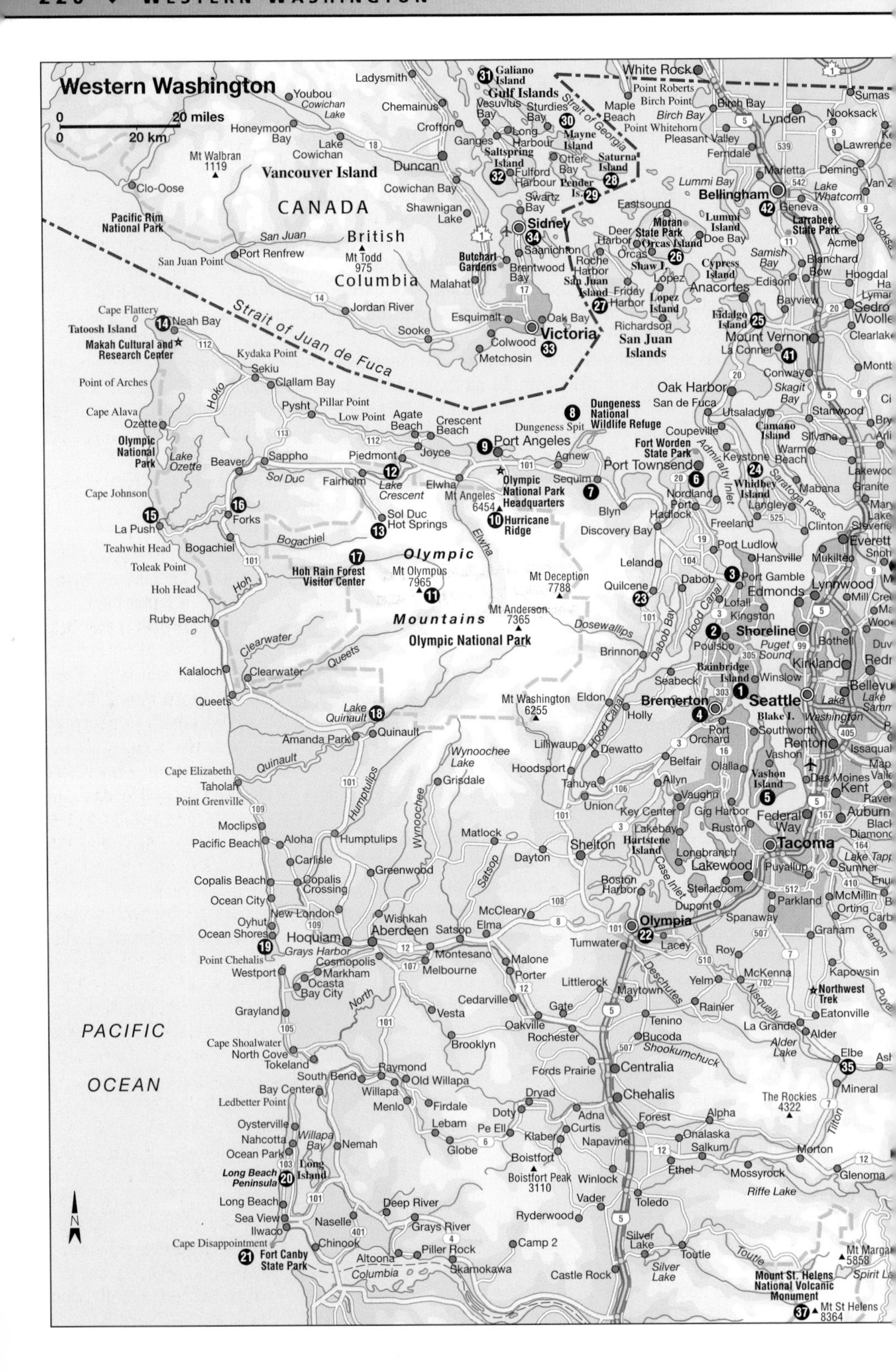
Western Washington
0 20 miles
0 20 km
N
Vancouver Island
CANADA
British Columbia
Strait of Juan de Fuca
Strait of Georgia
Gulf Islands
San Juan Islands
Olympic Mountains
Olympic National Park
PACIFIC OCEAN
Ladysmith
Youbou
Cowichan Lake
Chemainus
Galiano Island
Vesuvius Bay
Sturdies Bay
Mayne Island
Honeymoon Bay
Crofton
Ganges
Long Harbour
Saltspring Island
Otter Bay
Saturna Island
Lake Cowichan
Mt Walbran 1119
Duncan
Fulford Harbour
Pender Is.
Cowichan Bay
Swartz Bay
Clo-Oose
Shawnigan Lake
Sidney
Pacific Rim National Park
San Juan
Saanichton
Butchart Gardens
Brentwood Bay
Port Renfrew
Mt Todd 975
San Juan Point
Malahat
Jordan River
Esquimalt
Oak Bay
Victoria
Sooke
Colwood
Metchosin
Cape Flattery
Tatoosh Island
Neah Bay
Makah Cultural and Research Center
Kydaka Point
Sekiu
Clallam Bay
Point of Arches
Hoko
Pysht
Pillar Point
Low Point
Agate Beach
Crescent Beach
Cape Alava
Ozette
Olympic National Park
Lake Ozette
Beaver
Sappho
Sol Duc
Piedmont
Joyce
Port Angeles
Dungeness Spit
Dungeness National Wildlife Refuge
Olympic National Park Headquarters
Fairholm
Lake Crescent
Elwha
Mt Angeles 6454
Hurricane Ridge
Agnew
Sequim
Cape Johnson
Forks
La Push
Sol Duc Hot Springs
Bogachiel
Teahwhit Head
Toleak Point
Hoh Head
Hoh
Hoh Rain Forest Visitor Center
Mt Olympus 7965
Mt Deception 7788
Mt Anderson 7365
Dosewallips
Ruby Beach
Clearwater
Queets
Kalaloch
Lake Quinault
Quinault
Amanda Park
Mt Washington 6255
Wynoochee Lake
Cape Elizabeth
Taholah
Point Grenville
Humptulips
Wynoochee
Grisdale
Moclips
Pacific Beach
Aloha
Carlisle
Copalis Beach
Copalis Crossing
Ocean City
Greenwood
Matlock
Satsop
Dayton
New London
Oyhut
Ocean Shores
Wishkah
Aberdeen
Hoquiam
Grays Harbor
Point Chehalis
Westport
Cosmopolis
Markham
Ocasta
Bay City
Montesano
Melbourne
Malone
Porter
McCleary
Elma
Grayland
North
Cedarville
Vesta
Brooklyn
Oakville
Rochester
Cape Shoalwater
North Cove
Tokeland
South Bend
Raymond
Old Willapa
Willapa
Bay Center
Menlo
Firdale
Ledbetter Point
Oysterville
Nahcotta
Willapa Bay
Nemah
Lebam
Pe Ell
Globe
Ocean Park
Long Island
Long Beach Peninsula
Long Beach
Sea View
Ilwaco
Naselle
Deep River
Grays River
Cape Disappointment
Chinook
Fort Canby State Park
Altoona
Piller Rock
Skamokawa
Columbia
White Rock
Point Roberts
Birch Point
Maple Beach
Birch Bay
Point Whitehorn
Pleasant Valley
Ferndale
Sumas
Lynden
Nooksack
Lawrence
Deming
Marietta
Lummi Bay
Lake Whatcom
Bellingham
Geneva
Lummi Island
Larrabee State Park
Eastsound
Moran State Park
Orcas Island
Deer Harbor
Doe Bay
Orcas
Shaw I.
Roche Harbor
San Juan Island
Friday Harbor
Lopez
Lopez Island
Cypress Island
Samish Bay
Blanchard
Bow
Acme
Edison
Anacortes
Bayview
Fidalgo Island
Sedro Woolley
Clearlake
Richardson
Mount Vernon
La Conner
Conway
Skagit Bay
Oak Harbor
San de Fuca
Utsalady
Stanwood
Camano Island
Coupeville
Fort Worden State Park
Admiralty Inlet
Warm Beach
Port Townsend
Keystone
Lakewood
Whidbey Island
Saratoga Pass.
Mabana
Nordland
Port Hadlock
Langley
Clinton
Blyn
Discovery Bay
Freeland
Everett
Port Ludlow
Hansville
Mukilteo
Leland
Dabob
Port Gamble
Edmonds
Lynnwood
Quilcene
Lofall
Kingston
Dabob Bay
Hood Canal
Shoreline
Poulsbo
Puget Sound
Bothell
Kirkland
Brinnon
Bainbridge Island
Winslow
Seabeck
Seattle
Bellevue
Lake Sammamish
Eldon
Bremerton
Holly
Blake I.
Lake Washington
Southworth
Port Orchard
Renton
Issaquah
Lilliwaup
Dewatto
Vashon
Hoodsport
Belfair
Olalla
Vashon Island
Des Moines
Kent
Tahuya
Allyn
Vaughn
Union
Key Center
Gig Harbor
Federal Way
Auburn
Lakebay
Ruston
Shelton
Hartstene Island
Tacoma
Longbranch
Lakewood
Puyallup
Sumner
Case Inlet
Boston Harbor
Steilacoom
Dupont
Parkland
Orting
Olympia
Spanaway
Graham
Carbon
Tumwater
Lacey
Roy
McKenna
Kapowsin
Littlerock
Maytown
Deschutes
Yelm
Nisqually
Northwest Trek
Eatonville
Rainier
Gate
Tenino
La Grande
Alder
Alder Lake
Bucoda
Shookumchuck
Centralia
Fords Prairie
Elbe
Chehalis
Mineral
Dryad
Doty
Adna
Curtis
Klaber
Forest
Alpha
The Rockies 4322
Onalaska
Salkum
Napavine
Morton
Tilton
Boistfort
Boistfort Peak 3110
Winlock
Ethel
Mossyrock
Glenoma
Riffe Lake
Vader
Toledo
Ryderwood
Camp 2
Silver Lake
Toutle
Castle Rock
Mount St. Helens National Volcanic Monument
Mt St Helens 8364
Spirit Lake
1 2 3 4 5 6 7 8 9 10 11 12 13 14 15 16 17 18 19 20 21 22 23 24 25 26 27 28 29 30 31 32 33 34 35 37 41 42
5 9 11 12 14 17 18 20 99 101 103 104 105 106 107 108 109 112 113 167 164 305 303 401 405 410 507 510 512 525 539 542 702

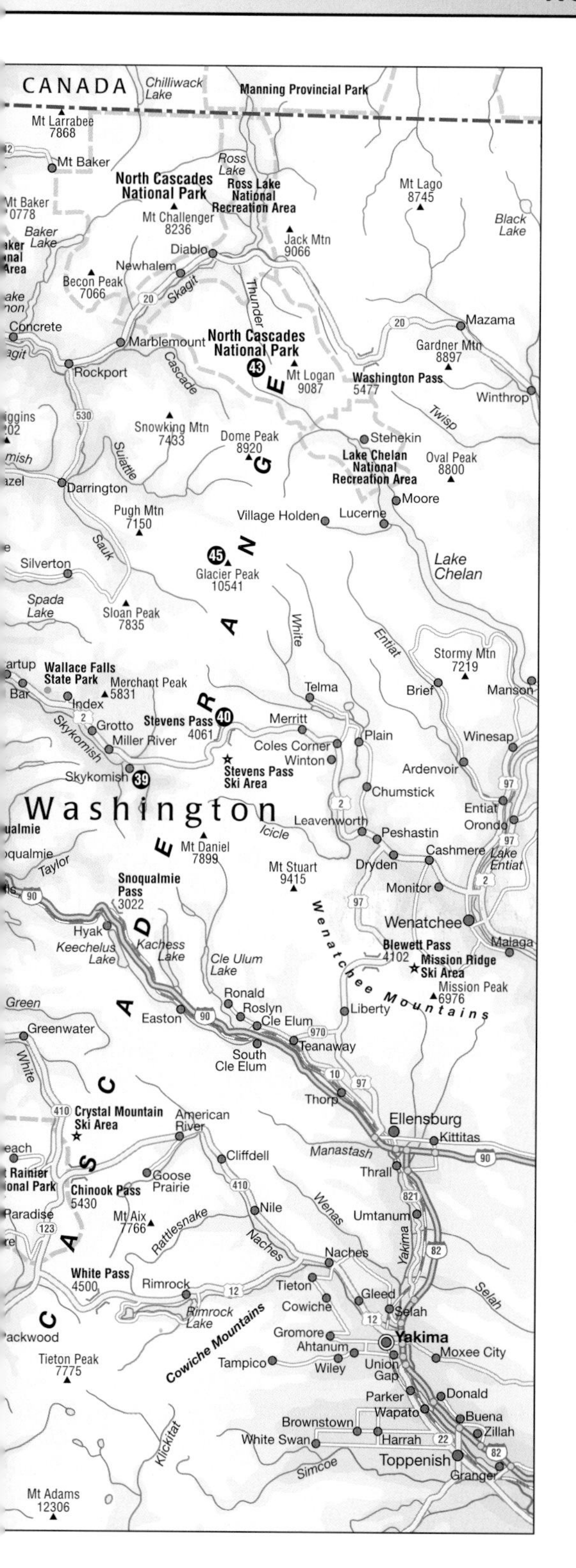

& Winery (open Wed–Sun, 12–5pm; tel: 206-842 9463; free) is a small, family winery becoming known for its European-style wines made solely from its own island-grown grapes.

On High School Street, the **Japanese Haiku Garden**, part of the Bainbridge Library grounds, commemorates the island's *issei* (first generation) Japanese-Americans. *Haiku*-inscribed plaques are scattered throughout the stone-and-bonsai garden: "Ice and water/their differences resolved/are friends again," reads one poem, hinting at the World War II internment. At the **Bainbridge Island Historical Society**'s small museum (open weekends May–Sept, 1– 4pm; tel: 206-842 2773; donations), two photographs vividly underscore the impact of the internment on island life. The photographs show Bainbridge High School's 1942 and 1943 graduating classes. In the first, about one third of the faces are Japanese; the second shows a smaller, all-white class.

Most descendants of the issei have moved away for opportunities on the mainland. One who hasn't is nursery-owner Junkoh Harui. His business, Bainbridge Gardens, restores the nursery his father started in the early 1900s from Japanese seeds – and then lost during the internment. The nursery sells a wide selection of trees, shrubs, perennials, bonsai and garden statuary.

Take Route 305 north towards the Agate Pass bridge to the Kitsap Peninsula, but before crossing the bridge, visit the **Bloedel Reserve** (open Wed– Sun, 10am–6pm; tel: 206-842 7631; admission fee). The former summer retreat of a Seattle mayor's widow is a 150-acre (60-hectare) reserve with woodland and meadows and wildlife habitat.

After crossing the Agate Pass Bridge onto the Kitsap Peninsula, a quick right on Suquamish Way leads to the **grave of Chief Sealth**, the Salish tribal chief for whom Seattle was named. Just up the highway is the **Suquamish Museum** (open daily May–Sept, 10am–5pm; admission fee) with its excellent collection of Salish artifacts.

Kitsap Peninsula

Along Route 305 is **Poulsbo** ❷, a Scandinavian fishing village turned tourist town. Nicknamed "Little Norway" because of its fjord-like setting on Liberty Bay and the Nordic families who emigrated here a century ago, Poulsbo is noted throughout the state for Poulsbo bread, baked fresh daily at Sluys Bakery.

If heading northward towards the Olympic Peninsula, before crossing the bridge over **Hood Canal** – a channel really – a worthwhile diversion is to **Port Gamble** ❸, which, until a few years ago, was one of the last lumber towns to boast a fully operational mill. Built by the Pope and Talbot timber families, who arrived by clipper ship from Maine in the 1850s, the town's original trading center has been converted into a combination gift store, cafe and museum. The tiny town, with its refurbished Victorian clapboard houses, is a picture of a prim-and-pretty New England village against a Northwest backdrop.

South from Poulsbo is the seaport town of **Bremerton** ❹. Founded in 1891 by William Bremer, a German immigrant, Bremerton is one of those Western towns that for years was controlled by one family. Platted by Bremer on land he had purchased, the town – today's downtown area – stayed in the hands of the Bremer family until the second of the two sons died in the 1986. Neither son married – in accordance with their mother's wishes, according to local lore – and after the second son died, local Olympia College inherited most of downtown.

To the outside world, Bremerton is known for the **Puget Sound Naval Shipyard**. The shipyard still is the single most important influence on the local economy and culture. But a gentrification movement is transforming downtown, and the result is an odd mixture of art galleries, specialty shops, and espresso cafes, on the one hand, and tattoo parlors, dingy bars, and boarded up buildings on the other.

BELOW: ferries service the Sound.

For many years, Bremerton's biggest tourist attraction was the battleship USS *Missouri*. In 1999, Bremerton lost the *Missouri* – the most highly decorated ship in World War II – to Honolulu, where it is now berthed next to the USS *Arizona*, and got in its place an interesting footnote to the Vietnam War: the destroyer **USS *Turner Joy*** (open Thur–Mon, 10am–5pm; admission fee), one of the ships in the Tonkin Gulf incident that escalated the Vietnam War. The nearby **Naval Museum** (open Tues–Sat, 10am–5pm, Sun from 1pm; tel: 360-377 4186; donations) focuses on World War II, with a special section devoted to the shipyard's contribution.

Join the locals at the "old Woolies." Here's a gentrification project that isn't for the gentry – a former Woolworth department store turned into an indoor flea market, with more than 40 vendors selling the usual mix of junk and treasure. The once-retired soda fountain has been brought back into service.

Vashon Island

Southwest of Bremerton, take the ferry to **Vashon Island** ❺, also accessible by ferry from Kitsap Peninsula or Tacoma. Without a bridge connecting it to the mainland, Vashon remains the most rural and least developed of Puget Sound's close-in islands, mostly because that's the way the residents want it. It has a few island-based companies: the roasterie for Seattle's Best, one of the area's most popular coffees, and K-2 Skis, which supplies the world's top skiers with equipment. But there isn't nearly enough industry to support the island's 10,000 residents, and most islanders end up commuting to work in Seattle, or maybe even Tacoma.

The island's sense of rural priority is nicely symbolized by a famous landmark: the bike in the tree. It seems years ago someone planted a bike in the fork of a tree and left it to rust. Today, the bike is completely engulfed by the tree, with only the handlebars sticking out the front of the trunk and part of the rear wheel sticking out the back. It's located in the woods near the Sound Food Cafe, on Vashon Highway a few miles south of downtown. Ask for directions at the cafe or the small general store across the street.

While Vashon's small downtown has yet to be overrun by specialty boutiques, there are enough book, art and antique shops for a few hours of browsing. The **Vashon Hardware Company and Tool Museum** (open daily 8am–7pm; tel: 206-463 3852; free) displays antique tools of every description, while selling modern equivalent. The owner is the third generation of his family to run the store.

In the 1960s and 1970s, Vashon was a counterculture retreat. "There was only one cop on the island, so you could get away with a lot," explains one alumni of that era. Today, mixed in with the locals is a community of artists, some of whose work is displayed in New York and elsewhere, not to mention in galleries scattered across the island. The **Blue Heron Art Center and Art Gallery** (open Tues–Sat, 11am–5pm; tel: 206-463 5131), on Vashon Highway SW, shows work by local and regional artists. ❑

Map on pages 220–1

Festivals each year celebrate the region's Scandinavian roots.

BELOW: Puget Sound and the Olympic Mountains.

A WALK ON THE WILD SIDE

Northwest wildlife ranges from black bears to moles, from sockeye salmon to crows, and from bald eagles to songbirds and waterfowl

Despite Seattle's urban – and suburban – growth, wildlife is still at home in this corner of the Northwest. Though expanding residential areas have shrunk the number and extent of natural wild habitats, a number of species have adapted to the changes and made their homes in many parks and green spaces.

Inside the city limits, the most common creatures you'll see are eastern gray squirrels, oposums, raccoons and an assortment of birds such as robins, seagulls, pigeons and crows. You may, however, spot a fox, a beaver or an otter. Get a little further away from the city center – in the suburbs, for example, and you increase your chances of spotting coyotes (they occasionally make a meal of someone's cat or small dog), cougar or deer. You might also run into a black bear as close as Tiger Mountain, near Issaguah.

BIRDING IN SEATTLE

Three nesting pairs of bald eagles are known to reside in the Seattle area, and are occasionally spotted near Green Lake, as well as in West Seattle. Popular birding spots in downtown Seattle include Lake Union, as well as Discovery Park and the Washington Park Arboretum, home to a variety of shorebirds and freshwater ducks. Discovery Park offers sandy and rocky beaches, sand cliffs, meadows, conifer forests, marsh areas and deciduous trees.

◁ **SEA ELEPHANT**
The northern elephant seal (*Mirounga angusirostris*) is an occasional visitor to Puget Sound, and usually travels solo.

▽ **UP A TREE**
Two black bear cubs (*Ursus americanus*) sit surrounded by autumn foliage. Bears live on Tiger Mountain, east of Issaquah on Interstate-90.

▷ **SPAWNING SOCKEYE**
In the fall, sockeye salmon (*Oncorhynchus nerka*) spawn in streams such as Issaquah Creek and the Sammamish Slough.

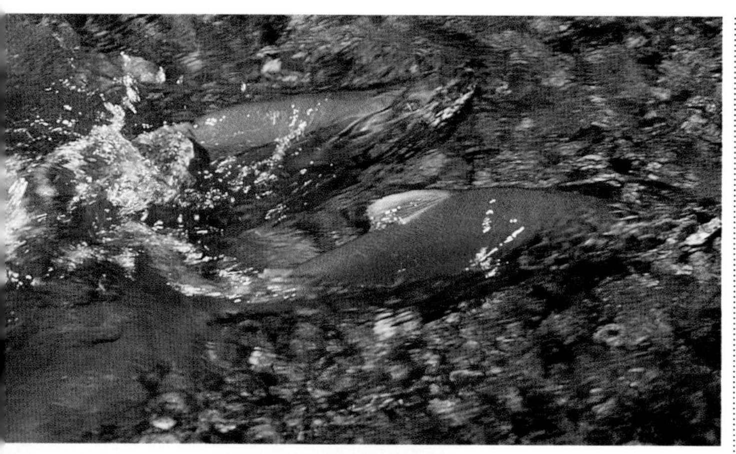

SWIMMING FOR HOME

Four species of salmon migrate through the Puget Sound area. King (or chinook), sockeye (red), coho (silver) and chum salmon leave saltwater to spawn in rivers and streams in the region. The fish travel along here from early June through November, but make their most spectacular appearance in Seattle in early July, when thousands of sockeye salmon fight their way from Puget Sound up the fish ladder at the Hiram Chittenden Locks, headed for the Cedar River and other streams. The fish ladder bypasses the locks, and provides viewing windows, along with an explanation of the salmon life-cycle. Celebrate salmon with Issaquah's Salmon Days Festival (first week of October). In Seattle, check out the Salmon Homecoming event in September.

◁ OTTER FAMILY
A mother and baby sea otter (*Enhyrda lutria*) rest on a kelp bed. Though wild in the area, the best places to find these playful animals are Woodland Park Zoo or the Seattle Aquarium.

. IN BLACK AND WHITE
/atch for the black dorsal ns of killer whales *Orcinus orca*) in Puget ound. The whales are ıore commonly sighted in ıe San Juan Islands.

EAGLE EYES
The bald eagle (*Haliaeetus leucocephalus*) can sometimes be seen near Green Lake and Discovery Park.

THE OLYMPIC PENINSULA

Although the Olympic Mountains are not extensive, their glaciers and rain forests are another world from Seattle and environs – and with a heck of a lot more rain each year

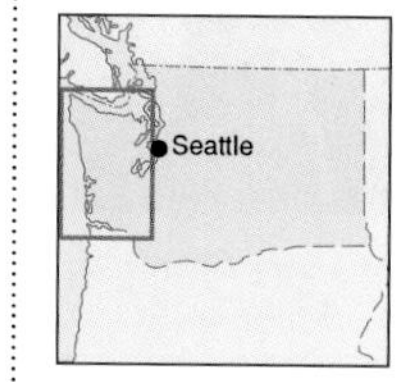

From anywhere in the Puget Sound area, it's hard to ignore the craggy outlines of the mountains to the west. Millions of years ago, the restless movements of tectonic plates threw up the mountains on the Olympic Peninsula. What plate tectonics had started, erosion and glaciers continue today, sculpting and molding the **Olympic Mountains**. In few other areas can the traveler go from rugged coast across prairies and through forests to timber line and snow-covered, glacier-capped peaks in such a short distance.

To reach the peninsula from Seattle, take a ferry to Bremerton (*see page 222*). From there, head north 19 miles (30 km) on State Route 3 and pass through Poulsbo, known as Washington's Little Norway for the Norwegian immigrants who settled there (*see page 222*). Continue on State Route 3 for about 7 miles (11 km) to the **Hood Canal Bridge**. The floating bridge is a major gateway to the Olympic Peninsula and is the only one erected over tidal waters and one of the longest in the world at 1½ miles (2.5 km). A section is pulled aside to let ships pass; a long, black Trident submarine heading out on patrol from the submarine base at Bangor may hold up traffic. Before crossing the bridge, take a short side trip to historic Port Gamble two miles (3 km) east of the bridge (*see page 222*). The former mill town is reminiscent of 19th-century New England with beautifully restored homes and wide, tree-lined streets. And well it should, for the mill owner developed the town to remind him of his roots in Maine.

PRECEDING PAGES: lighthouse on the Olympic Peninsula.
LEFT: rain forest in Hoh Valley.
BELOW: 1879 home in Port Townsend.

Port Townsend

Drive from the Hood Canal Bridge north about 30 miles (50 km) to reach **Port Townsend ❻**. Stop at the visitor center on the way into town for information about the many attractions. In 1851, settlers and developers organized the city on the shore of the large harbor here, discovered by Capt. George Vancouver in 1792 while surveying the coast for the British Admiralty. They had dreams that Port Townsend would be the largest West Coast port, wealthy and prosperous. By the end of the century, the young city was booming, but then the dreams – dependent on a railroad connecting the city to Tacoma that never came to pass – vanished from sight.

Urban renewal and development also missed the town, so Port Townsend has a large collection of historic Victorian-style buildings. Many of the homes have been converted to bed-and-breakfast inns. A walk along Water Street is past art galleries, antique and clothing stores, and restaurants that occupy the old commercial buildings. Some back up on the water, convenient for loading sailing vessels in the late 19th century. At the north end of Water Street is a marina and several marine-based industries.

St. Paul's Church, Port Townsend.

North of the city is historic **Fort Worden State Park**, located on 434 acres (175 hectares). Once it was the keystone of a network of forts first established in the 1880s by the U.S. Army to guard the entrance to Puget Sound, until the end of World War II. The fort is now a state park and conference center. You may recognize the parade ground area, with its many buildings: it featured prominently in the movie *An Officer and a Gentleman*. The **Coast Artillery Museum** (open daily 11am-5pm; donation) on the north side of the parade ground illustrates the history of the fort through uniformed mannequins, guns, models of cannons, and old photographs taken during the fort's heyday.

Accommodations are available in the restored officers' homes (tel: 365 385 4730) on the south side of the parade ground; the houses are decorated in the Victorian style and have one to five bedrooms. Other accommodations are in the restored barracks (comfortable but not luxurious), the hostel, or a campground.

If interested in military hardware, walk through the complex of concrete emplacements that once housed defensive cannon. One type of cannon at the fort firing a 12-inch (30-cm) shell raised up to shoot its projectile and then disappeared down into the emplacement for reloading; the largest cannon used at Fort Worden could fire a 16-inch (41-cm) projectile weighing 2,300 pounds (1,000 kg) nearly 30 miles (50 km).

Sharing the flat point with some of the emplacements is **Point Wilson Lighthouse**, built in 1922 to replace one built more than 40 years before. The **Marine Science Center** (open Tues–Sat, noon–6pm in summer, weekends noon–4pm at other times; admission fee) on the waterfront has exhibits and touch tanks of local marine life. The Marine Science Center also sponsors interpretive programs, marine-science activities, and summer camps for kids.

BELOW: Hastings House in Port Townsend, circa 1891.

West to Sequim and Port Angeles

Head south 13 miles (21 km) from Port Townsend on State Route 20 and then north and west on US 101 for another 13 miles to the sunny town of **Sequim** ❼ (pronounced *skwim*), in the Dungeness Valley. The town is in an arid area that was first homesteaded in 1854; a visionary pioneer irrigated the valley four decades later and Sequim then evolved into a farming community. The **Museum and Arts Center** (open Mon–Sat, 9am–4pm; donation) offers exhibits showing natural and human history in the valley – farming and Salish and pioneer life – as well as displays by local artists. Sequim's mild climate (which it shares with Port Townsend), due to the rain shadow of the Olympic Mountains and moderated by the ocean, has attracted many retirees to the area.

Head north 5 miles (8 km) on Ward Road to the **Olympic Game Farm** (open daily 9am, with variable closing times; tel: 360-683 4295; admission fee), where animals such as bears, bison, deer, elk, zebras and lions roam. Over the years it has supplied many animal "actors" for movies and television.

Further north is **Dungeness Spit** ❽ and its lighthouse. At 6 miles (8 km) and growing, the spit is the longest sand hook (in which a sand spit grows out from the shore and then parallels it) in the United States. Trails in the Dungeness Recreation Area encourage exploration of the area. A 6-mile (8-km) hike along the spit generally follows the shore of the saltwater lagoon formed by the spit. The lagoon itself is a national wildlife refuge for migrating water fowl. At the end of the spit is the New Dungeness Lighthouse, built in 1857.

Follow US 101 west 17 miles (27 km) to **Port Angeles** ❾, the largest port city on the northern Olympic Peninsula. Port Angeles offers a huge harbor with loading facilities for ocean-going ships to Asia and other Pacific Coast ports. The

Map on pages 220–1

Strait of Juan de Fuca , the narrow passage between the Olympic Peninsula and Canada's Vancouver Island, was named for a Greek captain sailing under the Spanish flag and who may have sailed the strait in 1592.

BELOW: Olympic National Park.

harbor is formed by Ediz Hook, another long sand spit with a Coast Guard air station at its end. The car ferry *Coho* (tel: 360-457 4491) operates year-round to Victoria (*see page 246*) on Vancouver Island, in Canada's province of British Columbia. A passenger-only ferry – *Victoria Express* – sails during summer.

Of particular interest are the **Clallam County Historical Museum** (open Mon–Fri, 8.30am–4pm; tel: 360-452 2662; donation), housed in an historic Georgian-style courthouse and with displays about local history, fishing industries, genealogy, and local Indian artifacts. Spectacular views of the Strait of Juan de Fuca and Vancouver Island spread to the north and the Olympic Mountains to the south.

Modern log home, Olympic Peninsula.

Olympic National Park

The **Olympic National Park Visitor Center** (open daily, 8.30am–6pm in summer, 9am–4pm the rest of the year) is in Port Angeles, with maps and other park information, along with displays depicting the area's wildlife, plants and geology, as well as Northwest Coast tribal culture.

To enter the park, follow Race Street in Port Angeles to the well-marked Hurricane Ridge Road and the steep 17-mile (27-km) ascent through forest to **Hurricane Ridge** ❿, 5,200 ft (1,600 meters) above sea level. From here are views of mountains, meadows with wildflowers, and forests. To the southwest is glacier-capped **Mount Olympus** ⓫, at 7,965 ft (2,428 meters) the highest peak in the Olympics. North 25 miles (40 km) across the Strait of Juan de Fuca is Vancouver Island and British Columbia. No roads lead to Mount Olympus, only hiking trails; in winter months, Hurricane Ridge is the only place in the Olympics for cross-country and downhill skiing.

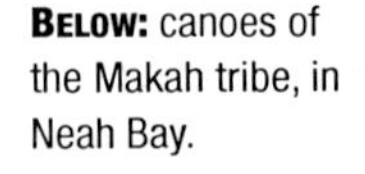

BELOW: canoes of the Makah tribe, in Neah Bay.

Return to US 101 and head west for 5 miles (8 km) beyond Port Angeles as the road curves south around **Lake Crescent** ⓬, an immense cobalt-blue glacier lake surrounded by tall-timbered forest. Lake Crescent Lodge, on the southern shore, is where Pres. Franklin D. Roosevelt stayed in 1937 just before he signed the act to create the 922,000-acre (373,000-hectare) Olympic National Park. Continue west along US 101 and turn south onto Soleduck River Road to **Sol Duc Hot Springs** ⓭ to enjoy the Olympic-size pool or hot mineral pools, a pleasant 102-109°F (39-43°C). A lovely 1-mile hike through the rain forest leads to Soleduck Falls and another none-too-fancy geothermal spring, Olympic Hot Springs. Rocks dam up the waters to form shallow soaking pools.

Neah Bay

Continue west on US 101 to **Sappho** and then north on State Routes 113 and 112 to **Neah Bay** ⓮. At the intersection with SR 112, turn and head west 27 miles (43 km) through Clallam Bay and Sekiu to Neah Bay, at the northwesterly tip of the peninsula. An alternative is to follow SR 112 from Port Angeles along the picturesque shore of Strait of Juan de Fuca, bypassing Lake Crescent.

The remote village of Neah Bay is on the **Makah Indian Reservation**. Ivan Doig's *Winter Brothers*, a journal of a man who lived with the Makah tribe during the 1800s, offers insight into the old Makah culture. The Makah call themselves Kwih-dich-chuh-ahtx, or people who live by the rocks and seagulls.

The Makah have lived in the area for thousands of years, relying on majestic red cedars for clothing, houses, tools, and sea-going canoes, in which they hunted gray whales on annual migration and seals. While the Makah still have the right by treaty to hunt whales, commercial fishing is a mainstay. Sports fishing for salmon and halibut is an important industry for the Makah and a big attraction for the several thousand anglers annually; over 200 commercial and sports-fishing boats make Neah Bay their home port. The Makah operate a fish hatchery and visitors are welcome to view salmon migrating up the fish ladders that are part of the hatchery. Check at the Makah Cultural and Research Center (tel: 360-645 2711; see below) for information.

Neah Bay is renowned for the **Makah Cultural and Research Center** (open daily in summer 10am–5pm, Wed–Sun 10am–5pm the rest of the year; tel: 360-645 2711; admission fee). The museum is filled with Northwest Indian artifacts, a replica of the longhouses that served as hubs of Makah village life, and photomurals from late 19th- and early 20th-century pictures by Edward S. Curtis, a photographer who began an essay in 1896 of the North American Indian and finished 34 years later with over 40,000 images.

Most of the 55,000-plus artifacts were discovered in an archeological dig on the Ozette Indian Reservation on the coast, south of Neah Bay and the Makah lands. Ozette is considered one of the important archeological finds in North America. The original village was buried by a mudslide more than 500 years ago; the clay soil sealed the contents of the houses and thus preserved them for posterity. The dig is currently closed because of a lack of funding.

Map on pages 220–1

In 1999, the Makah exerted their whaling rights and harpooned a gray whale from a dugout canoe – towed to the area by a power boat – after several failed attempts. The whale was given the coup de grace *by shots from a rifle.*

BELOW: looming over Rialto Beach.

TIP

Only three temperate rain forests exist in the world: Chile, New Zealand and a coastal band stretching from the Olympic Peninsula to southern Alaska. In North America, most rain forests have been logged. The western side of the Olympic Peninsula provides an opportunity to explore this ecosystem.

BELOW: rain forest, Olympic Peninsula.

Many beaches in the area are closed to non-American Indians. While at the Makah Cultural and Research Center, obtain maps of the reservation showing closed areas and also the car route and walking trail to **Cape Flattery**, on the northwestern tip of the Olympic Peninsula. The boardwalk trail threads through a forest to observation decks on the 60-ft (18-meter) cliffs of Cape Flattery. The vistas are spectacular, with waves crashing on rocky shores and pristine beaches. During spring and late fall, one may see gray whales migrating, and seals, birds and ship traffic.

Just offshore a few hundred yards is **Tatoosh Island**, home to seals and sea lions. It is also home to Cape Flattery Light, commissioned in 1857. The Makah didn't welcome the construction workers for the light, who had to build a blockhouse on the island before starting work. The light overlooks the funnel-like entrance to the Strait of Juan de Fuca and is a graveyard for many ships; storms, ocean currents and fog have caused ships to miss the strait, ending up on the Washington coast or on Vancouver Island.

South along the coast

South from the Makah Reservation's southern boundary, 57 miles (98 km) of cliffs, sea stacks and beaches are a vital and spectacular part of Olympic National Park, and also comprise a national wildlife refuge. Just north of Forks is a turnoff – SR 110 – to the coast, leading to Rialto Beach and the Quileute village of La Push. **Rialto Beach** is a favorite spot for fashion photographers to capture their lovely models, typically shivering in the winter winds. **La Push** ⓯ is known for its jagged rock-lined beach, interesting offshore sea stacks, and a famous and quite fine 16-mile-long (26-km) beach walk.

Century-old **Forks** ⓰, with a population of around 5,000, is located on a broad prairie on the northwest part of the peninsula and is the only sizable town on this side of the peninsula. It boasts more rainfall than any other community in the United States – around 140 inches (350 cm) a year. Attractions include the **Forest Timber Museum** (open daily 10am–4pm Apr–Oct; tel: 360-374 9663; donation), with displays of a pioneer kitchen, farm and logging equipment, vintage newspapers and photos, and a fire lookout tower. The town makes a good base for hikes through the rain forests and rugged coast.

The helpful **Hoh Rain Forest Visitor Center** ⓱, south of Forks off US 101 and about 20 miles (30 km) into the national park, offers a vast amount of information on the wildlife, flora and history of the temperate rain forest found here. Moisture-laden air from the Pacific drenches the area with more than 150 inches (380 cm) of rain annually – this is the wettest place in the 48 contiguous states. Three loop trails (and a wheelchair-accessible, paved mini-trail) lead into the rain forest with its moss-draped trees, ferns and a clear, glacial-fed river. Elk, deer and other animals are often seen from the roads or while hiking the trails.

Further south of the turnoff to the rain forest, the U.S. 101 swings west to the coast and follows cliffs overlooking a series of beaches, from **Ruby Beach** and the **Hoh Indian Reservation** in the north to **Kalaloch** (pronounced *clay-lock*) **Beach** in the south. Part of Olympic National Park's coastal strip, the coast has a rugged and picturesque beauty. Waves crash against rocks and offshore islands, casting tree trunks up on the shore like so many toothpicks. Four miles offshore is reef-girdled Destruction Island and its lighthouse, built in 1890. On a foggy day, the mournful cry of its foghorn disturbs thousands of auklets – small sea birds – that nest on the island.

Map on pages 220–1

Fungus in the forest.

BELOW: Long Beach.

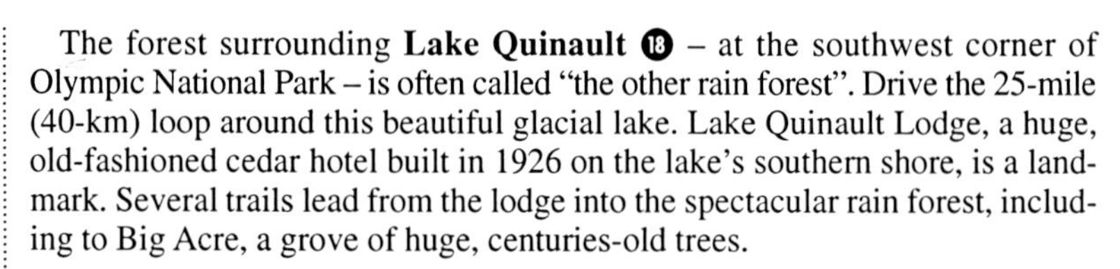

The forest surrounding **Lake Quinault** 18 – at the southwest corner of Olympic National Park – is often called "the other rain forest". Drive the 25-mile (40-km) loop around this beautiful glacial lake. Lake Quinault Lodge, a huge, old-fashioned cedar hotel built in 1926 on the lake's southern shore, is a landmark. Several trails lead from the lodge into the spectacular rain forest, including to Big Acre, a grove of huge, centuries-old trees.

North Head Light.

Ocean Shores

Head south to **Ocean Shores** 19, on a 6-mile-long (10-km) peninsula, entering through the city's peculiar but imposing stone-and-cement gateway. Originally homesteaded in the 1860s, Ocean Shores did not become an incorporated city until 1970, when investors, including singer Pat Boone, got the town under way. Today Ocean Shores is a town of motels and vacation homes.

Grays Harbor was discovered in 1792 by Capt. Robert Gray, an American trader who also discovered the Columbia River. The harbor is the only deep-water port on the outer Washington coast and is a major terminal for transporting lumber to Asian customers. The tall ship ***Lady Washington***, a replica of the ship sailed by Gray, now docks in the Grays Harbor Historical Seaport, a working shipyard that constructs and maintains such ships. Visitors may take a cruise on the *Lady Washington* Mon through Fri (tel: 360-532 8611).

Southward and eastward

A side trip south on US 101 and along the east shore of **Willapa Bay** leads to one of the nicest stretches of beach in Washington, **Long Beach Peninsula** 20, fronted by a 28-mile (45-km) stretch of ocean beach. The lively town of **Long Beach** is a miniature Coney Island – the main street is filled with huge chainsaw art sculptures (a near-naked mermaid, the Louis and Clark duo, and more). The historic town of **Oysterville** had its heyday during the Gold Rush in the 1850s, shipping oysters to San Francisco at $19 each in 1998 dollars.

BELOW: lighthouse on Cape Disappointment.

At the base of the peninsula is one of the most spectacular spots on the Washington coast: **Cape Disappointment** 21, overlooking the Columbia River and its treacherous mouth, a graveyard for an armada of ships and hundreds of sailors. Here is **Fort Canby State Park**, home to two lighthouses and the emplacements housing massive cannons that never fired a shot. **Cape Disappointment Light**, one of the first on the West Coast, has warned sailors of the dangers lurking at the mouth of the Columbia for over 150 years. **North Head Light** was built more than 40 years later to warn ships approaching from the north.

To close the loop trip around the Olympic Peninsula, head east from Grays Harbor to the state capital at **Olympia** 22 (*see* South of Seattle, *page 205*). A highway heads northward along the Hood Canal, known for its oysters, through the old timber town of **Shelton** (noted for Christmas trees and oysters) and Hoodsport. **Quilcene** 23, at the north end of Hood Canal on Dabob Bay, is home to the world's largest oyster factory. There fresh oysters and clams can be had to steam or to bake later. ❑

Mysterious Myths

Mysteries do fascinate us. Consider the popularity of the cult television series *Twin Peaks* and the discovery of the cellophane-wrapped corpse of a homecoming queen in the opening episode. Washington and British Columbia do have real mysteries... perhaps more than their share, including hairy ape men roaming the woods and sea serpents rising from the deep.

Sasquatch: Stories abound of giant, hairy hominids roaming forests from British Columbia to northern California, known as either Sasquatch or Big Foot. Such stories are the stuff of legends of the original Native Americans; depictions appear on totem poles. Descriptions among different tribes are remarkably similar, though they don't always agree if the creature is real or a spirit.

The first report of Sasquatch by a European was made by a Spanish naturalist, Jose Mariano Mozimo, in 1792 while exploring the British Columbia coast. He quoted natives as saying that Sasquatch inhabited the mountain country and had a monstrous body covered with black animal hair. They described it as having a head like a human but with eye teeth sharp like those of a bear. Massive arms ended in fingers with large curved nails. It was said that "his howls fell to the ground those who hear them, and he smashes into a thousand pieces the poor unfortunate, on whom a blow of his hand falls."

Early white settlers told of giant, shaggy creatures, huge footprints, awesome howls, evidence of fearsome strength, and nauseous smells. In more recent times, reports have told of peaceful encounters in which a Sasquatch avoided humans.

Indian and white witnesses describe the creature as 6 to 11 ft (3.4 meters) tall and weighing between 700 and 2,500 pounds (1,100 kg). They report that Sasquatch walks erect or slightly stooped with long arms that swing. Generally the hair is described as black or brown. Yet, there is not a shred of solid evidence to convince most researchers.

Cadborosaurus: Stories of sea serpents roaming the waters of the Pacific Northwest were told long before the coming of white men. The creatures are part of the lore of the Indian inhabitants of the coastal Northwest. Centuries ago, these people created petroglyphs of these creatures on rock surfaces. Paintings and wood carvings also depict the creatures, whether real or myth.

With the coming of European settlers, sightings of the creatures, mostly in Washington and British Columbia, continued. These reports are remarkably consistent, too, and agree with those of the Indians.

All describe serpent-like animals ranging up to 100 ft (30 meters) in length with heads like horses but with the down-turned snouts of camels. Some reports also told of short flippers and serrated fins down the back, often arched.

Two scientists with impeccable credentials have been collecting evidence and reports about Cadborosaurus or, more familiarly, Caddy, for years. Caddy was given its name by a Victoria newspaper editor in the 1930s due to the many sightings near Cadboro Bay, a coastal village near Victoria. ❑

RIGHT: myths rise out of the mists of time.

ISLANDS OF THE NORTH

Scores of seductive islands lie to the north of urban Seattle, some of them tiny and private and American, others large and Canadian with a city like Victoria, on Vancouver Island

From the window of an aircraft, islands and snow-capped mountains dominate the horizons. These varied landforms once resided in the Pacific south of the equator. Several hundred million years ago, large and small chunks of land – called terranes and propelled by sea-floor spreading and continental drift – sailed across the Pacific and docked on the west coast of ancient North America. In fact, much of North America west of the Rockies is formed from terranes. The impact of collisions forced up mountains, starting with the Rockies and most recently the Olympic Mountains and Vancouver Island.

During the last ice age, which ended around 10,000 years ago, a monstrous ice cap covered Canada and the northern United States. The ice over southern British Columbia was a mile thick. That ice, inexorably moving in a southerly direction, sculpted the landscape and carved deep valleys. As the ice melted at the end of the most recent ice age, the oceans rose about 300 ft (100 meters), flooding coastal valleys and leaving only mountain peaks above sea level. These are Canada's Gulf Islands and America's San Juan Islands, part and parcel of the same archipelago and sharing a benign climate.

PRECEDING PAGES: one of the San Juan Islands.
LEFT: snow on the light, San Juan Islands.
BELOW: boats in safe harbor.

The benign climate drew the earliest native peoples to Vancouver Island some 8,000 years ago. There, they lived undisturbed until English navigators like James Cook and George Vancouver, along with Spanish voyagers Dionico Galiano and Juan Francisco de la Bodega y Quadra, explored the Pacific Northwest in the 18th century. Traders followed, and eventually a flood of Europeans changed local culture forever.

The San Juan Islands

Only four of the 172 San Juan Islands – Shaw, Lopez, Orcas and San Juan – have regular ferry service and thus are easily accessible from Seattle, the Olympic Peninsula and Vancouver Island. Options to any of the islands, of course, include floatplane and chartered sailboat. Travel through the narrow channels and open water passes by sandy beaches, shallow bays, curving sand spits, grassy estuaries, and broad forested slopes. All the islands are resplendent with meadows, farms, forests, fields and outcroppings of rock surrounded by grasses. One may see orcas (killer whales), rafts of seabirds, harbor seals, otters, bald eagles and, through binoculars, brown rabbits.

Each island is unique, but the flat rural terrain of Lopez, Shaw and San Juan islands are best for bicycling. Orcas Island, dominated by Mount Constitution, is more difficult for bicyclists with its rolling hills, narrow shoulders and hairpin curves. Orcas Island was, contrary to expectations, not named for killer whales but rather for a Spanish nobleman, the patron of a Spanish explorer to the region in 1792.

Accessible from the Olympic Peninsula and Seattle is **Whidbey Island** ㉔, at 40 miles (65 km) the longest contiguous island in the United States. It boasts a colorful history, rolling hills, fertile farmlands and rocky beaches. A ferry at Mukilteo, 45 minutes north of Seattle, takes you on a short ride across the channel to **Clinton**, on Whidbey. If starting from the Olympic Peninsula, the Keystone Ferry from Port Townsend goes to Whidbey Island.

Rosario Resort on the island of Orcas.

Langley is a lovely town perched on a cliff overlooking Saratoga Passage, between the island and the mainland about 4 miles (6 km) away. Spectacular water and mountain views provide a picturesque backdrop to the stylish century-old shops, restaurants, art galleries and inns. Historic **Coupeville** displays its Victorian homes and quaint shops. **Oak Harbor** near the north end is the largest town on the island. Whidbey Naval Air Station is nearby.

At the northern tip of the island lies narrow **Deception Pass**, spanned by a 976-ft-long (297-meter), 180-ft-high (55-meter) steel bridge between Whidbey and **Fidalgo Island** ㉕ to the north. Deception Pass is rather treacherous, where swift, churning tidal currents are funneled through the pass of just 500 ft (150 meters). More than 3 million people visit the state park here.

Anacortes, at the tip of Fidalgo Island, is the other large town on the two islands. While most people know Anacortes for its ferry terminal, a gateway to the San Juan Islands and Vancouver Island, a closer look is worthwhile. Many homes are ornate 19th-century, and the old downtown area is interesting to explore. The views from the top of nearby Mount Erie are worth the drive.

Shaw Island has a small esoteric grocery store at the dock, maintained by nuns from Our Lady of the Rocky priory, a Franciscan nunnery, and a campground on the south shore. Shaw is embraced by Orcas and San Juan islands.

BELOW: ferry from Seattle arriving in Friday Harbor.

Since the 1890s, when the first passenger ferries came to the San Juans, **Orcas Island** ㉖ has been a visitor destination. Today, the tiny villages of Orcas, Eastsound, West Sound, Deer Harbor and Olga offer restaurants, shops and tiny grocery stores. Accommodating bed-and-breakfast inns are scattered throughout the island. Orcas has a well-stocked grocery store, hotel and several restaurants near the ferry dock. The only establishment resembling a traditional resort on Orcas is **Rosario**, the 1904 estate of ship-builder and former Seattle mayor Robert Moran.

Nearby **Moran State Park** was named after him following his gift to the state of Washington of more than 3,600 acres (1,450 hectares) of forested land, mountain lakes and streams surrounding Mount Constitution. A paved road and hiking trail wind up to the top of the mountain and a 50-ft-high (15-meter) stone lookout tower. At the top is a 360-degree view of the islands and, on a clear day, Mount Baker 50 miles (80 km) to the east in the Cascade Range.

Map on pages 220–1

Whidbey Island has been inhabited by American Indians for thousands of years, and by retired ship captains for decades.

San Juan Island

On **San Juan Island** ㉗, the ferry docks at **Friday Harbor**, a small village of quaint restaurants, hotels and shops. In Friday Harbor, visit the **Whale Museum** (open daily 10am–6pm in summer, 11am–4pm the rest of the year; tel: 360 378 4710; admission fee) at 62 First Street North, three blocks from the ferry landing. The museum's exhibits illustrate whale biology, behavior and sounds. Skeletons of an adult orca and a baby gray whale are on display. The museum also has an extensive photographic catalog of the dorsal fins and tail flukes of orcas resident in regional waters; the markings of each whale are distinctive, allowing researchers to identify individual animals.

San Juan Island was the site of a territorial dispute between Great Britain

LEFT: hotel at Roche Harbor on San Juan Island.
BELOW: Whidbey Island.

and the United States between 1859 and 1872; the remains of the camps of the opposing armies are incorporated within the **San Juan Island National Historical Park**. At the island's north end is charming **Roche Harbor**, once mined for limestone, used to produce concrete, iron and paper. It was the richest deposit west of the Mississippi River, and the quarries and kilns are still visible. A 100-year-old log cabin and an 1850s hotel – the Hotel de Haro, with its delightful flower garden – stand side by side at the harbor's edge.

TIP

BC Ferries operates a frequent service to the Gulf Islands from Tsawassen, south of Vancouver, and Swartz Bay, north of Victoria. The islands can also be reached by float plane or private boat. A variety of lodging exists – resorts, inns, B&Bs, hotels, cottages, camping, and a country estate.

Canada's Gulf Islands

The southern part of Canada's Gulf Islands – Saltspring, Galiano, Mayne, the Penders, and Saturna – are convenient to Victoria and mainland British Columbia. Naturally, the smaller the population of the island, the fewer the options, but activities range from shopping and fine dining to bicycling, hiking, golf and tennis, shopping, beachcombing, kayaking and boating, fishing and scuba diving. And if inclined to contemplation, then sit on the shore against a tree and watch the setting sun.

Saturna Island ㉘, the most southerly of the Gulf Islands, is large in area but small in population – slightly more than 300. The ferry from Swartz Bay on Vancouver Island docks at Lyall Harbour at the north end. The island is a rural hideaway with plenty of wildlife, quiet roads, scenic walks and accessible beaches. Rent a boat for a fishing expedition or a kayak to tour the shoreline of the island. Winter Cove Marine Park has an excellent harbor, a boat launch, picnic areas, walking trails, and a tidal marsh with lots of wildlife. A stiff hike takes you up 1,630-ft-high (500-meter) Mount Warburton Pike for a panoramic view of the Gulf and San Juan Islands.

The **Pender Islands** ㉙, with a population of around 2,000, are two islands

BELOW: starfish of the Gulf Islands.

connected by a wooden bridge over a narrow waterway. The ferry from Vancouver Island docks at Otter Bay on North Pender. Explore the islands by car, bicycle, scooter or on foot, discovering idyllic country roads and hidden coves and beaches. Bedwell Harbour on South Pender has a large resort with a full range of facilities including a marina. It is a port of entry for boaters entering Canada from the San Juans.

Mayne Island ㉚, southeast of Galiano and with a population of 900, became the center of commercial and social life in the Gulf Islands during the Fraser River/Cariboo Gold Rush in the 1850s. Would-be miners rested at **Miners Bay** before rowing in small boats across the Strait of Georgia. The center of life shifted to Saltspring around the end of the 19th century. Miners Bay boasts of a few shops, eateries and a museum (once the jail). Explore the island's byways by car or bicycle; there are interesting hiking trails to peaks and beaches with sandstone caves. At the northwest corner of the island, Active Pass Light and its grounds are now a park and a wonderful place to picnic and watch shipping.

Nineteen-mile-long (31-km) and skinny **Galiano Island** ㉛ lies east 2 miles (3 km) off Saltspring, with a population of only 1,000. Ferries dock at Sturdies Bay at the south end. To reach Galiano from the west, you sail through narrow Active Pass, an S-shaped passage with Mayne Island on the south. The currents are strong, with many eddies when the tides are flowing. Sea birds, eagles, herons and – sometimes – orcas can be seen. Ferries between Vancouver Island and mainland British Columbia use Active Pass, meeting in the middle.

Migrating birds and wildflowers draw bird watchers and naturalists in the spring. Hike through meadows and forests of Douglas fir to high points or along the shoreline and beaches. Kayakers and other boaters enjoy the protected west

Map on pages 220–1

Lodging on Salt Springs includes Hastings House, known for relaxed elegance. The replica of a Sussex-style, 16th-century manor house was built in 1939 by Warren Hastings, descendant of the first Governor General of British colonial India.

BELOW: seagull at nest with young.

Although with a mild climate, snow is not uncommon in the islands.

coast with its high cliffs and beaches. The waters of Active Pass and Porlier Pass at the north end attract scuba divers and fishermen.

Ganges, the commercial center and only town on the island, has a variety of shops, art galleries, pubs and restaurants. Saltspring is home for many artists, and their work is displayed at a summer-long arts-and-craft fair in Ganges. Several freshwater lakes offer swimming and fishing for trout and cutthroat. The two largest lakes are St. Mary's Lake, 3 miles (5 km) north of Ganges, and Cusheon Lake, south a few miles from town. Cyclists enjoy relatively flat roads, while hikers can find trails on the level, up mountain slopes, or along beaches.

Yes, **Saltspring Island** ㉜ does have salt springs – there are 14 ranging in size from a few feet to 100 ft (30 meters) in diameter, all located at the northern end. It is the largest of the Gulf Islands, with a population of around 10,000. Most residents live on the flatter northern part of the island. The southern part is punctuated by two mountain ranges separated by a narrow valley. The ferry from Swartz Bay docks at **Fulford Harbour** at the south end of that valley. Ferries from mainland British Columbia and the other Gulf Islands dock at Long Harbour, on the east coast. A ferry connects **Vesuvius Bay**, on the northwest coast, to Crofton, north of Victoria.

Victoria

On the southern tip of Canada's Vancouver Island and convenient to the San Juan Islands, **Victoria** ㉝ offers a lifestyle unique in Canada and rare in the United States. The rain shadows cast by the Olympic Mountains to the south in Washington and the mountains of Vancouver Island to the north of Victoria guarantee enough rain to keep plants and lawns green, but no more. The warm

BELOW: Victoria's waterfront at night.

California Current passing offshore further moderates the climate to prevent temperature extremes. The result is a small, classy town with a harbor that draws visitors from around the world.

When Hudson's Bay Company built a trading fort on the site of modern-day Victoria in 1843, an influx of Europeans with diverse backgrounds began, which still continues today. With the start of a gold rush on the mainland in 1858, people swarmed into Victoria, and many stayed. The boom collapsed and Victoria began to acquire its "cool" reserve from an influx of English settlers.

The city retains an English ambience with its tea rooms, double-decker buses, horse-drawn tallyho carriages, and, above all, flowers. Because of the residents' pride in their gardens, Victoria has adopted the moniker the City of Flowers – flowers in gardens, window boxes, road dividers, and, in summer, hanging from the blue lampposts in downtown Victoria. The world-famous Butchart Gardens north of Victoria is the crowning floral masterpiece (*see page 250*).

The **Inner Harbor**, dominated by the Empress Hotel and the Legislative buildings, is Victoria's center of activity. Float planes, tiny harbor ferries scurrying like water bugs across the calm waters, larger ferries arriving from Seattle, Port Angeles and Bellingham, and pleasure and fishing boats come and go. Both the **Legislative Building** and the **Empress Hotel** were designed by English architect Francis Rattenbury, who had made a fortune in the gold rush in northern British Columbia. The Legislative Building, completed in 1898, incorporates a mixture of European styles and is an imposing structure, especially at night when it is illuminated by 3,000 lights. A curious omission by Rattenbury was washrooms – there are none in the main building.

The Empress Hotel was one of a chain of hotels built across Canada by the Cana-

Map on pages 220–1

After some years in Victoria, Rattenbury returned to England, only to be murdered by his young footman, alleged to be the lover of Rattenbury's young second wife.

BELOW: dome of the Legislative Building.

dian Pacific Railroad. Construction started in 1904 on what had been muddy James Bay, spanned by a rickety wooden bridge that carried Government Street. The Causeway was built three years earlier to allow draining and filling of the bay and replacement of the bridge with a proper roadway. To reach solid ground beneath the mud of the bay, the Empress sits on 2,855 50-ft (15-meter) pilings of Douglas fir. The six-story hotel, designed in a French château style, opened in 1908.

The **Royal British Columbia Museum** (open daily, 9am–5pm; tel: 250-387 3701; admission fee) illustrates the culture of the region's original native inhabitants, ecology, early life in Victoria, and an Imax theatre. The culture of the indigenous Native Americans is centered on a replica of a Northwest longhouse, with canoes, mannequins garbed in tribal styles, a pit house, the reconstruction of an archaeological dig, models of original villages, and many artifacts. The natural history gallery depicts a huge mammoth, dioramas, and full-size exhibits of rain forests, coastal zones and tidal marshes.

Next door is **Thunderbird Park**, with a collection of totem poles and a carving shed, where Native American carvers work on totem poles and carve small artifacts for sale in art galleries. During fine weather, visitors and residents throng the Lower Causeway in front of the Empress Hotel, attracted by artists and street musicians.

Head north on Government Street, which fronts the Empress Hotel, with its many stores, most in 19th-century buildings, and be pulled into one by chocolate, Scottish woolens or Irish linens. A wonderful bookstore occupies an old bank building. A few steps further, aromas of fine cigars and pipe tobaccos waft from a 100-year-old tobacconist's store. At the corner of Fort Street is the four-story **Eaton Centre**, a huge indoor mall looking out of place in a 19th-century environment. Interested in antiques? Turn right on Fort Street and head up

TIP

Stop in at the Tourism Info Centre at the north end of the Lower Causeway for maps, brochures, lodging guides, information on sightseeing tours, whale watching, harbor cruises, and nature safaris. Open daily 8.30am-7.30pm.

Below: French styling at the classic Empress.

Antique Row, as this part of Fort Street is known, with its collection of antique stores – silver, china, paintings – and antiquarian bookstores.

Opposite the north end of Eaton Centre, a pedestrian walkway leads west to **Bastion Square**, the center of the site of Fort Victoria, no longer in evidence. Explore the **Maritime Museum** (open daily, 9.30am–4.30pm; tel: 250-385 4222; admission fee) in the old Law Courts building where Matthew Begbie, the so-called "hanging judge", held forth. Begbie was the first judge appointed in British Columbia, riding on horseback to mining camps and dispensing justice from a tent. The museum has three floors of nautical exhibits dedicated to the marine history of British Columbia, with an extensive collection of ship models and a gallery illustrating the Royal Canadian Navy.

Further up Government Street, Yates, Johnson and Pandora streets lead to Wharf and Store streets and the waterfront. This is **Old Town**, where many fine 19th-century buildings survived "urban renewal" in the decades following World War II. Now they house a collection of small businesses. Market Square, once a produce market, has been resurrected with its shops and restaurants.

Chinatown

Further along on Government is Fisgard Street and the colorful "Gate of Harmonious Interest," an arch emblazoned with Chinese art, capped with a red-tile roof, and supported by two red columns. Stone lions guard each side. This is the entrance to **Chinatown**, once the largest on the North American West Coast but a shrunken image of the original. As you amble down Fisgard, keep eyes open for Fan Tan Alley, only 3 ft (1 meter) wide and the narrowest road in Canada. Most of the Chinese immigrants who arrived in Victoria during the

The Hudson's Bay Company had a monopoly on the Northwest fur trade. James Douglas, with the Company, steamed into the harbor on the steamer Beaver. *He established a fort and trading post, naming both after recently crowned Queen Victoria.*

BELOW: tourist boat in the Inner Harbor.

Many gambling dens lined Fan Tan Alley, followed by bordellos and a network of hidden doors, secret entries and escape routes from police raids. The newspaper called the location Fan Tan Alley.

late 1800s and early 20th century were men. Deprived of women, they gambled and visited the bordellos. One popular gambling game with them was *fan tan.*

Walk back to the Causeway on Store and Wharf streets, where there are interesting stores and restaurants in period buildings, plus great harbor views. The Johnson Street Bridge (Blue Bridge) leads to the town of **Esquimalt** and the home of Canada's Pacific Fleet; Britain began using the deep-water anchorage in 1848, and it's been used ever since. Beyond Esquimalt are the communities of Langford, Colwood and Metchosin. In the **Colwood** area is Royal Roads University, a former military college. **Fort Rodd Hill National Historic Park** (daily 10am–5pm; tel: 250-478 5849; admission fee) was once a coastal defense complex, used between 1895 and 1956; visitors can roam the loop-holed walls, examine some of the weaponry, and explore underground magazines and barracks. **Fisgard Lighthouse,** on the shoreline of the fort, was built in 1860, the first in British Columbia.

To sample other areas of Victoria and some spectacular coastal views, drive west past the motels and hotels lining Belleville Street. Then follow the waterfront past Fisherman's Wharf, the Canadian Coast Guard base and the docks for ocean-going cruise ships at **Ogden Point**. You're now on Dallas Road, the beginning of Marine Drive (a marked scenic route, not a street). Between Dallas and the shore, a park allows walks along the cliffs and beaches fronting the Strait of Juan de Fuca. On the left is Beacon Hill Park with colorful flowers and a lookout with a view of the Strait and the Olympic Mountains.

Continue past modest cottages near the shore and pretentious houses clinging to hillsides. Keep an eye open for a pullout where you can rest and enjoy the panoramic view. Just beyond, the road becomes Beach Drive. The manicured fairways and greens of the ocean-front Victoria Golf Club line Beach Drive. You are now entering **Oak Bay**, sometimes said to be "behind the tweed curtain" for the many Britishers living there.

Below: autumn Northwest leaves.

Sidney

About 20 miles (30 km) north of Victoria is **Sidney** ㉞, the site of Victoria's international airport and a ferry connection to the San Juans. Next to the airport is the **British Columbia Aviation Museum** (open daily 10am–4pm; tel: 250 655 3300; admission fee), with a hangar full of historic aircraft, some being restored.

Butchart Gardens (open daily, 9am with varying closing times; tel: 250-652 4422; admission fee) offers 50 acres (20 hectares) of flowers in the Rose Garden, Japanese Garden and the Show Greenhouse. The centerpiece is the Sunken Gardens, originally created by the Butchart family in the quarry left by the family's limestone business. Near Butchart Gardens are the **Butterfly Gardens** (open daily 9.30am–5.30pm; tel: 250-652 3822; admission fee), an indoor tropical garden with numerous species of free-flying butterflies and birds. During cold weather, the butterflies are lethargic and seldom fly, and thus easily admired.

The **Saanich Historical Artifacts Society** (open daily, 9am–4pm in summer, to noon other times; tel: 250-652 5522; donations), also in the Sydney area, maintains exhibits of the Saanich Peninsula's rural past, including a blacksmith shop, sawmill, and a one-room log cabin. ❑

Totem Poles

Northwest Indians are carvers by tradition, and the totem pole is one of the more notable of their crafts. The extent of totem pole carving ranged from the Puget Sound area north to Alaska. The natives of British Columbia and Alaska, however, were the first to carve them. The history of these works is surprisingly brief, for it wasn't until the mid-1700s, when European explorers first encountered these remote people, that the unique sculptures began to appear. Although the local tribes were already expert carvers of canoes, tools, longhouses and furniture, they lacked the iron tools necessary to fell a massive tree in one piece and carve its length.

With the iron axes for which they traded, the coastal tribes could now take advantage of the trees that grew so tall and straight in their wet climate. Initially, the poles were made to stand against the front of a home, with figures facing out and a door cut through the base, so all would enter the house through the pole. In this case, the totem pole functioned as a family crest, recounting genealogies, stories or legends that in some way identified the owner.

Poles serve the function of recording the lore of the clan, much like a book. The top figure on the pole identified the owner's clan, and the succeeding characters (read from top to bottom) tell their stories. There is a story behind almost every image on a pole. If a legendary animal – Raven, the trickster, for example – had the power to transform into, say, a person, then the carver would depict Raven with both wings and limbs, or have a human face with a raven's beak.

Towards the end of the 1800s, the poles stood free on the beach or in the village outside the carvers' homes. Some villages were virtual forests of dozens – sometimes hundreds – of poles. (*See photograph on pages 20-21.*) The family that carved the pole gave a potlatch with feasting, games and gift-giving. These gatherings were costly and required a great deal of preparation and participation. The custom frustrated whites trying to "civilize" the Indians, especially missionaries who solved the problem by felling the poles. Employers, too, complained that their Indian workers were unreliable when a pole was being carved or a potlatch planned. Eventually, both the Canadian and U.S. governments banned potlatches and pole carving nearly died out. (The ban was finally lifted in the 1950s.)

The Tlingit, on the southeastern coast of Alaska, are especially noted for their poles. On a tour in 1899, a group of Seattle businessmen visited the Tlingit village of Tongas and took one of the poles. They erected it in Seattle, where, at 50 ft (15 meters), it became one of the city's most distinctive monuments. In 1938, Tlingit carvers copied the pole after the original was destroyed by fire; the copy is in Pioneer Square today.

Learning to read – and appreciate – totem poles is like learning to read a language. The poles speak of history, mythology, social structure and spirituality. They serve many purposes, for both individual and community, and continue to be carved by the descendants of the original carvers. ❑

RIGHT: totem poles record the lore of a clan.

THE CASCADES

A result of volcanism and colliding tectonic plates, the Cascades punctuate Seattle's eastern horizon with some nearly perfect mountains, especially the ever-present Mount Rainier

Map on pages 220–1

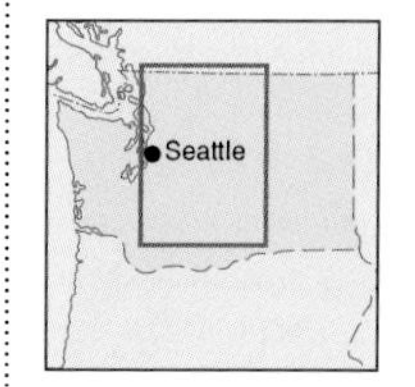

While Seattleites refer to other mountain peaks by name, 14,411-ft (4,392-meter) Mount Rainier, southeast of the city 70 miles (115 km), is called, simply, The Mountain. Visible from more than 100 miles (160 km) in any direction, its cone rises thousands of feet higher than other peaks in the Cascades and is the fifth-highest summit in the contiguous United States.

From the Tacoma area south of Seattle, follow the Nisqually River south to the tiny town of **Elbe** ㉟, the only train town this side of Strasberg, Pennsylvania. Here a cluster of cabooses, coaches and an antique steam engine sit in the Elbe trainyard – the cabooses are actually a motel, and the Mount Rainier Scenic Railroad is a train that chugs into the lush mountain forests three times a day, then transforms into an old-fashioned dining car on weekends. Just behind the depot is the "tiniest church in the world," according to *Ripley's Believe It or Not.*

Follow 706 out of Elbe to **Ashford**, a small town just outside the Longmire entrance to the park and the most convenient place to find lodging outside of the park. Alexander's Country Inn, an imposing 1912 hotel turned bed-and-breakfast establishment with an excellent dining room, or Mountain Meadows Inn, a rambling 14-acre bed and breakfast property complete with pond, pigs, a nightly campfire with toasted "smores" and the (remote) possibility of encountering Bigfoot, once heard nearby in the woods, are comfortable places to stay.

PRECEDING PAGES: climber on Mount St. Helens; Mount Adams is in the background. **LEFT:** mist in the Cascades. **BELOW:** hiker on Mount Rainier.

Mount Rainier National Park

First named Tahoma – "The Mountain That Was God" – by the Indians, then renamed **Mount Rainier** ㊱ in 1792 by English explorer Capt. George Vancouver, the mountain has inspired artists, mountain climbers and entrepreneurs alike with its monumental and breathtaking beauty. One single road loops around the mountain, through miles of the 378-sq.-mile (980-sq.-km) **Mount Rainier National Park** and timbered canyons. During the winter months, passes at Cayuse and Chinook are closed; between May and October the park is accessible year-round.

Climbing Mount Rainier is a challenge, and all but experienced climbers must undertake the ascent with a professional guide service. Mount Rainier, for all its majesty, is dangerous and many people have been killed trying to scale its snow-covered heights. Hiking through the park is excellent on the park's 300-plus miles of trail system.

Mount Rainier's compelling history dates back over 75,000 years ago when volcanism enabled the peak to reach 16,000 ft (5,000 meters) in height. Subsequent erosion by glaciers stripped 2,000 ft off its top. The mountain's present height of 14,411 ft (4,392 meters) makes it the tallest volcanic mountain in the conti-

If in the making of the West, Nature had what we call parks in mind – places for rest, inspiration and prayers – this Rainier region must surely be one of them. Of all the fire mountains which... once blazed along the Pacific Coast, Mount Rainier is the noblest.

– JOHN MUIR

nental United States. Today, Mount Rainier is host to the single largest glacier system – 26 glaciers – in the lower 48. Buried under more than 50 ft (15 meters) of snow annually, the glaciers can move as much as a foot every day, depositing boulders and debris in morainal mounds and grinding bedrock into powder. Considered dormant, the peak last erupted 500 to 600 years ago, with a lava flow just 150 years ago.

Access to the park is through the Nisqually Entrance and then **Longmire**, just inside the national park's southwestern border, where the modestly priced, 25-room National Park Inn is the only lodge open all year, a simple rustic inn and restaurant, with a wildlife museum containing stuffed animals on display. Longmire is the only place in the park to buy gas. Follow the road for a few miles where a short hike into the Grove of the Patriarchs leads to the tallest trees in the park.

Paradise, the most popular destination point in the park, lies northeast (at 5,400 ft/1,650 metres) and has paved parking, the **Henry M. Jackson Memorial Visitors Center**, gift shop and cafeteria. There are spectacular views of **Narada Falls** and **Nisqually Glacier**, as well as of Mount Rainier from the observation deck.

Head east on the road and then north at the **Stevens Canyon Entrance** in the park's southeast corner, cresting at 4,675-ft (1,425-meter) **Cayuse Pass**. Just beyond is the **White River Entrance**; turn left, or west, towards the **Sunrise Visitors Center**, the closest spot to Mount Rainier (at 6,400 ft) and with a visitors center. It offers a breathtaking entree to lush wildflower meadows. The Emmons Glacier, largest in the lower 48, is visible from a short trail from the visitors center.

Northward from the White River Entrance, just off the road on the western

BELOW: reflection of Mount Rainier.

edge of the park and outside its boundary, is **Crystal Mountain**, where some of the best ski slopes in Washington entice avid skiers to down-hill and cross country throughout the winter. In the summer, chair lifts are used to catch a glimpse of Mount Rainier, while tennis, horseback riding and easy park access all help to lure tourists.

Map on pages 220–1

Mount St. Helens

Only two hours from Elbe is **Mount St. Helens** ㊲, the active volcano that erupted with unexpected fury in May of 1980. Follow Highway 7 south to Morton and stop for travel information. Several roads lead to views of what remains of Spirit Lake, once the prime vantage point of the mountain, and the volcano itself; the volcanic landscape is spectacular and makes for a wonderful diversion from Elbe. From Seattle, the most direct route is south on Interstate 5. Ringing the area are the peaks of Mount Adams, Mount Rainier, and Mount Hood.

The 1980 explosion blew away a cubic mile of St. Helens' summit, reducing its elevation from 9,677 ft (2,949 meters) to 8,364 ft (2,549 meters) and flattening 230 sq. miles (595 sq km) of surrounding forest. Seventy people died. The toll on the wildlife is estimated at 5,000 black-tailed deer, 1,500 elk, 200 black bears, 15 mountain goats, and uncounted mountain lions, bobcats, and avian wildlife. The eruption's ash and steam ascended to 60,000 ft (18,000 km). Afterwards, wood to build 80,000 three-bedroom homes was salvaged. The volcano's peak is now a gaping mile-wide crater, 2,000 ft (600 meters) deep.

The area, easily reached via Interstate 5 from Seattle, is now designated the **Mount St. Helens National Volcanic Monument**. A visitors center includes an extraordinary 22-minute film of the volcano's eruption.

A logger in the mountains east of Seattle.

BELOW: bubbling brook in the Cascades.

THE RING OF FIRE

The beautiful volcanic peaks that pepper the Pacific Northwest – Rainier, Baker, Adams, St. Helens – are part of the 30,000-mile-long (48,000-km) Ring of Fire, essentially the volcanically active rim of the entire Pacific Basin. It extends down the west coasts of North America and South America, then up through Asia – Indonesia, Philippines, Japan – and across the Aleutian Islands to Alaska. Along this Ring of Fire are 70 percent of the planet's 500 or so historically active volcanoes.

This Ring of Fire is defined by the meeting of the earth's tectonic plates, pieces of the earth's crust fitting together like a jigsaw puzzle, but slowly moving over the hotter and softer material underneath. Where they collide results in mountain ranges, earthquakes and volcanoes. The Ring of Fire roughly follows the edges of the Pacific Plate, about the same size as the Pacific Ocean. Where the Pacific Plate collides with the Eurasian Plate gives rise to the volcanoes of Japan and the Philippines. Where it meets the American Plate – along the North American west coast – we find the San Andreas Fault of California and the volcanoes of the Pacific Northwest. While in our lifetime the explosion of Mount St. Helens is a catastrophic event, in geological time it is a common and expected occurance.

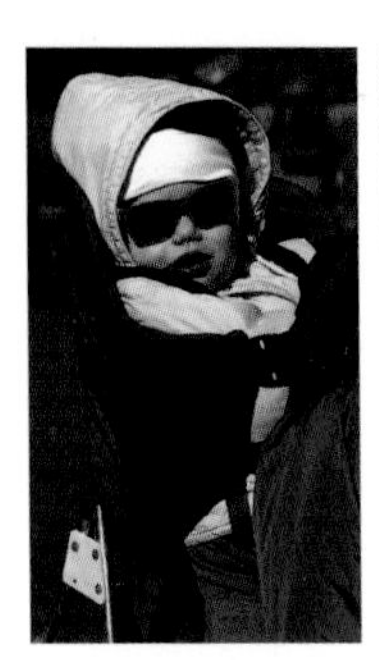

Shades in the high sky of the Cascades.

East into the Cascades

From Everett, north of Seattle, head east into the town of **Snohomish** 38, once an active logging town (founded in 1859, it is one of Washington's oldest communities) and an antique center of the Northwest. Its downtown historic district is loaded with antique stores, most within a four-block radius. Head east on US 2 and follow the Skykomish River through the conifer forests of the **Mount Baker-Snoqualmie National Forest**; the jagged peaks of the Cascade Range loom ahead.

The road is especially scenic in the fall, when vine maples lend a distinctive scarlet color to the landscape. At **Wallace Falls State Park**, a 7-mile (11-km) roundtrip trail leads to the impressive 365-ft (111-meter) cascade and a view of an imposing Mount Index, nearly 6,000 ft (1,800 meters) high. Kayaking, fishing and river-rafting are popular activities along the Skykomish, and many trailheads originate along the route. Stop at the US Forest Service Ranger Station in the town of **Skykomish** 39 for local maps and information. In winter, downhill and cross-country skiing are enthusiastically pursued at 4,061-ft (1,237-meter) **Stevens Pass** 40, 25 miles (40 km) past Skykomish, and at Mission Ridge, southwest of Wenatchee, on the eastern flanks of the Cascades.

North to La Conner

Take Interstate 5 north out of Seattle to Mount Vernon, north of Seattle, and then head west for the busy tourist town of **La Conner** 41, a fine example of what energetic townspeople can accomplish by promoting their history and staging annual events to restore a dying town. In the 1970s, local entrepreneurs filled their tiny shops on First and Second streets with art galleries, antique stores,

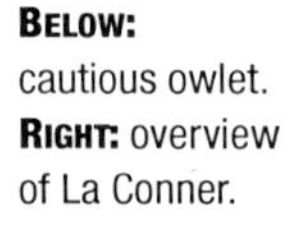

Below: cautious owlet. **Right:** overview of La Conner.

restaurants, boutiques and country stores. Now the best-known town in Skagit Valley, La Conner's claim to fame is tulips, as busloads of visitors make treks here each April for the Skagit Valley Tulip Festival, then head into town for the parades, flower shows, street fair and dances.

Because of the area's beauty, artists like Morris Graves, Mark Tobey and Guy Anderson chose to live here and paint remarkable landscapes of the area. The town hall, built as a bank in 1880, and the 1869 cabin of Magnus Anderson vie with the 22-room **Gaches Mansion** (1891) on Second Street for the town's most popular old structure. The Gaches Mansion is a wonderful example of Victorian architecture, right down to the widow's walk that overlooks the Skagit Valley. Just over the Rainbow Bridge outside town is **Hope Island** and Sneeoosh Beach, one of the most pristine beaches in the Pacific Northwest.

La Conner makes a perfect jumping-off point for further excursions. From here, one can head west, mostly by boat, to the San Juan Islands and Canada's Gulf Islands. South returns to Seattle and Tacoma, or Los Angeles. East climbs into the awesome Cascades, while north eventually passes into British Columbia. Cross Swinomish Channel by the Rainbow Bridge to visit one of the earliest Indian communities built by Christian missionaries.

Back on the mainland, head through the Skagit Valley to Chuckanut Drive, a fairly famous piece of roadway once part of the old Pacific Highway and now one of the most scenic drives in the state. The roadway curves north about 25 miles (40 km) and follows the water up to **Bellingham** ㊷; along this stretch are several top-notch restaurants mostly specializing in the region's oysters and seafood, not to mention pretty **Larrabee State Park**, south of Bellingham and Washington's first state park.

Map on pages 220–1

BELOW: spires of the Cascades.

North Cascades National Park

From La Conner, SR 20 shoots east into the Cascades Range, which lie east of Seattle, divide the eastern and western parts of the state, are 700 miles (1,100 km) in length, and extend from northern California, where they join the Sierra Nevada Range, to the Fraser River just south of Vancouver, in British Columbia. Visible on clear days to the east, the North Cascades' towering peaks are reminiscent of the Alps. The Cascades themselves are a jigsaw puzzle of different national parks, national forests, and wilderness areas. The northern extent of the Cascades, interestingly enough called the North Cascades, extends to the Canadian border.

Five hundred miles (800 km) of scenic highway loop through the 800-sq. mile (2,000-sq. km) **North Cascades National Park** ㊸, traversing snow-covered mountains, rushing rivers and the many pretty towns scattered along the way. The cliffs, glaciers and gorges of North Cascades National Park are bordered on the eastern edge by the arid hills of Okanogan National Forest. In the center of the horseshoe-shaped forest are the touristy towns of **Winthrop** and **Twisp**. Cross-country skiing centers in winter, in summer they turn into recreational vehicle ghettos.

Quite prominent on the skyline directly west of North Cascades National Park is **Mount Baker** ㊹, at 10,778 ft (3,285 meters) one of the several volcanoes that gives the Cascades a personality. The trail along Heliotrope Ridge offers views of the frozen rapids of Coleman Glacier. On the national park's southern end is **Glacier Peak Wilderness**, the heart of the North Cascades with 10,541-ft (3,212-meter) **Glacier Peak** ㊺. Its glaciers end in ice-blue lakes and meadows blanket small corners between broken rock spires. ❑

BELOW: skiing in the Cascade Range. **RIGHT:** Snoqualmie Falls and Salish Lodge.

COMMON SENSE AND SMARTS

The old proverb is good advice: Take nothing but pictures, leave nothing but footprints. As the number of visitors increases to national parks, the wear and tear on the environment is increasingly a concern. If intending to hike, climb or camp in one of the Northwest's national parks or forests, follow all rules and regulations established by the National Park Service and U.S. Forest Service.

In addition to the awareness of environmental ethics, visitors need to acknowledge common sense. Don't hike alone. Never approach wild animals, even if they seem tame and waiting just for your camera beside the road. Don't let dogs run loose. Know thy physical and mental limitations. Dress appropriately and anticipate the worst. Concentrate on what you're doing and where you're going. Take care near cliffs and rivers.

Don't attempt anything that you're uncomfortable with or for which you lack the skills or experience. Most accidents and injuries in the wilderness are caused by inattentive or incautious behavior. Heed all posted warnings and seek the advice of park rangers.

Air is thinner at higher altitudes. Unless acclimated, one may experience lack of breath, nausea, headache, fatigue and light-headedness.

INSIGHT GUIDES

Travel Tips

CONTENTS

Getting Acquainted

The Place

Area: Greater Seattle encompasses a geographic area stretching east across Lake Washington to the edge of the Cascade Mountains, west across Puget Sound to include communities on the Kitsap Peninsula and several islands (from which people commute to Seattle by ferry), south to Tacoma and north to Everett
Population: Close to 540,000 people make Seattle proper home. The greater Seattle metropolitan area population is slightly over 3 million
Language: US English
Time zone: Pacific Standard Time
Currency: US dollar ($)
Weights and measures: Imperial
Electricity: 110 volts
International dialing code: 01 (USA), 206 Seattle
Ethnic mix: Caucasians make up almost 75 percent of Seattle's population. Asian Americans comprise the city's largest minority group representing 12 percent of the population, followed by African Americans, Latinos and descendants of one of the original Native American tribes that lived along the shores of Puget Sound, the Duwamish

Climate

The temperature in western Washington (west of the Cascade Mountains) is usually mild. Daytime temperatures typically range from 75–79°F (23–26°C) in summer and 41–48°F (4.5–9°C) in winter. From October through April, Seattle gets 80 percent of its annual quota of rain. In summer, Seattle is frequently covered by some form of marine mist or fog in the morning that dissipates by the afternoon. Seattleites on average only receive the sun's light and warmth uninterrupted for the whole day about 55 times a year.

Snow tends to stay in the mountains, which keeps skiers and almost everyone else happy, but because of quirky weather patterns you can sometimes find yourself in a hail shower on one side of town while the other side experiences clear skies and a rainbow.

Time Zones

Seattle is within the Pacific Standard Time Zone (the same as California), which is two hours behind Chicago and three hours behind New York City. On the first Sunday in April, residents set their clocks forward one hour for Daylight Saving Time, and on the last Sunday in October set them back an hour to Standard Time.

On Pacific Standard Time, when it is noon in Seattle it is:

- 3pm in New York and Montréal
- 8pm in London
- 4am (the next day) in Singapore and Hong Kong
- 5am in Tokyo
- 6am in Sydney

Ethnic Mix

Caucasians make up almost 75 percent of Seattle's population. Asian Americans comprise the city's largest minority group representing 12 percent of the population followed by African Americans, Latinos and descendants of one of the original Native American tribes that lived along the shores of Puget Sound, the Duwamish.

Most Seattleites are conversant only in English. Yet locals tend to be outgoing and willing to try to help visitors despite a language barrier. There are few multilingual signs with the exception of Japanese, due to economic ties to Japan. At Sea-Tac Airport, for example, recorded verbal instructions on the subway trains are in English and Japanese. A separate information booth is staffed by people fluent in the Japanese language.

Most large hotels in Seattle offer a multilingual concierge or front-desk staff who can supply information regarding city and airport transportation, currency exchange and other visitor services.

If translation is a necessity, there are several places to turn to:

Transitional Assistance Program
(formally known as Traveler's Aid)
1100 Virginia Street
Suite 210
Seattle, WA 98101
Tel: (206) 461-3888
Helps with various problems such as accommodation, transportation or lost traveler's checks. Opening hours: Monday–Friday, 9am–4pm.

Language Bank-American Red Cross
1900 25 Avenue S.
Seattle, WA 98144
Tel: (206) 323-2345
Manages a 24-hour volunteer emergency service. Offers written and oral interpretation in 70 languages.

Washington Academy of Languages
98 Yesler Way
Seattle, WA
Tel: (206) 682-4463
Offers translation services for visitors. Opening hours: Monday to Thursday 8am–9pm, and Friday 8am–5pm.

The Seattle-King County Visitor's Bureau
800 Convention Place
Washington State Convention & Trade Center
Tel: (206) 461-5840
Website: www.seeseattle.org
Distributes a Seattle tourist brochure in Japanese and English and maps of the airport in Japanese and English.

Planning the Trip

Entry Regulations

Visas and Passports

To enter the United States you must have a valid passport; smart travelers make sure their passports are valid at least three months longer than their intended length of stay in the United States. Visas are required for all foreigners except Canadians and Britons, and should be obtained prior to entering the country. Canadian and Mexican citizens who possess a border pass do not need a visa or a passport.

Inoculations and other documents

Vaccinations are not required for entry unless the visitor is from, or has passed through, an infected area. In this case, a health record may be necessary.

Other documents that are invaluable are a driver's license and any type of health insurance or travel insurance cards. If you intend to do any driving, obtain an International Driving Permit. It's a useful accessory to your own country's driving document which may be viewed by local authorities as less than real.

Customs

An individual over the age of 21 is allowed to bring one bottle of liquor free of tax and 200 cigarettes duty free into the USA.

All gifts must be declared. There is a $400 exemption for visitors including US residents. For gifts worth $400–$1,000, visitors pay a 10 percent charge. Gifts worth upwards of $1,000 are charged a "duty right" tax variable by item.

Money

Traveler's checks

American dollar traveler's checks are the safest form of currency. If lost or stolen, most can be replaced. In addition, they are as acceptable as cash in most stores, restaurants and hotels. Banks will generally cash large amounts of traveler's checks. Always keep a record of the check numbers separate from the checks themselves. Remember to take your passport with you in case you are asked to produce it as identification.

To report stolen or lost traveler's checks you can call:

Visa
Tel: (1 800) 227-6811
Thomas Cook
Tel: (1 800) 223-7373
MasterCard
Tel: (1 800) 223-9920
American Express
Tel: (1 800) 221-7282.

Currency and credit cards

Foreign currency exchange is available at Sea-Tac (*see below*), major Seattle banks and at some major downtown hotels. Daily newspapers print exchange rates for most major currencies.

Having a credit card can be valuable for emergencies and transactions such as renting a car. Visa and MasterCard are widely accepted throughout the United States. In case of a lost or stolen card, use their toll-free numbers to report the incident immediately: **Visa** (Tel: (1 800) 336-8472) and **MasterCard** (Tel: 1-800 826-2181).

Getting There

BY AIR

Seattle-Tacoma International Airport, known as Sea-Tac, is located 13 miles (20 km) south of Seattle.

For information on the airport, its services, parking or security, call the **Sea-Tac International information line**, Tel: (206) 431-4444, (206) 433-5288, or (1 800) 544-1965.

Public Holidays

- **New Year's Day** January 1
- **Martin Luther King's Birthday** 3rd Monday in January
- **Lincoln's Birthday** February 12
- **President's Day** 3rd Monday in February
- **Memorial Day** last Monday in May
- **Independence Day** July 4
- **Labor Day** 1st Monday in September
- **Columbus Day** 2nd Monday in October
- **Election Day** 1st Tuesday after 1st Monday in November
- **Veteran's Day** November 11
- **Thanksgiving** 4th Thursday in November
- **Christmas** December 25

(*See Festivals for a calendar of events, page 285.*)

Access to Sea-Tac is via Interstate-5 (take exit 154 from south I-5 or exit 152 from north I-5), or via Highway 99/509 and 518. Stop-and-go traffic on I-5 is not uncommon, especially during rush hours, so the alternate route on the highway is often quicker.

At the airport

Many services are available at Sea-Tac to ease the transition from air to ground; some are especially helpful to foreigners.

Aside from restaurants, restrooms, gift shops, and resort-wear clothing stores, three Thomas Cook currency exchange booths are scattered throughout the airport. Two are in the main terminal: one behind the Delta Ticket counter in the B-concourse (open 6am–8pm) and another at the Alaska Airlines ticket counter (open 6am–6pm). The third booth is located in the south satellite (open 6am–2:30pm). Tel: (206) 248-6960 for more information.

At the US West Communications Center, located in both the main and north terminals, fax (outgoing only) and copy machines are

City	from Seattle	driving time
Spokane, WA	280 miles	5 hours approx.
San Francisco,CA	850 miles	15 hours approx.
Portland, OR	75 miles	3 hours approx.
Vancouver, BC	140 miles	3 hours approx.

This is a listed of estimated times and distances to several cities within a day or two driving a car under safe road conditions.

available, as are desks, a small conference room (on a first-come, first-served basis), and telephones for the hearing impaired.

A nursery with an enclosed carpeted play area for children, a crib and a nursing room with rocking chairs, will provide relief for travel-stressed parents and children.

A beauty salon/barber shop offers not only haircuts and manicures, but also showers.

There is a meditation room/chapel available on the mezzanine level that has a Sunday only service at 11.30am. For chaplain, Tel: (206) 433-5505.

On the second level of the terminal, **Traveler's Aid** offers an escort service at the airport for children, the elderly or handicapped for a fee. It also has information on transportation from the airport and tourist attractions in the area. Tel: (206) 433-5288.

Operation Welcome has interpreters fluent in 21 foreign languages to aid passengers through customs and immigrations. The service is located in the south satellite on the mezzanine outside immigration. Tel: (206) 433-5367. There are also several booths just for visitors from Japan. Tel: (206) 433-4679.

The **Seattle-King County Convention and Visitors Bureau** operates a tourist information booth near the baggage claim area. Tel: (206) 433-5218.

International Airlines

Major airlines flying into and out of Sea-Tac include:

Air Canada/Air BC:
Tel: (1 800) 776-3000.
Alaska Airlines:
Tel: (206) 433-3100,
(1 800) 252-7522.
American West:
Tel: (1 800) 235-9292
American Airlines:
Tel: (1 800) 433-7300
British Airways:
Tel: (1 800) 247-9297
Canadian Airlines:
Tel: (1 800) 426-7000
Continental Airlines:
Tel: (1 800) 231-0856
Delta:
Tel: (1 800) 221-1212
Hawaiian Airlines:
Tel: (1 800) 367-5320
Horizon Air:
Tel: (1 800) 547-9308
Japan Airlines:
Tel: (1 800) 525-3663
Korean Air:
Tel: (1 800) 438-5000
Lufthansa:
Tel: (1 800) 645-3880
Northwest Airlines:
Tel: (1 800) 225-2525
Qantas:
Tel: (1 800) 227-4500
Scandinavian Airlines:
Tel: (1 800) 221-2350
Southwest Airlines:
Tel: (1 800) 435-9792
TWA:
Tel: (1 800) 221-2000
US Air:
Tel: (1 800) 428-4322
United Airlines:
Tel: (1 800) 241-6522

Check the *Yellow Pages* under "Airline Companies" or Tel: 1-(206) 555-1212 for more information.

The lost and found is located on the mezzanine level in the main terminal. It is open Monday–Friday, 7.30am–5.30pm, Tel: (206) 433-5312.

Last but not least, Ken's Baggage, on the baggage level, under the escalators, between carrousels 9 and 12 will take care of odds and ends for travelers, such as coats and boots storage, dry cleaning services, UPS and Federal Express package services, as well as notary public, ticket- and key-holding services and much more. Hours: 5.30am–12.30am, seven days. Tel: (206) 433-5333.

BY BUS

Transcontinental bus lines providing services throughout Seattle and the US include the following:

Greyhound
811 Stewart Street
(corner of Eighth Avenue and Stewart Street)
Tel: (1 800) 231-2222
The ubiquitous Greyhound bus service offers the most comprehensive service of scheduled routes from Seattle and across the North American continent.

Green Tortoise
Tel: (1-415) 956-7500 or (1 800) 867-8647
Website: www. Greentortoise.com
This infamous bus service is an alternative form of bus travel connecting Seattle to San Francisco and Portland. Here, easy chairs replace bus seats, music plays in the background, and stops are scheduled for soaking in a hot springs and having a campfire cookout.
Tel: (1-415) 956-7500 or (1 800) 867-8647
Website: www. Greentortoise.com

Quick Shuttle
Tel: (1 800) 665-2122
This company operates five daily express runs between Vancouver, BC, and downtown Seattle and the airport.

BY RAIL

Amtrak is the USA's national rail network. It can be found in Seattle at Third Avenue and S. Jackson Street. Tel: 1-800–usa-rail.

Amtrak connects Seattle with the east via the "Empire Builder" from Chicago and the "Pioneer" from Denver, and with the south via the "Coast Starlight" from Los Angeles. The "Coast Starlight" is the most popular route with beautiful coastal scenery and stops in Tacoma, Olympia, Vancouver, Washington, and Portland, Oregon, along the way. Amtrak's "Mount Baker" run also connects Vancouver, over the Canadian border, and Seattle. In summer early reservations for this trip are essential.

BY ROAD

Major land routes into Seattle are the Interstate Freeway 5, known as "I-5" which stretches from the Canadian to the Mexican borders; and Interstate 90, or "I-90," which leaves downtown Seattle eastward right toward the cities of Chicago and Boston.

Federal and state highways are generally well-maintained and policed, with refreshment areas and service stations located at regular intervals. There are no bridge tolls or highway fees payable in or around Seattle.

Practical Tips

Tourist Information

A wealth of information on attractions, activities, accommodations and restaurants is available from the **Seattle-King County Convention and Visitors Bureau** in the Washington State Convention Center at 666 Stewart Street (Eighth Avenue and Pike Street). Tel: (206) 461-5840. Hours: 8.30am–5pm Monday– Friday, 10am–4pm on Saturday during summer. The bureau also operates an **information center** at **Sea-Tac Airport**, on the baggage level. Tel: (206) 433-5218. Hours: 9.30am–7.30pm daily.

USEFUL TELEPHONE NUMBERS

AAA of Washington
Tel: (206) 448-5353
American Youth Hostel
Tel: (206) 622-5443
FBI Tel: (206) 622-0460
Coast Guard Emergencies
Tel: (206) 217-6000
Crisis Clinic
Tel: (206) 461-3222
Mountain Road Conditions
Tel: (1 900) 407-pass
Seattle-King County Convention and Visitors Bureau,
Tel: (206) 461-5840
Seattle Post-Intelligencer
Tel: (206) 448-8000
Seattle Public Library
Main Branch
Tel: (206) 386-info
(for quick information)
Seattle Times
Tel: (206) 464-2121
Transitional Assistance
(formally Travelers Aid)
Tel: (206) 461-3888
US Post Office
Main Station
Tel: (206) 442-6340
Weather
Tel: (206) 526-6087

Embassies & Consulates

The following embassies are located in downtown Seattle. For information on other countries, contact your embassy or consulate before leaving home:

United Kingdom
First Interstate Center
999 Third Avenue, Suite 820
Seattle, WA 98104
Tel: (206) 622-9255
Canada
Plaza 600, Suite 412
Sixth Avenue and Stewart Street
Seattle, WA 98101-1286
Tel: (206) 443-1777
Mexico
2132 Third Avenue Seattle
WA 98121
Tel: (206) 448-3526

Business Hours

Most businesses in central and greater Seattle are generally open from 9am–5pm Monday–Friday and closed on Saturday, Sunday and public holidays.

Banks are usually open from 9am–3pm, Monday–Friday, with many in the center staying open on Saturday mornings. Most banks, government agencies, such as the post office and some other businesses close on public holidays (*see page 265*).

Religious Services

For referrals of religious services by denomination, contact:

The Church Council of Greater Seattle
4759 15th Avenue NE
Tel: (206) 525-1213

Media

Print

The major daily newspapers in Seattle are the *Seattle Post-*

Intelligencer and the *Seattle Times*. On Sunday, the two combine into one large edition. Friday tabloid sections in both papers are useful guides to weekend events. *Seattle Weekly*, a tabloid news-magazine, prints a guide to the week's recreation and entertainment, including visual arts, theater, music and film. Also included is dining and shopping information. *Puget Sound Business Journal* is a weekly newspaper that covers business activities in the Puget Sound area.

Foreign language newspapers include the *North American Post*, a Japanese daily, the *Seattle Chinese Post*, and *Hispanic News* (weekly).

Public libraries offer reading rooms stacked with periodicals and, at the main branch, a good selection of foreign newspapers and periodicals (ask at the Humanities desk). The main library is located at 100 Fourth Avenue (Fourth and Madison). Hours: 9am–9pm Monday–Thursday, 9am–6pm Friday–Saturday; 1–5pm Sunday, September to June. Tel: (206) 386-4636.

Newsstands that sell foreign publications include:

Steve's Broadway News
204 Broadway E.
Tel: (206) 324-READ

Steve's Fremont News
3416 Fremont Avenue N.
Tel: (206) 633-0731

Read All About It International Newsstand
98 Pike Street (in Pike Place Market)
Tel: (206) 624-0140

Television and Radio

Excluding cable television, seven major stations serve the Seattle area. The public broadcast station is KCTS. It does not air commercials, but supports itself through public donations and grants.

There are numerous radio stations in the city to cater to all tastes (see below).

Postal Services

The main post office in Seattle is located at 301 Union. Tel: (206) 442-6340. Hours: 8.30am–5pm Monday–Friday. Travelers uncertain of their address in a particular town may have mail addressed in their name, sent care of General Delivery at the main post office of that town. Mail will be held there for pick up.

Be sure to include a five-digit zip code for all addresses within the US. Information about zip codes may be obtained from any post office. Overnight delivery service and Express Mail, is also provided by the post office and some private companies. Check in the *Yellow Pages* under "Delivery Service."

Stamps may also be purchased from vending machines, as well as at post offices, which can often be found in hotels, stores, airports, and bus and train stations.

Telephone Services

For long distance calls within the 206, 425 and 253 area codes, the ten-digit phone number must be preceded by a "1".

For long-distance calls outside the local 206 area code, first dial a "1", the area code and then the phone number.

For assistance in long distance dialing, first dial zero and an operator will assist you. Phone numbers that are preceded by "1 800" are free of charge only when dialed from within the US.

To dial other countries (Canada follows the US system), first dial the international access code "011", then the country code, for example:

Australia (61)
France (33)
Italy (39)

Seattle television and radio channels

Television:

Channel: 4	KOMO	ABC affiliate
Channel: 5	KING	NBC affiliate
Channel: 7	KIRO	CBS affiliate
Channel: 9	KCTS	PBS
Channel: 11	KSTW	independent
Channel: 13	KCPQ	independent
Channel: 22	KTZZ	independent

Radio:

AM stations:

570 KVI	popular music, sports
630 KCIS	religious music, interviews
710 KIRO	news, sports
820 KGNW	religious
880 KIXI	hits from 1940s–60s
950 KJR	classic hits
1000 KOMO	news, adult contemporary
1050 KBLE	religious
1090 KING	news, talk shows
1150 KEZK	business, talk, news
1210 KBS	goldies from 1950s–70s
1250 KKFX	rhythm and blues
1300 KMPS	country
1420 KRIZ	urban contemporary music, blues, jazz, gospel
1590 KZOK	oldies

FM stations:

88.5 KPLU	jazz and news. Public Radio affiliate.
89.5 KNH	contemporary, run by Seattle School District
90.3 KCMU	alternative music, world beat
93.3 KUBE	contemporary hits
94.1 KMPS	country
94.5 KUOW	classical, ethnic, swing, talk shows
95.7 KLTX	soft rock
96.5 KXR	adult rock
97.3 KBSG	rock from 1950s–70s
98.1 KING	classical
98.9 KEZX	jazz, soft rock, folk, reggae
100 KISW	rock
100.7 KSEA	easy listening
101.5 KPLZ	oldies, sports, traffic
102.5 KZOK	classic rock
103.7 KBRD	easy listening
105.3 KCMS	contemporary Christian music
106.9 KKNW	progressive, jazz, new age
107.7 KNDD	cutting edge, alternative rock

Japan (81)
Mexico (52)
Spain (34)
UK (44)
If using a US phone credit card, such as Sprint or AT&T, dial the company's access number, then "01", then the country code.
Sprint Tel: 10333;
AT&T Tel: 10288.

Telegraph and fax

Telegraph services are available through Western Union. Tel: (1 800) 325-6000.

Fax machines can be found at most hotels and at the airport. Fax companies are located throughout the city. See the *Yellow Pages* under "facsimile" for information.

Emergencies

SECURITY AND CRIME

The streets of Seattle and most adjoining neighborhoods are safe during the day. However, at night caution is advised. It is best not to walk alone at night on deserted city streets. Lock your car and never leave luggage, cameras or other valuables in view.

Never leave money or jewelry in your hotel room, even for a short time. Use the hotel's safety deposit service. Carry only the cash you need, using traveler's checks whenever possible.

LOSS OF BELONGINGS

If valuables are lost or stolen, report them to the local police department. A description of the items will be filed, and if the items turn up the police will return them as soon as possible.

Lost Luggage:

Most airlines and other transportation companies have insurance for lost customer luggage, but it doesn't hurt to ask the company what its policy is. Be sure to mark all luggage with identification tags. If luggage left at the airport is turned in to Sea-Tac's lost and found (*see page 265*), someone from that department will usually bring the luggage to the hotel if returning to the airport is inconvenient.

MEDICAL SERVICES

The medical care in Seattle is excellent, but it is prohibitively expensive if a long hospital stay is required.

If an illness strikes or medical attention is needed, it pays to have temporary health insurance which has been issued prior to your trip. Check with your current insurance provider for additional travel coverage for the US.

Emergency Services

For police, fire or medical emergencies, dial **911**.

Most hospitals have a 24-hour emergency room service. Here are some major hospitals in the Seattle area that can provide emergency care:

In Seattle

Children's Hospital and Medical Center
4800 Sand Point Way, NE
Tel: (206) 526-2000
Harborview Medical Center
325 Ninth Avenue (corner of Jefferson Street)
Tel: (206) 731-3000
Providence Medical Center
500 17th Avenue
Tel: (206) 320-2000
Swedish Medical Center/ Ballard
NW Market, Barnes Street
Tel: (206) 782-2700
Swedish Medical Center
747 Broadway
Tel: (206) 386-6000
University of Washington Medical Center
1959 NE Pacific Street
Tel: (206) 598-3300
Virginia Mason Hospital
925 Seneca Street
Tel: (206) 624-1144

In Bellevue

Overlake Hospital Medical Center
1035 116th NE, Bellevue
Tel: (425) 688-5000

In Kirkland

Evergreen Hospital Medical Center
12040 NE 128th, Kirkland
Tel: (425) 899-1000

Referrals

King County Medical Society
Tel: (206) 621-9393 (physician referral).
Seattle-King County Dental Society
Tel: (206) 443-7607 (dentist referral).

Translation Services

Hospital interpretation services offers a 24-hour translation service for hospital patients. Call **ALS Translation and Interpreting**
Tel: (425) 462-8660.

Pharmacies

Certain drugs can only be prescribed by a doctor and purchased at a pharmacy. Bring any regular medication with you and check the *Yellow Pages* under "Pharmacies" for listings.

Tipping

Tips are intended to show appreciation for good service and should reflect the quality of service rendered. The accepted rate is 15–20 percent of the bill in restaurants for waiting staff (10 percent for barstaff), 10–15 percent for taxi drivers and hairstylists. Porters and bellhops generally warrant 50 cents to $1 per bag; valets $1 to $2.

Getting Around

Maps

The King County Convention and Visitor's Bureau in the Washington State Convention Center offers free maps. If these maps are insufficient for a particular destination, the American Automobile Association, better known as "Triple A" can offer advice for planning trips, the best routes to take and detailed maps for a fee.
AAA, 330 Sixth Avenue N.
Tel: (206) 448-5353.

The Thomas Guides contain detailed street maps in a book format. They are available in most bookstores.

From the Airport

Shuttle buses and taxis can be found outside the terminal on the baggage claim level. The exact location of shuttle buses varies depending on destination and carrier. Check with the information booth at the north end of the main terminal on the baggage level. Taxis can be picked up at the north end of the terminal also.

STITA (Seattle-Tacoma International Taxi Association) provides services to and from the airport. Tel: (206) 246-9999. The trip from the airport to downtown (or vice versa) costs about $30.

Bus or van companies that link the airport with metropolitan Seattle or Bellevue include:

The Grayline Airport Express, Tel: (206) 624-5077. Operates buses every 20–30 minutes between the airport and major downtown hotels.

Greyhound, Tel: (206) 628-5556 or (1 800) 231-2222. Has several runs to and from the airport and to its downtown station at Eighth Avenue and Stewart Street.

Shuttle Express, Tel: (206) 622-1424. Provides door-to-door van service to and from the airport 24 hours daily throughout the metropolitan Seattle area.

Metro Transit, Tel: (206) 553-3000. Buses link the airport with various points throughout the city and provide the least expensive method of transportation. The 194 bus is the most direct, bringing passengers downtown to bus tunnel stops in about 30 minutes. The 174 bus makes local stops on its way downtown. Both buses run on the half hour, seven days a week.

Quick Shuttle, Tel: (206) 684-9373. Operates fast bus connections between the airport, downtown Seattle (Travelodge, 8th & Blanchard) and Vancouver (Sandman Inn, 180 W. Georgia) eight times daily. Trips between the two cities take 4 hours.

Washington Limousine Service, a well-established and reliable service, is available by reservation only. Tel: (206) 523-8000.

Local Transportation

Buses and streetcars

Metro Transit bus has both peak and non-peak hour fares. Monthly passes are available. Metro also provides a "Ride Free Area" in the downtown core bordered by the I-5 to the east, the waterfront to the west, Jackson Street to the south and Battery Street to the north.
Metro Transit, Tel: (206) 553-3000 or (206) 684-1739 for TTY/TDD users.

Metro also operates a **waterfront streetcar**, a 1927 vintage trolley which runs 1½ miles (3 km) along the waterfront every 20–30 minutes from Myrtle Edwards Park to the Pioneer Square district. The ticket requires exact change.

You can also purchase a **Metro Visitors' Pass** at various Metro Customer Assistance offices which allows one day's unlimited travel on buses and streetcars and the monorail. Tel: (206) 624-PASS.

Monorail

The **Monorail**, which was built for the 1962 World's Fair, runs every 15 minutes between Seattle Center and Fourth and Pine streets to Westlake Center. The ride is just under 1 mile (2 km) and takes only 90 seconds. It's clean and spacious with large windows.

Taxis

There are **taxi stands** at major hotels, bus depots, train stations and the airport. Taxi fares are regulated. There is an initial hire charge, with each additional mile (½ km) then costing a flat rate.
Taxi Companies:
Farwest Cab Tel: (206) 622-1717
Broadway Cabs Tel: (206) 622-4800
Graytop Cab Tel: (206) 282-8222
Yellow Cab Tel: (206) 622-6500

Car Rental companies

Alamo: Tel: (206) 433-0182.
Avis: Tel: (206) 433-5231
airport: (1 800) 831-2847.
Budget: Tel: (1 800) 345-6655
airport: (1 800) 527-0700.
Enterprise: Tel: (206) 246-1953
airport: (1 800) 736-8222.
Hertz: Tel: (206) 433-5275
airport: (1 800) 654-3131.
National: Tel: (206) 433-5501
airport: (1 800) 227-7368.

Driving

Car rental

A wide selection of rental cars is available. Rental offices are located at the airport and downtown. Generally, a major credit card is required to rent a car and the driver must be 25 years and possess a valid driver's license. Local rental companies sometimes offer less expensive rates. Be sure to check insurance provisions before signing any paperwork.

Road Tips

Driving around Seattle can be tricky. There are many one-way streets and steep hills, but also beautiful views in the downtown area, which is generally considered to lie between

Denny Way and Yesler. Avenues run north-south, while streets run east-west. Streets and avenues can be designated with numbers or names. When trying to locate an address, be sure to note whether the address includes directionals (north, south, east or west). For example, E. Madison Street or Queen Anne Avenue N. will indicate the east or north part of town.

Avoid driving during the rush hours of 7am–9am and 4pm–6pm. Although extra express lanes operate on parts of I-5 and I-90 to help alleviate the backup, it is a time-consuming and sometimes frustrating experience.

A right turn is permitted, after stopping, at a red light unless street signs indicate otherwise.

Parking laws in Seattle require that when facing downhill, the front wheels are turned into the curb and when facing uphill, front wheels are turned outward. Doing so will decrease the likelihood of the car rolling downhill. Also be sure to set the emergency brake.

Street signs, usually on corners, will indicate what type of parking is permitted for that side of the street. However, red-painted curbs mean no parking is allowed and yellow curbs indicate a loading area for trucks or buses only.

There are plenty of traffic police around (except when you need them) who earn their living by passing out fines and having cars towed away. Picking up a towed car is not only inconvenient, but costly (from $40–100 depending on where the car was parked).

Pedestrians always have the right of way. Although legal, except on freeways, picking up hitchhikers or hitchhiking is potentially dangerous.

Specialty Tours

GUIDED TOURS

Argosy Cruises, Pier 55, Suite 201, at the foot of Seneca Street. Tel: (206) 623-4252. Offers 12 different narrated cruises from one-hour trips along Seattle's waterfront and shipyards, to longer tours that pass through the Chittenden Locks into Lake Union to view the houseboats, fishing vessels and sailboats. Another cruise takes in the homes of the wealthy on Lake Washington.

Boeing Plant/Paine Air Field, Highway 526, Everett. Tel: (206) 544-1264. E-mail: everett.tourcenter@boeing.com; www.boeing.com/companyoffices/about us/tours. Paine Air Field is located about 30 miles (48 km) north of Seattle, exit 189 off I-5 and 3.5 miles (5.5 km) west on Hwy 526. Tours of this commercial aviation plant take place in the world's largest building, where visitors can observe the manufacture of 747s, 767s and 777s. Tours last one hour, beginning with a 25-minute video presentation of Boeing's history. Admission is charged and space is limited; tickets are available on a first-come, first-served basis.Six tours each weekday beginning at 8.30am. Tours are scheduled for 9, 10, and 11am, and 1, 2 or 3pm. In the summer, tickets for the day's tours can be gone by 9 or 10am. Children under 4 ft 2 inches (127 cm) in height are not permitted under any circumstances.

Brewery tours: The Redhook Ale Brewery, 14300 NE. 145th Street, Woodinville, brews one of Washington's more popular micro-beers. Tel: (425) 483-3232. Tours are given every hour from noon till 5pm in summer. **Pyramid Ale House**, 1201 1st Avenue S., Tel: (206) 682-3377, offers tours and tastings every day. Other micro-breweries that offer tours are: **Maritime Pacific Brewing Co.** Tel: (206) 782-6181. Tours from 1–4pm, Saturdays only; and **Seattle Brewers** Tel: (206) 762-7421.

Chinatown/International District Tours are run by Chinatown Discovery, Tel: (206) 236-0657. Three-hour guided tours include a seven-course "*dim sum*" lunch at a local restaurant. Mini-tours are scheduled daily in the summer. Admission is charged. www.seattlechamber.com/ chinatowntour

Gray Line of Seattle, 720 S. Forest, Tel: (206) 624-5077 or (1 800) 544-0739 (and the Sheraton Hotel lobby) offers numerous tours including San Juan Islands, Mount Rainier and North Bend and Snoqualmie Falls (of *Twin Peaks* fame).

Private Eye on Seattle Mystery and Murder Tour; Tel: (206) 622-0590 A narrated tour of Seattle's more publicized and gruesome crime scenes. Not for the faint hearted. www.privateeyetours.com

Skagit Tours operated by the city's utility company, Seattle City Light, offers a 4-hour excursion to the Diablo hydro-electric project in the North Cascades. It includes an explanatory slide show, inclined train trip, boat cruise on Lake Diablo, and bus ride to Ross Dam followed by an all-you-can-eat chicken dinner. Three departures daily, Thursday–Monday. Reservations required, Tel: (206) 684-3030. Admission is charged.

Tillicum Tours, depart from Pier 56. Tel: (206) 443-1244. A 4-hour tour combines harbor sightseeing with a trip to Blake Island Marine State Park. The park is host to Tillicum Village featuring the Northwest Coast Indian Cultural Center and Restaurant. Once there, tours include an Indian-style salmon dinner and traditional tribal dances, with time left for shopping or a casual walk. Tours run daily from May through mid-October and on weekends the rest of the year. Reservations recommended. www.Tillicum.

Underground Tours, 610 First Avenue S. Tel: (206) 682-4646. A three-block, one-hour walking tour of Pioneer Square including passage through a number of basements where subterranean sidewalks and storefronts were missed by the 1889 fire before being covered by new constructions. Stairs involved and strollers not allowed; admission charged.

Seattle Architectural Foundation's Viewpoints, Tel: (206) 667-9186 Narrated walking tours in and around downtown Seattle have different themes: one might reveal the beauty and history surrounding a city park and another feature some of Seattle's historic buildings.

A series of "lunchtime tours" offer vantage points on the city or one of its new constructions. One tour takes you to Microsoft's campus to visit the software empire.

See Seattle Walking Tours, Tel: (206) 226-7641. Walks take in the more popular Seattle sites, including Pike Place Market, the waterfront, Pioneer Square and the International District. Walking@see-seattle.com or www.see-seattle.com

Seattle Walking Tour, Tel: (206) 885-3173 A tour led by local author Duse Mclean focusing on the history of Seattle's downtown architecture. dusem@aol.com

TRAIN TOURS

Spirit of Washington Dinner Train Tel: (425) 227-RAIL or (1 800) 876-RAIL . A 45-mile (72-km) rail tour along the eastern shore of Lake Washington in restored railcars and engine from the early 1900s with a full-service dinner.

Seattle Trolley Tours, Tel: (206) 626-5212. Offers a flexible form of downtown travel via motorized trolley cars. Get on and off at a number of designated areas downtown as many times you like for the cost of a ticket good for the whole day. Trolleys run every 30 minutes and provide narrated passage.

BUS TOURS

Bus companies that offer tours in the area (Mount Rainier, Mount St. Helens, wineries, Whidbey Island and San Juan Islands) include:

Contiki Holidays
Tel: (1 714) 740-0808

Gazelle International
7739 1st Street
Tel: (206) 762-8983

Gray Line of Seattle
720 S. Forest Street
Tel: (206) 624-5077, (206) 626-5208

Greyhound Travel Services
811 Stewart Street
Tel: (1 800) 231-2222.

Puget Sound Coach Lines
8721 S. 218th Street, Kent
Tel: (253) 246-3603.

BOAT TOURS

Argosy Cruises (*see page 271*).

Gray Line Water Sightseeing, Pier 57. Tel: (206) 626-5208. Two-hour cruises by downtown waterfront, Elliott Bay, the Lake Washington Ship Canal and Lake Union via the Chittenden Locks.

Ride The Ducks of Seattle, Tel: (206) 441-DUCK or (1 800) 817-1116. Tours aboard refurbished amphibious World War II vehicles take you through the streets of Seattle before plunging into Lake Union and powering past the houseboats lining its shore. www.rideltheducksofseattle.com

Whale-Watching Tours

Island Mariner Cruises: Tel: (360) 734-8866. Tours from Bellingham. The 80-mile (130-km) round trip takes about 7½ hours and tours are scheduled May 22 through mid-September. Spotting whales is a chance endeavor but Island Mariner boasts an 85 per cent success rate with the help of professional spotters.

Mosquito Fleet San Juan Orca Cruises, Everett; Tel: (425) 252-6800 or (1 800) 325-ORCA. Call for reservations. www.whalewatching.com

Anacortes by Orca Search, Tel: (206) 386-4320. Affiliated with Seattle Aquarium, requires advance reservations.

San Juan Boat Rentals, Tel: (360) 378-3499. Offers 3-hour tours out of Friday Harbor. Office is one block from the ferry dock, which makes it convenient for those who don't want to bring their car on the ferry.

Islander Cruises, Lake Union. Tel: (206) 455-5769. 3-hour Lake Union and Lake Washington cruise.

Spirit of Puget Sound, 2819 Elliott Avenue (Pier 70). Tel: (206) 674-3499. Two- to three-hour dining and dancing cruises on Puget Sound aboard a 600-passenger luxury liner. www.spiritcruises.com

Chartering boats

From rowboats and kayaks to fully crewed yachts, charters are available to suit all needs.

Northwest Outdoor Center, 2100 Westlake Avenue N., Lake Union. Tel: (206) 281-9694. Offers sightseeing tours of Lake Union houseboats, sunset tours, and San Juan Island cruises. Kayak and canoe rentals available on Lake Union. Open all year.

Emerald City Charters (Lets Go Sailing) Pier 56, Tel: (206) 624-3931 Runs tours in view of downtown Seattle on Elliott Bay aboard a 70-ft racing sloop. Sailing tours are scheduled May through October. A 2½-hour sunset trip sails daily. www.obsession@afts.com

Wind Works Sailing Center, Shilshole Bay Marina. Tel: (206) 784-9386. Full fleet of sailboats; lessons and skippers available.

PLANE TOURS

Seattle Seaplanes
1325 Fairview Avenue E
Tel: (206) 329-9638 or (1 800) 637-5553
Offers extensive tours of the Seattle area or destinations such as Mount Rainier, and charters to fishing camps in Canada.
www.seattleseaplanes.com

Boeing Field/King County International Airport
Tel: (206) 296-7380 for information on companies that operate at this airport.

Northwest Seaplanes
860 W. Perimeter Road, Renton
Tel: (1 800) 690-0086
Scheduled and charter flights from Lake Washington and Lake Union to the San Juan Islands and BC.

Sound Flight
Renton Municipal Airport
243 W. Perimeter Rd., Renton
Tel: (425) 255-6500
Floatplane tours of Seattle, the mountains, or the San Juan Islands.

Worldwide Helicopter Inc.
6726 Perimeter Road, Boeing Field
Tel: (425) 763-1120
An on-call, round-the-clock charter

service with flights throughout the US and Canada. Also offers sightseeing tours.

Kenmore Air
6321 NE. 175th Street, Seattle
Tel: (425) 486-1257 or (1 800) 543-9595
Website: www.kenmoreair.com
Daily flights to British Columbia, Kitsap Peninsula, San Juan and Whidbey islands and the resort inn at Semiahmoo. Also offers day excursions and overnight packages.

Peninsula Airways
Tel: (1 800) 448-4226
Daily flights and charters from Seattle to Alaska.

Possible Routes

TOURING BY CAR

What may be Washington State's most spectacular natural site is the 286-ft (87-meter) **Snoqualmie Falls** (100 ft/30 meters higher than Niagara) which cascade dramatically into the Snoqualmie River, 25 miles (40 km) east of Seattle. Take I-90 to the Snoqualmie Falls (exit 27) and follow the signs. Power from the falls provides enough energy to serve 16,000 homes. Overlooking the falls is the elegant **Salish Lodge** (rooms with fireplaces, whirlpool tubs and refrigerators) with a good restaurant famous for its hearty breakfasts. Room rates start at $300 a night. (tel:425-888-2556). In the park beside the falls is a café and souvenir shop. Not far away and considerably less expensive is the **Honey Farm Inn B&B**, Tel: (425) 888-9399. The inn no longer raises bees, but instead operates a full service bed-and-breakfast.

Heading across the Sound by ferry to Bremerton on the **Kitsap Peninsula** offers a variety of sightseeing excursions. Next to the ferry terminal is docked the historic US naval destroyer, *USS Turner Joy* with tours aboard daily from May through October. Once you have fully explored Bremerton's waterfront, take a much smaller ferry a stone's throw across the water to the little town of Port Orchard that's full of antiques. Under the charming wooden arcades of storefronts spanning the downtown waterfront you can grab a bite to eat.

From the same Pier 50 in Seattle where you caught the ferry to Bremerton you can take a ferry to the city of **Winslow on Bainbridge Island**. Within a stroll of the ferry dock are shops and restaurants. Just outside Winslow the **Bainbridge Island Winery**, Tel: (360) 842-5867, can be visited in the afternoons Wednesday through Sunday. From Winslow you can head north by car to the delightful "Norwegian" town of **Poulsbo**. Once a thriving fishing village, the old waterfront area has long since turned its sights to becoming a charming tourist destination (buses operate from the ferry dock as far as Poulsbo. Tel: (360) 373-BUSS for schedules. The local convention and visitors' bureau also offers a free booklet to the Kitsap Peninsula, Tel: (360) 842-3700.

Washington State is renowned for its excellent wines, and between April and December there are dozens of special celebrations at different **wineries**. Write to the Yakima Valley Wine Growers' Association, PO Box 39, Grandview, WA 98930; or call the Tri-Cities Visitors & Convention Bureau Tel: (509) 783-8383 for free schedules and maps. Closer to Seattle are popular wineries in the suburb of Woodinville, **Château Ste Michelle**, Tel: (425) 488-1133, is located on an historic 86-acre estate once home to a lumber baron. During the summer months Ste Michelle sponsors classical music concerts and a series of contemporary pop, jazz and vocal performers on the

Exploring the Mountains

A visit to **Mount St Helens** or to **Mount Rainier National Forest** by car would logically loop right around the region, beginning south on I-5, then southeast on Highway 7 to the old lumber town of Elbe, 60 miles (95 km) from Seattle. Here you might take a ride on the **Mount Rainier Scenic Railroad, (**Tel:(360) 569-2588) before stopping for dinner at Alexander's Country Inn, Tel: (360) 569-2300, part of a rebuilt Victorian home turned into a 12-room hotel. Alexander's had the distinction of hosting President Teddy Roosevelt as an overnight guest. The hotel and restaurant are located in tiny Ashford on Highway 706. Comfortable rooms can be found at the equally old **Mountain Meadows Inn B&B** (Tel: (360) 569-2788). Once home to an executive of the Pacific lumber company, the largest west of the Mississippi, the inn sits among 11 acres of old growth cedar six miles (9.5 km) from the park entrance.

Highway 7 continues down towards **Mount St Helens National Volcanic Monument**, Tel: (360) 274-2103, whose visitor center on Highway 504 (also called the Spirit Lake Memorial Highway), just 5 miles (8 km) east of I-5 at Castle Rock, is open daily. The exhibits are exceptional in their teachings of volcanos and documenting the Mount St Helen's eruption including aftermath effects upon the ecology. Another view of the mountain can be found here in Castle Rock at the **Cinedome**, Tel: (360) 274-8000, a three–story-high movie screen showing the film *The Eruption of Mount St. Helens.* Other spectacular vantage points to view the mountain and its steaming volcanic crater can be had from the million-dollar facility at Coldwater Ridge, Tel: (360) 274-2131, or the Johnson Ridge Observatory, Tel: (360) 274-2140.

Continuing on Highway 7 then brings you into **Mount Rainier National Park** with comfortable inns at both Paradise and Longmire. Advance room reservations are strongly recommended, Tel: (360) 569-2275.

estate's lawns which also lend themselves to picnics. Wine-tasting is open in the château from 10am–4:30pm daily. Across the street is the **Columbia Winery**, Tel: (425) 488-2776, the oldest producer of some of Washington's better wines, with tours daily from 10am–5pm featuring more wine tasting.

TOURING BY FERRY

The **Washington State Ferry** system, the largest in the country, covers the Puget Sound area, linking Seattle (at Pier 52) with the Olympic Peninsula via Bremerton and Bainbridge Island. State ferries also depart from West Seattle to Vashon Island and Southworth and from Edmonds, 7 miles (11 km) north of Seattle, to Kingston on Kitsap Peninsula. It also goes from Anacortes, 90 miles (145 km) northwest of Seattle, through the San Juan Islands to Victoria, on Canada's Vancouver Island. For information: Tel: (206) 464-6400 or (1 800) 843-3779. Passengers to Canada need a passport.

Clipper Navigation operates both a passenger-only ferry, the *Victoria Clipper*, year–round, and a slower ferry for car-passengers, the *Princess Marguerite III* (in summer only) between Seattle and Victoria, BC. During spring, summer, and fall, catch the *Victoria Clipper* daily at 7:30am, 8am, 8:30am and 4pm from Pier 69 on the Seattle waterfront. The ride is 2½ hours with food and shopping available on board. Reservations are necessary. Tel: (206) 448-5000. The car ferry departs from Pier 48 at 1pm daily and takes 4½ hours.

The **Black Ball Ferry** departs from Port Angeles on the Olympic Peninsula to Victoria, BC, four times a day in summer and twice daily the rest of the year. Ferries carry cars. Tel: (206) 622-2222.

Victoria–San Juan Cruises, Bellingham Cruise Terminal, Bellingham. Tel: (1 800) 443-4552. Passenger ferries to San Juan Island and Victoria, May to October; also day cruises.

Where to Stay

Hotels

There are few really inexpensive hotels in downtown Seattle, but there are many along Pacific South Highway to SeaTac airport. most about halfway between the airport and Seattle around 141st Street.

Hotels in this guide are listed by city region and are among the best in their categories, for either facilities or value for money.

NEAR THE AIRPORT

Ben Carol Motel
14110 Pacific Highway S.
Tel: (206) 244-6464
All the motels in this area are around half the price of even modest downtown equivalents. They are all clustered around a comfortable, family-type restaurant and close to an enormous 24-hour supermarket. The Ben Carol also has a pool. **$**

Best Western Airport Executel
20717 Pacific Highway S.
Tukwila
WA 98188
Tel: (206) 878-3300
Amenities include a heated indoor pool, sauna, Jacuzzi, exercise room, airport transportation, restaurant, lounge, morning newspaper and laundry service. **$$**

Comfort Inn
Sea-Tac, 19333 Pacific Highway S.
Tukwila
WA 98188
Tel: (206) 878-1100
Cable television, exercise room, Jacuzzi, airport transportation, laundry service, continental breakfast. **$**

Doubletree Hotel Seattle Airport
18740 Pacific Highway S.
Tel: (206) 246-8600 or (1 800) 222-8733
Website: www.dbltrehotels.com
With three restaurants,two lounges. and other amenities such as heated pool, video room, room service, airport shuttle, and the hotel's fresh chocolate chip cookies brought to your room as a welcome gift. **$$**

Seattle Marriott
Sea-Tac Airport, 3201 S. 176th Street
Tukwila
WA 98188
Tel: (206) 241-2000 or (1 800) 228-9290
Website: www.marriott.com
Heated indoor pool, sauna, hot tub, exercise room, airport transportation, cable television, restaurant and lounge, facilities for handicapped. **$$**

Seattle Airport Hilton Hotel
17620 Pacific Highway S.
Tel: (206) 244-4800 or (1 800) HILTONS
Website: www.hilton.com

WestCoast Sea-Tac Hotel
18220 Pacific Highway S.
Tel: (206) 246-5535 or (1 800) 426-0670
Website: www.westcoasthotels.com/seatac

Wyndham Garden Hotel
18118 Pacific Hwy S.
Tel: (206) 244-6666
Website: www.wyndham.com

DOWNTOWN SEATTLE

The Alexis
1007 First Avenue
Seattle
WA 98104
Tel: (206) 624-4844
Website: www.alexishotel.com
Located in an early 20th-century building near the waterfront. The Alexis is an elegant hotel of 109 rooms (15 with whirlpools) that prides itself on attention to detail and personalized service. Rooms facing the courtyard are the ones to ask for; those facing 1st Avenue tend to be noisy. Amenities include:

fireplaces, complimentary sherry, continental breakfast and morning newspaper, shoe shines and a reduced-price, guest membership at the nearby upscale Seattle Club. In the hotel is The Painted Table restaurant, where you will find jazzy décor and Northwest cuisine. Or try the Bookstore Bar to enjoy your favorite brew along with a lighter meal while browsing among the books or people-watching on 1st Avenue. **$$$**

The Edgewater Inn
2411 Alaskan Way
Seattle
WA 98121
Tel: (206) 728-7000 or (1 800) 624-0670
Built at the time of the World's Fair in 1962 and completely remodeled in 1989. This is Seattle's only downtown waterfront hotel; it stands on Pier 67. Amenities include an atrium lobby, stone fireplaces, and mountain lodge décor. Complimentary downtown shuttle, banquet and meeting facilities, 238 rooms. Restaurant features Northwest cuisine. Rates vary depending on water- or city-view rooms. **$$**

The Four Seasons Olympic Hotel
411 University Street
Seattle
WA 98101
Tel: (206) 621-1700/(1 800) 223-8772 (US) or (1 800) 821-8106 (Washington State)
Website: www.fourseasons.com
A grand hotel in the Italian Renaissance style, built in 1924 and renovated in 1982. It features 450 spacious guest rooms furnished in period reproductions. Enjoy high tea in the atrium-style Garden Court and shopping off the lobby in stores such as Laura Ashley or Bally. The hotel receives the AAA five-diamond award for service. Amenities include a health club, indoor pool, saunas, Jacuzzis, two restaurants, 24-hour room service, complimentary newspaper and shoeshine, bar, terry cloth robes, and supplies for parents with small children. Fee for valet parking and massage. **$$$**

Seattle Hilton-Downtown
Sixth and University streets
Seattle
WA 98101
Tel: (206) 624-0500 or (1 800) 445-8667
Amenities include: bay windows in each room; Top of the Hilton Lounge (a disco), 24-hour room service, valet/laundry service, concierge, restaurant and gift shop. **$$**

Holiday Inn Crowne Plaza
1113 Sixth and Seneca streets
Seattle
WA 98101
Tel: (206) 464-1980 or (1 800) 521-2762
Website: www.cplaza@wolfnet.com
Amenities include a health club with whirlpool, sauna, weight room on the fifth floor; a gift shop and a restaurant. 415 rooms. **$$**

Hotel Monaco
1101 4th Avenue
Seattle
WA 98101
Tel: (206) 621-1770 or (1 800) 945-2240
Website: www.monaco-seattle.com
With 189 rooms this new addition to Seattle prides itself on service and function. The hotel restaurant is the Southern-inspired Sazerac. The hotel is part of the Kimpton Group Hotels. **$$**

Hotel Vintage Park
1100 5th Avenue
Seattle
WA 98101
Tel: (206) 624-8000 or (1 800) 624-4433
Website: www.hotelvintagepark.com
Care in attending to guests is one feature of this highly organized hotel, where rooms are decorated in vintage style but with amenities such as fax machines, high-speed Internet connections and phones in the bathrooms. More personal touches include irons and ironing boards, robes, hair dryers and fast room service. **$$**

Inn at Harbor Steps
1221 1st Avenue
Seattle
WA 98101
Tel: (206) 748-0973 or (1 888) 728-8910
Website: www.foursisters.com
A hotel chain based in California called "Four Sisters" is geared toward country–inn experiences. The inn has only 20 rooms, but each has a fireplace, wet bar, and sitting area. Amenities include sauna, Jacuzzi and indoor pool along with complimentary *hors d'œuvres* and wine before dinner. **$$**

Inn At The Market
86 Pine Street,
Seattle
WA 98101
Tel: (206) 443-3600
Website: www.innatthemarket.com
Located in the Pike Place Market, most of the 65 rooms have splendid views of Elliott Bay. The inn surrounds a landscaped courtyard that boasts trendy shops, a spa and a restaurant, Campagne, serving French country cuisine. A fifth-floor deck – fake turf and potted plants – offers one of the best views in town. Amenities: complimentary downtown shuttle to shops; newspaper and coffee; room service from Campagne; deck overlooking bay from the fifth floor. **$$**

Price Guide

The following price categories indicated the price for a double room in high season:
$$$ More than $200 (expensive)
$$ $100–200 (moderate)
$ Under $100 (budget)

Mayflower Park Hotel
405 Olive Way
Seattle
WA 98112
Tel: (1 800) 426-5100 or (206) 623-8700
Website:
www.mayflower@seanet.com
European-style moderately sized hotel of 187 rooms. Adjacent to Westlake Center. Amenities include cable television, restaurant, lounge, and laundry service. **$$**

Pacific Guest Suites
915 118th Avenue SE.
Bellevue
WA 98005
Tel: (1 800) 962-6620 or (206) 454-7888

One-, two- or three-bedroom condominium suites located in Seattle, Redmond or Bellevue. Rooms have full kitchens, washer, dryer, fireplace, cable television, concierge and housekeeping. **$**

Residence Inn by Marriott
800 Fairview Avenue
Seattle
WA 98109
Tel: (206) 624-6000
The Inn offers 234 suites only, equipped with a full kitchen including microwave oven, coffee-maker, refrigerator, range-top stove and dishwasher (but the inn takes care of the dishes). Seventy per cent of the rooms overlook Lake Union. Amenities: continental breakfast in the atrium (complete with waterfall), fitness center with indoor pool, sauna, Jacuzzi, exercise room; free parking. **$$$**

Price Guide

The following price categories indicated the price for a double room in high season:
$$$ More than $200 (expensive)
$$ $100–200 (moderate)
$ Under $100 (budget)

Sheraton Seattle Hotel and Towers
1400 Sixth Avenue
Seattle
WA 98101
Tel: (1 800) 325-3535 or (206) 621-9000
Top floor (35th) has fitness center equipped with Jacuzzi, sauna, pool, bicycles and aerobics area and lounge with panoramic view of the city. Two restaurants: Banner's and Fuller's for formal dining. There is also a popular disco. **$$**

Sorrento Hotel
900 Madison Street
Seattle
WA 98104
Tel: (206) 622-6400 or (1 800) 426-1265
Website: www.hotelsorrento.com
This 1909 hotel was remodeled in 1981 after a castle in Sorrento, Italy, and rooms were refurbished with an Italian flavor. The 76 guest- rooms on seven floors are sophisticated and stylish, yet due to the moderate size, the hotel prides itself on attentive service. The Hunt Club restaurant continues the European theme. During summer months guests can enjoy dining outdoors in the hotel's courtyard. Afternoon tea with sandwiches and pastries is served daily in the fireside room accompanied by a pianist or guitarist. Other amenities: free limousine downtown, mobile phones, newspapers, shoe shines and valet parking. In-house florist, robes, valet and *shiatzu* massage. **$$**

Madison Renaissance Hotel
515 Madison Street
Seattle
WA 98104
Tel: (206) 583-0300 or (1 800) 278-4159
Website: www.renaissancehotels.com
Top two floors are the executive level rooms, with concierge service, complimentary breakfast and appetizers. Amenities include: outstanding views, fitness center with heated indoor pool, complimentary morning coffee and newspaper delivered to your room, 24-hour room service, laundry, and hair salon, two restaurants. **$$$**

Westin Hotel
1900 Fifth Avenue.
Tel: (206) 728-1000 or (1 800) 228-3000
Website: www.westin.com
This is the Westin chain's flagship hote, adjacent to Westlake Shopping Center. Amenities include two restaurants: Nikko, serving *sushi* and Japanese fare, and Roy's, for seafood with a flair for Asian sauces, first started in Hawaii. The rooms are spacious with views of Puget Sound or the city. There is a heated indoor pool, Jacuzzis, saunas and fitness center. Grayline Airport Express stops here. **$$$**

WestCoast Roosevelt Hotel
1531 Seventh Avenue
Seattle
WA 98101
Tel: (1 800) 426-0670
Website: www.westcoasthotels.com
A moderately priced hotel for downtown, it was built in Art Deco style in 1930, renovated in 1987. Rooms are not large, but the hotel is convenient to shopping and downtown sightseeing. **$**

Downtown Travelodge Motel
2213 Eighth Avenue at Blanchard.
Tel: (206) 624-6300
The Quick Shuttle bus from Vancouver stops here, which makes it a convenient overnight place if you are traveling between the two cities or planning to go to the airport. **$$**

NORTHEND

University Plaza Hotel
400 NE. 45th Street
Seattle
WA 98105
Tel: (206) 634-0100
In the heart of the University District, with 135 rooms. Amenities include: outdoor pool, cable TV, free parking, fitness center, beauty salon, laundry service, restaurant, lounge with entertainment. **$**

Chambered Nautilus Inn
5005 22nd Avenue NE.
Seattle
WA. 98105
Tel: (206) 522-2536
Website: www.chamberednautilus.com
This early 20th-century Georgian Colonial hotel near the university has six rooms furnished with antiques and private baths. Four of the rooms open onto porches with views of the Cascades. Amenities are over the top, with flowers, robes, bottled water, writing desks, and reading material from the 2000-plus books from the library. **$$**

Ramada Inn
Seattle at Northgate
2140 Northgate Way
Seattle
WA 98133
Tel: (206) 365-0700
Located seven miles (11 km) north of Seattle, adjacent to Northgate Mall. Amenities include: heated pool, restaurant, laundry, room service, handicapped facilities. **$**

University Inn
4140 Roosevelt Way NE.
Seattle
WA 98105
Tel: (206) 632-5055 or (1 800) 733-3855
This remodeled hotel is a well-run addition to the University District. Amenities include voice mail, off-street parking, free morning paper, data modem hook-up, and even small safes in guest rooms. Next to the hotel, the Portage Bay Café has a wonderful breakfast menu. **$$**

SOUTHEND

Best Western at South Center
15901 W. Valley Road
Tukwila
WA 98188
Tel: 000-226-1812
Next to the Southcenter Mall with many rooms overlooking Green River. Amenities include: fitness center with heated pool, wading pool, sauna, Jacuzzi, airport transportation, restaurant and lounge. **$**

Kirkland

Woodmark Hotel
1200 Carillon Point
Kirkland
WA 98033
Tel: (425) 822-3700
Features 100 rooms, some with views of Lake Washington, in a ritzy 31-acre shopping/office complex. Carillon Point also features a marina and the popular Ristorante Stresa and Yarrow Bay Restaurant and Beach Café. Amenities include: minibars, VCRs with free movies, terry cloth robes, complimentary breakfast with newspaper, and the Carillon Room restaurant. **$$**

Bellevue

Bellevue Hilton
100 112th Avenue NE.
Bellevue
WA 98004
Tel: (425) 455-3330
Built in 1980 in the heart of downtown Bellevue. Amenities include: heated indoor pool, saunas, Jacuzzi, airport transportation, cable TV. There are three restaurants and a lounge with entertainment. At weekends all standard rooms are inexpensive. **$$**

Best Western Bellevue Inn
11211 Main Street
Bellevue
WA 98004
Tel: (425) 455-5240
Amenities include: landscaped courtyard, heated pool, health club privileges, airport transportation, restaurant, suites with fireplace. **$**

Bellevue Club Hotel
11200 SE. 6th Street
Bellevue
WA. 98004
Tel: (425) 454-4424
Website: www.bellevueclub.com
As part of the athletic club, the hotel offers 67 rooms each with enormous bathrooms with spa-tubs and shower stalls. Amenities offered through the athletic club include: five indoor tennis courts, Olympic-size swimming pool, squash and racquetball courts, and exercise rooms. **$$**

Hyatt Hotel and Resort
900 Bellevue Way
Bellevue
WA 98005
Tel: (425) 462-1234
This luxury hotel in the Bellevue Place shopping center has 382 rooms and is the tallest hotel in Bellevue, with 24 floors. On the top two floors the hotel offers Regency Club rooms featuring special concierge service, continental breakfast and appetizers in the evening. Amenities include access to an adjacent health club for a small fee, and Eques, a fine dining restaurant. **$$**

Red Lion
300 112th SE.
Bellevue
WA 98004
Tel: (425) 455-1300 or (1 800) 547-8010
Red Lion offers 303 large rooms, some with balconies. Amenities include: heated pool, sauna and Jacuzzi; health club privileges, restaurant and nightclub. Lower weekend rates. **$$**

Residence Inn
14455 NE. 29th Place
Bellevue
WA 98007
Tel: (425) 882-1222
Offers one- and two-bedroom suites in a village-type setting amid landscaped grounds. Suites are equipped with kitchens, fireplaces and balconies or decks (depending on level). Other amenities: heated pool, Jacuzzis, laundry, airport transportation. **$$**

Issaquah

Holiday Inn
1801 12th Avenue
Issaquah
WA 98027
Tel: (425) 392-6421
Opposite Lake Sammamish State Park on the south end of the lake.

Amenities: seasonal pool, wading pool, sauna, Jacuzzi, restaurant and laundry facilities. **$**

Redmond

Redmond Inn
17601 Redmond Way
Redmond
WA 98052
Tel: (425) 883-4900
Amenities: cable TV, pool, Jacuzzi, restaurant, airport transportation, laundry.
$

Budget Hotels

For a wider range of inexpensive rooms in the downtown area, it is also worth considering the following:

Claremont Hotel
Virginia and Fourth
Tel: (206) 448-8600

Commodore Motor Hotel
2013 Second Avenue
Tel: (206) 448-8868

Days Inn Town Center
2205 Seventh Avenue
Tel: (206) 448-3434

EconoLodge
325 Aurora Avenue
Tel: (206) 244-0810

Moore Hotel
1926 Second Avenue
Tel: (206) 448-4852

Pacific Hotel
317 Marion Street
Tel: (206) 622-3900.

Price Guide

The following price categories indicated the price for a double room in high season:
$$$ More than $200 (expensive)
$$ $100–200 (moderate)
$ Under $100 (budget)

Poulsbo

Cypress Inn
Highway 305
Poulsbo, WA 98370
Tel: (360) 697-2119
Restaurant and coffee shop, outdoor pool, 65 rooms. **$**

Port Townsend

The Tides Inn
1807 Water Street
Port Townsend, WA 98368
Tel: (360) 385-0595 or (1 800) 822-8696
On the waterfront; 21 rooms, some with kitchenettes, Jacuzzis. **$**

The Port Townsend Inn
2020 Washington Street
Port Townsend, WA 98368
Tel: (360) 385-2211
Similar to Tides Inn, 26 rooms. **$**

Leavenworth

Obental Motor Inn
922 Commercial Street
Leavenworth, WA 98826
Tel: (1 800) 537-9382
There are 26 units, close to downtown and Cascades National Park. **$**

Evergreen Inn
1117 Front Street, Leavenworth
Tel: (1 800) 327-7212
The 39 units in three locations are all accessible to the Cascades. **$**

LaConner

LaConner Country Inn
107 South Second
La Conner, WA 98257
Tel: (360) 466-3101
Restaurant and 28 rooms. **$**

Bed & Breakfast

Bed-and-breakfast inns tend to be inexpensive or reasonably priced, with a more intimate atmosphere. Some rooms have a private bath; some a shared bath. Here is a small sampling of older, mostly Victorian places in the Seattle area.

Bacon Mansion
959 Broadway E.
Tel: (206) 329-1864 or (1 800) 240-1864
This Tudor-style mansion has seven rooms, five with private baths. Also set up to allow a small family or group visit is a carriage house on the grounds.

Capitol Hill Inn
1713 Belmont Avenue
Seattle, WA 98122
Tel: (206) 323-1955
Beautifully decorated with antiques, this 1903 mansion on Capitol Hill is close to shops and restaurants.

Challenger
Tel: (206) 340-1201
A very unusual tugboat-turned-B&B located on Lake Union. Eight state rooms are decorated with nautical charts and brass. The views of downtown and Lake Union are worth the stay. A continental breakfast is included.

Gaslight Inn and Howell Street Suites
1727 15th Avenue
Tel: (206) 325-3654
The early 20th-century mansion has 10 guest rooms each decorated in various styles or periods. Outside is a large heated pool. The proprietors are friendly and aim to please. No kids, pets, or smoking.

Hill House B&B
1113 E. John Street
Tel: (206) 720-7161 or (1 800) 720-7161
Built in 1903, this restored Victorian house has seven elegantly decorated rooms, five with private baths and handmade soap. Breakfast, cooked by innkeeper Herman Foster, can be a gourmet experience.

Salisbury House
750 16th Avenue E.
Tel: (206) 328-8682
Located in an historic Capitol Hill neighborhood near Volunteer Park, the house offers an inviting wraparound porch. The interior is just as special as its surroundings.

Prince of Wales
133 13th Avenue E.
Tel: (206) 325-9692
Good views of city, Sound and mountains.

Shafer-Baillie Mansion
907 14th Avenue E.
Tel: (206) 322-4654 or (1 800) 922-4654
Spacious grounds, gourmet breakfasts, antique furnishings.

Roberta's Bed & Breakfast
1147 16th Avenue E.
Tel: (206) 329-3326
Also near Volunteer Park, each of the five rooms in this house has a private bath. In the mornings Roberta brings you coffee before making a breakfast spread worth getting up for.

B&B Agencies

Several bed and breakfast agencies assist in selecting accommodation:

Pacific Bed and Breakfast Registry
701 NW. 60th Street, Seattle
WA 98107
Tel: (206) 784-0539

Traveler's Bed and Breakfast
PO Box 492, Mercer Island
WA 98040
Tel: 000-232-2345

Seattle Bed and Breakfast Inn Association
PO Box 95853, Seattle, WA
Tel: (206) 547-1020

Youth Hostels

Most hostels offer clean, no-frills, low-budget accommodation.

YMCA Accommodations
909 Fourth Avenue
Seattle, WA 98104
Tel: (206) 382-5000
A 178-room hostel. Use of YMCA facilities including lounge, hot tub, indoor pool, sauna, fitness center and laundry service. Membership fee per person plus 14.2 percent sales tax. Weekly rates are available. Bunks can be four to a room. Hostel members also receive discounts on rooms.

Commodore Hotel Youth Hostel
2013 Second Avenue
Seattle, WA 98121

Tel: (206) 448-8868
Well-kept older hotel of 100 rooms with inexpensive rates. Amenities include cable TV in each room, lobby area and free parking.

Seattle International AYH Hostel
84 Union Street
Seattle, WA 98101
Tel: (206) 682-0462
A 125-bed hostel. Amenities include: lounge, library and self-service kitchen, laundry available. Free membership for non-profit groups.

Campground/RV Parks

West Fay Bainbridge State Park
15446 Sunrise Drive NE.
Bainbridge Island, WA 98110
Tel: 000-842-3931
There are 26 sites available for RVs or tents and an additional 10 sites available for tents only. Amenities include: wide sandy beach on Puget Sound, walking trails through the 17-acre park, boat launch, two mooring buoys, facilities for handicapped, playground equipment, disposal station, picnic shelter and water hookup.

Kitsap Memorial State Park
Poulsbo, WA 98370
Tel: (360) 779-3205
Located approximately 4 miles (6.5 km) north of the charming Scandinavian town of Poulsbo. The park has 43 sites for tents or RVs with a 30 ft (9-meter) limit. Amenities include: flush and pit toilets; playground equipment, wooded trails, swimming, boat launch, fishing, disposal station.

South

Saltwater State Park
25205 Eighth Place S.
Tel: (1 800) 233-0321
On Puget Sound about 2 miles (1 km) south of Des Moines (18 miles/29 km south of Seattle) off Highway 509, the campground is inside the state park which has 88 acres and nearly 1,500 ft (450 meters) of Puget Sound beaches. There are 52 sites available for tents or RVs, but no hookups. Amenities include: free use of the park with swimming, boating, a dock, scuba diving, nature trails and a playground. There is also a grocery store, flush and pit toilets. Open all year.

North

Canyon Mobile Park & RV
3333 228 Street SE.
Bothell, WA 98021
Tel: (425) 481-3005
Primarily a mobile home park, but has 11 RV spaces available. Amenities include a recreation hall. Open all year.

Twin Cedars RV Park
17826 Highway 99 N.
Lynnwood, WA 98037
Tel: (425) 742-5540
There are 70 sites for RVs on this relatively quiet 3-acre campground. The level gravel sites are set off highway 99. Amenities include: television in recreation room, coin laundry, showers, propane, disposal station. Pets allowed. Open all year.

East

Trailer Inns Inc.
15531 SE. 37 Street
Bellevue, WA 98006
Tel: (425) 747-9181 or (1 800) 323-8899 (Holiday Travel Park network)
There are 100 RV sites on this 4-acre campground. The maximum footage for RVs is 35 feet (10.5 meters), with two sites allowing approximately one foot longer. Amenities include: token-operated laundry and propane, a television/game room, playground, hot tub and heated indoor pool. Pets allowed. A/C or heaters cost a little extra. Weekly and monthly rates are available. Open all year.

Vasa Park
3560 W. Lake Sammamish Road SE
Bellevue, WA 98008
Tel: (425) 746-3260
There are 16 tent sites and six RV/or tent sites at this 18-acre campground on Lake Sammamish. Maximum allotted stay is one week and check out time is 10am. Amenities include: a disposal station, beach for swimming, fishing and a playground. Pets allowed. Electrical hookups cost extra; water hookups are free. There are four sewer hookups at no extra charge. Open May 15–October 1.

Where to Eat

Restaurant Listings

Seattle has a wide range of eating establishments, as one would expect from a big city, ranging from deluxe, elegant dining to budget cafés. One of the specialties of the city is seafood – the Northwest's salmon and oysters are among the best in the country – which no visitor should miss. The following is a selection of some of the best dining experiences in the city.

Price Guide

The following categories are for a meal for two, without drinks:

$$$	$80 or more
$$	$40–$80
$	under $40

Downtown Seattle

Café Lago
2305 24 Avenue E.
Tel: 329-8005
Quality rustic Italian fare featuring crusty breads, antipasti, and pastas. Dinner Tue–Sun only. **$$**

Campagne
86 Pine Street
Pike Place Market
Tel: (206) 728-2800
Located in Pike Place Market, Campagne highlights the food of southern France with a French country ambiance. Daily specials are selected from seafood caught fresh that day and accompanied by fresh local produce. One of the top five restaurants in the city. **$$**

Chandler's Crabhouse and Fresh Fish Market
901 Fairview N.
Tel: (206) 223-2722
Delicious crab, shellfish and lobster. **$$**

Coastal Kitchen
429 15th Avenue E.
Tel: 322-1145
Rotating menu features delicious international cuisine and Northwest favorites. **$$**

Dahlia Lounge
1904 4th Avenue
Tel: (206) 682-4142
A mix of tastes and ingredients from various cultures combine to make some of the most memorable dining in town. Desserts are meant to be taken seriously. **$$**

Elliott's
Alaskan Way, Pier 56
Tel: 623-4340
Seafood with a view of the bay. Lunch and dinner. **$$**

Fuller's
1400 Sixth Avenue
Tel: 447-5544
In the Sheraton Hotel. Consistently rated one of Seattle's best overall restaurants. Northwest and Continental-style cuisine. **$$**

The Georgian Room
411 University Street
Tel: 621-7889
At the Four Seasons Hotel. First-class restaurant serving excellent Continental-style cuisine in elegant surrounds. **$$$**

Le Gourmand
425 NW. Market Street
Tel: 784-3463
Classic French cuisine incorporating Northwest ingredients. **$$**

The Gravity Bar
Broadway Market, Capitol Hill
Tel: 325-7186
Imaginative vegetarian dishes, wheatgrass juice and *espresso*. A great place to people-watch. **$**

The Hunt Club
900 Madison Avenue
Tel: 343-6156
In the Sorrento Hotel. Top-notch Northwest cuisine served in plush, clubby atmosphere. **$$$**

Il Bistro
93A Pike, Pike Place Market
Tel: 682-3049
Dark, Italian bistro in the Market. Dinner only. **$$**

Jitterbug Café
2114 N. 45th Street
Tel: (206) 547-6313
A diner with class, from the comfort-food menu to white linen napkins and servers in white blouses and ties. **$$**

Kabul
2301 N. 45th Street
Tel: (206) 545-9000
Afghanistani food prepared and served by the Malikyar family who emigrated to Seattle from Kabul, Afghanistan two decades ago. **$$**

Kaleenka
1933 1st Avenue
Tel: (206) 728-1278
The café-style restaurant serves traditional foods of the former Soviet Union. **$$**

Kingfish Café
602 19th Avenue E.
Tel: (206) 320-8757
Making a name for itself with the likes of Southern soul food. Lunch and dinner. **$$**

Price Guide

The following categories are for a meal for two, without drinks:

$$$	$80 or more
$$	$40–$80
$	under $40

Kokeb Ethiopian Restaurant
926 12th Avenue
Tel: 322-0485
Exotic and spicy cuisine from Ethiopia. Has a loyal following in the university crowd. Food is eaten with fingers. **$**

Lampreia
2400 1st Avenue
Tel: (206) 443-3301
One of the city's best restaurants, Lampreia focuses on dishes made of few ingredients, but combined to perfection. **$$$**

McCormick and Schmick's
1103 1st Avenue
Tel: (206) 623-5500
Seafood and Northwest cuisine, popular with locals for power lunches and cocktails. **$$**

Mikado Japanese Restaurant
514 S. Jackson Street
Tel: 622-5206
Excellent *sushi* and *robata* bar. Dinner only. **$$**

Painted Table
Alexis Hotel, 1007 First Avenue
Tel: 624-3646
Excellent, Northwest cuisine in plush atmosphere of the hotel. **$$$**

The Palm Court
1900 Fifth Avenue
Tel: 728-1000
Elegant formal dining among the palm trees at the Westin Hotel. Features Continental-Northwest cuisine. **$$$**

Pescatore
5300 34 Avenue NW.
Tel: 784-1733
Quality Italian and seafood restaurant overlooking Chittenden Locks. Outdoor deck for dining and boat-watching. **$$**

Ponti Seafood Grill
3014 3rd N.
Tel: (206) 284-3000
Voted best seafood and Northwest cuisine in a recent poll. **$$**

Ray's Boathouse
6049 Seaview Avenue NW.
Tel: 789-3770
One of Seattle's most popular seafood restaurants. Stunning view of Puget Sound and Olympic Mountains. **$$**

Rover's
2808 E. Madison Street
Tel: 325-7442
Fresh and contemporary French cuisine. Served in rooms of a frame house. Dinner only. **$$**

Saleh al Lago
6804 E. Green Lake Way N.
Tel: 524-4044
Classic Italian menu. **$$**

Salty's on Alki
1936 Harbor Avenue SW.
Tel: (206) 937-1600
Alder-smoked salmon stuffed with Dungeness crab, but it's the view at night that steals the show. **$$**

Sea Garden
509 7th Avenue S.
Tel: 623-2100; and
200 106th Avenue NE.
Bellevue
Tel: (425) 450-8833
Anything from the sea is game at these two restaurants, and done in Cantonese style. Don't be fooled by the non-descript interiorl. **$$**

Shanghai Garden
524 6th Avenue S.
Tel: (206) 625-1689
In the International District, this

Budget Dining

Other inexpensive restaurants recommended by *Seattle Times* food critics are as follows:

Agua Verde Café
1303 NE. Boat Street
Tel: (206) 545-8570

Boat Street Café
909 NE. Boat Street
Tel: (206) 632-4602

Catfish Corner
2726 E. Cherry
Tel: (206) 323-4330

Deluxe Bar and Grill
625 Broadway E.
Tel: (206) 324-9697

5 Spot
1502 Queen Anne Avenue N.
Tel: (206) 285-SPOT

Fremont Noodle House
3411 Fremont Avenue N.
Tel: (206) 547-1550

Grady's Pub & Eatery
2307 24th Avenue E.
Tel: (206) 726-5968

Queen Mary
2912 NE 55th Street
Tel: (206) 527-2770

Shultzy's Sausage
4124 University Way
Tel: 548-9461

Still Life in Fremont
709 E. 35th Street
Tel: (206) 547-9850

Teriyaki Bowl
3121 E. Madison
Tel: (206) 324-3224

brightly painted pink restaurant is host to some of the best Chinese food in Seattle. Anything with the homemade shaven noodles is a good bet. **$$**

Shucker's
411 University Street
Tel: 621-1984
Seafood restaurant at the Four Seasons Hotel, best known for its oysters, clams and mussels. **$$**

Third Floor Fish Café
205 Lake Street S., Kirkland
Tel: (425) 822-3553
Great views and well-prepared seafood. The piano bar fills the background. **$$$**

Wild Ginger Asian Restaurant and Satay Bar
1400 Western Avenue
Tel: 206 623-4450
The best prepared selections of Southeast Asian food in Seattle. **$$**

Bellevue

Andrés Gourmet Cuisine
14125 NE. 20 Street, Bellevue
Tel: (425) 747-6551
French and Vietnamese cuisine. Open lunch and dinner. **$$**

Duke's Bellevue Bar and Grill
23 Lake Bellevue Drive
Tel: (425) 455-5775
Northwest cuisine. Lunch, dinner. **$$**

I Love Sushi
11818 NE. 8th Street, Bellevue
Tel: (425) 454-5706
Success is founded on using the freshest of fish. Lunch, dinner. **$$**

Mediterranean Kitchen
103 Bellevue Way NE.
Tel: (425) 462-9422
The menu is Middle Eastern with large portions. **$**

Spazzo
10655 NE. Fourth Street, Bellevue
Tel: (425) 454-8255
Mediterranean grill fare.

Coffee Houses

Bauhaus Books & Coffee
301 E. Pine
Tel: (206) 625-1600

B&O Espresso
204 Belmont Avenue E.
Tel: (206) 322-5028

Caffè Ladro
2205 Queen Anne Avenue N.
Tel: (206) 282-5313; and
600 Queen Anne Avenue N.
Tel: (206) 282-1549

Café Septième
214 Broadway
Tel: (206) 860-8858

Chapters Coffee House
1109 N. 36th.
Tel: (206) 633-1825

Espresso Roma
4201 University Way NE.
Tel: (206) 632-6001

Macrina Bakery & Café
2408 1st Avenue
Tel: (206) 448-4032

Culture

Museums

The Burke Museum of Natural History and Culture
University of Washington campus, NE. entrance at 45th Street and 17th Avenue
Tel: (206) 543-5590
www.washington.edu/burkemuseum
The two permanent exhibits come from a collection of more than three million artifacts from Northwest Coast Indians, fossils, dinosaur skeletons and geological information. Hours: 10am–5pm daily, Thurs until 8pm. Closed: July 4, Thanksgiving and December 25. Admission free, except during special exhibits.

Center For Wooden Boats
1010 Valley Street
Tel: (206) 382-2628
www.eskimo.com/~cwboats
Located on the south shore of Lake Union, with its own marina. This maritime museum maintains a fleet of 75 vintage wooden boats, about half of which are available for rental on Lake Union. The center also runs workshops on wooden boat building, sailing and nautical skills. Also on show is the steam-powered *Walowa*, featured in the *Tugboat Annie* films of the 1930s starring Marie Driessler, based on Norman Reilly Raine's short stories. Raine's real-life model was Thea Foss, founder of the Foss Launch and Tug Co. (now Foss Maritime).

Coast Guard Museum
Pier 36, on Alaskan Way S.
Tel: (206) 217-6993
Nautical artifacts, ship models, lots of Coast Guard memorabilia and many old photographs. A 15-minute slide show is also presented. Hours: 10am–4pm Mon, Wed and Fri; 1pm–5pm Sat and Sun. Admission free.

Klondike Gold Rush National Historical Park
117 S. Main Street
(in Pioneer Square)
Tel: (206) 553-7220
www.nps.gov/klgo
This was the site for outfitting the 1897–98 Alaska Gold Rush. Artifacts, gold panning demonstrations and tours. Open: 9am–5pm daily. Closed: January 1, Thanksgiving and December 25. Admission free.

Museum of Flight
9404 E. Marginal Way, S.
Tel: (206) 764-5720
Located on the site where Boeing began. Museum features The Great Gallery room where vintage, experimental, fighting and cruising planes are suspended from the glass-domed ceiling all around the room. Short films depict Boeing's history and the history of flight. Hours: 10am–5pm daily, to 9pm Thur. Children under 6 free.

Museum of History and Industry
2700 24th Avenue
Tel: (206) 324-1125
Located in McCurdy Park on Lake Washington, it features exhibits on the history of Seattle, and the Pacific Northwest in addition to changing theme exhibits. It also features live radio broadcasts with jazz and progressive-style musicians. Hours: 10am–5pm Mon–Fri, and 11am–5pm Sat–Sun. Closed: January 1, Thanksgiving and December 25. Admission.

Nordic Heritage Museum
3014 NW. 67th Street
Tel: (206) 789-5707
Traces the history and contributions of Scandinavian settlers to the Northwest. Exhibits include: textiles, crafts, costumes, furniture, history of fishing and lumber industries. Phone ahead for guided tours. Hours: 10am–4pm Tues–Sat; noon–4pm Sun. Closed: January 1, Thanksgiving and December 24–25. Admission.

Pacific Science Center
Seattle Center
Tel: (206) 443-2880
A hands-on science museum for adults and children, with changing exhibits, IMAX theater, planetarium and unusual science gifts.

The Children's Museum
Lower Level, Center House
Seattle Center
Tel: (206) 441-1768
A hands-on learning experience where kids find out about other children's' cultures. The center also features a global village with kid-size houses and programs such as folk dancing, kite-making, story telling, and Native American children's games. The Discovery Bay station is especially for toddlers and infants. Open daily. Admission.
www.thechildrensmuseum.org

Wing Luke Asian Museum
407 7th Avenue S.
Tel: (206) 623-5124
Traces the history of Asian immigrants and their contributions to life in the Northwest. Also on display are paintings and crafts from Asian and Asian-American artists. Hours: 11am–4.30pm Tues–Fri, noon–4pm Sat–Sun. Until 8pm first Thur of each month. Closed: public holidays. Admission, except Thursdays.

Art Galleries

On the first Thursday of every month, Pioneer Square art galleries host "First Thursday." Visitors may gallery hop, view new works, sip wine and nibble cheese from about 6–8pm. Maps are available at most of the Pioneer Square galleries. Many galleries are closed Mondays.

Arthead Art Gallery
5411 Meridian Avenue N.
Tel: (206) 633-5544
Features regional artists of sculpture, photography and painting.

Carolyn Staley Fine Prints
313 1st Avenue S.
Tel: (206) 621-1888
Japanese woodblock prints and better quality old prints.

Art Museums

Frye Art Museum,
704 Terry Avenue
(corner Cherry Street)
Tel: (206) 622-9250
www.fryeart.org
Features paintings by 19th- and early 20th-century artists along with changing exhibits by contemporary artists. Frequently hosts poetry readings, chamber music and other performances. Open: 10am–5pm Mon–Fri, noon–5pm Sat–Sun. Admission free.

Henry Art Gallery
University of Washington
15th Avenue NE. & NE. 41st Street
Tel: (206) 543-2280
www.henryart.org
Features historic and contemporary works by American artists. Conducts a range of lectures and children's programs, and changing exhibits. Open 10am –5pm Tues–Sun; until 7pm Thur. Closed: Mon.

Seattle Art Museum
First Avenue and University Street
Tel: (206) 654-3100
Home to an internationally renowned collection of Northwest Indian art, and paintings by the Northwest Mystics group. There are also examples of early European, pre-Columbian, Islamic, African and Persian arts. Admission.

Seattle Asian Art Museum
1400 E. Prospect St, Volunteer Park
Tel: (206) 654-3100
Houses a spectacular Asian collection of Asian art. Hours: 10–5pm Tues–Sun. Until 9pm Thur. Tours are given daily at 2pm. Closed: Thanksgiving and December 25. Admission charge, but free on Thursday.

Bellevue Art Museum
Bellevue Way NE. and NE. 8th Street, Bellevue Square, Bellevue
Tel: (425) 454-3322
Located on the third floor of the upscale Bellevue Square shopping mall. Specializes in paintings and crafts of Northwest artists. Hours: 10am–6pm, Mon–Sat, 11am–5pm Sun. Until 8pm Tues. Admission, except Tuesdays. Note that the museum is due to move to a new location in 2001.

Center On Contemporary Art (coca)
65 Cedar Street
Tel: (206) 728-1980
Innovative and avant-garde works on display. Stages large exhibits off-site and performance art on-site.

Davidson Galleries
313 Occidental Avenue S.
Tel: (206) 624-7684.
Traditional landscapes and figurative work by contemporary Northwest painters. Also featured are antique and contemporary prints from around the world.

Elliott Brown Gallery
619 N. 35th Street, Suite 101
Tel: (206) 547-9740
Frequently exhibits glassworks by renowned international artists.

Foster/White Gallery
123 S. Jackson Street
Tel: (206) 622-2833
Exhibits ceramics, sculpture, and paintings by established Northwest artists and work in glass by artists of the Pilchuck School.

Francine Seders Gallery
6701 Greenwood Avenue N.
Tel: (206) 782-0355
Seders represents a large group of minority artists including works of Jacob Lawrence, Robert Jones, Gwen Knight and Michael Spafford.

G. Gibson Gallery
122 S. Jackson Street, 2nd floor
Tel: (206) 587-4033
Contemporary photography by both well known artists and young Northwesterners.

Greg Kucera Gallery
212 3rd Avenue S.
Tel: (206) 624-0770
Carries established Northwest artists with national recognition and hosts an exhibit once a year on a controversial topic.

Sacred Circle Gallery of American Indian Art
Daybreak Star Cultural Arts Center
Discovery Park
Tel: (206) 285-4425
An exquisite collection of works by highly respected Native American artists from Canada and the US.

Woodside/Braseth Gallery
1533 9th Avenue
Tel: (206) 622-7243
Paintings by Northwest artists.

William Traver Gallery
110 Union Street
Tel: (206) 587-6501
Works by Pilchuck Glass artists. Second floor displays paintings, photographs and sculpture by regional artists.

Eastside Galleries

Art Works Northwest
901 Kirkland Avenue, Suite C.
Tel: (425) 828-7500
Corporate and residential fine art studio.

Elements Gallery
10500 NE. Eighth Street, Bellevue
Tel: (425) 454-8242
Glassworks, jewelry, textiles and sculpture.

Howard/Mandville Gallery
120 Park Lane, Kirkland
Tel: (425) 889-8212
Northwest and international artists.

Gallery 410
553 Roosevelt Avenue
Tel: (360) 825-7451
Western and wildlife art.

Issaquah Gallery
49 Front Street N., Issaquah
Tel: (425) 392-4247
Paintings, pottery, jewelry, photography and art classes.

Music & Dance

The Opera House at Seattle Center is the headquarters of the Seattle Opera Association, which presents five full-scale operatic productions during its September–May season.

Seattle Opera Association
1020 John, Seattle
Tel: (206) 389-7676
www.seattleopera.org

Seattle Symphony Orchestra
305 Harrison Street, Seattle
Tel: 443-4747
The Seattle Symphony Orchestra schedules concerts regularly on Monday, Tuesday and Wednesday evenings, September–April, with matinées on Sunday and family concerts on Saturday mornings for the "Discover Music!" series. Gerard Schwarz is the conductor.

Pacific Northwest Ballet
301 Mercer, Seattle
Tel: 292-2787
When not in use for operas, you can enjoy performances by the Pacific Northwest Ballet, at the Seattle Center Opera House. Six productions from October–May and an annual production of *The Nutcracker*.

Theaters

Seattle has a thriving theater scene, both classical and fringe. The small fringe groups have formed **LOFT (the League of Fringe Theaters)** and run a 24-hour hotline for information on performances. Tickets are very reasonably priced. Tel: (206) 637-7373.

Other major Seattle theaters are:

Annex Theatre
1916 4th Avenue
Tel: (206) 728-0933

A Contemporary Theater (ACT)
700 Union Street, Seattle
Tel: (206) 292-7676
Close to Seattle Center. Seattle's leading repertory theater.

Empty Space Theater
3509 Fremont Avenue N.
Tel: (206) 547-7500

Fifth Avenue Theater
1308 Fifth Avenue, Seattle
Tel: 625-1900
Hosts touring Broadway shows, musicals and plays in an ornate and historic building.

Freehold Theatre
1525 10th Avenue, Seattle
Tel: (206) 323-7499

Intiman Theater
201 Mercer Street, Seattle
Seattle Center Playhouse
Tel: 269-1900

Kane Hall
University of Washington, DG-10
Seattle
Tel: (206) 543-4880

Meany Theater
University of Washington
George Washington Lane and NE. 40th Street, Seattle
Tel: (206) 543-4880

The Moore Theater
1932 Second Avenue, Seattle
Tel: (206) 443-1744

Nippon Kan Theater
628 S. Washington Street, Seattle
Tel: 224-0181
Building is on the National Register of Historic Places.

Buying tickets

You can purchase theater tickets at half price on the day of the show, but you run the risk of a sell-out and must take whatever seats you can get (if you're lucky they may be first row at half-price!) This also applies to dance performances and music concerts. Ticket venues include:

Ticket/Ticket: sells last minute tickets and charges a surcharge per seat. Will not give ticket information over the phone.

Broadway Market
Second Level, 401 Broadway E.
Tel: 324-2744. Open: 10am–7pm Tues–Sun. Cash only.

Pike Place Market Information Kiosk
Corner of First and Pike streets.
Half-price tickets.

Ticketmaster: half-price tickets beside the box office of theaters.

The Bon
Third Avenue and Pine or Northgate Mal.

Tower Records/Video
4321 University Way NE or 500 Mercer Street.
Tel: (206) 628-0888.
For tickets or information on performances.

On the Boards
1st Avenue W. and Roy Street
Tel: (206) 217-9888
Cutting edge performance art from around the globe.

Paramount Theatre
901 Pine Street, Seattle
Tel: (206) 682-1414
Presents well-known entertainers.
For tickets call: (206) 292-ARTS

Theatre Under The Influence
Union Garage, 1418 10th Avenue
Tel: (206) 720-1942

The University of Washington School of Drama
University of Washington
Stevens Way, Seattle
Tel: (206) 543-4880

Seattle Children's Theater
Charlotte Martin Theatre
Seattle Center, Seattle
Tel: (206) 441-3322
Productions for children of all ages on two stages, September through to June.

Seattle Repertory Theater
155 Mercer Street
Tel: (206) 443-2222
Located in the Bagley Wright Theater in Seattle Center, this is Seattle's flagship professional theater with productions of classic and contemporary works.

Theater Schmeater
1500 Summit, Seattle
Tel: (206) 324-5801

Washington Hall Performance Gallery
153 14th Avenue, Seattle
Tel: (206) 328-4862

Movie Theaters

Most cinemas feature first-run movies only. However, a handful of theaters will run, and sometimes specialize in, old "classics" and foreign films. In Seattle these theaters are:

The Uptown Cinema
511 Queen Anne Avenue N.
Tel: (206) 285-1022

Broadway Market
425 Broadway E.
Tel: (206) 323-0231

Egyptian
801 Pine Street
Tel: (206) 323-4978

Seven Gables
911 NE. 50th Street
Tel: (206) 632-8820

The Guild
45th at 2115 N. 45th
Tel: (206) 633-3353

The Harvard Exit
807 E. Roy Street
Tel: (206) 323-8986

The Metro Cinemas
NE. 45th Street and Roosevelt Avenue
Tel: (206) 633-0055

Neptune
1333 NE. 45th Street
Tel: (206) 633-5545

College and university campuses may also show off-beat films. For typical Hollywood blockbuster films, check out **Cineplex Odeon**'s 16-screen complex in downtown Seattle, Tel: (206) 622-6465.

Check the newspaper for theater listings and show times.

Nightlife

Several areas are hubs for evening entertainment where restaurants, clubs and shops open late. They are located around Lake Union or in the Pioneer Square district along the downtown waterfront, or around the University (especially along University Way), and along Broadway on Capitol Hill.

Downtown hotels offer some of the most elegant lounges such as: the **Garden Court of the Four Seasons Olympic Hotel**, the **Lobby Bar** of the Westin, and the **Camlin Hotel's Cloud Room** (on the top floor, naturally).

In Pioneer Square the trendiest and most pleasant bars have a historical flavor such as: **Dimitriou's Jazz Alley**, the **Merchant's Café, J & M Cafè** and the **Old Timers' Café**.

Bars & Music Venues

The Attic Alehouse and Eatery
4226 E. Madison Street
Tel: (206) 323-3131
A good selection of microbrews and neighborly conversation.

Alibi Room
85 Pike Street, Pike Place Market
Tel: (206) 623-3180
Hidden in Post Alley it draws the hip and single.

Axis
2214 1st Avenue
Tel: (206) 441-9600
One of Belltown's liveliest lounges.

Ballard Firehouse
5429 Russell Avenue NW.
Tel: (206) 784-3516
A performance space where you can hear rock, blues, or reggae. Excellent dance floor and porch.

Baltic Room
1207 Pine Street
Tel: (206) 625-4444
A lounge where the live music is

piano jazz and the words hip and cool come to mind.

The Breakroom
1325 E. Madison Street
Tel: (206) 860-5155
Premier venue for local rock bands.

Catwalk
172 S. Washington
Tel; (206) 622-1863
Gothic/Industrial club located in Pioneer Square. Open until 4am.

Crocodile Cafe
2200 2nd Avenue
Tel: 441-5611
Features local and international alternative rock bands.

Dimitriou's Jazz Alley
2033 Sixth Avenue
Tel: (206) 441-9729
Presents the top names in jazz in a sophisticated atmosphere.

Doc Maynard's
610 First Avenue
Tel: (206) 682-4646
Rock 'n' roll and rhythm and blues reign supreme at this Pioneer Square bar.

El Gaucho's Pampas Room
90 Wall Street
Tel: (206) 728-1140
Upscale jazz and dancing.

Elysian Brewing Co.
1211 E. Pike Street
Tel: (206) 860-1920
The beer is brewed on site and extremely good. On weekends live jazz can be heard.

Fenix Underground
315 2nd S.
Tel: (206) 467-1111
Alternates between live music and DJ driven dancing.

Four Angels Coffeehouse
1400 14th Avenue
Tel: (206) 329-4066
A place to hear acoustic folk music.

Gratful Bread Café
7001 35th Avenue NE.
Tel: (206) 525-3166
Could be Seattle's best folk club.

Hale's Brewery and Pub
4301 Leary Way NW.
Tel: (206) 782-0737
A showcase for locally brewed ales.

Il Bistro
93-A Pike St., Pike Place Market
Tel: (206) 682-3049
A place for after work or evening rendezvous. A European flair.

Kell's
1916 Post Alley
Tel: (206) 728-1916
Irish restaurant and pub with inspiring Irish sing-a-longs.

Larry's Greenfront
209 First Avenue
Tel: (206) 624-7665
Blues music.

Murphy's Pub
2110 N. 45th Street
Tel: (206) 634-2110
Irish pub with a great selection of brews and folk music.

New Orleans Creole Restaurant
114 First Avenue S.
Tel: 622-2563
Features creole, ragtime and jazz along with spicy foods.

Owl 'N' Thistle
808 Post Avenue
Tel: (206) 621-7777
An Irish pub with Celtic folk bands.

Owl Café
5140 Ballard Avenue, NW.
Tel: (206) 784-3640
A blues joint with a loyal following.

Showbox Nightclub
1426 1st, Seattle
Tel: (206) 628-3151
This venue has two huge dance floors, plus a live stage.

The Pink Door
1919 Post Alley, Pike Place Market
Tel: (206) 443-3241
A terraced rooftop where accordion music will soften your mood while drinking and eating *antipasti*.

The Triangle Lounge
3507 Fremont Place N.
Tel: (206) 632-0880
A Fremont haunt.

Top of the Hilton
Sixth Avenue and University Street
Tel: (206) 624-0500
Sophisticated disco features top 40 hits and city-light views.

Comedy Clubs

Comedy Underground
222 S. Main
Tel: (206) 628-0303
Presents nationally known comedians and local talent.

Giggles Comedy Night Club
Roosevelt & 53rd Street
Tel: (206) 526-JOKE

Festivals

Calendar of Events

The events listed below are free except where indicated otherwise.

JANUARY

New Year's Eve, celebrations at restaurants, hotels, nightclubs and homes all over town.

Chinese New Year
Tel: (206) 623-5124
www.wingluke.com
Based on the lunar calendar, is held sometime in January or February in the International District. Festivities include a parade with dragons, dancers, foods, fireworks.

FEBRUARY

Festival Sandiata, at Seattle Center during Black History month.

Artstorm, more than 200 art events held throughout Seattle during the last two weeks of the month including films, seminars and architectural tours.

Chilly Hilly Bike Ride, Bainbridge Island, the third Sunday in February. Hop aboard the ferry to Winslow for this 30-mile (50-km) ride sponsored by the Cascade Bicycle Club.

Fat Tuesday
Tel: (206) 622-2563
Pioneer Square's own Mardi Gras celebration. This week-long event, held the week before Lent, includes a parade, and music: Cajun, R&B and jazz in the clubs and in the streets. Nightclubs charge one cover price that lets people travel from club to club for the evening.

Northwest Flower and Garden Show

Tel: 800-229-6311
www.gardenshow.com
Washington State Convention and Trade Center, during President's Day weekend. On almost five acres of the convention center floor, landscape architects, nurseries and gardeners try their best to outdo each other at over 300 booths. Admission.

MARCH

Irish Week Festival, includes events such as the St Patrick's Day Dash, an easy 4-mile (7-km) run along the waterfront from F.X. McRory's on 100 Mercer Street to the Kingdome.

St Patrick's Day Parade, (17th)
Tel: (206) 329-7224
www.irishclub.org
Parade travels from City Hall, 600 4th Avenue, to Westlake Center, 1601 5th Avenue, featuring bagpipes, Irish dancers, marching bands and the laying of the green stripe down Fourth Avenue.

Whirligig
at Seattle Center
Tel: (206) 684-7200
www.seattlecenter.com
Hosts this indoor carnival for kids from about mid-February to early-April. Free entertainment; small fee for rides.

All Fools' Day Parade and Basset Bash, downtown Woodinville. Parade, great food, and basset hound shenanigans.

APRIL

Daffodil Festival and Grand Floral Parade
in Tacoma
Tel: (206) 627-6176
One of the country's largest floral parades.

Skagit Valley Tulip Festival
Tel: (360) 428-5959
www.tulipfestival.org
Held on 1,500 acres of colorful tulip fields. Bicycle and bus tours are popular.

Artsplash, at Redmond.

MAY

Northwest Folklife Festival
Tel: (206) 684-7300
www.nwfolklife.org
Memorial Day weekend at Seattle Center. Music, dancing, ethnic food and crafts from more than 100 countries. Many people take this opportunity to unpack their instruments and join some of the many jam sessions which spring up all around the Center's lawns.

Opening day of yachting season
Tel: (206) 325-1000
www.seattleyachtclub.org
Held first Saturday in May. Yachting Clubs bring out a parade of boats from Lake Union to Lake Washington. Also features a regatta of rowing teams.

International Children's Festival
at Seattle Center
www.seattlecenter.com
Children's performers and theatrical groups from around the world come to entertain at this week-long festival. Some events are free, but most charge admission.

Pike Place Market Festival
www.pikeplacemarket.org
On Memorial Day weekend. Clowns, jazz musicians, and a "kids' alley" full of craft activities round out the usual entertainment at the Market.

Seattle International Film Festival
Tel: (206) 464-5830
www.seattlefilm.com
All month long, at various theaters (concentrated in the University district and Capitol Hill).

University Street Fair
University Way
Tel: (206) 527-2567
Held the third weekend in May, the fair features hundreds of artists' booths in a 10-block area. Mimes, clowns and street entertainment.

JUNE

Fremont Arts and Crafts Fair
34th Street
Tel: (206) 547-7440
A well-known neighborhood fair, featuring live music, local crafts, jugglers, mimes, along with a zany street parade the weekend of summer solstice.

Mainly Mozart Festival
Meany Theater, University of Washington
Tel: (206) 543-4880
Mid-June. Seattle Symphony's three-week tribute to the master and other 18th-century composers in acoustically pleasing Meany Hall. The tickets are pricey but worthwhile.

Snoqualmie Railroad Days
Snoqualmie
Tel: (425) 746-4025
www.trainmuseum.org
Steam trains from the late-19th century. A 10-mile (16-km) ride from the Snoqualmie depot takes visitors up to the historic depot and quaint town of North Bend.

Mercer Island Summer Arts Festival
8236 SE. 24th Avenue
Mercer Island.
Usually held the last weekend in June. The downtown area overflows with display booths of local artists. Sponsored by the Mercer Island Visual Arts League.

Microbrewery Festival
at the Herbfarm, 32804 Issaquah Fall City Road, Fall City
Tel: (425) 784-2222
www.theherbfarm.com
Breweries from the Northwest, Canada and Utah offer sample brews, along with barbequed chicken, knockwurst and Bavarian-style beer music. Admission for taste testing.

Special Olympics
at various locations depending on the event
Tel: (206) 362-4949
Olympic-style events for the mentally disabled.

Summer Nights on the Pier
Pier 62–63
Tel: (206) 622-5123
www.summernights.org
A 3,000-seat outdoor facility hosts contemporary music through the summer.

In June, July, August and September the **Downtown Seattle Association** sponsors lunchtime concerts in various parks and plazas. For details, call the Daily Events Line: Tel: (206) 684-8582.

JULY

Fourth of July Parades: Downtown Bothell, Issaquah, Winslow (on Bainbridge Island) and other neighborhoods; check newspaper for listings.

Fourth of July-Ivar Festival and Fireworks
Myrtle Edwards Park
Tel: (206) 587-6500
www.keepclam.com
A fishing derby, concerts and food at this waterfront park during the day. A fireworks display over Elliott Bay at dusk.

Seafair
Tel: (206) 728-0123
www.seafair.com
Late July–early August. Seattle's most spectacular summer festival is really a bunch of events, parades and celebrations that take place over a 2½-week period (usually the third weekend in July to first week in August) in different parts of the city. Highlights include: the milk carton derby races at Green Lake, the Blue Angels Air Show (aerobatic flights), Hydroplane Races on Lake Washington, Bon Odori, festival of dances and food sponsored by the Seattle Buddhist church, Chinatown International District Summer Festival, Hing Hay Park, Soul Festival, including parade, and the Torchlight Parade, a grand, nighttime parade through downtown.

Bellevue Jazz Festival
City Park, 10201 NE. 4th Street
Northwest jazz artists entertain outdoors the three days beginning the third weekend in July. Tickets required; one concert in series free.

Bite of Seattle
Tel: (206) 232-2982
www.biteofseattle.com
Mid-July on the grounds at Seattle Center. A taste-testers delight with over 60 restaurants participating. Pay according to your tastes.

Emerald City Flight Festival
On Boeing Field, near the Museum of Flight (*see page 282*). Air shows, parachute drops and food.

Pacific Northwest Arts and Crafts Fair
301 Bellevue Square, Bellevue
Tel: (425) 454-3322
www.Bellevueart.org
Sponsored by the Bellevue Art Museum. Features exhibits and booths throughout the mall including artists-at-work demonstration booths, musical concerts at the fountain outside The Bon and entertainment for children.

King County Fair
at the fairgrounds in Enumclaw
Tel: (425) 296-4232
Begins third Wednesday in July and continues for five days of music, rodeos, logger competitions, crafts and food. The oldest county fair in the state.

Lake Union Wooden Boat Festival
1010 Valley Street, at the south end of Lake Union
Tel: (206) 382-2628
www.cwb.org
Features rowing, sailing and boat building competitions, workshops, food, crafts, and water taxis from the Center for Wooden Boats.

McChord Air Show
at the Air Force base in Tacoma
Tel: 253-984-5637

San Juan Island Dixieland Jazz Festival
at Friday Harbor
Tel: (360) 378-5509

AUGUST

Evergreen State Fair
Monroe
Tel: (360) 794-7832 or (1 800) 562-4367 (x 6700)
www.evergreenfair.org
Held third week in August–Labor Day weekend. A country fair with big-name country stars, plus rodeos, logging competitions, carnival rides, and a chili cook-off.

Seattle Tennis Club Open Tennis Tournament and Challenger Series
Tel: (206) 324-3200
During first week in August (order tickets well in advance).

Santa Fe Chamber Music Festival
Meany Hall
University of Washington
Tel: (206) 548-4880

Camlann Medieval Faire, Carnation.

Evergreen Classic Benefit Horseshow, Redmond.

SEPTEMBER

Bumbershoot
Tel: (206) 281-8111
www.onreel.org
Music and arts festival at Seattle Center, Labor Day weekend. Big names and local acts perform at this music event. A moderate entry fee is charged which entitles guests to attend hundreds of concerts in all styles throughout the Center complex.

Leavenworth Autumn Leaf Festival
Tel: 509-548-5807
Last weekend in September, with fall colors, parade, music and free events. Held in the Bavarian-style mountain village of Leavenworth, 120 miles (190 km) east of Seattle.

The Puyallup Fair
Tel: 253-841-5045
Western Washington's State Fair, about 35 miles (55 km) south of Seattle. A 17-day long country fair extravaganza.

OCTOBER

Festa Italia
Seattle Center, near Columbus Day.
Tel: (206) 684-8582.
Italian dancing and food

Greek Festival
St Demetrios Church
2100 Boyer Avenue E.
Tel: (206) 325-4347
Held in early October at this Byzantine church with folk dancing, arts and crafts and Greek cuisine.

Issaquah Salmon Day
Main Street
Tel: (206) 392-7024
www.frontstreet.org
The street is closed to traffic and open to arts and crafts booths with artists from all over the Northwest. Street entertainment, mime, clowns, and musicians are here as well as the salmon jumping up to the hatchery. Big salmon cookout.

Mushroom Show
Tel: (206) 543-2000
University of Washington Center for Urban Horticulture. Features 150–300 species of mushrooms.

Northwest Bookfest
Tel: (206) 378-1883

www.speakeasy.org/nwbookfest
A showcase for publishers and booksellers along with appearances and book signings by recognized authors, panel discussions and workshops.
Hallowe'en, parades, festivities and pranks at nightclubs and bars. Many shopping centers offer free candy for children roaming the mall in costumes.

NOVEMBER

Harvest Festival, late in the month.
Model Railroad Show
Pacific Science Center
Tel: (206) 443-2880
Held during Thanksgiving weekend.

DECEMBER

Christmas Ships
Tel: (206) 623-1445
www.argosycruises.com
Mid-December. Lighted and decorated boats parade around Lake Union and Lake Washington, making stops at public parks while choral groups entertain. Check newspaper for updated schedule.
A Christmas Carol at the ACT Theater, (A Contemporary Theatre)
700 Union Street
Tel: (206) 292-7676
An annual production of the ever-popular, classic Dickens tale.
Christmas tree-lighting and caroling in the Bavarian-style village of Leavenworth in the Cascade Mountains. Tel: 509-548-5807.
Community Hannukah Celebration
Stroum Jewish Center
Mercer Island
Tel: 232-7115
Arts and crafts, children's games and candle-lighting.

The Nutcracker presented by the Pacific Northwest Ballet, Opera House, Seattle Center. Runs from early December through New Year's. TicketMaster Tel: (206) 292-2787. www.ticketmaster.com

Shopping

Shopping Areas

Seattle's climate and outdoor recreational activities have brought about the success of the city's best-known stores such as Eddie Bauer (now a national chain), REI (the co-operative, with more stores opening across the country), the North Face and Patagonia. Many of the traditionalists in Seattle look like they just stepped out of one of these stores. Birkenstock sandals are favored during the drier months.

Several areas are well known for shopping. Among them is the **Pike Place Market**, the downtown retail district, along Broadway on Capitol Hill; and the **University District**. The latter features ethnic gift shops, specialty food markets, restaurants, bakeries and bookstores.

Washington has an 8.1 per cent sales tax that is added to the price of retail goods and food that is served in restaurants.

Shopping Malls

Alderwood Mall
Lynnwood
(near the north intersection of I-5 and I-405)
Tel: (425) 771-1121
Features The Bon, Nordstrom, J.C. Penney and Sears. Many furniture stores and smaller malls nearby.
Bellevue Square
NE. Eighth Street and Bellevue Way
Bellevue
Tel: (425) 455-2429
A 198-store mall featuring Nordstrom, The Bon, Frederick & Nelson, J.C. Penney.
Broadway Market
401 Broadway Avenue East
Tel: (206) 322-1610
Urban shopping complex featuring smaller boutiques and cafés.
The Bon
Third Avenue and Pine Street
Tel: (206) 506-6000
The flagship of one of Seattle's oldest and finest department stores. Good-quality, moderately priced clothing, jewelry, toys and sundry items on nine floors. There's also a post office, beauty salon, bakery and restaurants. A garage and a skywalk mean shoppers don't have to step outside on rainy days.
Country Village
23730 Bothell-Everett Highway
Bothell
Tel: (425) 483-2250
A collection of country farmhouses, remodeled for shopping with brick pathways, landscaped grounds with waterfalls, ponds, gazebos and flowers everywhere in spring and summer. Most stores have a country theme with goods such as quilts, antiques, cookware, yarns, furnishings, and clothing. There are also several cafés.
Edmonds Antique Mall
Located in the restored and historically flavored Old Mill Town. Craft, tourist shops and restaurants.
Gilman Village
Gilman Boulevard
Issaquah
Tel: (425) 392-6802
Country farmhouses and barns have been remodeled and made into a charming shopping village. Many stores have country-style gifts, clothing, artwork. Features the Gallery of Fine Woodworking, several cafés and restaurants.
Nordstrom
500 Pine Street
Tel: (206) 628-2111
www.nordstrom.com
Classical piano players at the baby grands are a trademark along with customer service. Quality clothing and accessories for all ages.
Northgate
555 NE. Northgate Way
This 116-store mall features The Bon, Nordstrom, Gene Juarez Salon, restaurants and bars.

Pike Place Market
First Avenue and Pike Street
Tel: (206) 682-7453
(*see page 291*).

Rainier Square
1301 Fifth Avenue
Tel: (206) 682-2104
Top-of-the-line fashion shops are here such as The Littler and Totally Michael's. Rainier Square adjoins the Hilton Hotel.

Southcenter Mall
I-5 and I-405, Tukwila
Tel: (206) 246-7400
The largest shopping center in the metropolitan Seattle area. Features Nordstrom, The Bon, among others. Many smaller shopping centers featuring furniture, electronics, clothing and food are in the vicinity of the mall.

Westlake Center and Plaza
Pine Street between Fourth and Fifth avenues
Houses 80 specialty shops. Adjacent to Nordstrom, The Bon Marché and Frederick & Nelson. Top floor features 15 fast-food stands from pizza and burgers to seafood and vegetarian cuisines. Specialty shops include the Disney Store, Brentano's Book Store, Williams-Sonoma (kitchenware) and the Museum of Flight branch store (*see page 282*).

Clothing

Baby & Co.
1936 First Avenue
Tel: (206) 448-4077
The ultimate in high-fashion women's wear.

Benetton
1420 5th Avenue
Tel: (206) 382-9393
Contemporary Italian fashions for men and women.

Brooks Brothers
1401 Fourth Avenue
Tel: (206) 624-4400
High quality men's clothing.

The Coach Store
417 University Street
Tel: (206) 382-1772
At the Four Seasons Olympic Hotel, the Coach Store is the maker of quality classic leather handbags, belts and accessories.

Michael's Bespoke Tailors
1203 2nd Avenue
Tel: (206) 623-4785.
High quality men's fashions.

Nelly Stallion
1622 Queen Anne North
Tel: (206) 285-2150
Fine women's clothing and accessories.

Yankee Peddler
4218 E. Madison
Tel: (206) 324-4218
Quality men's wear.

Photographic

Cameras West
1908 Fourth Avenue
Tel: (206) 622-0066
One of the best places in town to go shopping for cameras and accessories.

Food

A & J Meats
2401 Queen Anne N.
Tel: (206) 284-3885
High-quality meats including specialty cuts and preparation.

Café Dilettante
416 Broadway E.
Tel: (206) 329-6463.
Makes exquisitely-rich truffles, irresistible butter-cream filled chocolates, tortes and cakes.

Great Harvest Bread Co
5408 Sand Point Way NE.
Tel: (206) 524-4873
Wholewheat breads and sweets.

Honey Bear Bakery
2106 N. 55th
Tel: (206) 545-7296
Natural foods bakery and café.

Scandinavian Bakery
100 Mercer
Tel: (206) 784-6616
Scandinavian bakery with reputation for heavenly pastries.

Starbuck's Coffee and Tea
1912 Pike Place, University Village, also Bellevue, and small shops around town. Fine coffee, pastries, snacks and sandwiches.

Uwajimaya
519 Sixth Avenue S.
Tel: (206) 624-6248
Gourmet foods, records and books from Japan.

Measurement Chart

The US uses the imperial system of weights and measures.

1 inch	=	2.54	centimeters
1 foot	=	3048	meter
1 mile	=	1.609	kilometers
1 quart	=	9464	liter
1 ounce	=	28.3	grams
1 pound	=	453.5	grams
1 yard	=	9144	meter

Clothing Chart

Women's Dresses/Suits

American	Continental	British
6	38/34N	8/30
8	40/36N	10/32
10	42/38N	12/34
12	44/40N	14/36
14	46/42N	16/38
16	48/44N	18/40

Women's Shoes

American	Continental	British
4½	36	3
5½	37	4
6½	38	5
7½	39	6
8½	40	7
9½	41	8
10½	42	9

Men's Suits

American	Continental	British
34	44	34
–	46	36
38	48	38
–	50	40
42	52	42
–	54	44
46	56	46

Men's Shirts

American	Continental	British
14	36	14
14½	37	14½
15	38	15
15½	39	15½
16	40	16
16½	41	16½
17	42	17

Men's Shoes

American	Continental	British
6½	–	6
7½	40	7
8½	41	8
9½	42	9
10½	43	10
11½	44	11

Jewelry

Fast Forward
1918 First Avenue
Tel: (206) 728-8050
One-of-a-kind jewelry, fashioned mostly by local artists.
Friedlander Jewelers
Northgate Mall
Tel: (206) 365-8740
Established in Seattle in 1886. One of the most extensive offerings of watches, rings and crystal. Custom designs and repair.

Magazines & Books

Bulldog News
4208 University Way NE. and
401 Broadway (Broadway Mall)
Tel: (206) 322-NEWS
Huge selection of periodicals, foreign magazines and newspapers.
Elliott Bay Book Company
101 S. Main Street
Tel: (206) 624-6600
Four large rooms and two lofts with more than 100,000 titles. This is the second-largest independent bookstore in the state. Features readings by major authors, two cafés and a graphics store.
University Book Store
4326 University Way NE.
Tel: (206) 634-3400
www.bookstore.washington.edu
One of the largest in town with a comprehensive selection of books, maps and gifts.
Wide World Books and Maps
4411 Wallingford Avenue N.
Tel: (206) 634-3453

Music

Capitol Music Co.
718 Virginia
Tel: (206) 622-0171
Comprehensive selection of sheet music.
Tower Records
500 Mercer
Tel: (206) 283-4456
One of the best CDs and cassette selections in Seattle. Two other locations:
4321 University Way
in the University district
Tel: (206) 632-1187; or at
10635 8th Avenue
Bellevue
Tel: (425) 451-2557.

Outdoor Specialists

Eddie Bauer
Downtown
Tel: (206) 622-2766
Also has branch stores in most local malls.
The North Face
1023 First Avenue
Tel: (206) 622-4111
Backpacking clothing and gear.
REI (Recreational Equipment Inc.)
222 Yale Avenue North
Tel: (206) 223-1944
www.rei.com
Downtown location features a bike path for testing potential purchases and a 65-foot (20-meter) free-standing indoor rock climbing peak. Branch stores in Lynnwood and Bellevue.

Specialty Stores and Gifts

Ade Africana
612 Broadway E.
Tel: (206) 720-4879
African arts, fabrics and clothing.
Archie Mcphee
2428 NW. Market Street
Tel: (206) 297-0240
A plethora of zany cheap toys that for some reason you can hardly resist. Before you know it, you've collected a dozen small neon fish, a handful of tiny, thumbtack size umbrellas and one or two wacky glow-in-the-dark dinosaurs for purchase.
Crystal Connection
901 Fairview Avenue N.
Tel: (206) 682-7793
Northwest Indian art and jewelry, crystals, minerals and fossils. Hand-blown glass art.
Exclusively Washington
Pier 54
Tel: (206) 624-2600
Features works by Northwest artisans; sculpture, jewelry, clothing, pottery and Native American art.
Made In Washington
Pike Place Market (and malls)
Tel: (206) 467-0788 or (1 800) 645-3474
Everything in the store from crafts, local cookbooks, and wines is made in the State of Washington.
Metsker Maps
702 1st Avenue
Tel: (206) 623-8747
In need of a travel guide or map for any place that you might think may take some navigational help? It's probably here. Also look at the assortment of reproductions of antique maps or globes of all sizes, including those that light up to illuminate the world.
Museum of Flight Store
9404 E. Marginal Way S.
Tel: (206) 764-5720
An assortment of aviation gifts: model airplanes, selection of books, T-shirts, pins, photos. Main store at the museum, branch in Westlake Center.
Molbak's Greenhouse & Nursery,
13625 NE. 175th Street
Woodinville (and branches)
Tel: (425) 483-5000
Almost a destination in itself, this is Washington's largest indoor nursery. Offers a huge selection of plants, trees and shrubs. Also features a café, conservatory, gift shop, florist and patio furniture.
Sur La Table
84 Pine Street (across from Pike Place Market)
Tel: (206) 448-2244
Gourmet cookware.

Outdoor Activities

Waterside Activities

Aquarium
1483 Alaskan Way
(Pier 59 at Waterfront Park)
Tel: (206) 386-4320
Seattle's aquarium, a $5.4-million complex, features an underwater dome with a (360) degree view of Puget Sound sea creatures. The aquarium houses 14,541 sea mammals and creatures from around the world on its 200 acres. Open: 10am–7pm during summer and 10am–5pm for the rest of the year. Children under six, free.

Omnidome
Pier 59 at Waterfront Park
Tel: (206) 622-1868
This 180-degree screen surrounds viewers with natural history films, like the eruption of Mount St Helens. Hours: 10am–10pm, Apr–Oct; 11am–5pm, Nov–March. Admission.

Hiram M. Chittenden Locks
Tel: (206) 783-7059
Located in the Washington Ship Canal, the locks raise and lower large fishing vessels, pleasure boats and canoes alike to make the transition from Puget Sound to Lake Union and vice versa. This can be a 6- to 26-ft (2–8-meter) difference, depending on tides. A "fish ladder" with an underwater viewing room allows visitors to watch salmon jumping their way up the ladder and upstream to spawn. A 7-acre park and rose garden around the locks provide an ideal spot for picnicking and watching the passing boats. Open 7am–9pm daily. Free.

Fisherman's Terminal
1735 West Thurman Street
Presents an opportunity to observe first-hand the workings of one of Seattle's major industries. Visitors can stroll and observe hundreds of commercial fishing boats and their crews at work. A newly-built public plaza features signs that detail the development of the local fishing industry. Several excellent seafood restaurants are nearby. Free.

Downtown Waterfront
Piers 52–59
The Washington State ferries, Ye Old Curiosity Shop, fresh seafood restaurants, souvenir shops, and a park with elevated walkways that offer wonderful views of Puget Sound and the Olympic Mountains. Stroll along the waterfront past the Edgewater Inn, the *Victoria Clipper* (catamaran to Victoria, Canada) to Pier 70 and visit the shops and restaurants. Free.

Markets and Centers

International District
Home for many of Seattle's Asian communities, the district is located at the southern end of downtown Seattle. Highlights are Uwajimaya, a large Japanese supermarket and department store, the Wing Luke Asian Museum, Kobe Park and gardens, and the Chinese Pavilion in Hing Hay Park. Tours of the district are available (*see page 271*).

Pike Place Market
Pike Street and First Avenue
A bustling marketplace of fresh produce, seafood, artisans, gourmet food, street musicians, boutiques, restaurants and much local color. Many describe this as the heart of the city. The Pike Street Hillclimb, with its labyrinth of staircases and elevators, connects the market area with waterfront shopping and sightseeing. Free.

Seattle Center
Tel: (206) 684-8582
Built for the 1962 World's Fair and home of Seattle's most recognizable landmark, the Space Needle. The center's 74 acres form a cultural hub for the city's performing arts groups, housing the Opera House, home of the Seattle Opera Company, the Seattle Symphony Orchestra and the Pacific Northwest Ballet (*see page 283*); the Bagley Wright Theater, the Seattle Repertory Theater's new house, and the Playhouse, home of the Intiman Theater.

Also at the Center are the Fun Forest amusement park with a variety of children's rides and arcade games; the Pacific Science Center;, the Center House, with 50 shops and restaurants; the Coliseum and Key Arena, which host trade shows, concerts and are the home courts of the Seattle Sonics basketball team; the Northwest Craft Center; and more. You can reach the center in 90 seconds by monorail from Fourth Avenue and Pine Street, in the center of downtown's shopping district (*see page 270*).

Pacific Science Center
200 Second Avenue N.
Tel: (206) 443-2870
A hands-on museum with six buildings of science adventure for the whole family. Features the IMAX theater, laser shows, a planetarium, plus changing and permanent exhibits. Open: 10am–6pm Mon– Fri, until 7pm on Thur. Admission.

Skyscrapers

The Space Needle
Tel: (206) 443-2111
Offers panoramic views of Puget Sound, the Olympic Mountains, the Cascades, and Mount Rainier from its observation deck, 607 ft (185 meters) above ground. Two revolving restaurants at the top turn 360 degrees each hour. Hours: 9am–midnight daily. Admission, but there is no elevator charge for diners.

Smith Tower
Yesler Way and Second Avenue
Tel: (206) 622-4004
This 42-story building was the tallest building outside New York City in 1905 when it was completed. The Chinese Room on the 35th floor tells the story of Washington, Alaska and Seattle through intricately carved Chinese characters. An observation deck encloses the room and offers views of Seattle, the Olympics and, on a clear day, Mount Rainier. Hours: 10am–10pm daily. Admission.

Gardens and Zoos

University of Washington
Tel: (206) 543-2000
Its elaborate early 20th-century architecture, well-designed grounds, the Henry Art Gallery, the Medicinal Herb Garden – all reasons to stop by and visit this lovely campus. Gatekeepers hand out free maps of the grounds. Free.

Washington Park Arboretum
Tel: (206) 543-8800
A 200-acre wooded park with plant families from around the world. Guided tours are available by appointment. An authentic Japanese Garden and traditional tea house is located at the south end of the grounds. The arboretum is free and open year-round, but the Japanese Garden is open Mar–Nov only and has an admission charge. The visitors' center of the arboretum is open: 10am–4pm Mon–Fri, noon–4pm Sat–Sun.

Woodland Park Zoo
50th Avenue N. and Fremont Avenue
Tel: (206) 684-4800.
Winner of many awards for its design which simulates the natural habitats of animals, including the African savannah for lions, hippopotami, giraffes and zebra; there is a gorilla habitat, swamps, a petting-farm, pony-rides and an excellent gift shop. Open: 9.30am–dusk daily all year. Admission, children under 6 free.

EastSide

There are further outdoor attractions located in the Eastside area:
Bellevue: Historical Society, Tel: (425) 450-1046.
Bothell: Country Village Shopping Center, Tel: (425) 483-2250.
Carnation: Remlinger U-Pick Farms, Tel: (425) 451-8740.
Fall City: Herbfarm, Tel: (425) 784-2222.
Issaquah: Boehm's Candy Kitchen, Tel: (425) 392-6652; Cougar Mountain Zoo, (425) 391-5508.
Redmond: The Balloon Depot, Tel: (425) 881-9699.
Woodinville: Molbak's Greenhouse, Tel: (425) 483-5000.

Children

Seattle is a place where children are welcome. Signs around town say, "Seattle is a kids' place," and it's surely one reason Seattle is consistently rated a livable city in the national press. There are a variety of things for children to enjoy right in town and just a short trip away. Here are a few suggestions.

Lakes and Parks

Take the kids for a **ride on the ferry** on any one of the five routes in and around Seattle (*see page 274*). It's inexpensive and, through children's eyes, may be one of the highlights of a visit to Seattle. On board are wide decks to run around (ferries are quite informal), and enjoy the views and fresh sea air. The process of loading and unloading cars is fascinating for most (except tired commuters). The indoor areas are also wide and airy with comfortable benches and tables and large windows overlooking the Sound. Cafeterias on board serve sandwiches, burgers and drinks.

Hiking is another great pastime. Some excellent parks for this are the Arboretum, Foster Island Trail (from the Arboretum it leads to Montlake Cut and the Museum of History and Industry in McCurdy Park), Discovery Park, Volunteer Park, Marymoor Park, and beachcombing on Puget Sound beaches. For a mountainous hike, Tiger Mountain in Issaquah offers well-marked trails. Some trails there allow mountain biking, which older children enjoy. A stop by Gilman Village and Boehm's Chocolate factory (Tel: (425) 392-6652) in town make the adventure a treat.

Swimming is an option on Lake Washington beaches during the summer (*see page 296*). Paddle-boating, bicycling, hiking, picnicking, and swimming are some of the activities available at **Green Lake Park.** Just up the hill from Green Lake is the **Woodland Park Zoo and Garden** www.zoo.org.com.

Another place to watch animals is the **Seattle Aquarium** at Pier 59, downtown. www.seattleaquarium.org (*see page 291*).

Bicycling is ideal for children on the bicycle trails. There are smooth paved roads and no cars to worry about (just the occasional serious bicyclist trying to break a speed record). Try the Burke Gilman Trail, which can be picked up anywhere from Gas Works Park on the north end of Lake Union or the University of Washington area to Log Boom Park in Kenmore. The Sammamish River Trail at Bothell Landing is a quiet and scenic trail, which extends for 9 miles (14.5 km) to Marymoor Park. Green Lake's trail can get busy, so it's best to try for a weekday ride around the lake. (*See page 294 for bike rental information*).

Chandler's Cove, at the south end of Lake Union, is home to the Center for Wooden Boats which offers hourly rentals of classic wooden boats. Hop aboard the dry-docked *Wawona* next door, and see what an 1800s fishing vessel looked like. Chandler's Cove also contains several eateries, both fast food and quality restaurants, in addition to interesting shops (especially Pennsylvania Woodworks which features Amish furniture) and a lakeside playground.

The Chittenden Locks is another favorite attraction. Children love to watch how they work, see the boats line up, watch the salmon jumping up the fish ladder, and walk through the park and garden that surrounds the locks (*see page 291*).

Try a stroll through **downtown Kirkland** and rest for a while at **Marina Park**, watching the boats and enjoying the view of Lake Washington and Seattle beyond. Follow the signs along Lake Washington Boulevard for a pleasant stroll past restaurants, antiques shops and condominiums to still more lakeside parks. Two blocks west of downtown on Central Avenue is Park Place Shopping Center, with **Pinocchio's Toys** and **Park Place Books**, of special interest to children. Next to the center is **Peter Kirk Park** with grassy fields, a playground, an outdoor pool and a library.

Point Defiance Park (Tel: (253) 305-1000) in Tacoma is a 700-acre park containing a zoo, an excellent aquarium (especially the shark and beluga whale exhibits), **Nisqually Fort Museum** (a restored fur trading post and village circa 1830s), **Camp Six** (a lumber museum with a steam train that rides around the camp) and **Never Never Land** with 31 displays from the Mother Goose stories. There are also formal gardens, beaches to explore, numerous hiking trails with vistas of Puget Sound, Vashon Island and the Olympics. The **zoo** and **aquarium** are open 10am–7pm daily. Admission, children age two and under free. Tel: (253) 591-5335.

Town Centers

Pike Place Market (*see page 291*) is fascinating for children as well as adults. But hold hands, it's easy to get lost in the crowd. **Pioneer Square district** offers a variety of restaurants, art galleries, shops, cafés, and bookstores. It is also the place to begin the Seattle Underground Tour.

Edmonds is another town that's fun to stroll through, whether browsing the quaint shops that line Main Street, learning about the history of Edmonds in Old Mill Town, watching the ferries load and unload, or simply enjoying the color of the hanging baskets of flowers that line downtown streets. A long fishing pier extends out into the sound next to Olympic Beach. Curious children love to see what kind of fish people catch. It's also possible to walk along the waterfront from Olympic Beach to Marina Beach, passing Anthony's Homeport, a fine seafood restaurant, Tel: (425) 771-4400, and the Edmonds Yacht Club. From the beaches (Marina Park has playground equipment), enjoy the sea breezes and views of Puget Sound and the Olympic Mountains.

Museums for Children

The **Seattle Center** (*see page 291*) is a wonderland for children. A day or two here is well-spent. The Pacific Science Center, a hands-on museum with displays that children can manipulate to learn scientific principles, offers planetarium shows, laser-light shows and nature/adventure films in the dramatic IMAX theater. At the Center House with its numerous fast food cafés and tourist shops, is the **Children's Museum**.

Outside, the Fun Forest offers amusement park rides, arcade games and miniature golf. The elevator up to the Space Needle is a treat, as is the view if it's not cloudy. From Center House, take a ride on the Monorail to the heart of downtown's retail stores. In 2000, the Experience Music Project is scheduled to open. The Northwest music museum is a pet project of Microsoft co-founder and Seattle Seahawks owner, Paul Allen.

The **Museum of Flight**, located in Boeing airfield, approximately 10 miles (16 km) south of Seattle, is one the kids won't want to miss. The central room, called the Gallery, contains 20 airplanes including an early 1900 Wright Brothers' model, fighter jets and ultra-light gliders hanging from the glass ceiling (*see page 282*).

The **Puget Sound and Snoqualmie Valley Railroad** provides a living history adventure. The late-1800-vintage steam trains travel between North Bend and Snoqualmie for a half-hour trip through forests, farmlands and over streams. Trains run on Sunday from Apr–Oct; on Saturday from May–Sept; on Friday and Saturday from July–the first weekend in Sept.

While in Snoqualmie, 30 miles (48 km) east of Seattle, a trip to the falls is recommended. Children can explore the trails that surround the 268-ft (82-meter) falls and visit the gift shops and restaurants of the visitors' center. The **Salish Lodge** next to the top of the falls has a restaurant with a deck overlooking the falls and splendid accommodation for those who wish to stay overnight (*see page 273*).

Farms

At **Lake Serene Pony Farm** in Lynnwood. let the kids climb on the back of a pony. The farm conducts 20-minute trail walks for children aged 3–13 on Saturday by reservation. Address: 3915 Serene Way, Lynnwood. Tel: (425) 743-2112 (*see page 296*).

Carnation Research Farm, near the town of Carnation, is approximately 25 miles (40 km) northeast of Seattle. This 1,200-acre dairy farm is where the Carnation company conducts research for its pet foods, milling and genetics divisions. The maternity and calf barns, milking stalls and Friskies nutrition kennels are open for self-guided tours, as are the formal flower gardens and informal picnic areas.
Carnation Farm, 28901 NE Carnation Farm Road. Tel: (425) 788-1511. Open: 10am–3pm Mon–Sat, Mar–Oct. Free.

The Herbfarm, just outside of Fall City, is approximately 25 miles (40 km) east of Seattle. An extensive herb garden with over 630 varieties and a lovely gift shop with herbs, gardening books, supplies and dried flowers for sale, are the steady attractions here. Children will also enjoy the farm animals and grounds for picnics. The farm's extremely popular restaurant burned down in 1997, and in the interim will continue to offer their wonderful foods in partnership with Hedges Cellars, a restaurant in Issaquah, Tel: (425) 391-4060. The farm conducts hay rides, pumpkin picking, stories and games (like a maze made of hay) during its annual Hallowe'en Festival.
The Herbfarm, 32804 Issaquah-Fall City Road. Tel:(425) 784-2222.

Open 9am–6pm daily.

Springbrook Trout Farm is a place where anyone can catch a fish. The farm provides rods and bait and also cleans and wraps the fish for guests to take home and cook. Price depends on the size of your catch.

Springbrook Trout Farm, 19225 Talbot Road S., Renton. Tel: (253) 852-0360. Open 10am–8pm daily.

Amusement Parks

Designed for the children in all of us is Wild Waves and Enchanted Village Amusement Park in Federal Way, approximately 17 miles (27 km) south of Seattle.

The Wild Waves part of the park contains heated pools, plus one that makes waves, and many water slides and smaller pools for small children. The Enchanted Village has a farm, numerous cafés, a merry-go-round, ferris wheel, boat rides, train rides, and more. The store inside Wild Waves sells bathing suits and any other equipment (rafts, towels, T-shirts) needed.

Wild Waves and Enchanted Village Adventure Park
36201 Enchanted Parkway South, Federal Way, WA 98003. (Exit 142B off I-5.)
Tel: (253) 661-8000.
Open: 11am–8pm last week in June–first weekend in Sept; 10am–6pm last weekend in May–third week in June, Sat–Sun, Apr, early May and Sept after Labor Day weekend.

Sport

Participant Sports

BICYCLING

Seattle was rated by *Bicycling* magazine as the number one city in the US for biking.

The **Burke-Gilman Trail**, a paved road on an abandoned railroad bed, leads from Gas Works Park on Lake Union to Logboom Park on Lake Washington. The 12½-mile (20-km) trail follows Lake Washington down by the University and is popular with people of all ages, whether biking, jogging or walking. The **Sammamish River Trail** follows the Sammamish River from Bothell, through Woodinville farmland and ends at Marymoor Park at the north tip of Sammamish Lake. This trail runs for 9½ miles (15 km) and will soon connect with the Burke Gilman trail. A 2½-mile (4-km) stretch between the two trails is under construction.

Another popular bicycle route is the 3-mile (5-km) paved trail around **Green Lake**. It can be busy on sunny days, especially at weekends, with strollers, joggers, inline skaters and cross-country roller skiers. From Green Lake, bicyclists may choose to take the Ravenna Park Trail to the University.

Every third Sunday and first Saturday of the month from May–September, a 6-mile (9.5-km) stretch on **Lake Washington Boulevard** is closed to cars (from the Arboretum to Seward Park). Beautiful lakefront parks and scenery can be enjoyed on this paved road for family biking and hiking. Tel: (206) 684-7092.

Marymoor Park in Redmond has a velodrome for racing and held the 1990 Goodwill Games bicycle races. Races are held 7.30pm Fri, Apr–Nov. Tel: (425) 556-2300.

Numerous bicycle rides and races are held throughout the year. For information on current events telephone the **Cascade Bicycle Club**, Tel: (206) 522-BIKE.

For bicycle rentals near these trails, contact the following:

Gregg's Greenlake Cycle Inc.,
7007 Woodlawn NE.
Tel: (206) 523-1822

The Bicycle Center
4529 Sand Point Way NE.
Tel: (206) 523-8300

Alki Bicycle Co.
2611 California Avenue SW.
Tel: (206) 938-3322

Sammamish Valley Cycle
8451 164th Avenue NE. Redmond.
Tel: (425) 881-8442

Also check the *Yellow Pages* directory under "Bicycle Rentals".

BIRDWATCHING

Audubon Society
8028 35th Avenue NE.
Tel: (206) 523-4483
The society offers a checklist of birds in the area and a list of where to purchase birdseed mixed for native species. It also conducts field trips in Seattle's parks.

GOLF

Reservations to the following public golf courses is recommended:

Ballinger Park
23000 Lakeview Drive, Mountlake
Tel: (425) 775-6467
Nine-hole, par: 34-men, 36-women.

Bellevue Municipal
5450 140th NE.
Tel: (425) 451-7250
Eighteen-hole, par: 35-men, 36-women.

Foster
13500 Interurban S.
Tel: (206) 242-4221
Eighteen-hole, par: 69-men, 71-women.

Green Lake
5701 W. Green Lake Way N.
Tel: (206) 632-2280
Nine-hole, par: 27 men and women.

Jackson Park Municipal
1000 NE. 135th Street

Tel: (206) 363-4747
Eighteen-hole, par: 71-men, 73-women. Also, nine-hole, par 3.

Jefferson Park Municipal
4101 Beacon S.
Tel: (206) 762-4513.
Eighteen-hole, par: 70 men and women.

Maplewood Golf Course
4000 Maple Valley Highway, Renton.
Tel: (425) 277-4444
Eighteen-hole, par: 72-men, 73-women.

Tyee Valley
2401 S. 192nd Street
Tel: (206) 878-3540
Eighteen-hole, par: 71 men, 73-women.

Wayne
16721 96th Avenue NE, Bothell
Tel: (425) 485-6237
Eighteen-hole, par: 65-men, 66-women.

West Seattle
4470 35th SW.
Tel: (206) 935-5187
Eighteen-hole, par: 72-men, 74-women.

Seattle Golf Club
210 NW. 145th
Tel: (206) 363-5444
Nine-hole, par: 27 men and women.

HIKING

A good pair of walking shoes, some snacks and a drink are all you need (but binoculars and camera are nice to have along) to explore the area and see what the land looked like before construction took over.

Carkeek Park offers wooded trails leading to Puget Sound beach. Playground, picnic, restrooms and high bluff views of the Sound.

Discovery Park, W. Government Way and 36th Avenue W. Tel: (206) 386-4236. A 534-acre park of deep wooded ravines, forest, grassy meadows and two miles of beach at the base of Magnolia Bluff. Nature trails wind their way throughout the park. The US Coast Guard's West Point Light Station is accessible by a 1½-mile (2.5-km) trail and open for tours from noon–4pm Sat–Sun, and Wed–Fri by appointment. The Daybreak Star Indian Cultural Center, which includes the Sacred Circle Indian Art Gallery, features Indian arts and crafts. Open 8am–5pm Mon–Fri, 10am–5pm Sat–Sun. Admission is free. The park is open daily from dawn–11pm. Guided tours are offered, and a visitors' center is open daily 8.30am–5pm.

Foster Island Trail, from McCurdy Park or the Arboretum. An easy, level hike over wooden bridges and pontoons over Lake Washington to Foster Island.

Marymoor Park, north end of Lake Sammamish, Redmond. Extensive playing fields, playgrounds, trails, picnicking facilities, a bicycle velodrome, model plane airport and historical museum in this park.

Meadowdale Park, North Edmonds. Wooded hiking trail leads down to level, grassy picnicking area and sandy Puget Sound beach.

St Edward's Park, Juanita Drive, Bothell. Some open grassy grounds for picnicking, soccer or baseball are available on the site of this old Catholic seminary. Wooded trails lead down to still more trails along east shores of Lake Washington.

Tiger Mountain, Issaquah. There are numerous trails leading to alpine lakes and mountain vistas. Many of the trails also allow mountain biking.

Volunteer Park, E. Galer and 15th Avenue E., and E. Prospect and 14th Avenue E. (on Capitol Hill). Tel: (206) 684-4743. Home of Seattle's Asian Art Museum's collection. A conservatory has collections of cacti, orchids and exotic tropical plants and is surrounded by extensive formal gardens. A 75-ft (23-meter) water tower with a steep spiral stairway provides on a clear day a panoramic view of downtown Seattle, and the surrounding lakes and mountains. Open dawn–11pm. Conservatory open 10am–7pm May 15–Sept 15; 10am–4pm the rest of the year.

For hiking trails that take up an entire day or more, try the parks in the Cascade Mountains, especially Mount Rainier and Olympic National Park.

Hiking maps and information

REI, Recreational Equipment Inc.
Tel: (206) 223-1944
Outdoor recreational equipment retailer that sells maps and organizes trips.

US Forest Service/National Parks Service Outdoor Recreation Information Office
915 Second Avenue
Tel: (206) 220-7450

The Mountaineers
300 Third Avenue W.
Tel: (206) 284-6310
An outdoor recreation club that runs hiking trips. www.mountaineers

Washington Trails Association
1305 Fourth Avenue.
Tel: (206) 625-1367.
Has most information needed on trails in the state. www.wta.org

Sierra Club
8511 15th Avenue NE.
Tel: (206) 523-2147
www.sierraclub.org

Mountain Madness
7103 California Avenue SW.,
Tel: (206) 937-8389
Offers personalized outdoor adventure tours including mountain biking, fishing, mountain climbing and hiking.

Boating on the Lakes

Canoeing, kayaking, rowing, sail boarding and sailing are all available around Lakes Union and Washington. In addition, Green Lake offers paddleboating.

Rentals: University of Washington Waterfront Activities Center, Tel: (206) 543-9433. Offers canoe rentals.

Green Lake, Tel: (206) 684-0780. Offers rowboats and paddleboats.

Northwest Outdoor Center, 2100 Westlake N. Tel: (206) 281-9694. Offers sea kayak rentals, lessons and tours.

Sailboat Rentals and Yacht Charters, 1301 N. Northlake Way. Tel: (206) 632-3302.

HORSEBACK RIDING

Ranches offer guided tours through parks, like Bridle Trails, or mountains, like Squak and Tiger. Lengths of tours vary from one hour to all day.

Aqua Barn Ranch
15277 SE. Renton-Maple Valley Highway, Renton
Tel: (425) 255-4618

Hidden Valley Ranch
Valley Road
Tel: 509-857-2322

Eastside Equestrian Center
Kirkland
Tel: (425) 827-2992

Tiger Mountain Stables
24508 SE 133rd, Issaquah
Tel: (425) 392-5090

SCUBA DIVING

Although not perhaps automatically associated with a US city, **Brackett's Landing** in Edmonds has a sandy beach, next to the ferry landing, which is especially designed for scuba diving. The underwater park features a sunken 300-ft (90-meter) dock and five floating rests.

SKIING

Summit at Snoqualmie
Tel: (425) 434-7669
Three ski areas atop Snoqualmie Pass – Alpental, Snoqualmie Summit and Ski Acres – joined together to offer extensive choices of trails, linked by a free shuttle bus available Fri–Sun, and a single lift ticket. Night skiing is also available.
www.summit-at-snoqualmie.com

Crystal Mountain Resort
Highway 410, 40 miles (75 km) east of Enumclaw
Tel: (360) 663-2265
The site of the 1972 World Cup Championships. Offers a vertical of 3,100 ft (945 meters) and 32 trails from beginner to advanced. Weekend night skiing.

Stevens Pass
Tel: (360) 973-2441
Seventy miles (110 km) northeast of Seattle, 26 runs and a 1,800-ft (550-meter) drop.

White Pass
Tel: 509-453-8731
Near Yakima. A vertical of 1,500 ft (460 meters) plus night skiing.

Whistler
Tel: 800-944-7853
This internationally renowned resort is a four-hour drive from Seattle, north of Vancouver in Canada.

SWIMMING

Beaches on the Sound include: Golden Gardens and Carkeek Park on the north end of Seattle and Alki and Lincoln Park on the south end.

Lake beaches include: the north east end of Green Lake; or, on the western shores of Lake Washington, (from north to south): Matthews Beach Park, Magnuson Park, Madison Park, Madrona Park, Mount Baker Park, Seward Park, Pritchard Island Beach Park. On the east side of the lake are: Denny Park, Bothell; Juanita Beach and Waverly Park, Kirkland; Meydenbauer Beach Park and Chism Park, Bellevue; Kennydale Park, north Renton; Lake Washington Beach Park, Renton.

Sports in Public Parks

There are numerous playfields in Seattle for baseball, soccer, football, tennis and paddleball, and areas for chess games, bocce (lawn bowling), picnicking, kite-flying and exploring. Parks vary in what they offer. For information on parks in a particular area or information on facilities, contact the following:

King County parks
Tel: (206) 296-4232.

Seattle parks
Tel: (206) 684-8021.

Kirkland
Tel: (425) 828-1217.

Mercer Island
Tel: (206) 236-3545.

Issaquah
Tel: (425) 392-7131.

Redmond
Tel: (425) 556-2300.

Swimming is also available in public swimming pools. These pools, which are located throughout metropolitan Seattle, the suburbs and Bellevue and Redmond, are maintained by the parks department. Contact the following numbers for more information:

Seattle
Tel: (206) 684-8021.

King County
Tel: (206) 296-4232.

Bellevue
Tel: (425) 455-6885.

Kirkland
Tel: (425) 828-1218.

Mercer Island
Tel: (206) 236-3545.

Redmond
Tel: (425) 556-2300.

Spectator Sports

FOOTBALL

Seattle Seahawks
11220 NE. 53rd Street
Kirkland
Tel: 888-NFL-HAWK
Seattle's NFL (National Football League) team. Located at the Kingdome throughout the 1999 season. The Hawks play at Husky Stadium (below) while a new stadium, scheduled to open in 2002, is under construction.

Husky Stadium
Southeast end of University of Washington
Tel: (206) 543-2200
This 73,000-seat stadium hosts the UW's football team. The Husky Stadium has the added attraction of offering views of Lake Washington and the Cascade Mountains, while taking in the game.

SOCCER

Seattle Sounders
Memorial Stadium, Seattle Center.
Tel: 800-796-KICK.
The A-League 1995–96 soccer champions play their season from April to October. Come the year 2002 they will be sharing a new stadium with the Seattle Seahawks.
www.seattlesounders.com

BASEBALL

Seattle Mariners Baseball Club
Safeco Field, First Avenue S.
Tel: (206) 346-4000
www.mariners.org
The new 1999 $417-million ballpark mixes tradition with high tech, with real grass on the playing field and a spectacular retractable roof, an engineering marvel unto itself.
Open Apr–Sept.

The Everett Aquasox
Memorial Stadium, Everett
(Exit 192 off I-5)
Tel: (425) 258-3673.
www.aquasox.com
This class-A minor league team of the Mariners plays 38 games on a grass field from mid-June through early September at the outdoor Memorial Stadium in Everett. The stadium is intimate, compared to most baseball stadiums, seating only 3,600. The ballpark food here was rated one of the best in the country.

Tacoma Rainiers
Cheney Stadium, 2502 S. Tyler St.
Tel: 800-281-3834
www.rainiers.fanlink.com
The Seattle Mariners Triple-A farm club play 72 games from April through to September.

BASKETBALL

Seattle Supersonics
KeyArena, Seattle Center
Tel: (206) 628-0888
www.sonics.nba.com/sonics/
Seattle's NBA (National Basketball Association) team. The season begins in November and playoffs begin in May. The Key Arena, which seats 14,250, is the city team's home arena.

University of Washington, Women's Husky Basketball
Hec Edmundson Pavilion
Tel: (206) 543-2200
www.gohuskies.com
The women's basketball season begins in November and ends in March. Seattle is scheduled to get a new team through the WBA (Women's Basketball Assocation) team for the 2000 season.

HOCKEY

Seattle Thunderbirds
Seattle Center KeyArena
Tel: (206) 448-PUCK or (206) 728-9121
Season runs from late Sept–Mar (or May if they make the playoffs).
www.seattle-thunderbirds.com

RACING

Emerald Downs
Exit 1 I-405, West Valley Highway, Auburn
Tel: (253) 288-7000 or (888) 931-8400
Emerald Downs features thoroughbred racing amid beautiful grounds. Races are held Wed–Sun, Apr–Sept. Approximately 10 races are held per day. The north end of the grandstand is free, but clubhouse boxes offer the best view. Wednesday to Friday racing begins at 5pm, but gates open at 3.30pm. Saturday, Sunday and holidays races begin at 1pm, with gates opening at 11.30am.

Saturday and Sunday mornings the track also holds a tour of the backstretch. For tour reservations Tel: (1 800) 7-DOO-DAH. There are seven restaurants at the track serving cuisine that ranges from hot dogs to fine dining. Wine, beer and cocktails are also available as is a children's area. www.emdowns.com

HYDROPLANE RACING

During **Seafair** hydroplane races take place north of Seward Park on Lake Washington. Boats reach speeds of over 150 mph (240 kmph) on the top of the water and follow a 2-mile (3-km) oval course. Tickets are available in advance or (more expensive) at the gate to prime viewing spots along the beach. There are very privileged seats available for large sums of money at the Captains Club.
Tel: (206) 728-0123.
www.seafair.com

Further Reading

General

British Columbia: A Centennial Anthology by Reginald Eyre Watters, editor. McClelland & Stewart (1958).
A Guide to the Indian Tribes of the Pacific Northwest by Robert H. Ruby and John A. Brown. University of Oklahoma (1986).
The Hidden Northwest by Robert Cantwell. Lippincott (1978).
Long Old Road by Horace R. Caton. University of Washington Press (1970).
Red Man's America by Ruth Murray Underhill. University of Chicago Press (1971).
Roadside Geology of Washington by David D. Alt and Donald W. Hyndman. Missoula, Montana: Hyndman Mountain Press Publishing Company (1990).
Seattle & Environs by Cornelius Harford. Pioneer Historical Publications (1924).
Seattle Cityscape by Victor Steinbrueck. University of Washington Press (1962).
Sexless Oysters and Self-tipping Hats: 100 Years of Invention in the Pacific Northwest by Adam Woog. Seattle: Sasquatch Books (1991).
Skid Road: An Informal Portrait of Seattle by Murray Morgan. Seattle and London: University of Washington Press (1988 revised edition).
Washington, The Evergreen State by John W. Goddard. Scribners (1942).

History

The American Fur Trade of the Far West by Hiram R. Chittenden. Press of the Pioneers (1935).
Boeing in Peace and War by E. E. Bauer. Enumclaw, Washington: taba Publishing (1990).
Boeing Trivia by Carl M. Cleveland. Seattle: CMC Books (1989).

The Columbia by Stewart H. Holbrook. Rinehart (1956).
Exploring Washington's Past: A Road Guide to History by Ruth and Carmela Alexander Kirk. Seattle and London: University of Washington Press (1990).
Ivar: The Life and Times of Ivar Haglund by Dave Stephens. Seattle: Dunhill Publishing (1988).
Origin of Washington Geographic Names by Edmond S. Meany. University of Washington Press (1923).
Pacific Northwest Indian Wars by Ray Hoard Glassley. Binford & Mort, (1953).
Puget's Sound: A Narrative of Early Tacoma and the Southern Sound by Murray Morgan. Seattle and London: University of Washington Press (1979).
The Seattle General Strike by Robert L. Friedheim. University of Washington Press (1964).
Seattle: Past to Present by Roger Sale. Seattle and London: University of Washington Press (1989).
Sons of the Profits: Doc Maynard, the Man who Invented Seattle by William C. Speidel. Seattle: Nettle Creek Publishing Co. (1990).
Surveyor of the Sea: Life of Voyages of Captain George Vancouver by Bern Anderson. Seattle, Washington, University of Washington Press (1960).
Timer and Men: The Weyerhaeuser Story by Ralph L. Hidy. Macmillan (1975).
Totem Tales of Old Seattle by Gordon Newell. Superior Publishing (1956).
Washington: A Bicentennial History by Norman H. Clark. W.W. Norton (1976).
Women & Men on the Overland Trail by John Mark Faragher. Yale University Press (1979).

Nature

Great Northwest Nature Factbook by Anne Saling. Bothell: Alaska Northwest Books (1991).
Hiking the North Cascades by Fred T. Darvill. Sierra Club (1982).
Mountaineering: The Freedom of the Hills by Ed Peters. The Mountaineers (1982).
Nature Walks in and around Seattle by Stephen R. Whitney. Seattle: The Mountaineers (1987).
The Northwest Green Book by Jonathan King. Seattle: Sasquatch Books (1991).
Of Men and Mountains by William O. Douglas. Harper (1950).
Pacific Salmon Fishing by John N. Cobb. Bureau of Fisheries (1917).
Pacific Salmon and Steelhead Trout by R.J. Childerhose. Seattle: University of Washington Press (1981).
Trees of Seattle: The Complete Tree-finders' Guide to History by Arthur Lee Jacobson. Seattle: Sasquatch Books (1989).
The Way of Herbs by Michael Tierra. Washington Square Press (1980).

Travel

Kidding Around Seattle: A Young Person's Guide to the City by Rick Steves. Santa Fe, New Mexico: John Muir Publications (1991).
Seattle Best Places edited by David Brewster and Stephanie Irving. Seattle: Sasquatch Books, (1991 fifth edition).
Washington Handbook by Dianne J. Boulerice Lyons. Moon Publications.
Washington State by Charles P. LeWarne. University of Washington Press (1986).

Other Insight Guides

Other Insight Guides which highlight destinations in this region include *Inside Guide: The Pacific Northwest* and *Insight Guide: Vancouver.*

Assembled by a team of over 30 local writers and photographers, *Insight Guide: The Pacific Northwest* is bold, beautiful and packed with information.

Insight Guide: Vancouver. This young, beautiful city isolated from the rest of Canada is both explained and explored by a team of local residents.

ART & PHOTO CREDITS

George Baetjer 79R
Chas D. Benes 231
Chris Bennion 195
Courtesy of Boeing Corporation 40, 104, 199
Bodo Bondzio front flap bottom, 4BL, 6/7, 57, 78, 93, 101, 102, 120L, 131, 149T, 164, 171T, 176/177, 212/213
Zdenka Bondzio 31
British Film Institute 41L
Barry Broman 96, 119L, 119T, 120T, 126, 127T, 128L, 129, 132, 134, 134T, 135, 146, 146T, 148, 156, 156T, 157T, 159, 163, 180, 185, 187, 188L, 188R, 189, 208, 218, 219, 222, 223
Bruce Bernstein Collection/Courtesy of the Princeton University Library 19, 23, 24, 25, 27, 74, 118, 120
Ed Cooper front flap top, back cover center right, 42, 62/63, 64, 66, 67, 69, 75, 77, 79L, 89, 95, 100, 117, 119R, 122, 136T, 149, 161, 173, 200, 206, 226/227, 228, 229, 230, 232T, 233, 234, 235, 236, 236T, 237, 238/239, 240, 241, 243L, 251, 258R
Stuart Dee 250
Chuck Flaherty 76R
Natalie B. Fobes 10/11, 54R, 110/111
Lee Foster 192T
D & J Heaton 41R
Historical Society of Seattle and King County/Museum of History and Industry 26L, 28, 29, 32/33, 34, 36, 37, 38, 39, 43, 85, 223T
Catherine Karnow 2/3, 4/5, 106/107, 133, 158, 166/167
Lewis Kemper 235T
Tom & Pat Leeson 257, 259
James McCann 80
Vautier de Nanxe 35
NASA 70
Jonathan Nesvig 12/13, 53, 54L, 55, 196/197, 201T, 204, 204T, 207, 242, 244, 245, 246, 252/253
Richard Nowitz spine top, back flap top
Pat O'Hara 230T
Anita Peltonen 127
Province of British Columbia 108/109
Joel W. Rogers spine center, back flap bottom, 1, 2, 8/9, 14, 18, 50, 56, 86, 90/91, 92, 112, 114/115, 128R, 130, 133T, 151, 154, 243R, 260
John Running 94, 232
Charles Seaborn 76L
Seattle Art Museum/Paul Macapia back cover left, 2BL, 22
Charles Shugart 247, 248
Smithsonian Institution, National Anthropological Archives 20/21
Tony Stone Images 65
Courtesy of Text 100 105
Tom Till 4BR, 60/61
Courtesy of Underground Tours 26R
Joe Viesti 84, 249
Jamie Wakefield spine bottom, back cover bottom, back flap top, 5BL, 44/45, 46/47, 48, 49, 51, 52, 68, 71, 82/83, 88, 98/99, 103, 120R, 121, 123, 123T, 124, 125, 128T, 130T, 136, 137, 140/141, 144, 145, 147, 150, 152/153, 155, 158T, 160L, 160R, 160T, 161T, 162, 164T, 165, 168, 169, 170, 172, 172T, 175, 178/179, 184, 186, 189T, 190, 190T, 191, 192L, 192R, 193, 193T, 194, 198, 201, 202, 202T, 203, 205, 209, 210T, 211, 214/215, 216, 242T, 246T, 254, 256, 257T, 258T, 261, 262
Art Wolfe 81, 255, 258L
Konrad Wothe/Oxford Scientific Films 5BR
R.F. Zallinger/Museum of History and Industry

Picture Spreads

Pages 58–59: *Top row left to right:* Peter Newark's American Pictures, Natalie B Fobes, Peter Newark's American Pictures, Peter Newark's American Pictures; *Centre row:* all by Natalie B Fobes; *Bottom row left to right:* Peter Newark's American Pictures, Natalie B Fobes, Peter Newark's American Pictures
Pages 72–73: *Top row left to right:* Natalie B Fobes, Andrea Pistolesi, Buddy Mays/Travel Stock, Andrea Pistolesi; *Centre row left to right:* Buddy Mays/Travel Stock, Kerrick James; *Bottom row left to right:* Andrea Pistolesi, Natalie B Fobes, Natalie B Fobes
Pages 138–139: *Top row left to right:* Natalie B Fobes, Natalie B Fobes, Buddy Mays/Travel Stock, Buddy Mays/Travel Stock; *Centre row left to right:* Deni Bown/Oxford Scientific Films, Blaine Harrington; *Bottom row left to right:* Andrea Pistolesi, Natalie B Fobes, Natalie B Fobes
Pages 224-225: *Top row left to right:* T Kitchin & V Hurst/NHPA, David C Fritts/Oxford Scientific Films, Kevin Schafer/NHPA *Centre row left to right*: Mark Hamblin/ Oxford Scientific Films, Daniel J Cox/Oxford Scientific Films; *Bottom row left to right:* Richard Herrmann/Oxford Scientific Films, Jeff Foott/Oxford Scientific Films, Lon Lauber/Oxford Scientific Films

INSIGHT GUIDE Seattle

Cartographic Editor **Zoë Goodwin**
Production **Stuart A Everitt**
Design Consultants **Carlotta Junger, Graham Mitchener**
Picture Research **Hilary Genin**

Map Production Colin Earl

Index

Numbers in italics refer to photographs

a

b

c

d

e

f

g